I0796794

Hiking Metro Atlanta's Hidden Forests

Hiking Metro Atlanta's Hidden Forests

AN HOUR OR LESS FROM DOWNTOWN

Jonah McDonald and Zana Pouncey

MILESTONE PRESS
AN IMPRINT OF
THE UNIVERSITY OF GEORGIA PRESS
ATHENS

Published by Milestone Press,
an imprint of the University of Georgia Press
Athens, Georgia 30602
www.ugapress.org
© 2025 by Jonah McDonald and Zana Pouncey
All rights reserved
Set in 9.5/12 Bodoni Egyptian Pro
by Rebecca A. Norton
Maps by Alexander Bowen and Jon Davies
Printed and bound by Sheridan Books, Inc.
The paper in this book meets the guidelines for permanence and durability of the Committee on Production Guidelines for Book Longevity of the Council on Library Resources.

Most University of Georgia Press titles are available from popular e-book vendors.

Printed in the United States of America

29 28 27 26 25 P 5 4 3 2 1

EU Authorized Representative
Easy Access System Europe—Mustamäe tee 50, 10621 Tallinn, Estonia, gpsr.requests@easproject.com

Library of Congress Cataloging-in-Publication Data

Names: McDonald, Jonah, 1979– author | Pouncey, Zana author
Title: Hiking Metro Atlanta's hidden forests : an hour or less from downtown / Jonah McDonald and Zana Pouncey.
Description: Athens : Milestone Press, an imprint of the University of Georgia Press, 2025.
Identifiers: LCCN 2024061741 | ISBN 9781889596440 paperback
Subjects: LCSH: Hiking—Georgia—Atlanta Metropolitan Area—Guidebooks | Trails—Georgia—Atlanta Metropolitan Area—Guidebooks | Atlanta Metropolitan Area (Ga.)—Guidebooks | LCGFT: Guidebooks
Classification: LCC GV199.42.G462 A8563 2025 | DDC 796.5109778/231—dc23/eng/20250326
LC record available at https://lccn.loc.gov/2024061741

CONTENTS

NORTHSIDE

I-75 NORTH

I-575 NORTH

GA 400 NORTH

I-85 NORTH

BONUS HIKES

PREFACE

Jonah McDonald

Over 20 years ago, I arrived in Atlanta by way of the Appalachian Trail. After hiking this rugged 2,000-mile path from Maine to Georgia and establishing my new home in the city, I spent weekends driving hundreds of miles away from Atlanta in search of the peace and beauty that nature offers. On weekday afternoons, I sought out trails in the forests of Atlanta and wandered beside creeks, over ridges, and through some of the most impressive old-growth forests I've found anywhere. I have come to believe that short hikes close to home can be as life-changing as extended backpacking trips. And I have found that Atlanta is the perfect metropolitan area for hiking.

In the decade since the original *Hiking Atlanta's Hidden Forests: Intown and Out* was published, Atlanta has reclaimed its identity as "The City in the Forest." This identity has spread throughout the metro area, where we now find great hiking trails from Dacula to Villa Rica, from Peachtree City to Milton, and from Kennesaw to Stonecrest. In writing this book, I've been privileged to explore trails in Butts, Carroll, Cherokee, Clayton, Cobb, DeKalb, Douglas, Fayette, Forsyth, Fulton, Gwinnett, Monroe, Paulding, and Rockdale Counties. As a city of Atlanta resident, I've enjoyed visiting vibrant communities and hiking peaceful trails all around my city.

My wife, Dana, has been my constant hiking partner, and the publication of *Hiking Atlanta's Hidden Forests* also coincided with the birth of our daughter, Annie Mae. Now I try to keep up with my energetic kid, who leads our family on hikes. I now experience these trails—and our city—through the eyes of my child.

Finally, I am honored to introduce you to my coauthor, Zana Pouncey, who is a delight to work with, a great hiking partner, and a fantastic trail guide. Her experience, passion, and knowledge have helped make this book even more thorough, accurate, and inclusive than it would have been if I had been on this writing journey alone.

I hope these trails change your life as they have changed mine.

Zana Pouncey

I grew up in Georgia, and when I was a kid, exploring the outdoors was my favorite pastime. I earned a degree in environmental science from Emory University and have had the opportunity to study and hike in some of the world's most beautiful and remote wildernesses, from the Rockies to the rainforest. But my love of hiking formed while I was traversing the trails around the city. My appreciation for Atlanta's eclectic neighborhood trails was solidified while I worked at an after-school program that traveled to a new hiking destination every week. It was there that I first encountered Jonah's work: we used the original *Hiking Atlanta's Hidden Forests* as a guide to plan hikes.

I got to know Jonah almost 10 years later at an environmental education conference. We then became professional colleagues. It has been an honor and pleasure to join him in creating this resource for the community.

Environmental advocacy and accessibility are driving forces in my career and a motivation for writing this guidebook. When I was younger some part of me always understood that it wasn't typical for black women to go hiking alone, but it never crossed my mind that I (or anyone else) didn't belong on the trails or in the woods. Spending time in nature has always been a spiritual experience for me. Scientific data support my experience that being in nature is good for our mental and physical health. I want the trails and woods of Atlanta to reflect the city's diversity of people and cultures.

My hope is that this guidebook can help people of all levels of hiking experience to find a moment of peace and serenity on a trail in their community or neighborhood. I hope to also bring a bit of love and awareness to some of the lesser-known parks and trails around the metro area. From waterfalls, wetlands, meadows, and mountains, I hope this guidebook helps you find your new favorite hike.

ACKNOWLEDGMENTS

When we set out to write two hiking guidebooks in one year, we didn't quite know what we were getting ourselves into. Despite the fun and adventure of hiking over 125 trails, this project consumed a great deal of time and was only possible because of the patience, support, and encouragement we received from our families. So thank you, Dana, Annie Mae, and Matthew. You are our favorite hiking partners, collaborators, and cheerleaders.

Our extended families also accompanied us on this project, offering suggestions, edits, hike testing, and a listening ear. Even in the midst of work, health, and personal challenges, you supported us in this project. Thank you, Ron, Susan, Jesse, Cindy, Marie, David, Mark, Marlene, Andrea, and Todd. Thank you, Winfred, Zena, and Tate.

We couldn't have even started writing this guidebook if the trails weren't cared for by the community. Nature center staff, park rangers, parks and recreation workers, hiking clubs, mountain bike advocates, scout troops, neighborhood associations, and many, many individual volunteers have gone above and beyond to protect and maintain these greenspaces. To everyone who cares for metro Atlanta's forests, we are in your debt.

Every hike route in this book has been tested and edited by volunteers who are passionate about hiking in Atlanta: Eddas Bennett, Shaundon Moore, Dana Goldman, Annie Mae McDonald, Mark Goldman, Marlene Goldman, Marty Levine, Katie Hendrickson, Sandi Still, Marianne Skeen, Andrew Tsivoglou, Rachel Countryman, Darling Ngoh, Tegan Callahan, Greg Kennedy, Delano Callahan, Lori Ayling, Danielle Bunch, Christy Espy, and others tested hikes, took photos, and helped us hone the routes and our writing.

It is exciting to expand the scope of the original *Hiking Atlanta's Hidden Forests: Intown and Out*. Our editors at the University of Georgia Press, Nathaniel Holly, Laura Price Yoder, and Jon Davies, have provided so much guidance and support during our process of researching and writing this book.

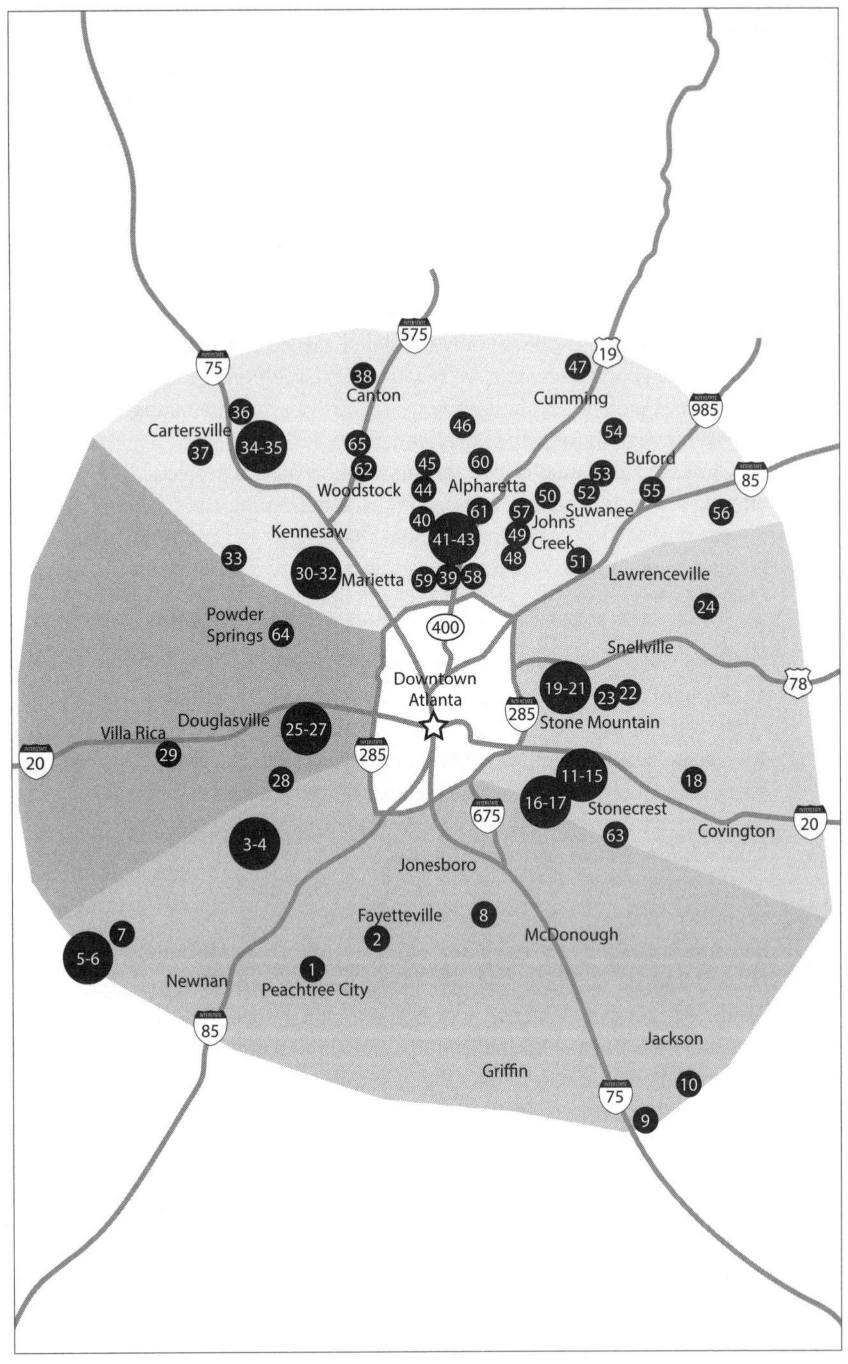

575
75
19
985
85
400
78
285
20
675
38
Canton
47
Cumming
36
Cartersville
34-35
37
46
54
65
Buford
62
45
60
53
Woodstock
44
Alpharetta
52
55
56
50
Suwanee
57
40
61
Johns
Creek
41-43
49
Kennesaw
33
30-32
Marietta
59
39
58
48
51
Lawrenceville
24
Powder
Springs
64
Snellville
Downtown
Atlanta
19-21
23
22
Stone Mountain
Douglasville
25-27
Villa Rica
29
28
11-15
18
16-17
Stonecrest
Covington
63
3-4
Jonesboro
Fayetteville
8
7
2
McDonough
5-6
1
Newnan
Peachtree City
Jackson
Griffin
10
9

1. Line Creek Nature Area
2. The Ridge Nature Area
3. Bear Creek Falls
4. Henry Mill Falls
5. Bobcat & Flat Rock Trails
6. Riverside & Wild Turkey Trails
7. McIntosh Reserve Park
8. Newman Wetlands Center
9. High Falls State Park
10. Dauset Trails
11. Mountaintop & Mountain View Trails
12. Forest & Mile Rock Trails
13. Vaughters' Farm & Retreat House Trails
14. Laurel Creek Trail
15. Cascade & Wilburn Farm Trails
16. Outcrop & Watershed Trails
17. Alexander Lakes Trail
18. Big Haynes Creek Nature Center
19. Walk-Up Trail
20. Cherokee Trail
21. Songbird Habitat Trail
22. Yellow River North Loop
23. Yellow River South Loop
24. Tribble Mill Park
25. Sweetwater Creek Red Trail
26. Sweetwater Creek White Trail
27. Sweetwater Creek Yellow & Orange Trails
28. Boundary Waters Park
29. Clinton Nature Preserve
30. Summit Trail
31. Cheatham Hill Loop
32. Kolb Farm Loop
33. Pickett's Mill Battlefield State Historic Site
34. Homestead & Sweet Gum Trails
35. Iron Hill Trail
36. Pine Mountain Recreation Area
37. Etowah Indian Mounds State Historic Site
38. Etowah Hiking Trails
39. Big Trees Forest Preserve
40. Chattahoochee Nature Center
41. Gold Branch
42. Vickery Creek
43. Island Ford
44. Leita Thompson Memorial Park
45. Lakhapani Preserve
46. Birmingham Park
47. Sawnee Mountain Preserve
48. Simpsonwood Park
49. Jones Bridge
50. Medlock Bridge
51. McDaniel Farm Park
52. Chattahoochee Pointe Park
53. Settles Bridge Park
54. Bowmans Island & Laurel Ridge Trail
55. Gwinnett Environmental and Heritage Center & Ivy Creek Greenway
56. Little Mulberry Park
57. Autrey Mill Nature Preserve and Heritage Center
58. Dunwoody Nature Center
59. Lost Corner Preserve
60. Providence Park
61. Big Creek Greenway
62. Noonday Creek Trail
63. Rockdale River Trail
64. Wildhorse Trail
65. Olde Rope Mill Park

HIKES AT A GLANCE

	Hike distance	Miles from downtown	Difficulty	Popularity
SOUTHSIDE				
I-85 SOUTH				
Line Creek Nature Area	3	35	Easy to moderate	★★★★☆
The Ridge Nature Area	4	26	Easy to moderate	★★★☆☆
Bear Creek Falls—Cochran Mill Park	4	27	Moderate	★★★★★
Henry Mill Falls—Cochran Mill Park	7.5	28	Strenuous	★★★★☆
Bobcat & Flat Rock Trails—Chattahoochee Bend State Park	4	54	Moderate	★★★★☆
Riverside & Wild Turkey Trails—Chattahoochee Bend State Park	6.5	54	Moderate to strenuous	★★★★★
McIntosh Reserve Park	5	46	Moderate	★★★★☆
I-75 SOUTH				
Newman Wetlands Center	1.35	23	Easy	★★★★★
High Falls State Park	4	51	Moderate	★★★★☆
Dauset Trails	6	54	Moderate	★★★★☆
EASTSIDE				
I-20 EAST				
Mountaintop & Mountain View Trails—Davidson-Arabia Mountain Nature Preserve	5	20	Moderate	★★★★★
Forest & Mile Rock Trails—Davidson-Arabia Mountain Nature Preserve	2.2	20	Easy to moderate	★★★★★

Facilities	Primary trail surface	Fees	Views	Water	History
	Dirt		Line Creek, Lake McIntosh	River, lake	Mule carving
	Dirt			Wetland	
	Dirt Gravel Rock outcrop	$5	Bear Creek Falls	Waterfall & creek	Mill ruins & dam
	Dirt	$5	Henry Mill Falls	Waterfall, creek	
	Dirt Rock	$5		Creek	
	Dirt	$5	Chattahoochee River	River	
	Dirt Gravel	$5	Chattahoochee River	River	Chief McIntosh's homestead & grave, Council Bluffs
	Boardwalk Dirt			Wetlands	
	Dirt Boardwalk	$5	High Falls	Lake, river, & waterfall	Mill site & powerhouse ruins
	Dirt Gravel Boardwalk			Creeks, ponds	
	Dirt Rock outcrop Paved Boardwalk		Mountaintop	Lake	
	Dirt Rock outcrop			Lake & pond	Quarry ruins

	Hike distance	Miles from downtown	Difficulty	Popularity
Vaughters' Farm & Retreat House Trails—Davidson-Arabia Mountain Nature Preserve	4.5	19	Moderate	★★★★☆
Laurel Creek Trail—Davidson-Arabia Mountain Nature Preserve	2.5	20	Easy to moderate	★★★☆☆
Cascade & Wilburn Farm Trails—Davidson-Arabia Mountain Nature Preserve	3.5	18	Moderate	★★★☆☆
Outcrop & Watershed Trails—Panola Mountain State Park	2	20	Easy to moderate	★★★★☆
Alexander Lakes Trail—Panola Mountain State Park	2	21	Moderate	★★★★☆
Big Haynes Creek Nature Center	4	32	Moderate	★★★★☆
US 78 EAST				
Walk-Up Trail—Stone Mountain Park	2	20	Strenuous	★★★★★
Cherokee Trail—Stone Mountain Park	5	20	Moderate to strenuous	★★★★☆
Songbird Habitat Trail—Stone Mountain Park	1.5	20	Easy	★★★★☆
North Loop—Yellow River Park	4.5	23	Moderate to strenuous	★★★★☆
South Loop—Yellow River Park	3.75	23	Moderate to strenuous	★★★★☆
Tribble Mill Park	6	42	Moderate	★★★★★
WESTSIDE				
I-20 WEST				
Red Trail—Sweetwater Creek State Park	2	19	Easy to moderate	★★★★★
White Trail—Sweetwater Creek State Park	5	19	Moderate to strenuous	★★★★☆

Facilities	Primary trail surface	Fees	Views	Water	History
	Dirt Rock outcrop		Hilltop	Lake	Barn
	Dirt Paved			Creek & cascades	
	Dirt Paved		Hilltop	Pond, creek, & cascade	Farmhouse ruins
	Dirt Gravel Boardwalk	$5	Mountain outcrop	Creek	
	Paved Boardwalk	$5	Upper & Lower Alexander Lake	Lake	Barn
	Dirt Gravel		Wetland Overlook	Wetland & creek	Historic homestead
	Rock outcrop	$20	Mountaintop		
	Dirt, Outcrop	$20	Venable Lake, Stone Mountain	Lake	Grist Mill, Pine Lodge Chimney
	Dirt	$20	Meadow		
	Dirt			Waterfall, creek	
	Dirt Paved		Yellow River	River	
	Paved Dirt		Ozora Lake	Lakes, waterfall	Mill site
	Dirt Stairs Rock outcrop	$5	Sweetwater Creek	Creek	New Manchester Mill
	Dirt Gravel Stairs	$5	Sweetwater Creek Jack's Lake Dam	Creek & lake	Ruins, New Manchester Mill

	Hike distance	Miles from downtown	Difficulty	Popularity
Yellow & Orange Trails—Sweetwater Creek State Park	3	19	Moderate	★★★★☆
Boundary Waters Park	7	22	Moderate to strenuous	★★★★☆
Clinton Nature Preserve	5	30	Moderate to strenuous	★★★★☆
NORTHSIDE				
I-75 NORTH				
Summit Trail—Kennesaw Mountain National Battlefield Park	2–6	25	Strenuous	★★★★★
Cheatham Hill Loop—Kennesaw Mountain National Battlefield Park	3.75	24	Moderate	★★★★☆
Kolb Farm Loop—Kennesaw Mountain National Battlefield Park	6	24	Moderate	★★★★☆
Pickett's Mill Battlefield State Historic Site	3.75	34	Moderate	★★★★☆
Homestead & Sweet Gum Trails—Red Top Mountain State Park	5.5	38	Moderate to strenuous	★★★★★
Iron Hill Trail—Red Top Mountain State Park	4.5	37	Moderate	★★★★★
Pine Mountain Recreation Area	5	42	Strenuous	★★★★☆
Etowah Indian Mounds State Historic Site	2.25	44	Easy to moderate	★★★★★

Facilities	Primary trail surface	Fees	Views	Water	History
	Dirt	$5	Sweetwater Creek New Manchester Mill	Creek	Native American shelter rock
	Dirt Paved		Chattahoochee River	River & lake	
	Dirt Gravel Rock outcrop			Lake	1800s log house & bunkhouse
	Dirt Paved	$5	Mountaintop		Civil War memorial monuments & replica cannons
	Dirt Gravel	$5		Creek	Civil War memorial monument & earthworks, soldier graveyard, battlefield site
	Dirt Gravel	$5		Creek	Civil War earthworks & monuments
	Dirt	$3.50–$6	Ravine, meadow	Wterfall, creek	Civil War battlefield, mill site, log cabin
	Dirt	$5	Lake Allatoona	Lake, creeks	Homestead ruins
	Dirt	$5	Lake Allatoona	Lake	Abandoned campground, iron mines
	Dirt		Mountaintop	Creeks	
	Dirt Grass Boardwalk	$2–$6	Top of mounds	Etowah River	Historic mounds & museum

	Hike distance	Miles from downtown	Difficulty	Popularity
I-575 NORTH				
Etowah Hiking Trails	7.3	41	Strenuous	★★★☆☆
GA 400 NORTH				
Big Trees Forest Preserve	1.25	19	Easy	★★★★☆
Chattahoochee Nature Center	2.25	24	Easy to moderate	★★★★★
Gold Branch–Chattahoochee River National Recreation Area	3.5	22	Moderate	★★★★☆
Vickery Creek–Chattahoochee River National Recreation Area	4.5	21	Moderate	★★★★★
Island Ford–Chattahoochee River National Recreation Area	6	22	Moderate	★★★★★
Leita Thompson Memorial Park	2.5	28	Easy to moderate	★★★★★
Lakhapani Preserve	1.5	30	Easy to moderate	★★★☆☆
Birmingham Park	2	36	Easy to moderate	★★★★☆
Sawnee Mountain Preserve	3.5–9.0	47	Strenuous	★★★★★
I-85 NORTH				
Simpsonwood Park	2.5	25	Moderate	★★★☆☆
Jones Bridge–Chattahoochee River National Recreation Area	5.25	26	Moderate	★★★★☆
Medlock Bridge–Chattahoochee River National Recreation Area	1.75	25	Easy to moderate	★★★☆☆
McDaniel Farm Park	2.3	25	Easy to moderate	★★★★★
Chattahoochee Pointe Park	3.3	35	Easy	★★★★★

Facilities	Primary trail surface	Fees	Views	Water	History
	Dirt		Etowah River	River, creeks	Sutallee Trace, carved rocks, historic church, cemetery
	Dirt Paved			Creek	
	Dirt Boardwalk Paved	$14–$20	Chattahoochee River	Ponds, wetlands, river	Historic homesite
	Dirt	$5	Chattahoochee River, Morgan Falls Dam	River, wetlands	
	Dirt Paved	$5	Chattahoochee River, Roswell Mill Dam	River & dam	Roswell Mill
	Dirt	$5	Chattahoochee River	River, creek, pond	
	Crushed gravel			Creek & lake	
	Dirt			Lake & creek	
	Dirt Gravel			Creek	Barn
	Dirt		Mountaintop	Creeks, pond	Abandoned mines
	Dirt Gravel		Chattahoochee River	River, creek	Methodist Retreat Center
	Dirt	$5	Chattahoochee River	River	
	Dirt	$5	Chattahoochee River	River	
	Paved			Creek	Historic farm & buildings
	Gravel Boardwalk		Chattahoochee River	River, creek	Site of historic farm

	Hike distance	Miles from downtown	Difficulty	Popularity
Settles Bridge Park	4	36	Moderate	★★★★☆
Bowmans Island & Laurel Ridge Trail—Chattahoochee River National Recreation Area	9.75	44	Strenuous	★★★★☆
Gwinnett Environmental and Heritage Center & Ivy Creek Greenway	7.75	36	Moderate	★★★☆☆
Little Mulberry Park	6	41	Moderate to strenuous	★★★★★
BONUS HIKES				
SHORT BUT SWEET HIKES				
Autrey Mill Nature Preserve and Heritage Center	1–2	28	Easy	★★★★☆
Dunwoody Nature Center	1.5	20	Easy	★★★★★
Lost Corner Preserve	1	19	Easy	★★★★☆
Providence Park	1–2	30	Easy	★★★★☆
PAVED MULTIUSE TRAILS				
Big Creek Greenway	1–15	24	Easy to moderate	★★★★★
Noonday Creek Trail	1–2.75	31	Easy	★★★★★
Rockdale River Trail	1–18	30	Easy to strenuous	★★★☆☆
Wildhorse Trail	1.7	23	Easy	★★★☆☆
TRAILS SHARED WITH MOUNTAIN BIKES				
Olde Rope Mill Park	1–17	32	Easy to strenuous	★★★★★

Facilities	Primary trail surface	Fee	Views	Water	History
	Dirt Paved		Chattahoochee River	River, lake, creek	Settle's Bridge
	Dirt Gravel	$8	Chattahoochee River, Lake Lanier	River, lake, waterfall	Buford Dam
	Dirt Paved Boardwalk		Waterfall, suspension bridge	Creeks, wetlands	Mill dam, historic house
	Paved Dirt		Ravine waterfall & Miller Lake valley	Waterfall & creeks	Stone structures
	Dirt Boardwalk			Creek, cascade	Mill ruins & historic buildings
	Dirt		Creek viewpoint	Creek	
	Paved Dirt			Creek	1800s-era cottage & spring house
	Dirt Paved		Providence Lake	Lake	
	Paved			Wetland	
	Paved Boardwalk			Creek, wetland	
	Paved		South River	River, wetland	Monastery of the Holy Spirit
	Paved			Creek	
	Dirt Paved		Little River	River, creeks	Mill ruins & dam

Hiking Metro Atlanta's Hidden Forests

AN INTRODUCTION TO METRO ATLANTA HIKING

Why Hike in Metro Atlanta?

As you hike the woodland coves, creekside trails, wooded hilltops, and rocky mountains described in this guidebook, it's easy to forget that every trail in this book is in a suburban neighborhood. Nearby are homes, businesses, highways, industry, and even skyscrapers. Each hike is within an hour's drive of downtown, but these suburban hidden forests transport you so much farther away. This guidebook can help you integrate hiking into your everyday life. If you want to walk your dog after work or are in search of a Sunday afternoon excursion for your family, you'll find a trail not too far from home to explore. And if you want a full day of hiking without spending a half day in the car, you will discover that metro Atlanta's hidden forests are the perfect place to go.

HIKING FOR EXERCISE

Hiking on forest trails is one of the best physical activities available. Walking is cardiovascular exercise that promotes overall fitness, tones muscle, burns fat, strengthens joints, and develops balance. The uneven surface of hiking trails provides a more thorough workout than a walk on flat pavement. Dirt, grass, wood chips, and even gravel trail surfaces are also easier on joints than sidewalks.

HIKING FOR NATURE

Do you love big trees? Wildflowers? Bird-watching? Waterfalls? Atlanta may be one of the 10 largest metropolitan areas in the United States, but it is also a haven for nature. Our creeks and urban sprawl have left ample space between neighborhoods in which animals and plants thrive. The trails in this book are the perfect way to commune with nature without dedicating your whole day to driving.

HIKING FOR HISTORY

In the past, Atlanta has bulldozed historic structures to make way for new development. But in the metro area's hidden forests, you can still find relics of history: million-year-old geological formations, century-old trees, and human ruins, including old homesteads, dams, and

Civil War battlefields. Using this book, you can hike through quarry ruins, observe 19th-century homesteads, and behold 1,000-year-old indigenous burial grounds. What a fun way to learn Atlanta's history!

HIKING FOR CONNECTION

Hiking trails throughout the metro Atlanta area can help build connections across boundaries of geography, race, and ethnicity. We Atlantans are often siloed in our neighborhoods or areas of town. A Sandy Springs resident may feel no need to visit Stockbridge. A Fulton County homeowner may not have a reason to explore Villa Rica. When we welcome new hikers to the trails near our home or when we explore a park nestled in a town we've never visited, we take a literal step to break down barriers and build connections.

Safety, Ethics, and Etiquette

WHAT TO WEAR

Though some hikers swear by high-tech boots and specialized clothing, the hikes in this guidebook don't require a shopping spree at an upscale outdoor retailer. Wear what you have around the house and follow these general guidelines:

Dress for the season and weather. In warm weather, wear short sleeves, a sun hat or baseball cap, and breathable clothing that allows airflow. Though shorts are cooler, wearing lightweight pants in the summer can help you avoid annoyances such as ticks, chiggers, and poison ivy. In the winter, long sleeves and long pants are a good idea, but layering is key. It's good to be able to peel off a layer as you warm up from the exercise, and it's wonderful to put that warm layer back on when you begin cooling down afterward. Much body heat is lost through the head, and fingers can chill quickly, so a warm hat and gloves are especially effective means of staying warm in cold weather. A rain jacket, a poncho, or even an umbrella is important to bring in case of rain.

Choose appropriate footwear. Wearing the right shoes can make or break a hike. Unless you have ankle sensitivities, athletic shoes work as well as hiking boots for any of the hikes in this book. If you seek more hiking-specific footwear, look for trail runners or light hikers that combine the lightweight materials of sneakers with the ankle support and rugged sole of boots. Socks are an important factor in avoiding blisters. Choose athletic or hiking socks that fit well and come up over your ankle. Most hikers prefer woolen and synthetic-blend socks because they wick away moisture, keeping your feet cool and dry.

WHAT TO BRING

The following checklist can help you leave the house prepared for your hike in any weather:

- Backpack or waist pack
- Water (one liter per person at least)
    - For hot summer hikes, electrolyte powder or tablets can help keep you hydrated. You can find these at most grocery stores.
- Food (lunch or snacks such as energy bars, trail mix, fruit, etc.)
- Navigation (guidebook, map)
- Clothes
    - Waterproof jacket, poncho, and/or umbrella
    - Fleece, sweatshirt, coat, warm hat if the weather is cold
- Sun protection (sunscreen, sun hat, sunglasses)
- Insect repellent
- First-aid kit (bandages, blister pads, insect-bite remedy, etc.)
- Plastic bag (to pack out trash)
- Cell phone (in waterproof case or bag)

DOGS

Nearly all the hikes in this book are dog-friendly destinations (and the few that prohibit dogs are noted as such). Hiking with your pet can add to your enjoyment and safety. Bringing your dog does decrease your likelihood of seeing birds and other wildlife, but hikers with dogs often connect and strike up friendships more easily than solo hikers.

Leashing your pet is both required by law and important for making everyone feel welcome on these trails. Some people are afraid of dogs (yes, even afraid of your sweet pooch). Some dogs are reactive when approached by an off-leash canine. Even if your pet is friendly and responds immediately to voice commands, please be a good neighbor and leash your canine companion. Nearby off-leash dog parks are noted throughout this book.

Despite the law and etiquette, you will likely come across hikers who are walking with loose dogs. Use common sense when approaching (or being approached by) an unleashed dog and politely ask the owner to leash the pet.

Following leash laws also can help protect our waterways. Pet waste is a significant cause of creek pollution in the metro area. Dog waste left in the woods is washed into streams by rainstorms and adds foreign bacteria and other pollutants. Bring waste bags and carry your dog's waste to an appropriate trash receptacle.

SAFETY

Preparation, vigilance, and common sense are the foundation of safe hiking. You are in charge of your own safety while exploring the trails in this guidebook. Below are some tips that may help you as you go.

Poison ivy is common in the metro Atlanta area. The uncomfortable effects of exposure make it important to learn how to identify its three leaflets and hairy roots and vines. Wear long pants when hiking, and avoid touching the plant. If you think you have touched poison ivy, wash your skin thoroughly. Over-the-counter products can help avoid the rash caused by poison ivy, but they must be used soon after you make contact.

Snakes live throughout Georgia. Most are harmless and nonvenomous, but venomous copperheads may be seen on these trails in spring, summer, and fall. Though it's rare to have close encounters with snakes, vigilance is the key to avoiding them. Stay on the trail and look where you're putting your feet—do not step blindly over a large log or rock. Pay special attention when walking through marshy or open areas where snakes may choose to sun themselves. If a snake bites you, take a photo of the animal and call 911 immediately.

Insects you may encounter while hiking are primarily an annoyance, not a danger. Spiders, bees, hornets, wasps, and yellow jackets can best be avoided by not disturbing their homes—and staying on the trail. Mosquitoes, ticks, and chiggers can be the biggest annoyance in the forests in and around Atlanta. After your hike, check your body for ticks, especially in warm dark places on your body such as armpits and along waistbands and sock lines. Not all ticks carry Lyme disease, and ticks do not transmit the disease until at least 24 hours after biting you. So search for and remove ticks quickly and put your mind at ease. Chiggers are very small insects that cause itchy bumps that last for days. It is rare to get chigger bites when walking on maintained trails. When walking through tall grasses or brush, wear long pants and shower soon after hiking to wash away any chiggers that might have found you. Though mosquitoes are found everywhere in Atlanta, insect repellent is the best way to avoid their itchy bites.

Injuries most common to hiking are minor ankle sprains, blisters, weather-induced conditions such as heat exhaustion, and cuts caused by a fall. Watch where you are stepping, choose appropriate footwear, and use hiking sticks to lessen the likelihood of falls, sprains, and blisters. Most of these can be treated on-site with a small first-aid kit, but some injuries might need professional attention. And remember not to push yourself past your physical limits or take unnecessary risks for the perfect selfie. All of the hikes in this guidebook are in areas with mobile phone coverage. Call 911 if you need help.

Hiking alone on urban or suburban trails is not so different from walking alone on city streets. Pay attention to your surroundings, walk and speak with confidence, and trust your gut. Hiking in any metro Atlanta park after dark is not recommended and in most cases not allowed. If you're feeling particularly anxious about hiking alone, bring a dog, carry pepper spray, or invite a friend along.

Mobile phone reception is generally good throughout the metro Atlanta area, so carrying your phone can provide peace of mind and a direct connection to law enforcement. Always tell someone where you are going, and consider using a mobile phone app to share your location with a friend or family member. Call 911 if you need help while hiking, and pay attention to trail markers and other landmarks that can help you share your location with the emergency operator.

LEAVE NO TRACE PRINCIPLES

"Take only photos, leave only footprints" is an excellent motto for hikers. Urban hikers often add "and pack out trash." The Center for Outdoor Ethics promotes a philosophy that asks hikers to consider their impact on our natural places and take steps to actively leave no trace of their presence on the trail. While hiking through the urban and suburban greenspaces in this guidebook, you will often see signs of humans—old tires, beer bottles and cans, shopping bags, and other trash. As a visitor to these trails, you can also be a steward of the land by carrying a plastic bag and packing out any trash you find. The seven principles of Leave No Trace are:

1. Plan ahead and prepare
2. Travel on durable surfaces
3. Dispose of waste properly
4. Leave what you find
5. Minimize campfire impacts
6. Respect wildlife
7. Be considerate of others

For more information about Leave No Trace, visit www.lnt.org.

HOW TO USE THIS BOOK

This guidebook was written to break down the barriers that might stop you from enjoying metro Atlanta's trails.

Not enough time: In the pages that follow, you'll find hikes that don't require a full-day commitment or multihour drive. From an afternoon stroll to a weekend trek, there's a hike to fit your goals.

Not enough information: This book provides all the pertinent information you'll need to plan for and enjoy your hike. You can follow the recommended route exactly or use the maps and landmarks to design your own adventure.

No guidance: We have designed, tested, and refined every hike route in this book. Web searches and crowdsourced apps can overwhelm you with options and still leave you unsure about trail conditions. We have taken the guesswork out of choosing a hike.

Accessibility: Not every hiking trail is right for every person. Are you a wheelchair user? Are you bringing a baby along? Are you a first-time hiker? Do you deal with balance issues? This book offers a wide variety of hiking trails with options suitable for the needs of just about any hiker. Each chapter details what you can expect in terms of elevation, difficulty, and trail surface.

How to Get There

Each chapter includes a section that provides at a glance the information you need to get to the trailhead. The distance from downtown Atlanta is the actual driving distance from the Georgia Capitol, not an "as the crow flies" straight line. For your reference, we also have included the city, county, and major highway that are closest to the trailhead. You can punch the address into your favorite map app and navigate to the trailhead. Once you get to the park, you can refer to this book's specific directions for parking and finding the trailhead.

Public Transit

Though Atlanta is known for its sprawling neighborhoods, its public transit system has not quite caught up to the city's needs. However, hikes that are accessible via MARTA, Atlanta's system of public trains and buses, have been noted in this book. Find the right bus or train route in this book, then use MARTA's website (www.itsmarta.com) or Google Maps' Transit function (maps.google.com) to plan your route.

Hike Distance and Type

The Hike Distance listed is for the route recommended in this book. Remember, there are almost always more trails available at each greenspace, so you can add mileage by designing your own route or by hiking the recommended route more than once. Most hikes start and end at the same trailhead and are described as loop (one nonintersecting loop), figure-8 loop (a double loop that intersects), triple loop (three intersecting loops), lollipop loop (a loop with an out-and-back portion), or out-and-back (one linear trail with mileage that includes both the hike out and the hike back).

Difficulty Rating

Hike difficulty is subjective and is also based on many variables. We have provided an overall difficulty rating for each hike along with specific information to help you gauge how challenging a hike might be for you. These factors include but are not limited to how experienced you are with hiking, your level of fitness, the weather, how easy or difficult navigation is on the trails, the type of terrain and trail surface, and the amount of elevation change.

Safety Rating

How comfortable you feel on these trails is also subjective, but we have analyzed each hike to provide a 1-5 scale rating for four aspects related to our feeling of safety. One star is the least sense of safety, five stars represents a high sense of safety.

- Usage
    - How common is it to pass other people on this trail?
    - Do women hike alone in this park? With or without dogs?
    - Are people using the park for activities other than hiking?

- Visibility
  - How open or secluded is the trail?
  - How close to or far from the road is the trail?
  - How far ahead or behind can you see?
- Upkeep
  - Is the trail receiving regular maintenance? Are trails overgrown?
  - Are trails well marked?
- Parking
  - Is the parking area visible from the road? Is it in an open area?
  - Are there many cars or few cars in the parking area?
  - Are there cameras or staff on-site?

Dogs

Be sure to refer to this section of each chapter if you enjoy hiking with your pup. We've included information on whether leashed dogs are welcome on each trail and if there are nearby off-leash dog parks you can visit afterward.

Land Manager, Facilities, Hours, Fees

The hike route is not the only information you need to prepare for a hike. We've included information about the hours each trail is open and if there are any fees for use. A list of facilities can help you plan for bathroom breaks, water, picnicking, or pre- or posthiking activities such as fitness stations, sports fields, tennis courts, and playgrounds. If you need more information or clarification of the rules of each park, you can reach out to the entity that manages the trail, park, or facility.

Landmarks

What's better than a hike that's close to home? A hike that includes a scavenger hunt! The three landmarks listed for each hike give you a tip about what interesting and unique features you'll encounter along the trail. See if you can locate all three landmarks on every hike. These landmarks include historical ruins, unique ecological areas, waterfalls, overlooks, and other interesting features. In particular, we've identified unique and special trees along most trails.

Sentinel tree: This term, coined by author Jonah McDonald, describes a tree that is especially notable by virtue of its size, age, rarity, or other memorable characteristic.

Hike Route Description and Map

How you use the hike description will depend on your past hiking experience, confidence, and personality. Will you follow our directions to the letter? Will you wing it and use the map only as needed? Will you create your own route based on our recommendations? No matter your hiking style, reading the full hike description and reviewing the map before your hike will give you important information about trail conditions, landmarks, and possible impediments.

The hike description is written in narrative form, as if you were talking with the authors themselves. But even though the style is conversational, the content is precise. Still, changes occur in nature all the time, so you might encounter a newly fallen tree, a broken bridge, or even a brand new trail.

Each map is simple in design but includes a great deal of information. In addition to our recommended route, we have included all other trails in each greenspace, as well as connecting roads. You'll also find bridges, boardwalks, and other landmarks noted. If you use this book for nothing else, these maps are just about the most thorough and accurate ones you can find anywhere.

SOUTHSIDE

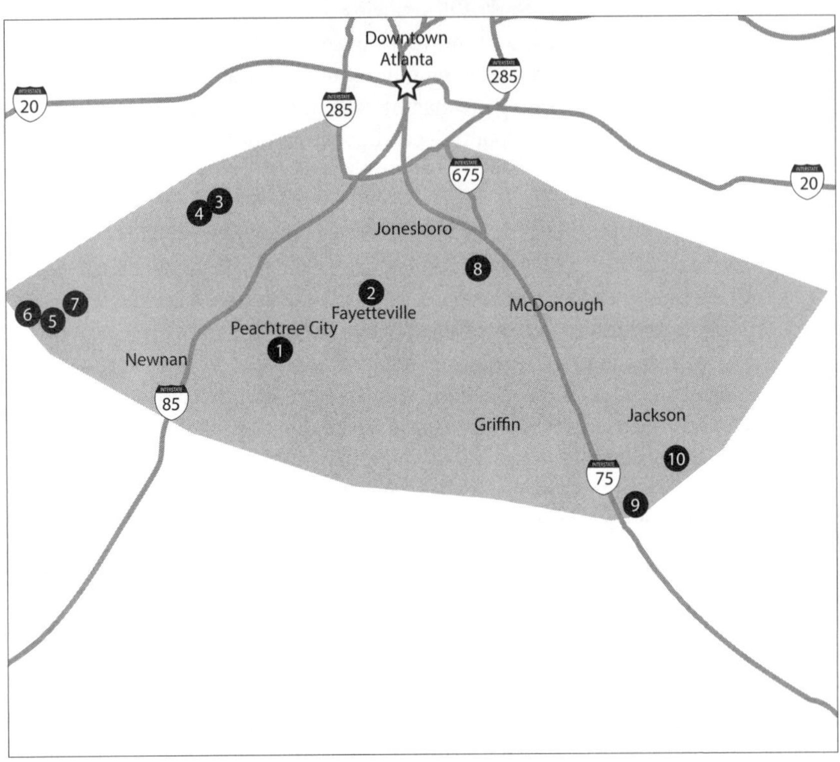

1. Line Creek Nature Area
2. The Ridge Nature Area
3. Bear Creek Falls
4. Henry Mill Falls
5. Bobcat & Flat Rock Trails
6. Riverside & Wild Turkey Trails
7. McIntosh Reserve Park
8. Newman Wetlands Center
9. High Falls State Park
10. Dauset Trails

I-85 SOUTH

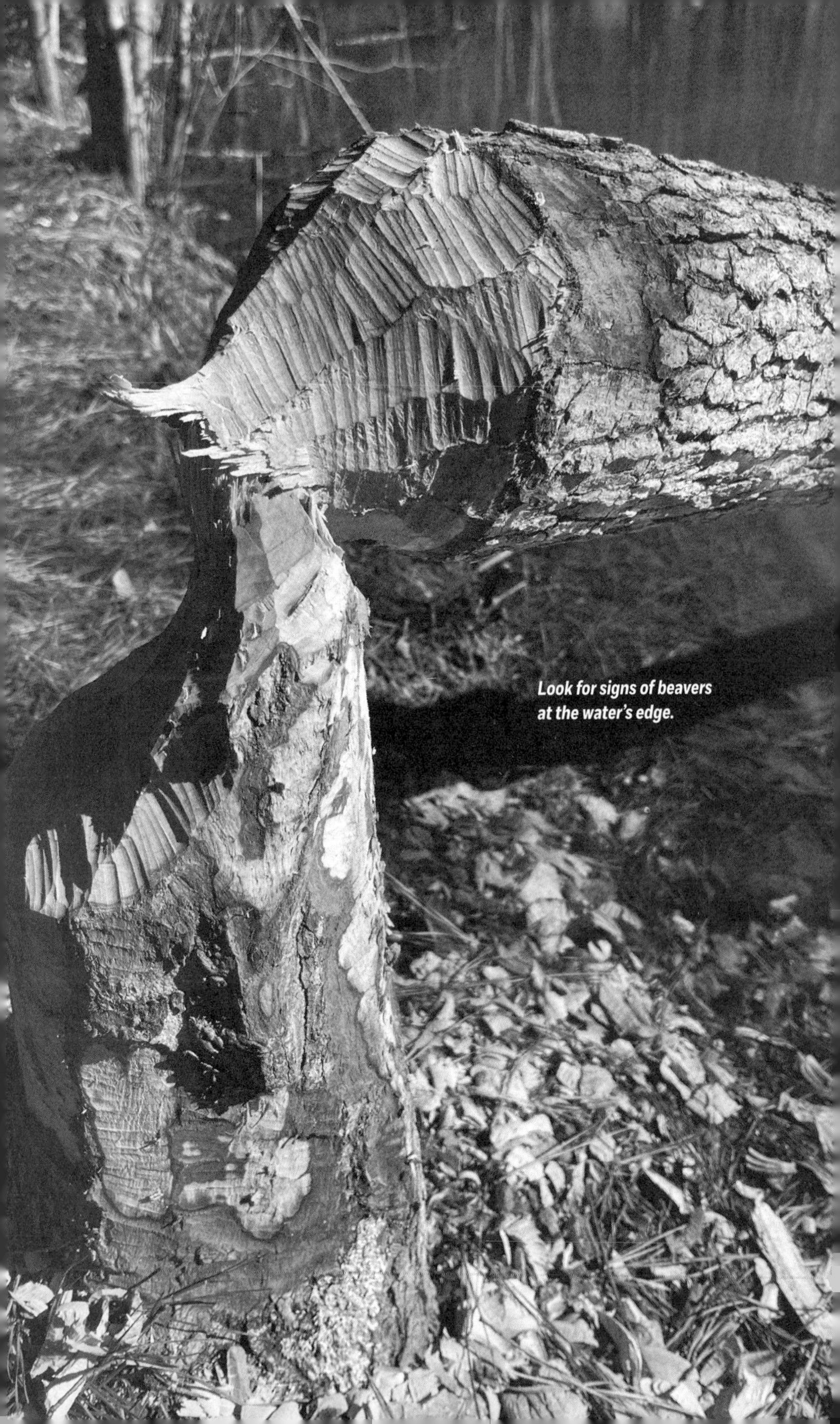
Look for signs of beavers at the water's edge.

Line Creek Nature Area

Line Creek Nature Area is a prime example of a hidden forest. Located less than a mile from shopping centers and restaurants, this 70-acre nature preserve has wetlands, stunning creekside views, historic sites, and granite outcrops. This route allows you to experience the highlights of the preserve as you hike through old-growth hardwood forests along the creek.

HOW TO GET THERE

Driving Distance from Downtown Atlanta: 35 miles
Address: 2754 GA 54, Peachtree City, GA 30269
Closest Interstate: I-85
City, County: Peachtree City, Fayette
Parking: Large gravel parking area

HIKE DISTANCE

3-mile lollipop loop

DIFFICULTY

Overall: Easy to moderate
Navigation:: Blazes on trees; signposts at most junctions
Terrain: Hard-packed dirt trails; rock outcrop crossings
Elevation Change: Minimal elevation change with a few rolling hills

SAFETY

Usage ★★★★☆
Visibility ★★★☆☆
Upkeep ★★★★☆
Parking ★★★★☆

HOURS

Dawn to dusk

DOGS

Leashed dogs allowed

FACILITIES

- Toilets at parking area
- Picnic area, trash bins, benches

FEES & PERMITS

None

LAND MANAGER

Peachtree City Parks & Recreation

Can you find the "mule" carving on the granite outcrop?

Landmarks

MULE CARVING

This rock outcrop on the Mule Trail is one of the first places to view Line Creek up close. As you cross the outcrop, see if you can find the "mule" carving in the rock. As noted on the signpost, it was carved by Glen Allen in the early 1980s.

HISTORIC DAM SITES

Halfway through the hike, pass two historic dam sites from the early 1800s. Though the dams are no longer intact, you can still see the large rocks that were used to build the dams.

SENTINEL AMERICAN BEECH

This sentinel American beech stands at the edge of the water. It's among the largest trees in this section of forest. Though beech trees usually have smooth gray bark, this one is tinted green from moss, which grows on but does not harm the tree.

Hike Route

Facing the parking area driveway, begin your hike at the front left corner of the parking lot at the signpost for Pond Trail. Fifty feet into the hike, go right and downhill toward the gazebo and observation deck for a close view of the sparkling pond. After exiting the deck, turn left and follow green blazes, immediately crossing two bridges. Hike along the edge of the pond, looking out for signs of beavers and downed trees.

Reach a junction at the edge of the pond and turn right onto Ridge Trail. In 100 feet at the next junction, go right and stay left at the next junction. In 0.1 mile, go right and downhill toward the creek, then go left at a junction at the bottom of the hill, following the red blazes for Mule Trail.

Cross a small rock outcrop. Take either path when the trail splits. The paths reconnect in 100 feet before crossing a larger rock outcrop. Look for the "mule" carving in the stone. In 0.2 mile, come to a junction with Ridge Trail. Bear right, following the yellow blazes for Shoal Trail. In 0.2 mile, reach a large rock outcrop along Line Creek with great views of the running creek. Continue on the dirt path past a bench.

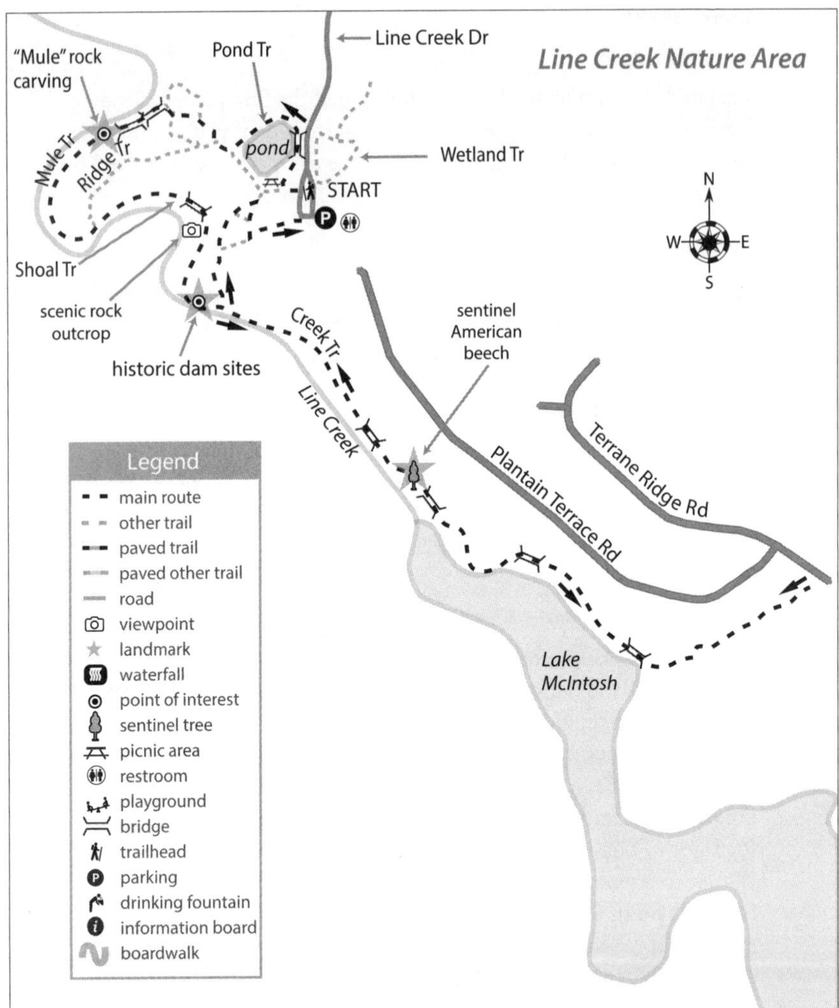
Line Creek Nature Area
"Mule" rock carving
Pond Tr
Line Creek Dr
Wetland Tr
pond
Mule Tr
Ridge Tr
START
N
W
E
S
Shoal Tr
scenic rock outcrop
historic dam sites
Creek Tr
sentinel American beech
Line Creek
Plantain Terrace Rd
Terrane Ridge Rd
Lake McIntosh
Legend
main route
other trail
paved trail
paved other trail
road
viewpoint
landmark
waterfall
point of interest
sentinel tree
picnic area
restroom
playground
bridge
trailhead
parking
drinking fountain
information board
boardwalk

At a three-way junction, stay left and come to the site of a mill dam built in the 1820s. In just a few yards, reach the second mill dam site, this one erected in 1824. At this junction of Shoal and Creek Trails, stay straight across the outcrop and reenter the forest on Creek Trail. A few yards in, the trail splits into a choose-your-own-adventure option: you can hike either low and close to the creek or higher along the ridge. Both trails lead to the same destination.

Hike along Creek Trail with a residential area to your left and Line Creek to your right. Cross a footbridge, then look to the right for a large sentinel American beech. Enjoy this scenic section of trail traversing old hardwood forest along the water's edge, where the creek empties into Lake McIntosh. Hike for 0.4 mile, crossing several bridges and passing benches. The trail ends at a second parking area behind a residential area. Turn around here and retrace your steps to the junction with the 1824 mill dam.

Turn right and take the rock surface trail uphill to where it reaches a junction with a dirt path. Stay on the rock surface trail and then turn right at the next junction. Take this trail back to the parking area, generally staying left at any subsequent junctions to end your hike.

Keep an eye out for wildlife as you hike.

The Ridge Nature Area

Tucked into a suburban Fayetteville neighborhood is the Ridge Nature Area, a 308-acre nature preserve with many miles of trail through a variety of ecosystems and habitats. Hike through hardwood old-growth forests, past wetlands, and along Ginger Cake Creek for a quiet escape just minutes from busy roads. The gentle slopes and variety of trails make this a popular location for hikers, birders, runners, and families.

HOW TO GET THERE	**Driving Distance from Downtown Atlanta:** 26 miles **Address:** 390 Burch Road, Fayetteville, GA 30215 **Closest Interstate:** I-85 **City, County:** Fayetteville, Fayette **Parking:** Gravel parking lot along a long gravel drive
HIKE DISTANCE	4-mile loop
DIFFICULTY	**Overall:** Easy to moderate **Navigation:** Blazes on trees; marked posts at most junctions **Terrain:** Hard-packed dirt trails that can be very muddy after a rain **Elevation Change:** Mostly flat with a few minor hills
SAFETY	**Usage** ★★★★☆ **Visibility** ★★★☆☆ **Upkeep** ★★★☆☆ **Parking** ★★★☆☆
HOURS	Dawn to dusk
DOGS	Leashed dogs allowed
FACILITIES	• Toilets in parking area • Picnic area, trash cans, dog waste station, little free library
FEES & PERMITS	None
LAND MANAGER	Southern Conservation Trust and City of Fayetteville

Landmarks

MEDITATION GROVE

Find the meditation grove at the end of Three Oaks Trail next to a wetland and in a secluded section of forest. Sit on the bench and take a few moments to enjoy the serenity of the forest. You are surrounded by mature oak trees estimated to be over 200 years old.

WETLAND

The wetland is fed by Whitewater Creek and is a habitat for a variety of animals from amphibians to birds. If you're patient, you may see deer, owls, or wading birds making use of the abundant food sources here.

OLD GROWTH GROVE

In contrast to much of the rest of this greenspace, this section of Muscogee Trail winds through an old-growth hardwood forest. These trees are some of the largest in the preserve and mark the section of forest that wasn't disturbed by logging after the Georgia Land Lottery, which redistributed Muscogee land to white settlers.

Hike Route

Begin your hike at the information board by the green picnic benches, just past the restrooms. Behind the information board, look for a post labeled Ridge Loop Trail and go right, following the yellow blazes. Hike for 0.15 mile with the park road on your right to reach a junction at another information board. Turn left onto Whitewater Trail and follow the blue blazes to a junction with Wildwood Trail. Go left onto Wildwood Trail, following the purple blazes.

In 0.1 mile, turn right onto Ridgewood Trail, following the white blazes. Soon after, at the next junction, turn left onto Whitewater Trail, which is marked with blue blazes. Hike through the low boggy floodplain for 0.2 mile to reach a junction marked with a post for Three Oaks Trail. Turn right and take this spur deeper into the forest for 0.2 mile.

The trail ends at the edge of a wetland near a bench and interpretive sign about oaks with a poem by Joyce Kilmer. After enjoying the tranquility of this section of forest, retrace your steps back to the main trail and turn right onto Whitewater Trail. In 100 feet, reach a junction with Muscadine and Meadow Trails. Stay to the right, following the blue blazes for Muscadine Trail. Hike through the low floodplain, reaching the edge of the wetland on your right.

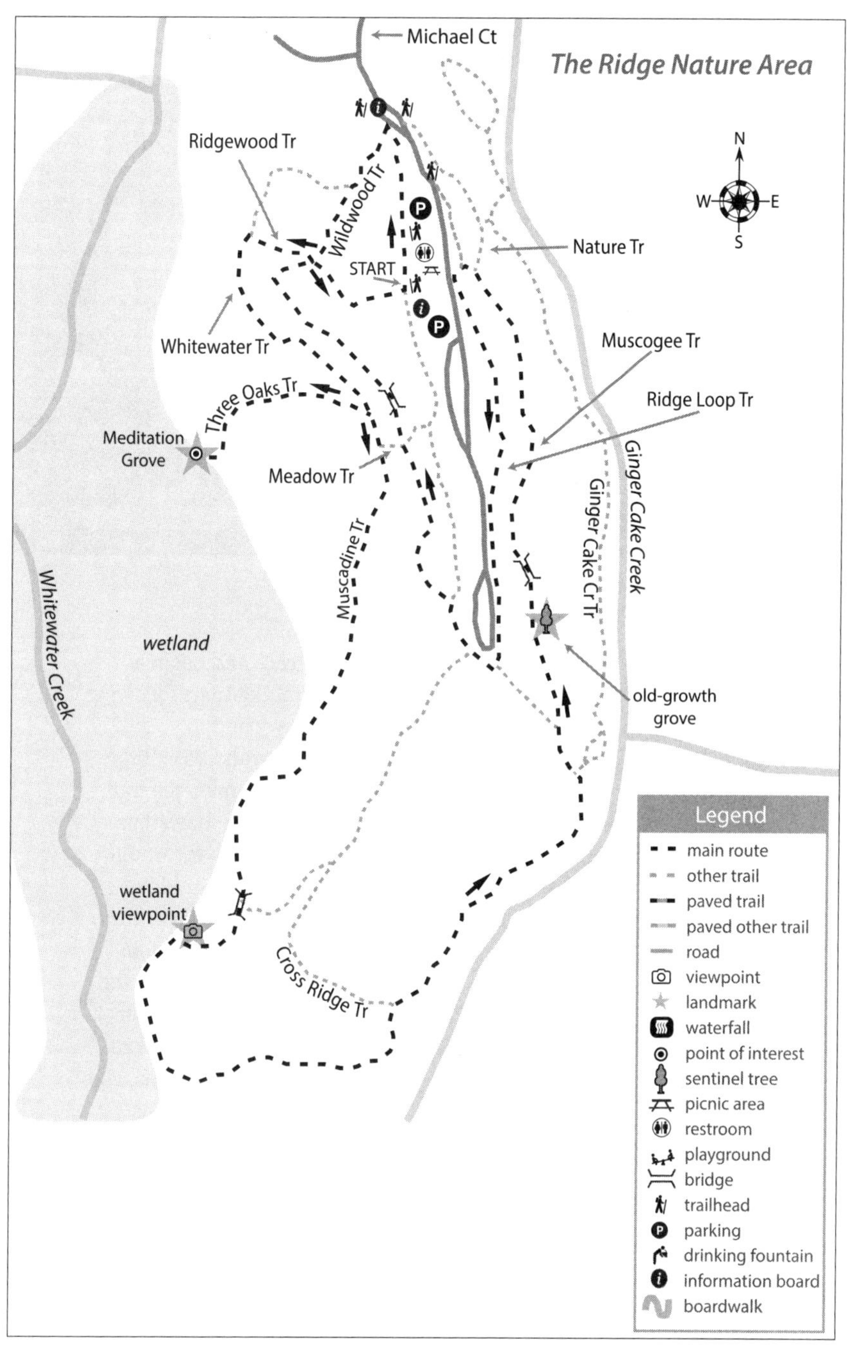
The Ridge Nature Area
Michael Ct
Ridgewood Tr
Wildwood Tr
START
Nature Tr
Whitewater Tr
Muscogee Tr
Ridge Loop Tr
Three Oaks Tr
Meditation Grove
Meadow Tr
Ginger Cake Creek
Ginger Cake Cr Tr
Muscadine Tr
Whitewater Creek
wetland
old-growth grove
wetland viewpoint
Cross Ridge Tr
N
W
E
S
Legend
main route
other trail
paved trail
paved other trail
road
viewpoint
landmark
waterfall
point of interest
sentinel tree
picnic area
restroom
playground
bridge
trailhead
parking
drinking fountain
information board
boardwalk

The Ridge is a mecca for fungi. How many species will you spot along the trail? Photo by Darling Nogh.

Pass two benches and several multitrunked trees and begin a slight uphill climb before the trail levels out again. Continue following the blue blazes with ravines on your left and the wetland to your right. After crossing a footbridge, reach a junction with Cross Ridge Trail and stay to the right on Muscadine Trail. As you hike, the trail brings you closer to the edge of the wetland than you've been thus far. Slow down here, as this is a good opportunity to look for wading birds or other wildlife.

From here, the trail gradually slopes uphill and curves away from the wetland before descending again. Be aware that at the bottom of the hill the trail can become washed out after a heavy rain. At the next junction with Cross Ridge Trail, stay right. Hike along Ginger Cake Creek for 0.3 mile to a junction with Ginger Cake Creek Trail. Stay left, following the purple blazes for Muscadine Trail. At the next junction, turn right onto Muscogee Trail, marked with red blazes.

Hike through some of the oldest sections of the forest in this park, passing several large mature oaks and tulip trees. Cross a footbridge and in 0.15 mile reach a junction with Nature Trail at a covered bench. Go left and uphill. This will bring you to a junction just before reaching the parking area. Turn left onto Ridge Loop Trail, following the yellow blazes. Hike along the top of the ridge, getting a different vantage point of the floodplain below.

At a junction with Muscadine Trail, stay straight, taking the trail with yellow and purple blazes. Stay straight at the immediate next junction. In 0.1 mile at a junction with Muscadine Trail, stay to the left, following the purple blazes. Notice the change in ecology on this section of trail, which has more pines and young trees.

In 0.2 mile, come to a four-way junction with Wildwood Trail and continue straight. Cross a small footbridge and in another 0.2 mile come to a four-way junction with Ridgewood Trail. Go right here, following the white blazes back to the intersection where you originally started. Exit the trail and return to the parking area to end your hike.

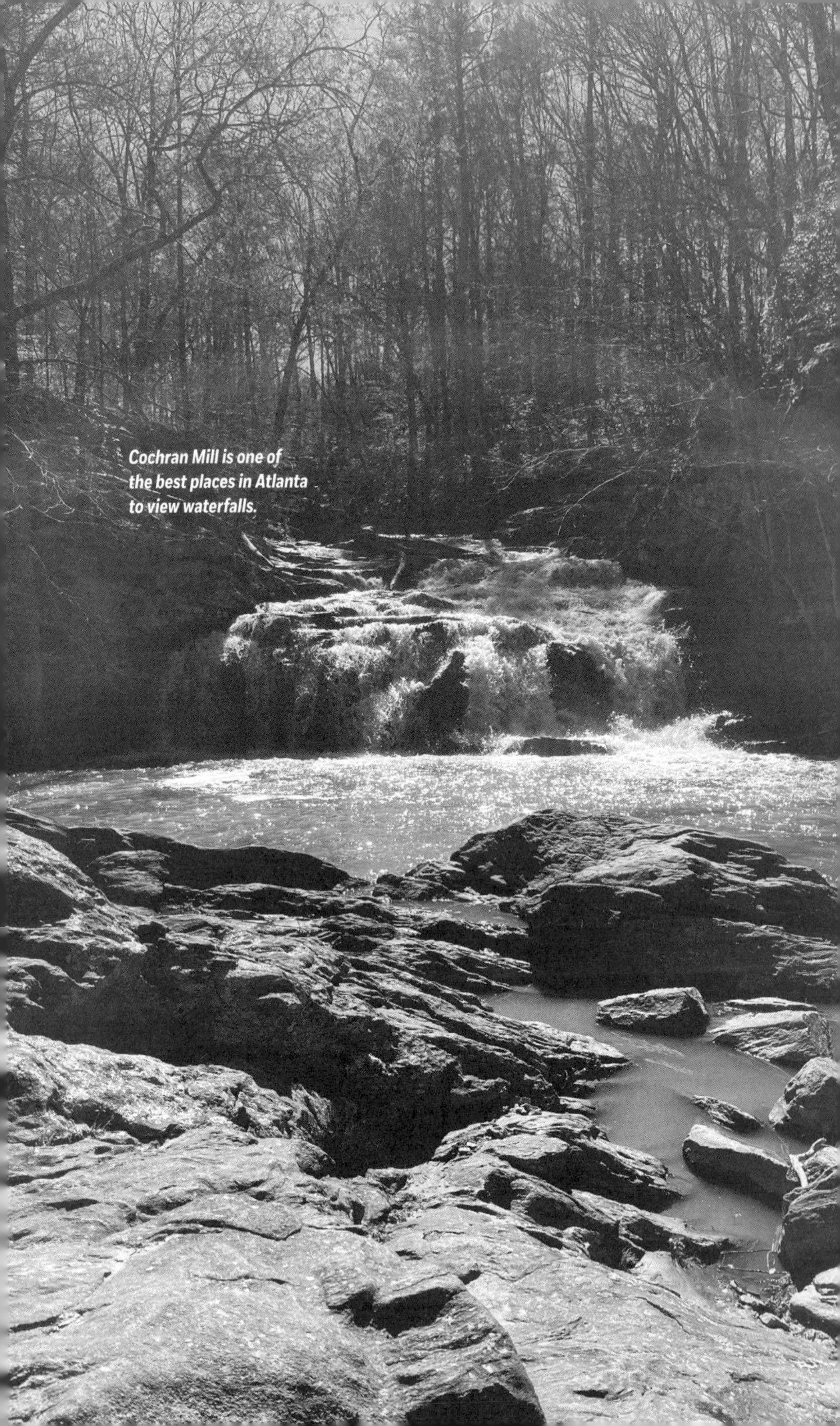
Cochran Mill is one of the best places in Atlanta to view waterfalls.

Bear Creek Falls

COCHRAN MILL PARK

The trails on the east side of Cochran Mill Park are some of the best hiking trails in Atlanta for waterfall enthusiasts. Bear Creek and Little Bear Creek spill over rock outcrops and old mill dams in beautiful cascades. The trail leads you along creeks, through rolling Piedmont hills, and past multiple waterfalls. And don't forget another major attraction: the nature center's reptile exhibit and raptor enclosure.

HOW TO GET THERE

Driving Distance from Downtown Atlanta: 28 miles
Address: 6875 Cochran Mill Road, Chattahoochee Hills, GA 30268
Closest Interstate: I-85
City, County: Chattahoochee Hills, Fulton
Parking: Large gravel parking lot

HIKE DISTANCE

4-mile figure-8 loop

DIFFICULTY

Overall: Moderate
Navigation: Maps at most junctions; marked posts and blazes along route
Terrain: Hard-packed dirt trail, wide gravel trail, and rock outcrops that can be slippery when wet
Elevation Change: Rolling hills with a few short but steep ascents and descents

SAFETY

Usage ★★★★★
Visibility ★★★★☆
Upkeep ★★★★★
Parking ★★★★★

HOURS

Dawn to dusk

DOGS

Leashed dogs allowed

FACILITIES

- Toilets at parking area
- Picnic areas, playground

FEES & PERMITS	$5 daily fee—purchase at payment kiosk next to information sign
LAND MANAGER	City of Chattahoochee Hills Parks & Recreation

Landmarks

BEAR CREEK FALLS

Those looking for waterfalls will get their heart's desire at the multiple falls and viewpoints along this hike. You will experience these waterfalls from all vantage points, above, below, and beside them. Each one is different, and that makes this hike great.

SENTINEL AMERICAN BEECH

This sentinel American beech stands on the opposite bank of Little Bear Creek from the trail. Thankfully, except for one signature ("Bobby"), the large trunk is free of carvings.

SENTINEL WATER OAK

This tree, 200 yards down a side trail to the right, looms over a much younger forest. The rounded shape of its crown demonstrates that it was the only tree growing in this area when the land was a farm.

Hike Route

Carefully exit the parking area and use the pedestrian crosswalk to cross Cochran Mill Road to the trailhead on the wide gravel trail. Cross a bridge over Little Bear Creek. The first falls are to your right at a large rock outcrop and mill ruins.

Hike left away from the falls and reach a junction. Go right and uphill. The trail switchbacks bring you to a higher viewpoint of the falls. If you'd like, take the junction on the right to a spur that leads out to another section of rock outcrop and waterfall viewpoint. It's a steep scramble over rocks but worth the view and opportunity to sit by the rushing water.

Return to the trail, turning right to hike along the bank of the creek. Look to the right for a leaning American beech tree on the opposite bank of the creek. In 100 yards, reach junction OR44 and go left. Soon after, at junction OR45, go right.

Hike for half a mile through rolling hills to come to a junction with a second waterfall in front of you. Go left and hike along the ridge with views of the second waterfall below you. At the next junction (OR50), in 0.25 mile, bear to the left.

At the bottom of the hill at junction OR49, stay straight and walk

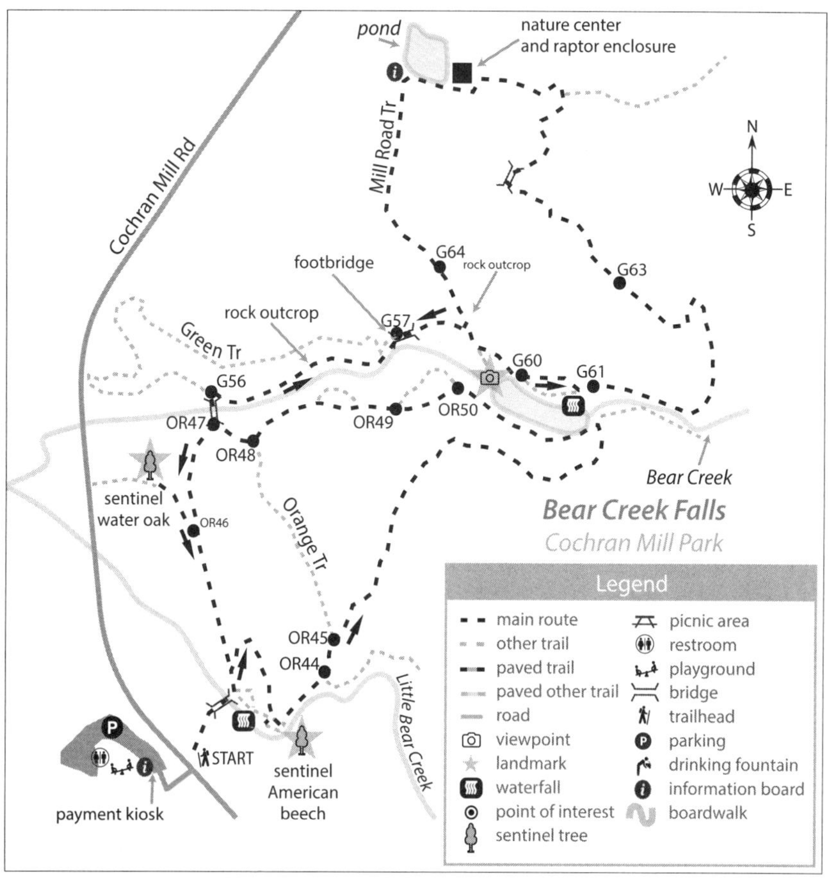

on the wooden planks to cross through a low wetland area. Hike uphill and along the ridge past a post marked G, staying to the left past two junctions on your right. Reach junction OR48 at the bottom of the hill in 0.2 mile and turn right.

The next junction (OR48) will appear immediately. Go right and cross a bridge. Then turn right onto Green Trail at junction G56. Hike along the banks of Bear Creek. Cross a rock outcrop in 0.1 mile; look to the left for the green blazes. Be careful crossing the rock outcrops as they can be especially slippery when wet.

In 0.15 mile, reach junction G57 and stay right across a small footbridge. At another rock outcrop in 0.1 mile, bear right for a closer view of the falls. After viewing the falls, retrace your steps on the outcrop and turn right at a post onto a dirt path that skirts the edge of the falls. You may be tempted to reconnect on the trail from the falls

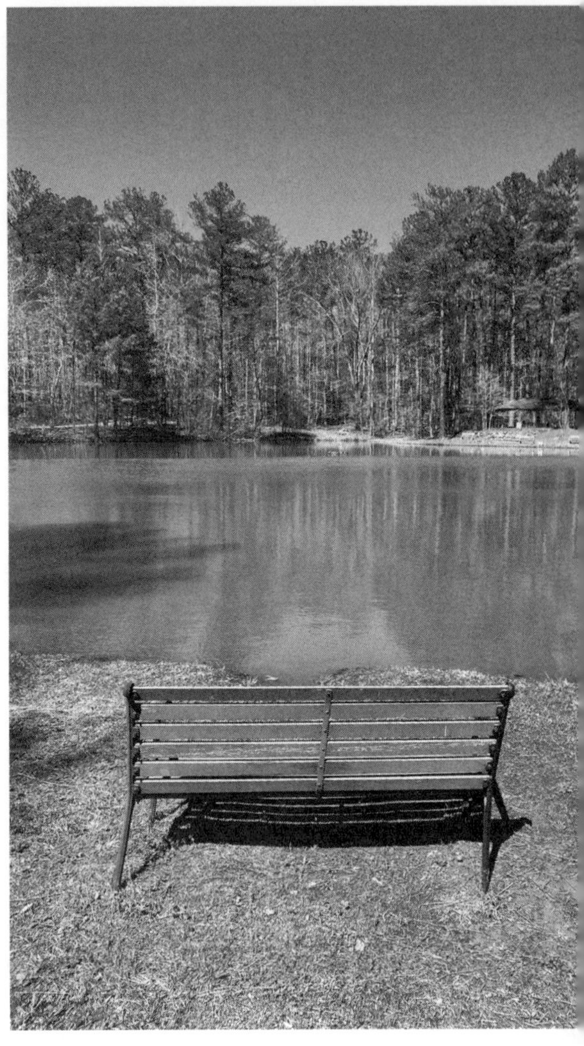

Waterfalls aren't the only scenic view on this hike.

viewpoint, but please don't, because the rock is very slippery here, and the water from the falls runs very close to the edge of the trail.

At junction G60, hike the left fork for the easier, less slippery route to the top of the falls. Continue bearing left at junction G61. After this junction, the trail begins to curve away from the creek and ascend the hill.

In 0.4 mile at the top of the hill, pass a post marked G63 and continue straight. Reach the bottom of the ridge in 0.2 mile and bear right to cross a footbridge. At the next junction, stay to the left, following the green blazes, and hike for 0.1 mile to reach the raptor enclosure behind the nature center.

Take the gravel trail around to the front of the nature center and hike the wide gravel trail next to the pond. Go left back into the forest in 0.1 mile at an information kiosk. Hike this wide trail for 0.25 mile back to the rock outcrop.

Go right and downhill, retracing the way you previously hiked back to junction G56. Turn left, cross the bridge, and then hike to the right.

Hike to the next junction (OR46) and take a sharp right to follow the spur to the sentinel water oak 200 yards down the trail on the right. It is the largest tree in this section of forest and easy to spot.

Retrace your steps and turn right onto the main path. When you reach the clearing near the first waterfall you encountered, cross the bridge and take the path back to the parking area to end your hike.

You'll find a fabulous waterfall at the midpoint of this hike.

Henry Mill Falls

COCHRAN MILL PARK

Cochran Mill Park is an 800-acre greenspace in Chattahoochee Hills that has miles of trails that attract bikers, equestrians, runners, and hikers. This adventurous hike route highlights the beauty and biodiversity of the park, passing wetlands, rock outcrops, meadows, streams, and old-growth forests. The apex of the hike is Henry Mill Falls, a sweeping waterfall at the Henry Mill ruins.

HOW TO GET THERE

Driving Distance from Downtown Atlanta: 28 miles

Address: 6875 Cochran Mill Road, Chattahoochee Hills, GA 30268

Closest Interstate: I-85

City, County: Chattahoochee Hills, Fulton

Parking: Large gravel parking lot

HIKE DISTANCE

7.5-mile figure-8 loop

DIFFICULTY

Overall: Strenuous

Navigation: Blazes on trees; occasional signposts along the trail

Terrain: Hard-packed dirt trail, gravel trail, and rock outcrop

Elevation Change: Rolling hills, but no major ascents or descents

SAFETY

Usage ★★★★★

Visibility ★★★☆☆

Upkeep ★★★★☆

Parking ★★★★★

HOURS

Dawn to dusk

DOGS

Leashed dogs allowed

FACILITIES

- Toilets at parking area
- Picnic areas, playground

FEES & PERMITS $5 daily fee—purchase at payment kiosk next to information sign

LAND MANAGER City of Chattahoochee Hills Parks & Recreation

Landmarks

SENTINEL SYCAMORE

This sycamore stands out as a sentinel giant in a thicket of privet near the entrance to a meadow. Its trunk leans, then bends upward. Notice the typically flaky bark at the base and smooth white branches at the top.

SENTINEL WATER OAK

Of the many large water oaks along this trail, this one on the right just beyond a creek crossing really stands out. With five large trunks, it is one of the largest living organisms in this area.

HENRY MILL FALLS VIEWPOINT

The halfway point of this hike is a scenic rock outcrop overlooking Henry Mill Falls. Have a snack or soak your feet in the water—it's definitely worth taking a few moments of rest at this rushing waterfall.

Hike Route

Follow the gravel parking area to the back end of the lot near the playground and horse trailer parking. Look for the trailhead at the edge of the forest, marked by a signpost. Take the trail into the forest, following the yellow trail markers and blazes for 0.3 mile. At the junction with the gravel road, turn right.

In 50 feet, take the trail to the right and use the bridge to cross Cedar Branch Creek. At the end of the bridge, turn right at junction Y5. Pass an unmarked junction on the left, and at the next junction (Y6) stay left on the trail. In 0.3 mile, just before the trail enters a large meadow, look to the right for a large leaning sentinel sycamore. Continue past the sycamore and into the meadow, following the trail as it curves around the left edge of the clearing.

Leave the meadow and pass through an open corridor, with a wetland on your right. Hike past junction Y7 and campsites on your left. At the next marked junction, look right across the meadow for where the trail reenters the forest. Take this path at a post labeled Y11 and follow the yellow blazes. In 0.1 mile, cross a small stream. Once on the opposite side of the bank, look to your right for a large sentinel

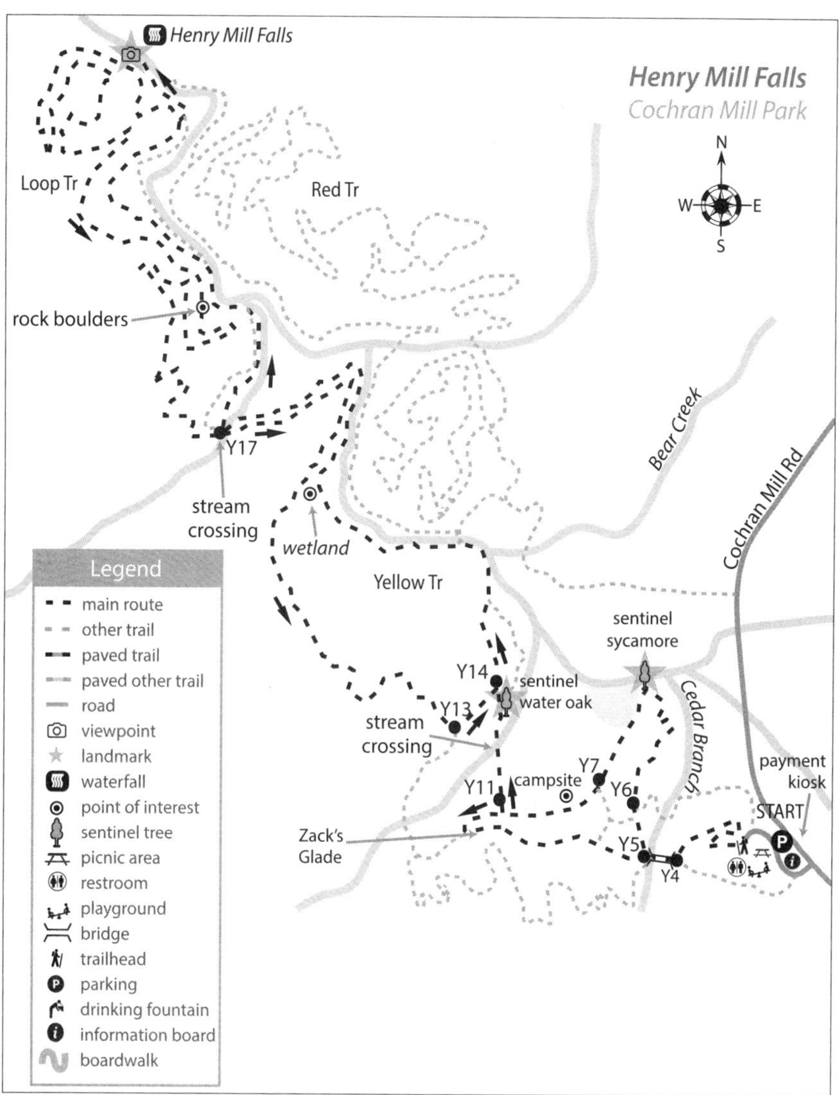
Henry Mill Falls
Henry Mill Falls
Cochran Mill Park
N
W
E
S
Loop Tr
Red Tr
rock boulders
Y17
stream
crossing
wetland
Yellow Tr
Bear Creek
Cochran Mill Rd
sentinel
sycamore
Y14
sentinel
water oak
Y13
stream
crossing
Cedar Branch
payment
kiosk
Y7
Y11
campsite
Y6
START
Zack's
Glade
Y5
Y4
Legend
main route
other trail
paved trail
paved other trail
road
viewpoint
landmark
waterfall
point of interest
sentinel tree
picnic area
restroom
playground
bridge
trailhead
parking
drinking fountain
information board
boardwalk

All creatures can find enjoyment at Henry Mill Falls.

water oak on the bank of the stream. This is one of the largest trees in this forest.

Continue hiking, following the yellow blazes. At the next junction stay straight. This section of the trail can be muddy and narrow, but continue following the yellow blazes to stay on the trail. At a post in 0.2 mile the trail begins to run parallel to Bear Creek. At a junction in 0.1 mile with Red Trail, go left, following the signs for Yellow Trail. As you hike, you may begin to hear the sound of frog calls as you approach a wetland.

Hike along the banks of Bear Creek until the trail curves away from the water and heads deeper into the forest, paralleling the return route of Yellow Trail. When the two parallel trails intersect at a stream crossing, bear right. Immediately after crossing the stream, turn right at the junction, following the sign for Henry Mill Falls. There are two trails on the right here—take either, as they lead to the same place and have similar mileage. In 0.4 mile at a junction where the two trails join, continue on Yellow Trail, hiking with the creek to your right and large boulders uphill on your left.

At a junction in 0.1 mile, go left, passing a large beech tree. Hike for 0.4 mile to reach a junction with a sign for the falls and Loop Trail. Go right, taking the spur trail to the falls. In 0.2 mile the trail ends at Henry Mill Falls. There are plenty of rocks where you can sit and enjoy the serene beauty of the landscape. After taking in the view, hike back to Yellow Trail, bearing right at the first junction, then right again to begin the second half of this hike.

The trail climbs a ridge via switchbacks, giving you another opportunity (in fall and winter) to view the waterfall and creek below you. The trail continues to switchback through this section of forest for one mile, eventually paralleling the section of Yellow Trail you hiked earlier. Continue on the high ridge and walk along the fern-covered hillside with the creek below you. The trail winds its way higher up the ridge and past large rock formations before descending into the floodplain.

In 0.7 mile, go left and follow the sign for Yellow Trail and the parking area. When you come back to the junction with post Y17, recross the stream and stay right at the immediate junction. Hike the high ridge with a different view of the creek and wetland area you hiked near before. Then the trail descends the ridge into the floodplain.

Reach junction Y13 and go left. At the next junction (Y14) go right, retracing your steps on the section of trail you took earlier to reach the open meadow. Cross the meadow and go right, circling around the stone memorial for Zack's Glade. Turn left onto the gravel path and take it back to the pedestrian bridge over Cedar Branch Creek. Continue on the gravel trail back to the parking lot or turn left at the Y4 post and retrace your steps on Yellow Trail back to the parking area to end your hike.

Flat Rock Trail leads through a gorgeous area of rock outcrop and wildflowers.

Bobcat & Flat Rock Trails

CHATTAHOOCHEE BEND STATE PARK

With a name like Chattahoochee Bend, you'd imagine that this state park's trails are entirely along the river. But if all you hike here is Riverside Trail, you're missing a spectacular and surprising adventure along Wild Turkey, Brown Thrasher, Bobcat, and Flat Rock Trails. These trails wind through hardwood forests and along peaceful creeks to reach an extensive rock outcrop that rivals the beauty of Arabia Mountain, Panola Mountain, or even Stone Mountain. This park uses controlled burns for forest management, and though you won't walk through fires, you may see signs of recent burns.

HOW TO GET THERE

Driving Distance from Downtown Atlanta: 54 miles
Address: 425 Bobwhite Way, Newnan, GA 30263
Closest Interstate: I-85
City, County: Newnan, Coweta
Parking: Large parking area at the park office

HIKE DISTANCE

4-mile figure-8 loop

DIFFICULTY

Overall: Moderate
Navigation:: Trail maps available at trailheads; color-coded blazes and trail markers at most junctions
Terrain: Hard-packed dirt trails with sections on rock; two creek crossings on rocks
Elevation Change: Rolling hills with some short but steep ascents and descents

SAFETY

Usage ★★★☆☆
Visibility ★★★★☆
Upkeep ★★★★☆
Parking ★★★★★

HOURS

Park open 7:00 am to 10:00 pm; office open 8:00 am to 5:00 pm

DOGS

Leashed dogs allowed

FACILITIES	• Toilets at trailhead • Playground, picnic areas, campgrounds, cabins, mountain bike trails, boat ramp
FEES & PERMITS	$5 daily ParkPass—purchase at gastateparks.org
LAND MANAGER	Georgia State Parks

Landmarks

WOODLAND CREEK

This small creek along Wild Turkey Trail has been protected from development and farming. As a result, you can find important native plants such as Carolina silverbell and rivercane and many species of spring wildflowers growing along the creekside trail.

FLAT ROCK OUTCROP

This area of exposed rock is a unique habitat where special flowering plants called diamorpha can grow in indentations called solution pits, where gravel, dirt, and water build up.

SENTINEL CHESTNUT OAK

Look for this giant tree with a bend at the base of its trunk about 30 feet below the trail as you hike through a steep-walled valley. Chestnut oaks have leaves with scalloped edges. Their acorns are an important source of food for woodland mammals.

Hike Route

Start your hike at the information board to the left of the park office. After 50 feet, reach a junction with Wild Turkey Trail, turn right, and hike uphill. The trail soon crests the hill and descends for 0.2 mile, past the 1-mile trail marker, to reach a woodland creek where you'll have to balance on rocks to cross.

The trail parallels this creek through a beautiful area where you'll find trillium, mayapple, Carolina silverbell, and rivercane growing. When you reach the Brown Thrasher Trail junction, stay straight on Wild Turkey Trail. The trail ascends a ridge through a pine forest where you'll see signs of a recent controlled burn. Pass the 0.5-mile trail marker, crest the ridge, and hike past several large exposed boulders before reaching another junction with Brown Thrasher Trail. Stay straight toward a trailhead and parking lot.

Face the information board, and you'll see a paved multiuse path on the right. This hike continues through the parking lot, crosses

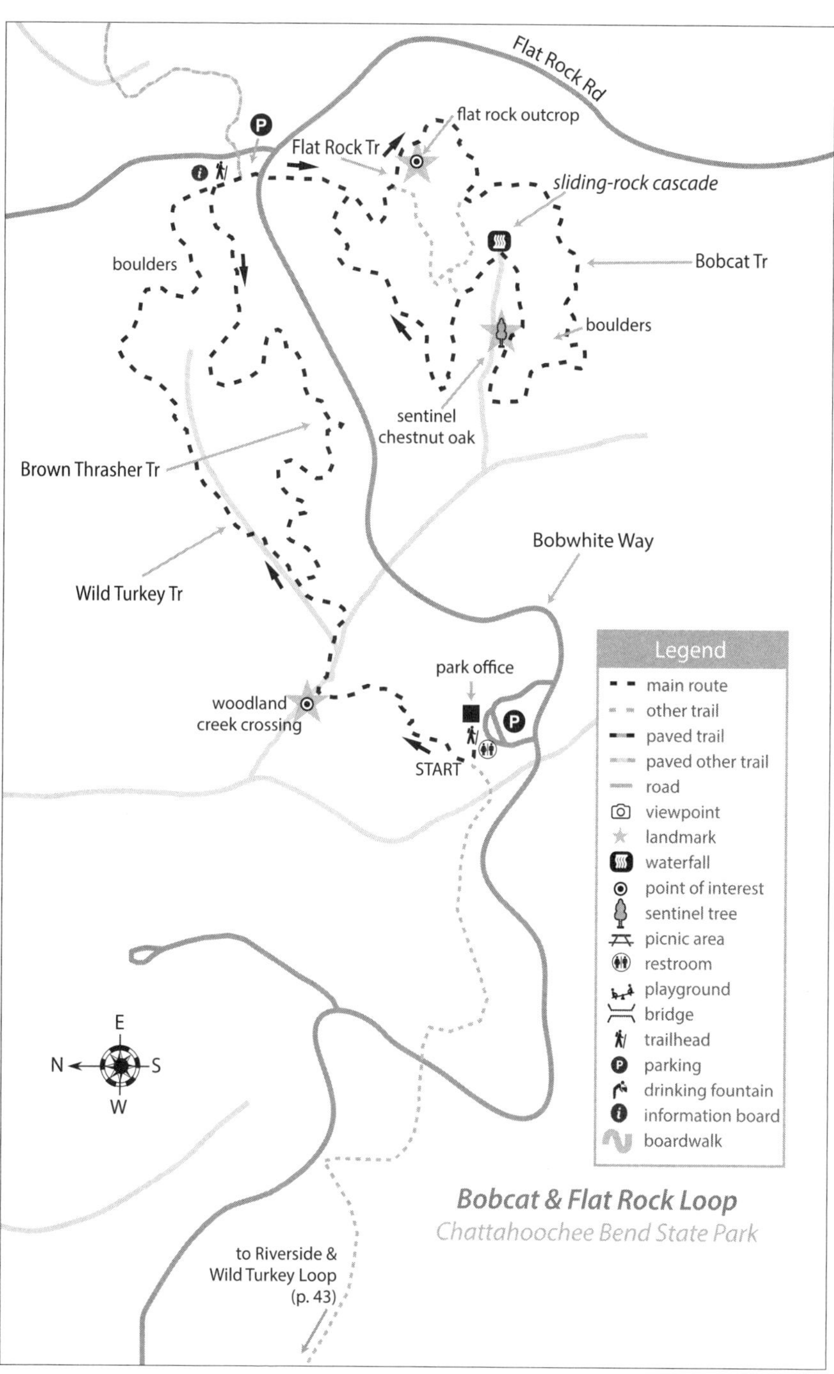
Flat Rock Rd
flat rock outcrop
Flat Rock Tr
sliding-rock cascade
Bobcat Tr
boulders
boulders
sentinel
chestnut oak
Brown Thrasher Tr
Wild Turkey Tr
Bobwhite Way
park office
woodland
creek crossing
START
Legend
main route
other trail
paved trail
paved other trail
road
viewpoint
landmark
waterfall
point of interest
sentinel tree
picnic area
restroom
playground
bridge
trailhead
parking
drinking fountain
information board
boardwalk
E
N
S
W
Bobcat & Flat Rock Loop
Chattahoochee Bend State Park
to Riverside &
Wild Turkey Loop
(p. 43)

Bobcat Trail passes several large, unique boulders on the hillside.

Bobwhite Way, and reenters the forest on the other side of the road to begin Flat Rock Trail. This trail follows blue blazes.

In 0.1 mile, stay straight at a junction with the yellow-blazed Bobcat Trail. Hike another 0.1 mile to reach a junction and follow the signs for Flat Rocks to the left. Hike straight across the rock outcrop, taking care not to step in the solution pits, where diamorpha and other sensitive plants and organisms grow. Follow the red blazes on the rock to reach a wide trail on the far side. Pay close attention to your route, as the red blazes can be hard to find.

Just after the red-blazed Flat Rock Trail reenters the forest on a single-track dirt trail, you will reach a junction with Bobcat Trail. Turn left to hike Bobcat Trail, blazed with yellow diamonds. This trail skirts the edge of several more rock outcrops before dipping into the forest again. In 0.3 mile, the trail winds between several large boulders. In another 0.2 mile, the trail curves right and enters a steep ravine with mountain laurel growing along the creek. The trail stays high on the side of the ridge and then passes a sentinel chestnut oak downhill about 30 feet on your left. This is by far the largest tree in this area of the woods. Look for a large tree with a curve at the base of its trunk.

Continue along the ravine until you finally cross the creek at the base of a small sliding-rock cascade, then begin hiking uphill through another area of boulders. Stay straight at a junction with a trail on the right that connects with Flat Rock Trail. Follow yellow diamond blazes as Bobcat Trail descends, curves sharply to the right, and then ascends slowly through an oak and hickory forest to reach a junction with Flat Rock Trail at the top of the ridge.

Turn left on Flat Rock Trail, hike to Bobwhite Way, and cross the road and the parking lot to reach the information board. Continue straight on the blue-blazed Wild Turkey Trail, then turn left at the first junction with Brown Thrasher Trail. Follow green diamond blazes to walk Brown Thrasher Trail along a ridge with many mature chestnut oaks. Longleaf pine trees also grow on this ridge. Hike 0.8 mile to a junction with Wild Turkey Trail. Turn left and follow Wild Turkey Trail 0.4 mile to return to the park office, where you'll end your hike.

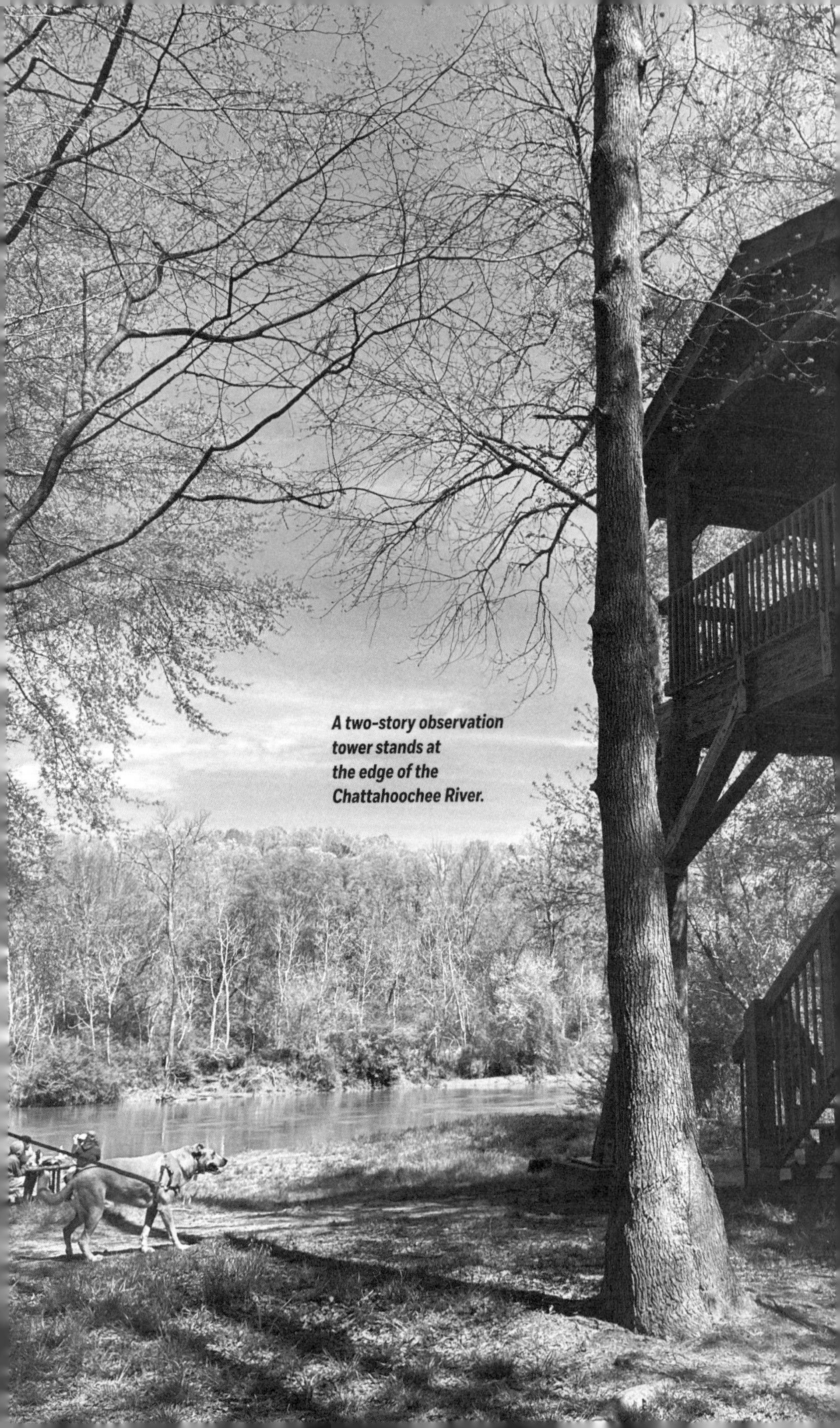

A two-story observation tower stands at the edge of the Chattahoochee River.

Riverside & Wild Turkey Trails

CHATTAHOOCHEE BEND STATE PARK

Riverside Trail is the most iconic trail in Chattahoochee Bend State Park. You'll hike parallel to the majestic river for miles among large trees, muscadine grapevines, and wildflowers. Instead of following the entire out-and-back Riverside Trail to the actual bend in the Chattahoochee River for which this park is named, this route loops back along Tower Trail and Wild Turkey Trail through peaceful forests, along rolling hills, and past creeks and ponds.

HOW TO GET THERE

Driving Distance from Downtown Atlanta: 54 miles
Address: 425 Bobwhite Way, Newnan, GA 30263
Closest Interstate: I-85
City, County: Newnan, Coweta
Parking: Large gravel parking area at the end of Bobwhite Way near the boat launch ramp

HIKE DISTANCE

6.5-mile lollipop loop

DIFFICULTY

Overall: Moderate to strenuous
Navigation: Trail map available at park office and trailhead; color-coded blazes and trail markers at most junctions
Terrain: Hard-packed dirt trails with some muddy sections; most creek crossings on bridges, but several on rocks or logs
Elevation Change: Mostly flat with some rolling hills

SAFETY

Usage ★★★★★
Visibility ★★★★☆
Upkeep ★★★★☆
Parking ★★★★★

HOURS

Park open 7:00 am to 10:00 pm; office open 8:00 am to 5:00 pm

DOGS

Leashed dogs allowed

Riverside Trail provides many opportunities to view the majestic Chattahoochee.

FACILITIES	• Toilets at trailhead • Playground, picnic areas, camping, cabins, observation tower, mountain bike trails, boat ramp
FEES & PERMITS	$5 daily ParkPass—purchase at gastateparks.org
LAND MANAGER	Georgia State Parks

Landmarks

OBSERVATION TOWER

This giant two-story observation tower next to the Chattahoochee River provides views of the river and surrounding forest from a unique vantage point. This is also a good lunch spot.

SENTINEL WHITE OAK

Generally, you'll find the biggest trees in this park along Riverside Trail, but this giant white oak tree on Wild Turkey Trail is especially impressive. Look for the large shaggy gray plates of bark and branches covered with resurrection fern.

BEAVER POND

Turkey Creek has been dammed by a family of beavers to create this scenic pond. Depending on the season, you'll hear tree frogs, see blooming wildflowers, and watch waterfowl enjoying the beaver pond.

Hike Route

Start your hike at the information board in the gravel parking lot near the playground. Follow the crushed gravel path through the day use area, past the playground and pavilions, to reach the restrooms in 100 yards. Cross Bobwhite Way onto Riverside Trail.

In less than 0.1 mile, reach a junction with Wild Turkey Trail at a bridge and good climbing tree. Turn left and cross the bridge to continue on Riverside Trail. In 0.1 mile, the trail curves right and begins to parallel the Chattahoochee River. Cross a bridge in 0.25 mile, then reach a junction with a cutoff trail on the right that leads to Wild Turkey Trail. Stay left toward the wetland and bridge. Cross the bridge and stay left.

Hike 0.4 mile to reach an amazing observation tower and picnic area. Enjoy this amenity, then continue on Riverside Trail to a junction with Tower Trail on the right. Go straight and pass the 1-mile marker here. Hike Riverside Trail for 1.25 mile. This stretch of trail has several river viewpoints and large trees. It's a lovely place to look for wildflowers and listen to birds. Creek crossings are on small bridges, rocks, or logs. Eventually, the trail turns sharply inland and ascends the ridge to reach the 2.5-mile marker and a junction with a service road. Go left and continue another 0.35 mile to a picnic table with a view of the river. You can continue another 2.25 miles to the end of Riverside Trail at the Chattahoochee Bend canoe put-in, but that adds almost 5 miles to this already 6.5-mile hike, so know your abilities and be safe.

This route turns back at the picnic table. Hike 1.5 miles back to the Tower Trail junction and turn left. Follow orange diamond blazes and hike through a young pine forest. This section of trail can be muddy. Hike 0.5 mile until you reach Wild Turkey Trail near the park's cabins. Stay right and follow the signs for Wild Turkey Trail as it curves sharply right and crosses two wooden footbridges.

Wild Turkey Trail is marked with blue blazes but crosses the

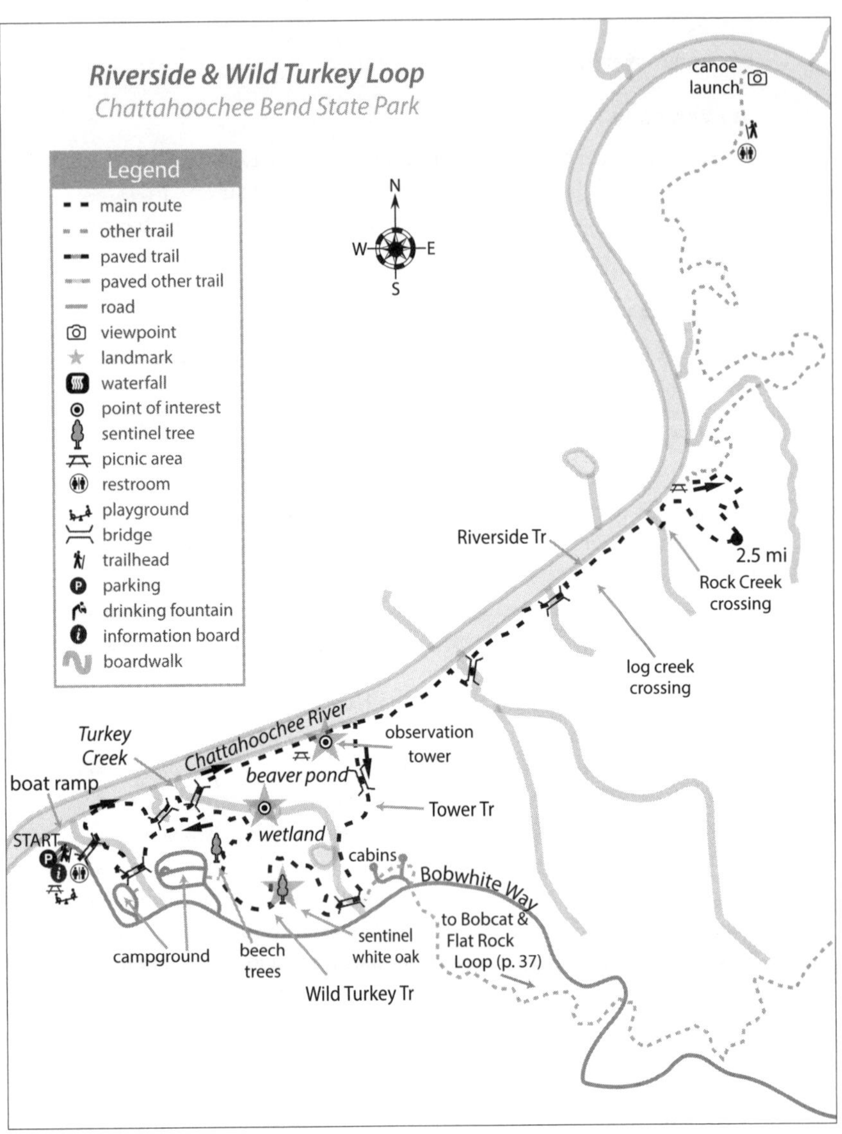
Riverside & Wild Turkey Loop
Chattahoochee Bend State Park
Legend
main route
other trail
paved trail
paved other trail
road
viewpoint
landmark
waterfall
point of interest
sentinel tree
picnic area
restroom
playground
bridge
trailhead
parking
drinking fountain
information board
boardwalk
N
W
E
S
canoe launch
Riverside Tr
2.5 mi
Rock Creek crossing
log creek crossing
Chattahoochee River
observation tower
Turkey Creek
boat ramp
beaver pond
Tower Tr
START
wetland
cabins
Bobwhite Way
to Bobcat & Flat Rock Loop (p. 37)
sentinel white oak
campground
beech trees
Wild Turkey Tr

Garter Snake mountain bike trail multiple times. When in doubt, stay straight and look for blue blazes.

After crossing the footbridges, enter a more mature section of forest, passing hardwood trees, native azaleas, a creek, and a viewpoint of a beaver-created wetland. After the wetland overlook and just before a Garter Snake Trail crossing, pass a sentinel white oak tree as big as any in Atlanta.

Over the next 0.4 mile, cross Garter Snake Trail several more times and stay straight at a trail on the left that leads to the campground. Reach the edge of the scenic beaver pond and parallel the water for 0.1 mile. Stay straight on the blue trail past a junction on the right that leads to Riverside Trail.

In 0.25 mile at a junction between two campgrounds, cross a bridge and turn right to follow the blue-blazed Wild Turkey Trail around the campground to a junction with Riverside Trail. Turn left and hike back, across Bobwhite Way, to the parking area to end your hike.

Take in sweeping views of
the Chattahoochee River.

McIntosh Reserve Park

McIntosh Reserve Park is nearly 1,000 acres and located in Carroll County. With several picnic pavilions, a splash-and-spray water park, campgrounds, and miles of trails, the park has a variety of options for anyone seeking time in nature. History buffs will enjoy learning about Muscogee (Creek) chief William McIntosh, who owned this land until his death in 1825. This hike will take you through rolling hills and old-growth forests and along the Chattahoochee River. This is a popular park for equestrians, so stay aware of your surroundings and give horses the right-of-way.

HOW TO GET THERE

Driving Distance from Downtown Atlanta: 46 miles

Address: 1046 West McIntosh Circle, Whitesburg, GA 30185

City, County: Whitesburg, Carroll

Parking: Trailhead near gravel splash-and-spray parking area

HIKE DISTANCE

5-mile loop

DIFFICULTY

Overall: Moderate

Navigation: Blazes on trees

Terrain: Hard-packed dirt and gravel trails

Elevation Change: Rolling hills, but no major ascents or descents

SAFETY

Usage ★★★★☆

Visibility ★★★★☆

Upkeep ★★★★☆

Parking ★★★★☆

HOURS

8:00 am to 8:00 pm

DOGS

Leashed dogs allowed

FACILITIES

- Toilets at splash-and-spray water park and old ranger station; portable toilets at River Trail parking and camping area

- Vending machine at splash-and-spray parking area, picnic pavilions, splash pad, campsites

FEES & PERMITS	$5 daily fee—purchase at entrance station
LAND MANAGER	Carroll County Parks & Recreation

Landmarks

MCINTOSH CABIN AND GRAVESITE

In the center of the reserve is the replica McIntosh cabin and gravesite. Chief McIntosh was a leader and representative in the Lower Creek (Muscogee) tribe and helped broker the Council Bluffs Treaty. McIntosh's legacy is complicated by his signing of the Indian Springs Treaty, which ceded Muscogee lands west of the Flint River, including his own land. Read the several interpretive signs to learn more about his life and impact.

ROCK OUTCROP

This rock outcrop overlooking the Chattahoochee River was a gathering place for Muscogee chiefs and councilmen. The metamorphic rocks formed as a result of the fault line. In the spring, white lilies bloom abundantly among the rocks.

RIVER VIEWPOINT PAVILION

The pavilion along River Trail is a perfect overlook to view this wide and slow section of the Chattahoochee River. The river was a major trading avenue for the indigenous nations in the region.

Hike Route

Begin your hike at the splash-and-spray parking area. From the parking area, turn right onto the wide gravel road and hike past the splash pad and between two ponds. Pass a picnic pavilion and campsites and begin to follow the purple blazes to the Moonshiner's Alley Loop trailhead.

In 0.15 mile, at a junction with a trail on the left, stay on the wide gravel trail. Reach a clearing where the gravel ends, and take the trail into the forest marked by a purple blaze. Stay right at the immediate next junction. Hike a forested trail lined with ferns. At a junction with Outer Boundary Trail on the right, stay to the left. From here the trail ascends and traverses a pine forest.

Come to a junction with a purple blazed trail in 0.4 mile and stay

Visit a replica of Chief McIntosh's log cabin, where many council meetings were held.

to the right on the blue-blazed Outer Boundary Trail. In 0.1 mile, the trail comes to the road near the entrance station. Carefully cross the road and follow blue and white blazes along the trail on the right near a firewood shed. At a junction in 0.1 mile, go right, then take a left at the next junction onto a wide gravel service road. Hike downhill following the white blazes on Pine Ridge Trail.

At the bottom of the hill you will reach a junction to your left and a fence in front of you marking private property. Turn left on Pine Ridge Trail, following the white blazes. Hike down into the floodplain and past groves of mature beech trees. When you reach a tree on the right with unmarked wooden posts nailed into it, look left for a junction with white blazes. Take this trail on the left, and in 0.1 mile, turn left at the next junction.

Reach a junction with Horse Park Loop Trail (yellow blazes) and go left for 100 yards. There will be a tool storage and work yard in front of you. Go right and hike downhill. At a junction at the bottom of the hill, turn right. The trail parallels the road before exiting the forest at the horse trailer parking area. From here the trail continues

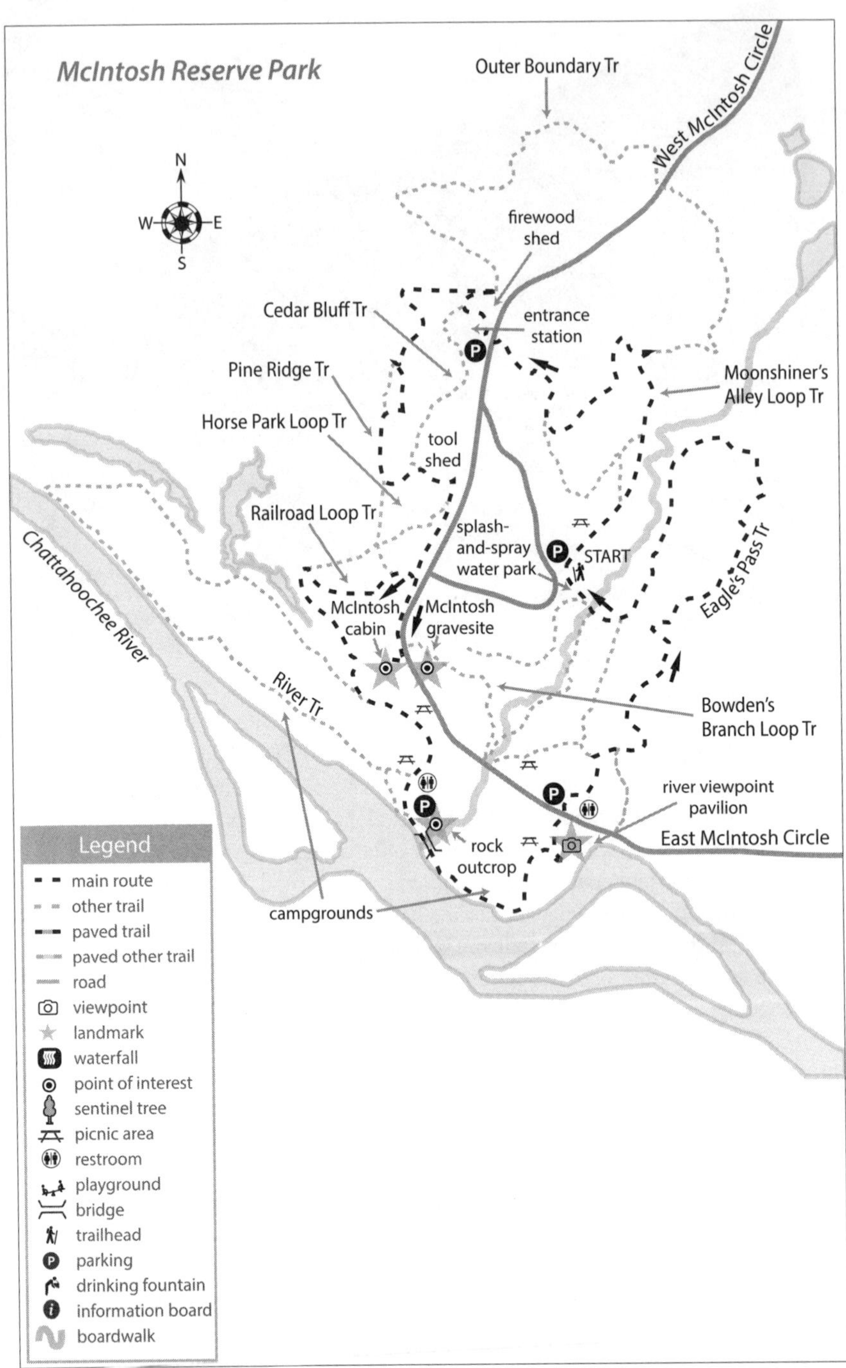
McIntosh Reserve Park
Outer Boundary Tr
West McIntosh Circle
N
W
E
S
firewood shed
Cedar Bluff Tr
entrance station
Pine Ridge Tr
Horse Park Loop Tr
Moonshiner's Alley Loop Tr
tool shed
Railroad Loop Tr
splash-and-spray water park
START
Eagle's Pass Tr
Chattahoochee River
McIntosh cabin
McIntosh gravesite
River Tr
Bowden's Branch Loop Tr
river viewpoint pavilion
East McIntosh Circle
rock outcrop
campgrounds
Legend
main route
other trail
paved trail
paved other trail
road
viewpoint
landmark
waterfall
point of interest
sentinel tree
picnic area
restroom
playground
bridge
trailhead
parking
drinking fountain
information board
boardwalk

immediately on the right just before a signpost. But before continuing on the trail, stay straight and carefully walk along the edge of the parking area to reach Chief McIntosh's log cabin.

There's informational signage outside the cabin, and you are able to walk inside the first floor of the home, but please remember to be respectful of the historic landmark. Directly across the road from the cabin is Chief McIntosh's gravesite. Carefully cross the road to view his resting place.

After you've explored the historical landmarks, return across the horse trailer parking area and reenter the trail on the left past an information board. Stay left and take a right at the next junction with a trail that leads to the horse trailer parking area. Follow the yellow and green blazes to hike along the top of the ridge and downhill, with a wetland below to your left. Stay left at a junction with the yellow trail and continue to the very bottom of the hill.

Turn left onto Railroad Loop Trail, marked by green blazes, and hike through the floodplain. When you reach a junction, go right, following the green blazes downhill. Take the trail to the left as it opens out to a large field. Directly across from you is a gray stone building and gravel road. Walk toward the road and building, turning right before reaching the road to walk along the edge of the road. Where the road forks to the right and left, take the road to the left at a No Vehicles sign onto River Trail. On your right are campsites.

Hike along this wide gravel path past rock outcrops on your left, the site of the signing of the Council Bluffs Treaty. Continue on River Trail and cross a bridge, immediately coming to a junction. Stay to the right to hike along the banks of the Chattahoochee River. At a four-way junction in 50 yards, stay straight or to the right—the two trails reconnect. Continue hiking this scenic section of trail, staying to the far right at any junctions and passing by campsites along the river.

After the last campsite, the trail begins to curve to the left away from the river. At the next junction, turn right to take the spur toward the river viewpoint pavilion to take in sweeping views of the meandering river below. Once you've enjoyed resting and watching the Chattahoochee, return to the trail and turn right. Carefully cross the road into the parking lot of the old ranger station.

There are bathrooms here if you need them. Behind the bathrooms, look for Eagle's Pass Trail at a signpost marked Waterpark. Follow the orange blazes onto Eagle's Pass Trail. In 50 yards, you will reach a junction with another signpost. Go to the right and at the immediate next junction stay to the left to follow the signs toward the water park.

Continue to follow the orange blazes. Pass an unofficial junction on the right and in a few yards pass another unofficial junction to the left. It's okay if you accidentally take these junctions; they will reconnect with the main trail. From here the trail descends into the floodplain past a stream before climbing again. This section of forest has several eastern white pines—look for their large pine cones in the fall. Continue on Eagle's Pass Trail for 1 mile, coming to a junction with a post marked for ranger headquarters and the water park. Go right toward the water park. In 0.1 mile at the next junction, go right and carefully cross the stream to return to the parking area and end your hike.

I-75 SOUTH

The beautiful Newman Wetlands Center is part of Clayton County's innovative water treatment system.

Newman Wetlands Center

The Newman Wetlands Center is an exceptional greenspace created by the nationally known Clayton County Water Authority, an industry leader in wastewater treatment. These wetlands are beautiful and provide excellent habitat for many species of animals and plants. They are also a crucial part of Clayton County's innovative water treatment system, which utilizes the natural environment to provide clean and efficient drinking water for county residents.

HOW TO GET THERE

Driving Distance from Downtown Atlanta: 23 miles
Address: 2755 Freeman Road, Hampton, GA 30228
Closest Interstate: I-75
City, County: Hampton, Clayton
Parking: Paved parking area

HIKE DISTANCE

1.35-mile loop

DIFFICULTY

Overall: Easy
Navigation: Map available at the learning center; trail markers posted at junctions
Terrain: Boardwalk, crushed gravel, and dirt trails
Elevation Change: Minimal elevation change, except on Turkey Ridge Trail, which has one short but steep ascent and descent

SAFETY

Usage ★★★★★
Visibility ★★★★★
Upkeep ★★★★★
Parking ★★★★★

HOURS

- Open Monday through Saturday
- Trail hours: March through October, daily 7:00 am to 7:00 pm; November through February, 8:00 am to 5:00 pm
- Learning center hours: 8:00 am to 5:00 pm
- Trails may be closed due to severe flooding or repairs

DOGS	No pets or therapy animals allowed; working certified service dogs are permitted
FACILITIES	• Toilets in the learning center and near the parking lot • Water fountain, learning center, picnic area, outdoor classroom
FEES & PERMITS	None
LAND MANAGER	Clayton County Water Authority

Landmarks

SENTINEL BALD CYPRESS GROVE

Two species of cypress trees are planted here: pond cypress and bald cypress ("bald" cypress because they are one of the few needle-leaf trees that lose their needles in the winter). The "cypress knees" that stick out above the water are still a mystery to scientists. One theory is that they provide a source of air, since the trees typically grow in standing water.

WOOD DUCK OVERLOOK

From this viewpoint, you can see the large area around Pate's Creek that has been periodically flooded by beavers, providing excellent habitat for wood ducks, other birds, and many species of reptiles and amphibians.

HAMMOCK OVERLOOK

A "hammock" is an ecological term for an area that is higher than the surrounding land and often provides habitat for hardwood trees that cannot survive in a wetland.

Hike Route

This hike is well marked with plenty of interpretive signs. You can also pick up a map from the learning center. Be aware that trails may be closed due to severe flooding or repairs.

Enter the crushed gravel trail through the gazebo entryway and follow it down a very small hill to the wetlands. You'll see an old mill saw on your right, and then the trail curves around to a junction just after the boardwalk begins. Turn left here to begin the loop. Look to the left to see a sentinel bald cypress grove. Notice the knobby "cypress knees" poking above the water at the base of each tree.

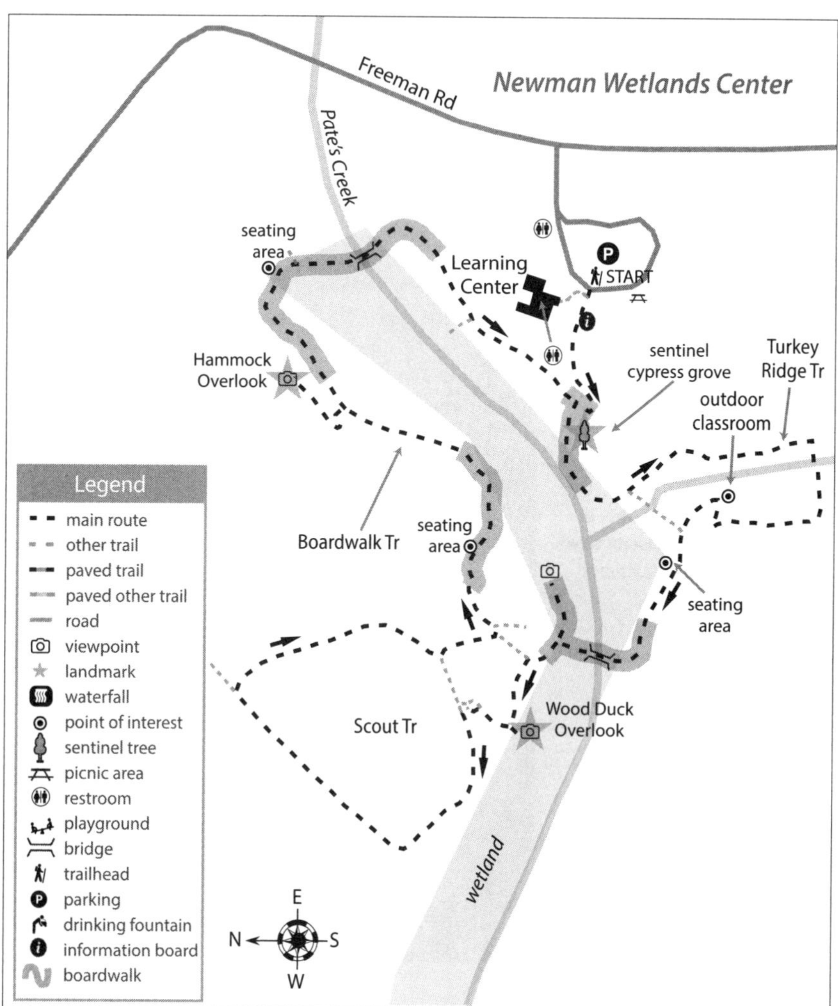
Newman Wetlands Center
Freeman Rd
Pate's Creek
seating area
Learning Center
START
Hammock Overlook
sentinel cypress grove
Turkey Ridge Tr
outdoor classroom
Boardwalk Tr
seating area
seating area
Scout Tr
Wood Duck Overlook
wetland
Legend
main route
other trail
paved trail
paved other trail
road
viewpoint
landmark
waterfall
point of interest
sentinel tree
picnic area
restroom
playground
bridge
trailhead
parking
drinking fountain
information board
boardwalk
E
N
S
W

Pause to take in the peaceful view from Hammock Overlook.

In 100 yards, the boardwalk transitions to crushed gravel, and you'll reach Turkey Ridge Trail. This 0.2-mile trail ascends the ridge through a grove of large hardwood trees, including beech, oak, and tulip trees. Turn left on Turkey Ridge Trail and hike uphill steeply to a forest road. Turn right and continue uphill, then curve right and hike back downhill to an outdoor classroom.

Reach Boardwalk Trail just after the outdoor classroom and turn left. Once the boardwalk begins again, look for signs of beaver activity. Cross a covered bridge over Pate's Creek, then arrive at Beaver Trail junction. Turn right and hike 50 feet to a viewpoint that is great for bird-watching. Turn back to the main trail and go straight to reach Scout Trail junction. Turn left toward Wood Duck Overlook.

Stay on Scout Trail past Wood Duck Overlook and turn left at the next junction to continue on Scout Trail. In 0.1 mile, the trail curves right on a mowed grass trail through a young forest. In another 0.1 mile, turn right off the wide grassy trail onto a gravel path to continue on Scout Trail. Turn left at the next junction to reach Boardwalk Trail and turn left again past a short spur trail on the right.

Cross a 100-yard boardwalk to reach a junction with Hammock Overlook Trail. Turn left here to visit the overlook, then return to Boardwalk Trail and turn left to continue the direction you were going, reentering a boardwalk. Hike 0.15 mile on the boardwalk through a particularly beautiful section of wetland.

After the boardwalk ends, hike the crushed gravel trail to where the boardwalk begins again. Turn left onto the gravel trail and hike back uphill to the learning center, where you'll end your hike.

High Falls on the Towaliga River is one of the best places in this park.

High Falls State Park

If you are into waterfalls, this state park is for you. It includes a giant human-made dam with water cascading over the top and the natural, rocky High Falls for which the park is named, so you'll be able to gaze at waterfalls to your heart's content. The iconic Falls Trail loop shouldn't be missed. And the 2-mile Tranquility Trail loop certainly lives up to its name, with rolling hills, bubbling brooks, and peaceful forests. After hiking, you might even rent a boat for a paddling adventure on High Falls Lake.

HOW TO GET THERE

Driving Distance from Downtown Atlanta: 51 miles
Address: 76 High Falls Park Drive, Jackson, GA 30233
Closest Interstate: I-75
City, County: Jackson, Monroe
Parking: Paved parking across the river on the left and near the park office

HIKE DISTANCE

4-mile double loop

DIFFICULTY

Overall: Moderate
Navigation: Map available at park office; trails are marked with diamond blazes
Terrain: Mostly hard-packed dirt trails with short sections of gravel, boardwalk, and pavement
Elevation Change: Rolling hills with several short but steep ascents and descents

SAFETY

Usage ★★★★☆
Visibility ★★★★☆
Upkeep ★★★★★
Parking ★★★★★

HOURS

Park open 7:00 am to 10:00 pm; office open 8:00 am to 5:00 pm

DOGS

Leashed dogs allowed

FACILITIES	• Toilets at park office and near trailhead parking • Picnic tables and pavilions, boat rentals, campground, miniature golf, swimming pool, playground
FEES & PERMITS	$5 daily ParkPass—purchase at gastateparks.org
LAND MANAGER	Georgia State Parks

Landmarks

HIGH FALLS

This waterfall has been an important site for centuries. A Native American trail ran along the modern route of High Falls Road, and white settlers built a gristmill above the falls and a hydroelectric powerhouse below them.

POWERHOUSE RUINS

This now-ruined powerhouse was in operation for 53 years during the 20th century. Huge cast-iron pipes fed water from above the falls to the water wheels below to generate around 3,600 kilowatts of electricity.

TRANQUILITY CREEK

The creek that you cross in the first quarter mile of the Tranquility Trail is truly tranquil. Sit and rest on the bench to breathe in the forest air and listen to the peaceful sounds of nature.

Hike Route

Start your hike on the far side of the river from the park's trading post and office. Park beyond the fee station, then walk back down to the road past great views of the High Falls dam. Carefully cross at the crosswalk to arrive at an information board. Turn right on the wooden stairs and follow the trail downhill past several waterfall viewpoints.

At the base of the falls, take a side trail on the right that leads to a wooden observation platform next to the Towaliga River. Then hike back uphill and go right on the main trail. At the first junction marked with red diamond blazes with arrows, turn left and hike to a junction near a wooden bridge. Cross the bridge to the right and hike to where the trail splits. Take the right fork. There are many unofficial trails along this section of the hike, but if you follow the red diamond blazes, you'll stay on this route. In 0.3 mile, pass a viewpoint of the lowest section of the waterfall. The trail then curves left and uphill.

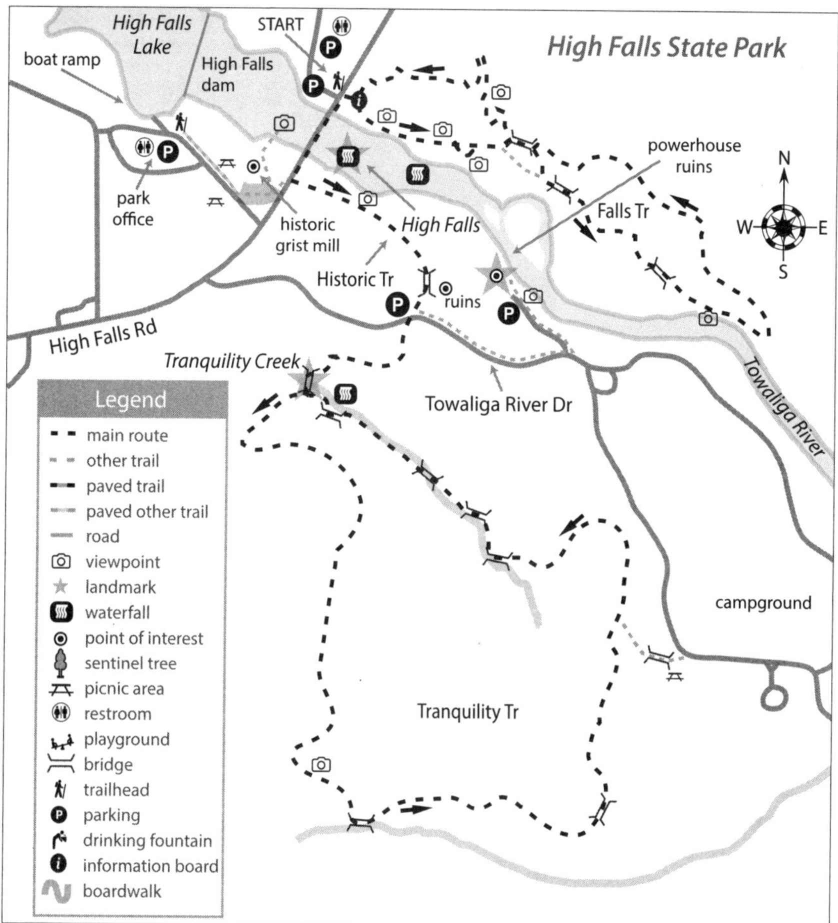

In 0.5 mile, bear right at a junction, cross a bridge, then turn right to switchback up a steep hill. Continue following red diamond blazes for 0.3 mile to get back to the information board and road.

To hike the Historic Trail and Tranquility Trail, turn left and hike the sidewalk across the High Falls Road bridge. After the bridge, a trail on the right leads to the site of a historic gristmill and great views of the dam. This route turns left onto the gravel Historic Trail, blazed with green diamonds.

In 0.1 mile, pass an overlook with great views of High Falls. In another 0.1 mile, cross a bridge above the historic ruins of pipe support structures, then arrive at a small parking lot at the campground road. (If you want to see the old powerhouse, turn left

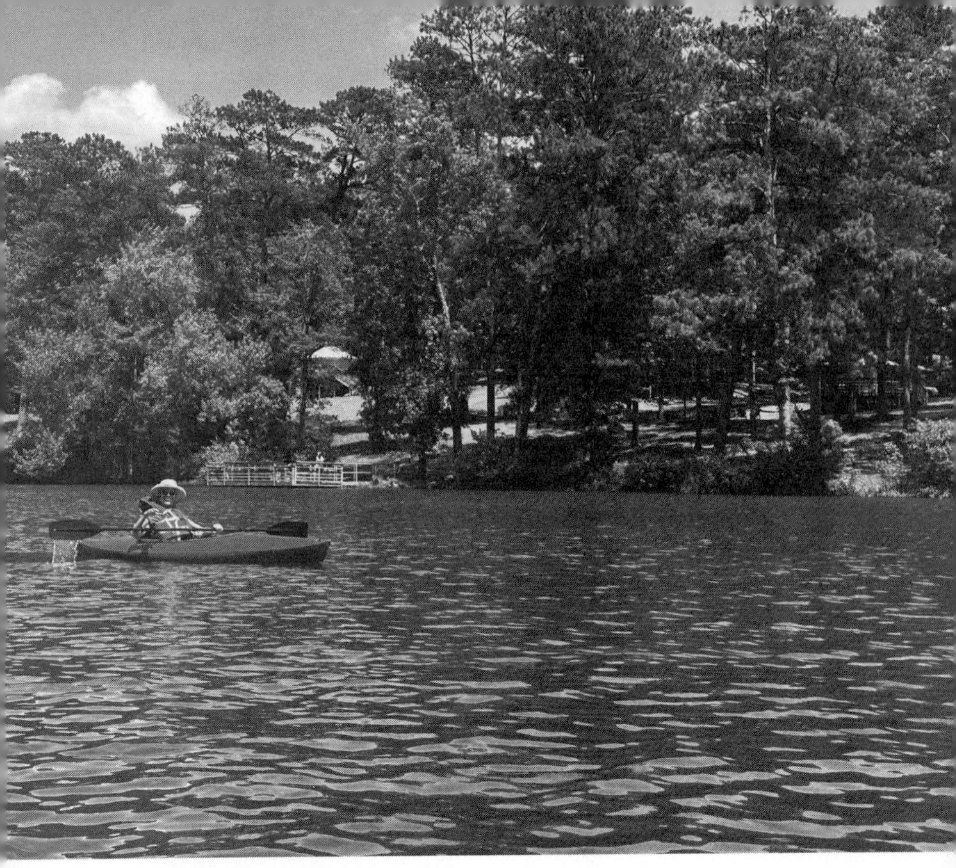

Paddling on High Falls Lake is a great activity after your hike.

and hike 0.15 mile down the steep road to a gravel parking lot and the ruins along the Towaliga River.)

This route crosses the road and begins Tranquility Trail, marked by orange diamond blazes. Hike downhill for 0.2 mile to a bench and bridge near a small creek. This is truly a tranquil place. Take a seat and listen to the sounds of the creek and the chirping of the birds, then proceed across the bridge. Hike steeply up a short hill to a junction and then turn right and continue uphill.

Along the Tranquility Trail loop, you'll pass many interpretive signs about the plants and animals common to this forest, including white-tailed deer, tulip tree, loblolly pine, lichen, box turtle, red maple, barred owl, opossum, and beaver. Continue uphill for 0.1 mile. The trail then enters more rolling terrain. In 0.4 mile, just after a lichen sign, arrive at benches and a ravine viewpoint. Then the trail descends steeply.

In 0.5 mile, reach a junction with a trail on the right that leads to a picnic table and the campground. Continue straight on Tranquility Trail. In 0.4 mile, the trail begins paralleling the creek, then ascends above the creek to a bench overlooking a small cascade.

Just after the cascade, you'll reach the junction with the other half of the Tranquility Trail loop. Turn right, cross the bridge, and hike uphill 0.2 mile to reach the campground road. Cross the road and hike Historic Trail back to High Falls Road. Cross the road bridge on your right to return to your vehicle and end your hike.

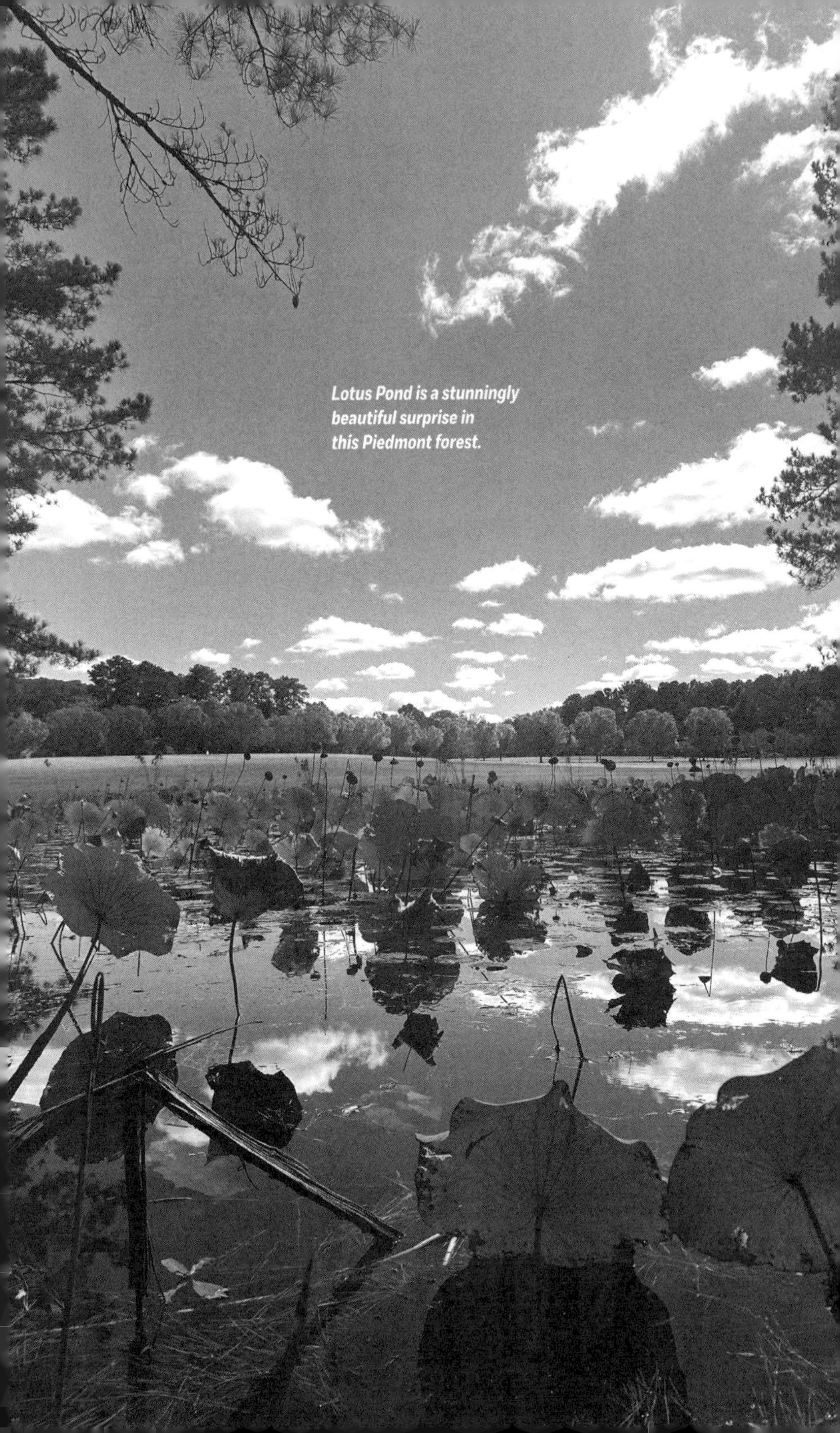

Lotus Pond is a stunningly beautiful surprise in this Piedmont forest.

Dauset Trails

This amazing and extensive system of trails is only an hour's drive from downtown Atlanta and is well worth the trip. From the educational trails near the nature center to the peaceful Piedmont forests of the hike-and-bike trail system, there is something for everyone at Dauset Trails. There are so many hiking options that you'll be able to explore a different route each time you visit. Plus, Dauset Trails is now part of the Creeks Trail System, which leads east to Indian Springs State Park and north to Jackson Elementary School.

HOW TO GET THERE

Driving Distance from Downtown Atlanta: 54 miles

Address: 360 Mount Vernon Church Road, Jackson, GA 30233

Closest Interstate: I-75

City, County: Jackson, Butts

Parking: Paved parking near the nature center; alternative gravel parking area at 400 Mount Vernon Church Road

HIKE DISTANCE

6-mile loop with options for up to 15 miles of hiking

DIFFICULTY

Overall: Moderate

Navigation: Trail maps at information boards and available for download; complicated trail system without blazes; many trail junctions are marked with signs or numbers

Terrain: Mostly hard-packed dirt trails with short sections of hard-packed gravel, paved, and boardwalk trails

Elevation Change: Rolling hills, but no major ascents or descents

SAFETY

Usage ★★★☆☆

Visibility ★★★☆☆

Upkeep ★★★★★

Parking ★★★★★

HOURS	• Gated nature center area open Tuesday through Sunday, 9:00 am to 5:00 pm • Hike-and-bike trails and alternative parking area open dawn to dusk
DOGS	• Pets not allowed on nature center trails • Leashed dogs allowed on hike-and-bike trails
FACILITIES	• Restrooms at trailhead near playground • Nature center, live animal displays, playground, picnic areas, water fountain, information boards, portable toilet at alternative parking area
FEES & PERMITS	None; however, donations are accepted
LAND MANAGER	Dauset Trails Nature Center

Landmarks

LOTUS POND

American lotus flowers have the largest blossom of any North American native plant, and their roots have long been prized as a food source by indigenous people. This plant thrives in small, shallow ponds like the one along Tree Trail.

PIEDMONT ANIMALS

At Dauset Trails Nature Center you can meet up close many of the woodland animals of the Piedmont region. The injured and now unreleasable birds and mammals are housed in enclosures along Animal Trail. Can you find a bobcat, red fox, raccoon, bald eagle, and great horned owl? What other creatures will you see?

SENTINEL POST OAK

This giant post oak near a picnic table and information board on one of the hike-and-bike trails sits at the top of the hill and is one of the biggest trees in this forest. Identify post oaks by the cross-shaped lobes of their leaves. Their bark peels less than that of white oaks. This tree also has a bicycle wheel displayed on its trunk. Resurrection ferns grow on its branches.

Hike Route

This hike is designed to lead you past the most amazing sites within this 1,800-acre property. Starting and ending within the fenced nature center area allows you to hike the Tree Trail, Woodland Garden Trail, and Animal Trail before completing a 5-mile loop on the hike-and-bike trails.

Dauset trails are shared between hikers and bikers.

If the timing of your visit does not allow access to the nature center area, then park in the alternative hike-and-bike parking area at 400 Mount Vernon Church Road and use the map to hike Moonshine Trail to Turkey Trot Trail to access the route described in this book.

Begin your hike at the playground and restrooms near the nature center parking area. Walk between the restrooms and play structures to reach an information board and the start of Tree Trail. This trail leads you 0.8 mile past 31 different species of trees, all labeled for your edification. Hike straight past the information sign, passing tree 1 and tree 2. The trail winds through rolling hills before arriving at a wide junction near the fenceline. Bear left, with the fence on your right, to reach Lotus Pond. Follow the tree marker signs to circle a small pine forest, then circle back on the edge of a large field, passing the other side of the lotus pond and a small gazebo. Stay along the edge of the field, then turn left into the forest. After passing tree 27, turn right and hike back to the clearing. Turn left, then left again to hike past trees 28-31 and reach the parking lot.

Straight across the parking lot is an entrance to Woodland Garden Trail. Carefully make your way across the parking area and enter this trail, then turn right on the crushed gravel path. Hike Woodland

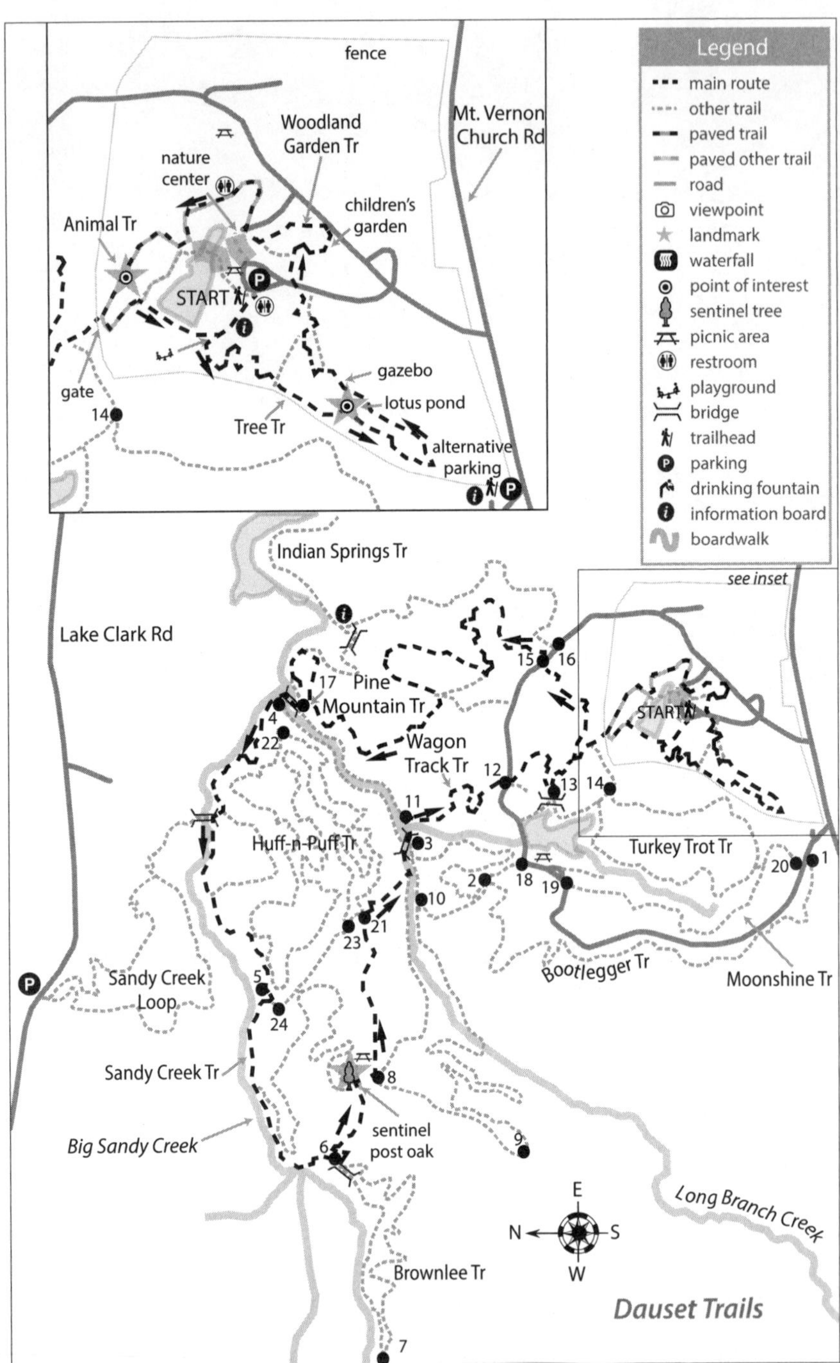
Legend
main route
other trail
paved trail
paved other trail
road
viewpoint
landmark
waterfall
point of interest
sentinel tree
picnic area
restroom
playground
bridge
trailhead
parking
drinking fountain
information board
boardwalk
fence
Woodland Garden Tr
Mt. Vernon Church Rd
nature center
Animal Tr
children's garden
START
gazebo
lotus pond
gate
Tree Tr
alternative parking
see inset
Indian Springs Tr
Lake Clark Rd
Pine Mountain Tr
Wagon Track Tr
Huff-n-Puff Tr
Turkey Trot Tr
Sandy Creek Loop
Sandy Creek Tr
Big Sandy Creek
Bootlegger Tr
Moonshine Tr
sentinel post oak
Long Branch Creek
Brownlee Tr
Dauset Trails
E
N
S
W

Garden Trail to a wooden entrance sign near the nature center. Walk toward the nature center, then turn right on a paved path to enter Animal Trail. Where the trail splits near the eagle enclosure, turn right and hike to the hike-and-bike trails gate, near the red fox enclosure. This gate is locked at 4:30 pm, so be sure you can return by that time. Pull up on the bar to open the gate and begin the next portion of this hike.

Walk 100 feet to the first junction. Stay straight, then turn right at the next junction. Hike 0.25 mile to a gravel road crossing and junction 15. Cross the road and go straight on Pine Mountain Trail. In 0.45 mile, arrive at a junction with a hiker sign. Go right and hike 0.8 mile to reach a junction above Big Sandy Creek. Take the sharp left turn and in 100 yards reach a junction with several trail signs. Go straight, following the sign toward Mount Vernon Church Road, to reach junction 17. This time, turn right, following the Lake Clark Road sign.

Cross a bridge over Long Branch Creek to reach junction 4. Turn right, following an arrow pointing to Lake Clark Road. In 0.3 mile, turn right at a junction, following a sign toward Lake Clark Road. When you reach a bridge over Big Sandy Creek, do not cross. Instead, bear left to hike Sandy Creek Trail, parallel to the creek.

Stay right or straight at each subsequent junction until you reach junction 6. If you go right here, you can add 1.2 miles to your hike on Brownlee Trail loop. Otherwise, turn left, following a red trailhead sign. Hike uphill for 0.25 mile to reach an information board, picnic table, and the sentinel post oak. Turn right and reach junction 8 in 100 feet.

Go left at junction 8, following a red trailhead sign to hike a wide forest road that descends slowly. At junction 21, turn right and follow a sign to Mount Vernon Church Road trailhead. In 0.1 mile, reach Long Branch Creek. Turn left and hike 100 yards to a bridge over the creek. Cross the bridge to reach junction 3. Go left here, not toward the red trailhead sign this time.

At junction 11, turn right on Wagon Track Trail and hike 0.3 mile to reach a gravel road. Cross the road at junction 12 and take the left trail fork. At junction 13, cross the bridge on the left, then turn left and hike uphill for 0.1 mile. Turn right at the next junction, then stay straight to reach the nature center fenceline and gate.

Enter the gate and turn right on the paved path. At the bald eagle enclosure, turn right on the boardwalk that leads across the lake, through the picnic area, and back to the playground and restroom, where you'll end your hike.

EASTSIDE

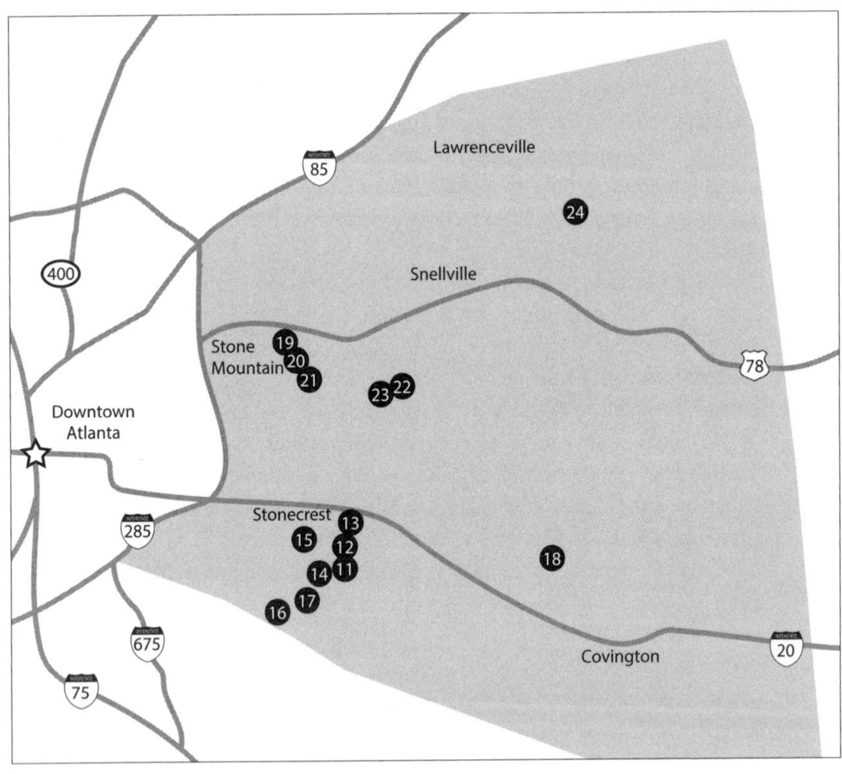

11 Mountaintop & Mountain View Trails
12 Forest & Mile Rock Trails
13 Vaughters' Farm & Retreat House Trails
14 Laurel Creek Trail
15 Cascade & Wilburn Farm Trails
16 Outcrop & Watershed Trails
17 Alexander Lakes Trail
18 Big Haynes Creek Nature Center
19 Walk-Up Trail
20 Cherokee Trail
21 Songbird Habitat Trail
22 Yellow River North Loop
23 Yellow River South Loop
24 Tribble Mill Park

I-20 EAST

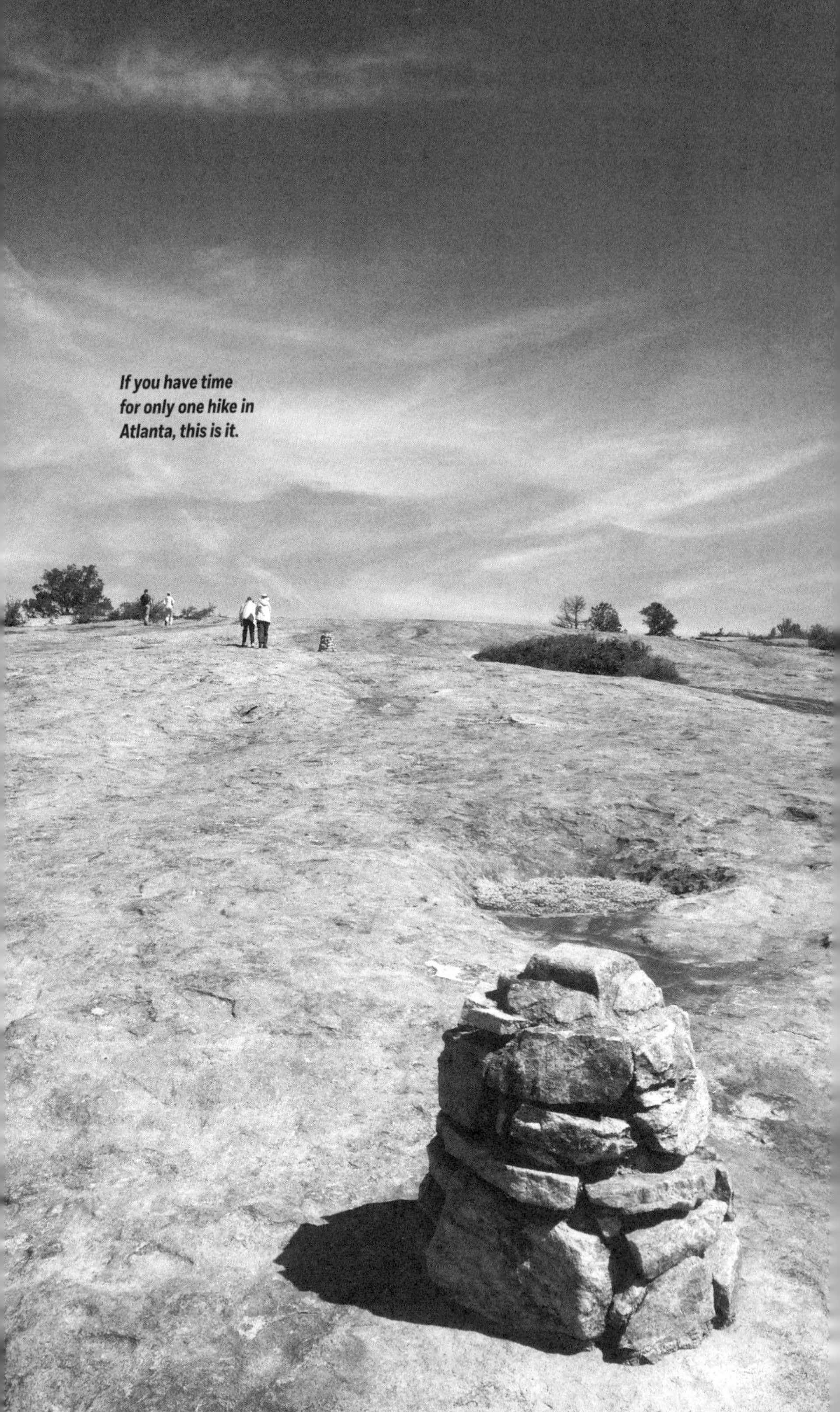

If you have time for only one hike in Atlanta, this is it.

Mountaintop & Mountain View Trails

DAVIDSON–ARABIA MOUNTAIN NATURE PRESERVE

Though Arabia Mountain is the oldest and least famous of the three monadnocks (granite mountains) in the Atlanta area, its summit and surrounding land are spectacularly beautiful, pristine, and peaceful. More accessible than Panola Mountain and without the crowds and development of Stone Mountain, Arabia Mountain is a place where many nature lovers have fallen in love with Atlanta. If you have time for only one hike at the Davidson–Arabia Mountain Nature Preserve, choose this one.

HOW TO GET THERE

Driving Distance from Downtown Atlanta: 20 miles

Address: 3787 Klondike Road, Stonecrest, GA 30038

Closest Interstate: I-20

City, County: Stonecrest, DeKalb

Parking: Large gravel parking area near the nature center and trailhead; small parking lot near the AWARE Wildlife Center (4158 Klondike Road) that might have space during off-peak hours

Hike Distance: 5-mile lollipop loop

DIFFICULTY

Overall: Moderate

Navigation: Map at trailhead and cairns and blazes that mark trail routes; navigation is more tricky when following blazes on the rock surface of Mountain View Trail

Terrain: Paved trail, boardwalk, rock surface, and hard-packed dirt trails

Elevation Change: Mostly flat, except for the short but steep ascent and descent on Arabia Mountain

SAFETY

Usage ★★★★★

Visibility ★★★★★

Upkeep ★★★★★

Parking ★★★★☆

HOURS

7:00 am to sunset

DOGS

Leashed dogs allowed

FACILITIES	• Pit toilet • Nature center, information kiosk, picnic tables, drinking fountain
FEES & PERMITS	None
LAND MANAGER	DeKalb County Recreation, Parks, & Cultural Affairs in partnership with Arabia Mountain National Heritage Area

Landmarks

DIAMORPHA

"What's the red stuff?" This sign is a perfect place to begin looking for diamorpha, a small but iconic plant that can be seen up close here at Arabia Mountain. The solution pits of Georgia monadnocks are the primary habitat of this small red plant, which puts on an amazing show each year. In late winter and early spring, only its succulent red stems are visible; in the summer, the plants become dry and brittle. But when its white flowers bloom in late spring, it is one of the most spectacular sights in the state.

ARABIA MOUNTAIN SUMMIT

This mountain rises only 950 feet above sea level, but its peak is one of the most peaceful spots in the Atlanta metro area. This is also the city's oldest monadnock (granite mountain)—400 million years old!

WILDLIFE VIEWING PLATFORM

After hiking to the top of Arabia Mountain, you'll discover that this spot on the far side of the lake is an excellent vantage point from which to see all the ground you've covered. A Chronolog station on the platform invites you to take a photograph, which helps rangers document the changes in the environment.

Hike Route

Much of this hike is on uneven rock surfaces and can be slippery and dangerous in wet weather. During or after a rain, consider hiking Laurel Creek Trail (p. 95), Cascade & Wilburn Farm Trails (p. 101), or Vaughters' Farm & Retreat House Trails (p. 89) instead.

Begin your hike at an information kiosk in front of the nature center and hike straight on the paved multiuse path between the nature center and picnic area. At a junction near a fire ring, turn left and hike 0.4 mile to a crosswalk at Klondike Road.

Carefully cross this busy road and hike the boardwalk 0.5 mile

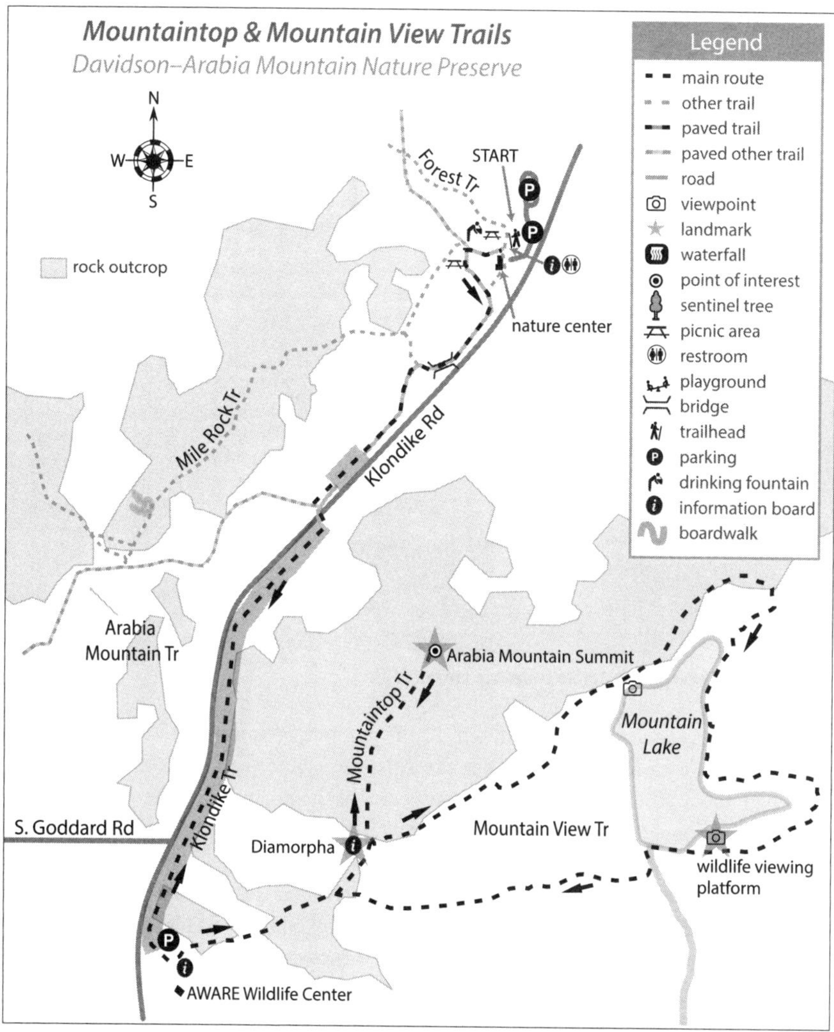

to the small parking lot next to the AWARE Wildlife Center. Turn left and walk through the gravel parking area to the information kiosk. Enter the rock outcrop and follow rock cairns on the otherwise unmarked trail. Take care not to step in the solution pits, where delicate flowers and plants flourish.

After 0.3 mile, pass a cairn with a blue blaze. This is a junction with Mountain View Trail. Stay left and follow the cairns to the base of the mountain past an interpretive sign about diamorpha. Continue to follow the cairns up the mountain.

Reach the last cairn after 0.2 mile and continue hiking another 100

The solution pits on Arabia Mountain are full of life.

yards to the top of the mountain. At the summit, look around. To the west on a clear day you can see the Atlanta skyline. To the southwest is Panola Mountain, another monadnock. To the northeast is the second peak of Arabia Mountain. It has been quarried and is not as pristine as the one you are standing on.

Turn around and hike back down the mountain. Just after passing the diamorpha sign, look to your left for the blue blazes of Mountain View Trail. Turn left and follow these blue blazes around the rock at the base of the mountain. The trail skirts the edge of the forest at the base of the mountain for 0.2 mile before turning right into the woods. After 0.1 mile in the forest, the trail crosses an intermittent stream, then reemerges onto the granite outcrop.

Pass a viewpoint at the edge of the lake in 0.1 mile. Beyond this viewpoint the trail continues to skirt the lake but a little higher on the mountain. The blue blazes painted on the rock are somewhat harder to find, so pay attention. In 0.2 mile, the trail descends to the right and enters the forest.

The trail follows an intermittent stream and then the edge of the lake, making a slight turn inland in 0.2 mile to avoid an area of mucky ground. You will soon reach a grove of pines with a bed of pine straw on the ground, which makes a good picnic spot. Follow blazes on trees to cross a small stream and hike uphill to an old roadbed. Turn right and walk 0.1 mile to a wildlife viewing platform that also provides great views of Mountain Lake and Arabia Mountain.

Continue on the trail past the wildlife viewing platform and across the lake's dam. At the far side of the dam turn left and hike downhill. Follow blazes across a small rock outcrop. The trail crosses an intermittent stream on the rock at the edge of the woods. Bear left uphill into the woods; the path merges onto a wide forest road. Follow blue blazes uphill another 100 yards to a field. The trail skirts the right side of the field past oak and cherry trees and reenters the woods in 0.1 mile.

In just over 100 yards, reemerge onto the rock outcrop to meet up with the cairns of Mountaintop Trail. Turn left and follow the cairns 0.25 mile back to the parking area and the AWARE Wildlife Center. Then hike the boardwalk and paved Arabia Mountain Trail back to the nature center, where you'll end your hike.

Arabia Lake is one of the prettiest places in the nature preserve.

Forest & Mile Rock Trails

DAVIDSON–ARABIA MOUNTAIN NATURE PRESERVE

Though not as iconic as the Mountaintop Trail, this hike is one of the most interesting in the whole preserve. Leading through forests, past the scenic Arabia Lake, and across an extensive quarried rock outcrop, these trails lead to many places that will make you stop and say, "Wow!" With colorful foliage reflected in the lake in the fall, yellow, red, and blue flowers in the spring, and croaking frogs in the summer, this loop hike is exciting in all seasons. The random polished slab of rock, the drill holes, and the ruined quarry buildings give you a glimpse of the history of the place.

HOW TO GET THERE	**Driving Distance from Downtown Atlanta:** 20 miles **Address:** 3787 Klondike Road, Stonecrest, GA 30038 **Closest Interstate:** I-20 **City, County:** Stonecrest, DeKalb **Parking:** Large gravel parking area near the nature center and trailhead
HIKE DISTANCE	2.2-mile loop
DIFFICULTY	**Overall:** Easy to moderate **Navigation:** Map at trailhead; trails marked with blazes and signposts at most junctions; and rock cairns on Mile Rock Trail **Terrain:** Forest Trail is hard-packed dirt; Mile Rock is rock surface, plus a short stretch on paved trail **Elevation Change:** Minimal elevation change—very level
SAFETY	**Usage** ★★★★★ **Visibility** ★★★★☆ **Upkeep** ★★★★★ **Parking** ★★★★☆
HOURS	7:00 am to sunset
DOGS	Leashed dogs allowed

FACILITIES	• Pit toilet • Nature center, information kiosk, picnic tables, drinking fountain
FEES & PERMITS	None
LAND MANAGER	DeKalb County Recreation, Parks, & Cultural Affairs in partnership with Arabia Mountain National Heritage Area

Landmarks

ARABIA LAKE

This picturesque lake is fed by Stephenson Creek and was used by the navy during World War II for underwater demolition exercises. Across the lake is an area of forest recovering from a 2019 forest fire.

QUARRY ADMINISTRATION BUILDING RUINS

The Davidson Granite Company operated on this land from the 1920s to 1970s and produced slabs of gneiss that were prized for their beauty. Eventually, the quarry became one of the largest producers of grit for the poultry industry. These buildings, built of Arabia gneiss, housed the quarry office.

FROG POND

A small spring bubbles from the rock here and, combined with rainwater, forms a small pond where amphibians and reptiles thrive. An interpretive sign tells you more about the species that have been found here.

Hike Route

Begin your hike at an information kiosk in front of the nature center and go right on a short boardwalk, following yellow-blazed Forest Trail. In 0.2 mile, arrive at the paved multiuse Arabia Mountain Trail.

Cross the paved path and reenter the woods, following a sign for the lake. Parallel the paved path for a few yards, then curve left at a No Bikes sign. This trail skirts the forested edge of a large rock outcrop on your left. When you arrive at the Mary Wade Grave Trail junction near a sentinel loblolly pine tree, turn right and hike to the grave past three large, impressive boulders. After visiting the grave, turn around, hike back to Forest Trail, and turn right.

Hike 0.3 mile to a junction with a wide, unmarked trail. Stay left and follow a sign for Arabia Lake. Then stay left at another junction,

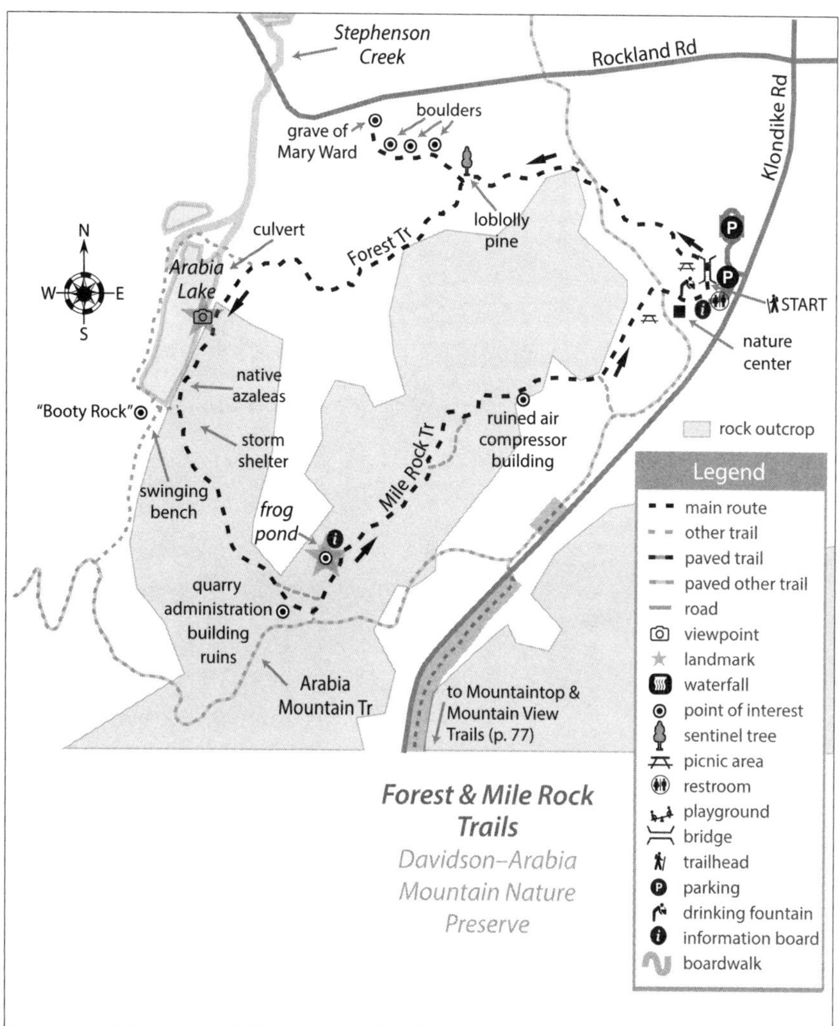
Stephenson Creek
Rockland Rd
Klondike Rd
grave of Mary Ward
boulders
loblolly pine
Forest Tr
culvert
Arabia Lake
N
W
E
S
START
nature center
native azaleas
"Booty Rock"
storm shelter
swinging bench
frog pond
Mile Rock Tr
ruined air compressor building
rock outcrop
quarry administration building ruins
Arabia Mountain Tr
to Mountaintop & Mountain View Trails (p. 77)
Legend
main route
other trail
paved trail
paved other trail
road
viewpoint
landmark
waterfall
point of interest
sentinel tree
picnic area
restroom
playground
bridge
trailhead
parking
drinking fountain
information board
boardwalk
Forest & Mile Rock Trails
Davidson–Arabia Mountain Nature Preserve

Rock cairns lead the way along Mile Rock Trail.

following another sign for the lake. Pass an old metal culvert on your right and follow the lakeshore for 0.2 mile, crossing a rock outcrop with a great view of the lake. Near the end of the lake, pass native azaleas growing on the right, then hike onto the outcrop toward the storm shelter.

This storm shelter is your last shaded spot for almost 0.75 mile. Look across the rock and hike toward the cairns that mark the route of Mile Rock Trail. Be careful not to step in the many solution pits, where delicate plants flourish in the rainwater the pits collect. In 0.25 mile, you'll see cairns on the rock outcrop and a trail that leads into the trees. Take this short, forested trail to reach the ruins of the historic quarry office buildings. Then turn left to follow the cairns back onto the outcrop.

Pass the frog pond and continue following the cairns across the outcrop, then down into a lower quarried area with tall rock walls. In 0.2 mile, pass another old quarry building that used to house an air compressor, then reenter the woods.

At the first junction in the forest, follow a sign for the nature center to the left. (Going right leads to the multiuse path.) In 0.15 mile, reach a junction with the paved multiuse path near the nature center. Go right and then over the bridge to reach the information kiosk and finish your hike.

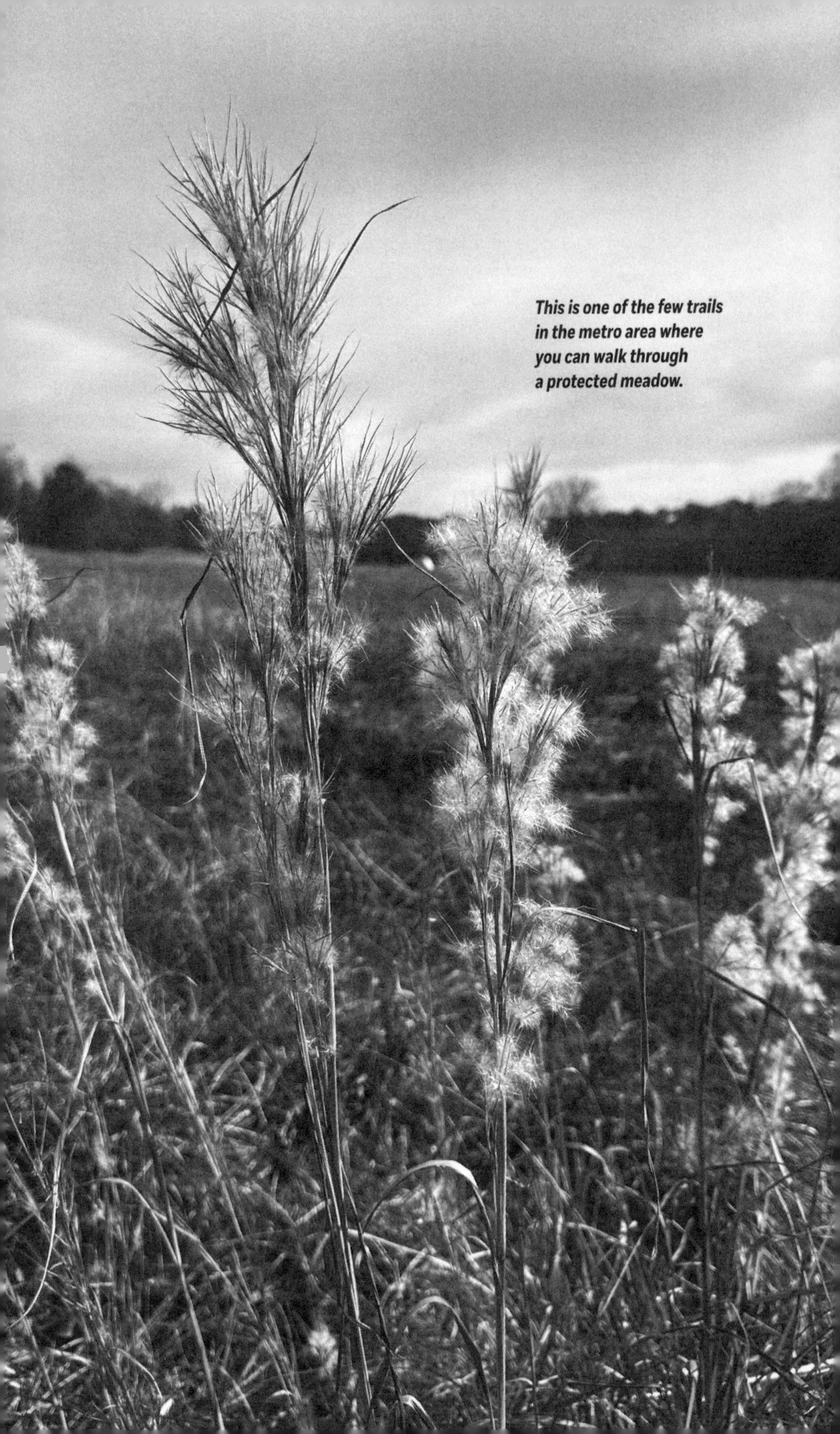

This is one of the few trails in the metro area where you can walk through a protected meadow.

Vaughters' Farm & Retreat House Trails

DAVIDSON–ARABIA MOUNTAIN NATURE PRESERVE

You can get everything you want from a hike along these trails! Panoramic views, historic ruins, a peaceful forest and meadows, a rock outcrop, a lake, and a picturesque barn can all be found along this network of five trails. Historic Vaughters' Farm was once a dairy farm and is now protected and managed by Georgia State Parks and DeKalb County. And this whole area is part of a national heritage area. This hike is a wonderful introduction to the beauty, history, and nature within the Arabia Mountain National Heritage Area.

HOW TO GET THERE

Driving Distance from Downtown Atlanta: 19 miles

Address: 3366 Klondike Road, Stonecrest, GA 30038

Closest Interstate: I-20

City, County: Stonecrest, DeKalb

Parking: Gravel parking area across Klondike Road from the Vaughters' Farm meadow and barn

HIKE DISTANCE

4.5-mile figure-8 loop

DIFFICULTY

Overall: Moderate

Navigation: Blazes on posts, trees, and rocks mark the route; signposts at most junctions

Terrain: Grass, hard-packed dirt, and rock trails, with one small creek crossing

Elevation Change: Rolling hills with several short but steep ascents and descents

SAFETY

Usage ★★★☆☆

Visibility ★★★★☆

Upkeep ★★★★☆

Parking ★★★★☆

HOURS

7:00 am to sunset

DOGS

Leashed dogs allowed

FACILITIES	• Pit toilet • Picnic tables, water fountain, information signs, bicycle rack
FEES & PERMITS	None
LAND MANAGER	DeKalb County Recreation, Parks, & Cultural Affairs and Georgia State Parks in partnership with Arabia Mountain National Heritage Area

Landmarks

HIGH POINT VIEW

At this vantage point, near the House Ruins Trail junction, you can look out over the protected forests and fields of the Arabia Mountain National Heritage Area and imagine what DeKalb County used to be like before urbanization. This viewpoint also happens to be higher above sea level than the peak of Arabia Mountain itself!

HOUSE RUIN

Though not much is known about this ruin, some close examination will show you that it is not built of quarried Arabia gneiss but instead of fieldstones removed from local farmland. You can even see nails that are still present in the remaining wood. Notice that these square-headed nails were likely hand-forged and date back to the 1800s.

RETREAT HOUSE LAKE

Stephenson Creek begins within the Vaughters' Farm property and is dammed to form two of the three lakes within this nature preserve, including Retreat House Lake. Beavers have taken up a home here and built an ecosystem thriving with amphibians, fish, birds, mammals, and reptiles.

Hike Route

Start your hike by carefully crossing Klondike Road at the crosswalk to access the paved multiuse Arabia Mountain Trail. Turn right on the paved path and hike 0.1 mile to reach the grassy entrance to Vaughters' Farm on the left. Hike around the barn to reach a junction with Meadow Loop Trail and turn right.

Hike uphill through the upper end of the meadow, which has many great views to the south. Just before arriving at the crest of the hill near a picnic table and House Ruins Trail junction, look south (downhill) for an expansive view of the forested terrain of the

The historic Vaughters' Farm barn is one of the most iconic sites in the Arabia Mountain National Heritage Area.

Davidson–Arabia Mountain Nature Preserve. This spot is also the highest point in the preserve at over 1,000 feet above sea level.

Turn right and follow the white blazes along the 0.4-mile House Ruins Trail. Pass the boundary between Georgia State Parks and DeKalb County property, marked with yellow paint; the trail then curves right and heads downhill. Pass a spring in a cove below private homes, then reach the ruins of an old house. The foundation, fireplace, and chimney are still standing. These ruins are very close to private property, so please be respectful of the neighbors. Turn around and hike back to Meadow Loop Trail. Keep your eye out for blazes, because the trail route is not as obvious on the way back.

At the junction, turn right and hike downhill 100 feet to a junction with Woodland Trail. Turn right and follow the orange blazes generally downhill through a mature oak and hickory forest. In 0.5 mile, enter a rock outcrop. Follow the orange blazes painted on the rock and be careful to avoid the solution pits, where delicate flowers and plants flourish. In 0.2 mile, near the edge of the rock outcrop,

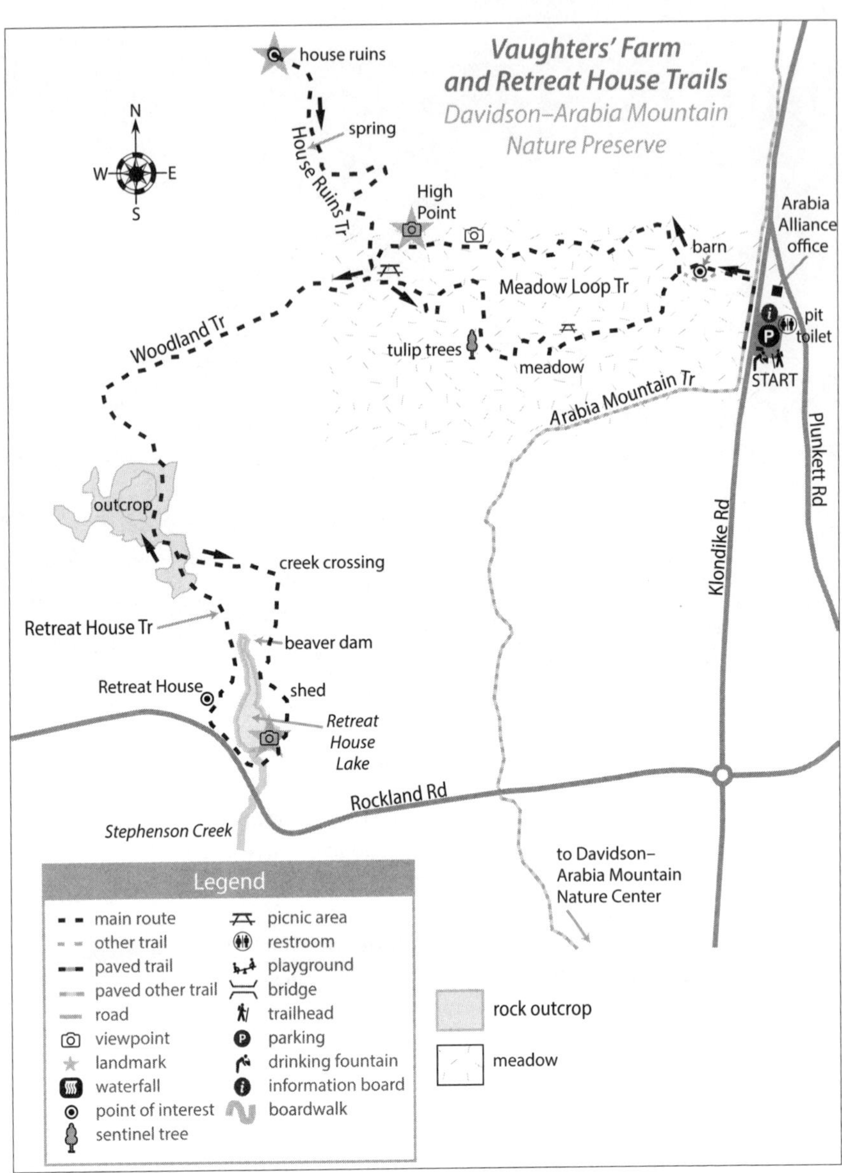
Vaughters' Farm
and Retreat House Trails
Davidson–Arabia Mountain
Nature Preserve
N
W
E
S
house ruins
spring
House Ruins Tr
High
Point
Arabia
Alliance
office
barn
Meadow Loop Tr
Woodland Tr
tulip trees
meadow
pit
toilet
START
Arabia Mountain Tr
Plunkett Rd
Klondike Rd
outcrop
creek crossing
Retreat House Tr
beaver dam
shed
Retreat House
Retreat
House
Lake
Rockland Rd
Stephenson Creek
to Davidson–
Arabia Mountain
Nature Center
Legend
main route
other trail
paved trail
paved other trail
road
viewpoint
landmark
waterfall
point of interest
sentinel tree
picnic area
restroom
playground
bridge
trailhead
parking
drinking fountain
information board
boardwalk
rock outcrop
meadow

look carefully for blazes at your feet. The last orange blaze of Woodland Trail is on the rock near the first two pink blazes of Retreat House Trail. Turn left at the last orange blaze to follow the pink blazed Retreat House Trail along the edge of the outcrop and then into the woods. If you accidentally hike counterclockwise, pink blazes will lead you back to this point.

Cross a creek in 0.15 mile. Pass an old farm shed in 0.2 mile, then reach the far end of Retreat House Lake, with a nice view. Cross the lake outflow and follow the pink blazes as the trail snakes between the dam and Rockland Road.

When you reach the gravel driveway for the Retreat House, turn right and hike to the right past the front door of the house. This house used to be the park ranger's residence, but Ranger Tyronne Burkette renamed it Retreat House to promote it as a community asset. Pink blazes show the way to continue on Retreat House Trail parallel to the lakeshore. Pass a beaver dam on the right and then reenter the rock outcrop. Almost immediately, reach the orange blaze of Woodland Trail and turn left. Hike Woodland Trail across the outcrop and back the way you came to Meadow Loop Trail.

Turn right on Meadow Loop Trail. From here it is 0.75 mile through the lower end of the meadow to get back to the paved Arabia Mountain Trail. Along the way you'll pass a grove of large sentinel tulip trees, a picnic table, a defunct tractor, and the barn once again.

Turn right on the paved path, then cross Klondike Road at the crosswalk to end your hike.

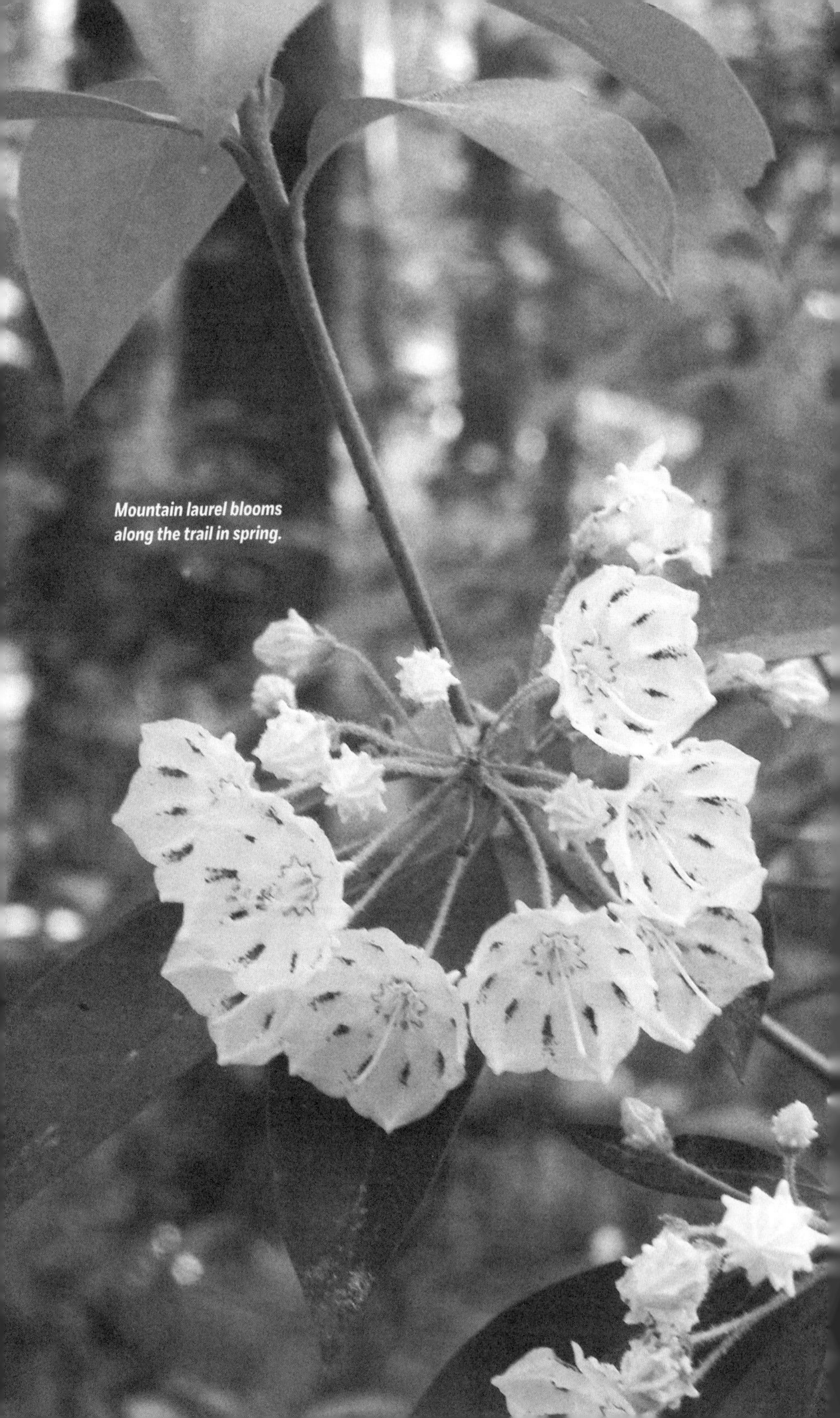

Mountain laurel blooms along the trail in spring.

Laurel Creek Trail

DAVIDSON–ARABIA MOUNTAIN NATURE PRESERVE

The least-hiked trail at Davidson–Arabia Mountain Nature Preserve is also one of its prettiest. Mountain laurel evokes images of fast-flowing creeks and remote mountain hollows, and this hike lives up to that image. The route follows a quiet, forested ridge, then meets up with a bubbling creek with two cascades, thickets of mountain laurel, and the feeling of exploring a forgotten hollow in the Appalachian Mountains. Then, just like that, you're back on a paved path next to an elementary school—it's like magic!

HOW TO GET THERE

Driving Distance from Downtown Atlanta: 20 miles

Address: 6775 South Goddard Road, Stonecrest, GA 30038

Closest Interstate: I-20

City, County: Stonecrest, DeKalb

Parking: Street parking along South Goddard Road; parking in the Murphy Candler Elementary School lot on weekends only

HIKE DISTANCE

2.5-mile lollipop loop

DIFFICULTY

Overall: Easy to moderate

Navigation: White blazes mark the trail, and most junctions have signs

Terrain: Hard-packed dirt trails with a paved portion at the beginning and end

Elevation Change: Several short but steep ascents and descents

SAFETY

Usage ★★☆☆☆

Visibility ★★★☆☆

Upkeep ★★★★☆

Parking ★★★★☆

HOURS

7:00 am to sunset

DOGS

Leashed dogs allowed

FACILITIES
- No toilets
- Picnic table

FEES & PERMITS None

LAND MANAGER DeKalb County Recreation, Parks, & Cultural Affairs in partnership with Arabia Mountain National Heritage Area

Landmarks

LAUREL CREEK CASCADE

This small cascade flows next to a thicket of mountain laurel, a flowering shrub that prefers to grow in rocky alpine soil. The rocky land surrounding Arabia Mountain provides a similar habitat for this beautiful evergreen plant.

SENTINEL TULIP TREE

This tulip tree (commonly known as tulip poplar) on the far bank of Laurel Creek is the largest tree in this area of forest—over 11 feet in circumference! There is no easy way to get across the creek to see this giant up close, but if you're creative, then you probably can find a way.

LAUREL CREEK RAPIDS

Laurel Creek is small, but as it flows over a cascade of rock, the water speeds up and forms "rapids," which are very picturesque. The trail ends at the top of the cascade, so be very careful if you choose to climb down to take photographs.

Hike Route

Begin hiking downhill on the paved multiuse path. Continue 0.1 mile before reaching the trailhead for white-blazed Laurel Creek Trail on the right.

Follow Laurel Creek Trail through a pine forest, then up a steep hill for 0.25 mile. When you reach a picnic table at the top, go right and hike 0.3 mile through rolling hills. Then begin a steep 0.3-mile descent to reach the creek.

When you arrive at Laurel Creek, you'll see a grove of mountain laurel, from which the trail and creek get their names. To the right, a short spur trail leads to a bubbling cascade and large boulder, which marks the start of private property. Turn left to hike 0.25 mile along

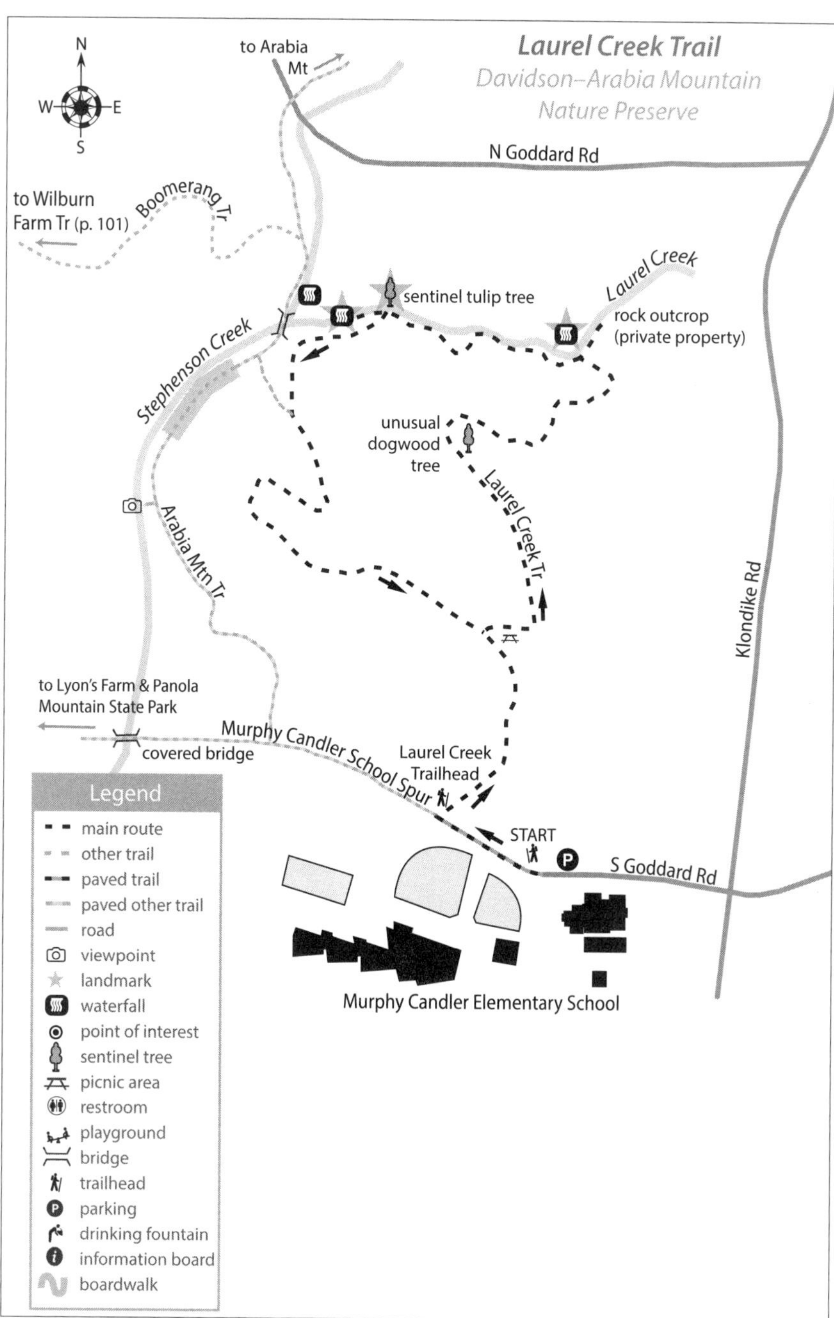

Laurel Creek Trail
Davidson–Arabia Mountain Nature Preserve
N
S
W
E
to Arabia Mt
N Goddard Rd
to Wilburn Farm Tr (p. 101)
Boomerang Tr
Laurel Creek
sentinel tulip tree
rock outcrop (private property)
Stephenson Creek
unusual dogwood tree
Laurel Creek Tr
Arabia Mtn Tr
Klondike Rd
to Lyon's Farm & Panola Mountain State Park
covered bridge
Murphy Candler School Spur
Laurel Creek Trailhead
START
S Goddard Rd
Murphy Candler Elementary School
Legend
main route
other trail
paved trail
paved other trail
road
viewpoint
landmark
waterfall
point of interest
sentinel tree
picnic area
restroom
playground
bridge
trailhead
parking
drinking fountain
information board
boardwalk

Colorful folk art greets you at the Murphy Candler Elementary School trailhead.

the creek, looking at the exposed roots of many large trees, to a junction with a sign that reads Rapids.

To your right, across the creek, is the sentinel tulip tree. Go straight through a laurel thicket to reach the Laurel Creek rapids (another small cascade) in about 100 yards. Returning to the trail junction, turn right and hike uphill, away from the creek.

In 0.2 mile, reach a junction. The right trail leads to the paved multiuse path and a larger cascade on Stephenson Creek. Turn left, cross a small creek after 0.1 mile, then continue uphill to the junction with a picnic table at the top of the hill.

Stay straight on the wide trail and hike for 0.25 mile, back to the multiuse path. Turn left to return to the parking area and end the hike.

The stone chimney is the only part of the historic Wilburn farmhouse still standing.

Cascade & Wilburn Farm Trails

DAVIDSON–ARABIA MOUNTAIN NATURE PRESERVE

This side of the Davidson–Arabia Mountain Nature Preserve is truly beautiful. This figure-8 loop leads you past cascading rapids running over a smooth granite outcrop, then up onto a ridge above a historic farm where you can see a view of Arabia Mountain. At the ruined farm, you can explore the remains of a farmhouse, a collapsed barn, a boxed spring, a scenic pond, and some special trees. The route ends with a relaxing walk down the paved multiuse path. It's a hike with something for everyone.

HOW TO GET THERE

Driving Distance from Downtown Atlanta: 18 miles
Address: 4028 Evans Mill Road, Stonecrest, GA 30038
Closest Interstate: I-20
City, County: Stonecrest, DeKalb
Parking: Small paved parking lot off Evans Mill Road

HIKE DISTANCE

3.5-mile figure-8 loop

DIFFICULTY

Overall: Moderate
Navigation: Map at trailhead; painted blazes mark the trail, and some junctions have signs
Terrain: Hard-packed dirt trails and paved multiuse path
Elevation Change: Several extended ascents and descents

SAFETY

Usage ★★★☆☆
Visibility ★★★☆☆
Upkeep ★★★★☆
Parking ★★★☆☆

HOURS

7:00 am to sunset

DOGS

Leashed dogs allowed

FACILITIES

- No toilets
- Picnic tables, information board, drinking fountain, benches, bike racks

FEES & PERMITS

None

LAND MANAGER DeKalb County Recreation, Parks, & Cultural Affairs in partnership with Arabia Mountain National Heritage Area

Landmarks

SENTINEL SYCAMORE

American sycamore trees usually grow close to water, so it's no surprise to find this one near the creek. This tree lost its top when it was young but continued growing limbs parallel to the ground, giving it a shape like a candelabra.

POLE BRIDGE CREEK CASCADE

Downstream from the remains of the historic Evans Mill is a beautiful cascade. The creek drops over 20 feet as it flows over a granite outcrop. This is one of the most beautiful spots in the Davidson–Arabia Mountain Nature Preserve.

FARMHOUSE RUINS

Among the broken timbers of this wood-frame farmhouse, you'll find an old well and a still-standing chimney made of Arabia Mountain stones. Across from the farmhouse is an eastern red cedar that is a giant among its species and was probably planted by the Wilburn family, who once occupied the farmhouse.

Hike Route

Before beginning the hike, take a short walk on the dirt trail parallel to Evans Mill Road, just before the paved multiuse path begins. This spur leads to a picnic area near the site of the historic Evans Mill and a sentinel sycamore tree on the right next to an interpretive sign. Remains of the old dam can be seen at the edge of the creek.

Back at the beginning of the multiuse path, walk for 50 feet to where the parking lot ends and turn right on Cascade Trail next to a bicycle-shaped bike rack.

Cross a wooden bridge to reach the cascades for which the trail is named. Continue hiking as the trail leaves the creek and ascends the ridge in 0.2 mile. In another 0.4 mile, reach a junction with the multiuse path. Cross the pavement and go straight to begin Wilburn Farm Trail.

After a 0.4-mile steady uphill climb, reach a junction with an old farm road. Turn right to reach a junction at the top of a large, cleared slope. From here you can see the peak of Arabia Mountain

This unusual sycamore tree looks a little like a candelabra.

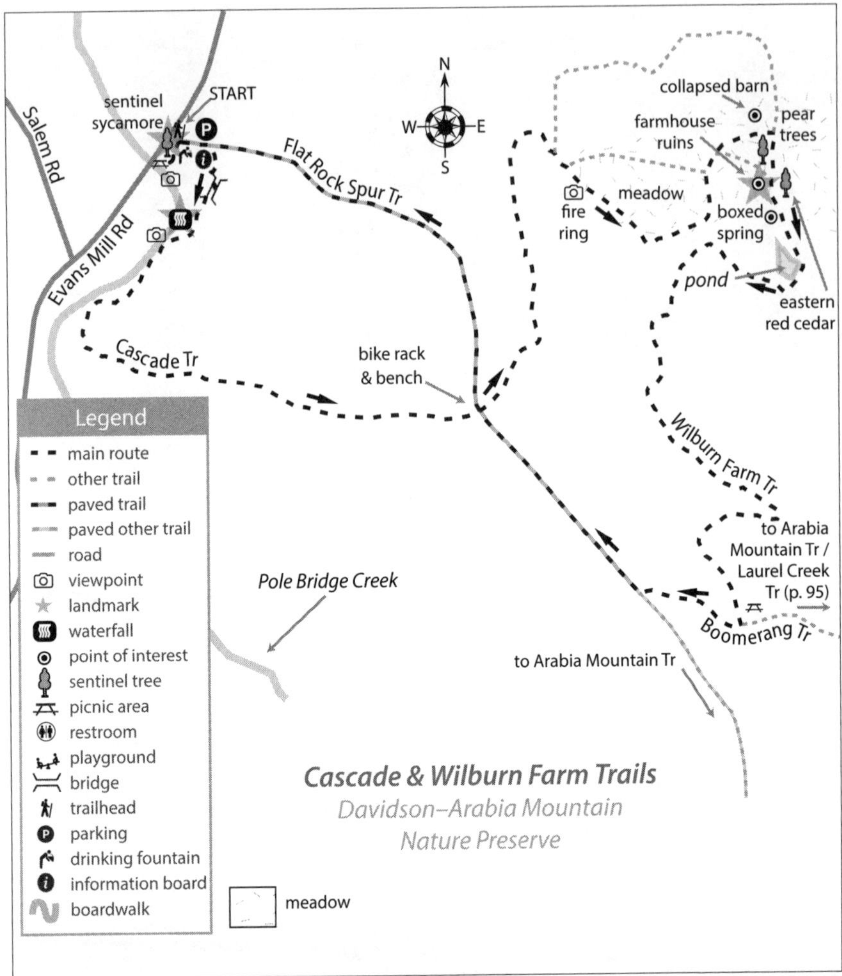

to the east. There are two paths through the field below, which can be somewhat overgrown in the summer, depending on how recently they've been mowed. Continue straight to pass benches and a fire ring, then hike down the hill on the right side of the field and reach a junction in 0.3 mile. Go straight, then left to walk toward the collapsed barn.

When you reach the barn, look across the field to the right to locate the collapsed farmhouse. Follow the trail toward the farmhouse for just over 100 yards to reach the two sentinel pear trees on the right at the next junction, next to the farmhouse chimney. You can take a photo of your face through the hole in one of these trees.

Continue straight, passing a sentinel red cedar on the left across from the farmhouse. Fifty yards beyond the farmhouse as the trail begins to descend and about 30 feet off the trail to the right, there is a spring that was boxed with stones for easier use by the farmers, if you care to explore and find it.

In another 0.1 mile past the farmhouse you'll reach a spring-fed pond with a small bench close to the water where you can sit and take in the beauty. Cross a small wooden bridge and follow the trail across the dam. The trail then winds through a lush Piedmont forest for 0.8 mile to a junction with a picnic table and the red-blazed Boomerang Trail.

If you go left, you can connect with the paved Arabia Mountain Trail, from which you can reach a spur trail that leads to Laurel Creek Trail. To continue the Cascade & Wilburn Farm Trails hike, turn right on Boomerang Trail.

In 0.15 mile, you'll reach a junction with the multiuse path. Go right and walk 0.9 mile back to the parking area to end your hike.

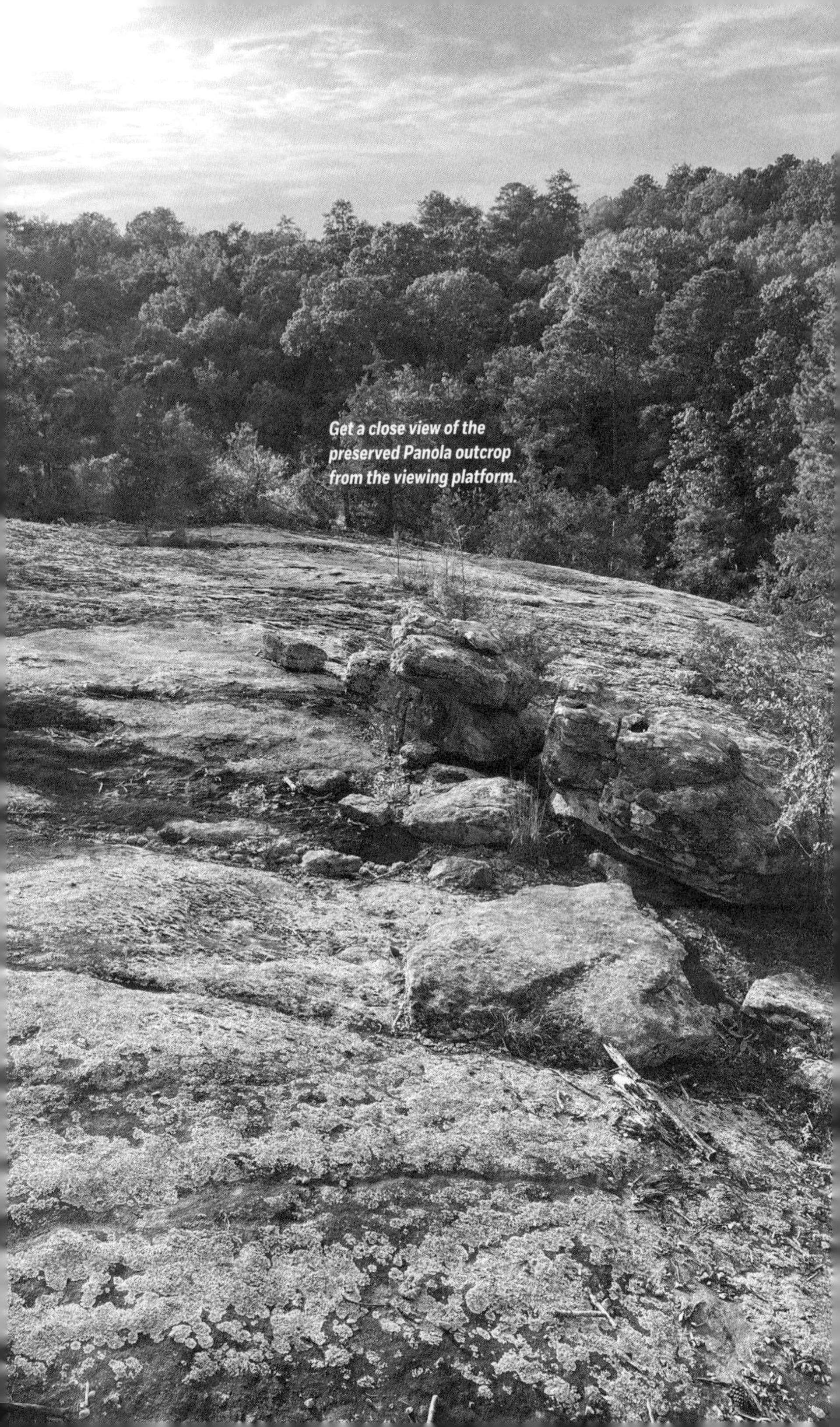

Get a close view of the preserved Panola outcrop from the viewing platform.

Outcrop & Watershed Trails

PANOLA MOUNTAIN STATE PARK

Panola Mountain is a 100-acre granite outcrop where visitors can hike nature trails, bike the paved multiuse trail, or picnic at one of the many pavilions near the nature center. The granite outcrop at Panola is being carefully preserved, and hikers can only walk on the rock on a ranger-led guided hike. Unlike other monadnocks (granite mountains) in the region, very little quarrying happened here. Because of its pristine condition, the outcrop at Panola is worth viewing from the overlook. The Outcrop and Watershed Trails start at the nature center, loop through the important and delicate ecosystems of Panola, and offer views of the mountain itself.

HOW TO GET THERE

Driving Distance from Downtown Atlanta: 20 miles
Address: 2620 Georgia 155 SW, Stockbridge, GA 30281
Closest Interstate: I-20
City, County: Near Stockbridge, in Rockdale County
Parking: Large paved parking area

HIKE DISTANCE

2-mile figure-8 loop

DIFFICULTY

Overall: Easy to moderate
Navigation: Blazes along route
Terrain: Hard-packed dirt and gravel trails
Elevation Change: Mostly flat with a few rolling hills

SAFETY

Usage ★★★☆☆
Visibility ★★★★☆
Upkeep ★★★★★
Parking ★★★★★

HOURS

7:00 am to 7:00 pm

DOGS

Leashed dogs allowed

FACILITIES

- Toilets across from parking area
- Water fountain, playground, picnic pavilions, nature playground, little free library, outdoor fitness stations

FEES & PERMITS	$5 daily ParkPass—purchase at gastateparks.org
LAND MANAGER	Georgia State Parks

Landmarks

SENTINEL MULTITRUNKED WHITE OAK TREE

This white oak tree sits at the edge of a creek bed and is one of the largest trees in the forest. Count its five trunks! White oak trees can provide habitat for over 300 species of caterpillar.

ROCK OUTCROP OVERLOOK

Because hikers can only walk on the outcrop with a park ranger, the granite ecosystem at Panola Mountain has stayed well preserved. From the overlook, you can see the delicate and intricate ways the granite rock supports life and the various stages of ecological succession.

PRICKLY PEAR CACTI

Cacti growing on rock? Prickly pear cacti are native to Georgia and thrive in the dry soil on granite outcrops. In the summer they produce an edible purple fruit, which you can view from the trail at this marked viewpoint.

Hike Route

To reach the hiking trails from the parking lot, turn left at the front doors of the nature center and take the wide gravel trail under an awning. To the left is a playground and outdoor classroom. Take the trail to the right, passing more nature-themed play areas to reach the map board at the end of the gravel trail.

Begin your hike by taking the Watershed Trail to the right side of the map board, following the red arrows. Stay straight in 100 feet at an unofficial trail leading to the parking lot. At another unofficial junction in 100 feet stay straight. Pass a signpost and follow the red blazes for 100 yards to a three-way junction with red arrows. Stay to the right.

Hike downhill and parallel to the creek. Cross a bridge and hike through the forest for 0.15 mile before crossing another bridge. The trail curves along a small creek. After crossing a third bridge, immediately look about 50 yards to the right of the trail, where you'll see a sentinel multitrunked white oak on the edge of the creek.

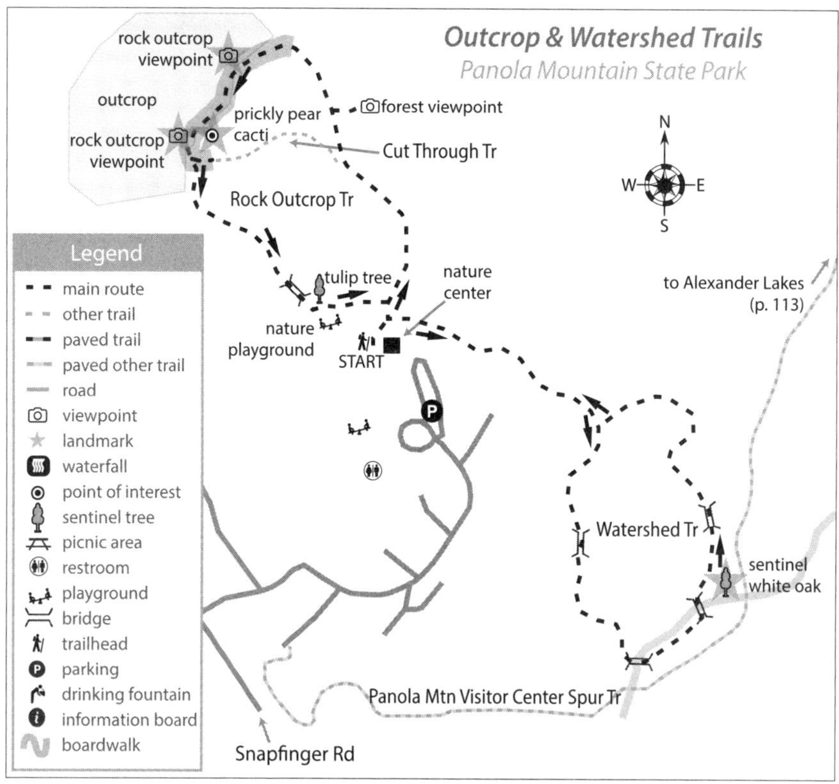

Continue hiking uphill, crossing a footbridge in 0.1 mile. From here, the trail climbs steadily and returns to the junction at the beginning of this loop. Turn right and retrace your steps to the map board near the nature center.

Stay to the right and begin hiking Rock Outcrop Trail, marked with white blazes. At the first junction, stay straight, following signs for Rock Outcrop Trail. Hike to a junction with Cut Through Trail and stay to the right. Hike the Rock Outcrop Trail downhill, passing a small spur on the right to an overlook of the floodplain where you can view the "layers" of the forest. Trees and plants that grow to different heights add diversity and stability to this ecosystem.

In 0.15 mile, reach a fenceline at the bottom of the hill with the outcrop on your right. As noted on the signposts, please stay on the trail and do not venture out onto the outcrop. The granite outcrop is a sensitive ecosystem that is being preserved by the state park. Hike along the fence and reach an outcrop viewpoint platform in 100 feet.

Many organisms such as this moss ecosystem flourish on the outcrop.

Return to the main path and in another 100 feet reach a second viewing platform. Read the informational signage about the ecological succession happening on the granite below. On a clear day, if you look right and to the west, you may see Stone Mountain, another well-known granite outcrop in this area.

After soaking in the view, return to the main path and reach a junction with the Cut Through Trail. Turn left onto Cut Through Trail and immediately at an interpretive sign on the left, look for prickly pear cacti on the exposed rock.

Retrace your steps back to Rock Outcrop Trail and turn left into the woods. Hike past a tulip tree with a large cavity on the right and come to a small footbridge. Just past the footbridge on the left is a large sentinel multitrunked tulip tree marked with an interpretive sign. Hike for another 0.1 mile, then turn right at a junction that connects back to the map board. Go right to reach the nature center and parking area to end your hike.

Large boulders along the trail beg to be climbed.

Alexander Lakes Trail

PANOLA MOUNTAIN STATE PARK

The Alexander Lakes loop is part of Panola Mountain State Park and connects with the Rockdale River Trail and the Arabia Mountain Trail. On nice days, people come to the lakes to fish, hike, bike, paddle, or picnic. Add this hike to one of the many other activities offered at this state park, and you'll have a full day of outdoor fun. This route not only offers great views of the lakes but also passes historic structures and unique ecological features.

HOW TO GET THERE

Driving Distance from Downtown Atlanta: 21 miles
Address: 5015 Flat Bridge Road SW, Stockbridge, GA 30281
Closest Interstate: I-20
City, County: Near Stockbridge, in Rockdale County
Parking: Large paved parking lot

HIKE DISTANCE

2-mile loop

DIFFICULTY

Overall: Moderate
Navigation: Trail markers and signage along route
Terrain: Paved multiuse trail and boardwalk
Elevation Change: Rolling hills, with a few extended ascents and descents

SAFETY

Usage ★★★★★
Visibility ★★★★☆
Upkeep ★★★★★
Parking ★★★★☆

HOURS

7:00 am to sunset

DOGS

Leashed dogs allowed

FACILITIES

- Toilets at parking area
- Water fountain, bike repair station, picnic pavilion

FEES & PERMITS

$5 daily ParkPass—purchase at gastateparks.org

LAND MANAGER

Georgia State Parks

Native flowers bloom along the edge of Alexander Lake.

Landmarks

TREE BURL

On the right side of the trail is a tree with a large, tumor-like growth on its trunk. Though some may consider burls an eyesore, wood from burls can be highly valued by woodworkers for its unique internal designs. Burls often don't harm the tree and are in fact the result of a tree defending itself against infection.

HISTORIC BARN

The trail runs through a historic barn. You can view the empty stables as you hike through the interior.

LAKE OVERLOOK

Bring your binoculars, because this spot on the boardwalk is a quiet place to birdwatch or fish on the far side of upper Alexander Lake.

Hike Route

Begin your hike by exiting the far end of the parking lot closest to the lakes. Hike on the wide paved path over the long bridge, enjoying the open view of upper and lower Alexander Lakes. The trail inclines

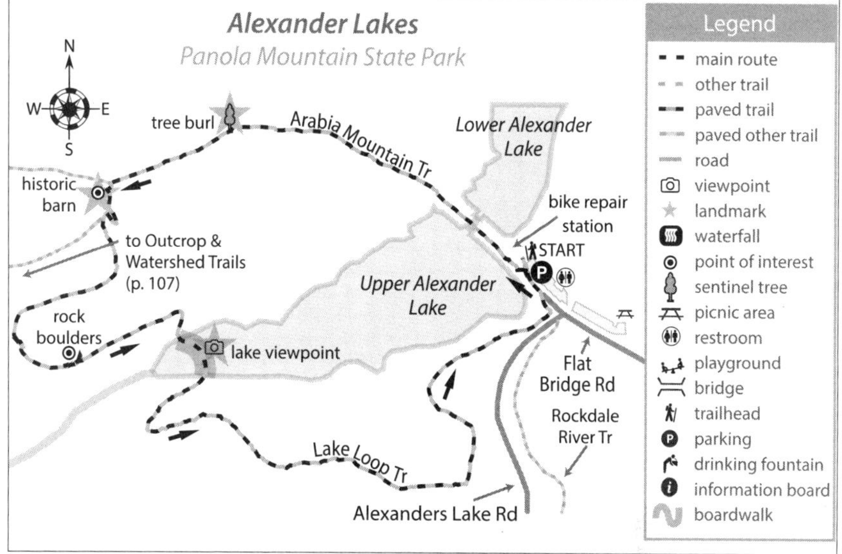

steadily and passes a junction with Scout Lake campground on the right in 0.25 mile.

In 0.1 mile, at a signpost on the right side of the trail 100 feet into the forest, is a tree with a large growth on its trunk. This growth is called a burl and is a common occurrence. Continue hiking to the next junction and a mileage post. Turn left and hike through the interior of an old barn.

After exiting the barn, take a left at the subsequent junction. From here, the trail begins a steep descent past large boulders on the left side of the path. Some of these large rocks are close to the trail, if you're in the mood for climbing. Reach the bottom of the hill and cross a long boardwalk over the far side of the lake.

Take a moment to enjoy the view at one of the lake lookout points along the boardwalk. When the boardwalk ends, the trail begins a steep incline. Hike uphill for 0.2 mile to where the trail begins to level out near a large field. Then the trail makes its way downhill to skirt the edge of the lake.

Where the trail intersects with Flat Bridge Road and Alexander Lakes Road, take the stairs in front of you or the paved section to the left to return to the parking area.

This structure invites hikers to contemplate the history of the land.

Big Haynes Creek Nature Center

This hike through the Big Haynes Creek Nature Center, which is part of the Georgia International Horse Park, will take you past pristine wetlands, blooming meadows, and a granite outcrop. With so many trails to choose and ecological beauties to enjoy, one could spend all day exploring this 173-acre nature preserve. Whether on foot, in a kayak, on a mountain bike, or on horseback, voyagers of all kinds are sure to find joy in the forests of Big Haynes.

HOW TO GET THERE

Driving Distance from Downtown Atlanta: 32 miles
Address: 855 Costley Mill Road NE, Conyers, GA 30013
Closest Interstate: I-20
City, County: Conyers, Rockdale
Parking: Large gravel parking lot

HIKE DISTANCE

4-mile loop

DIFFICULTY

Overall: Moderate
Navigation: Numbered posts along route
Terrain: Wide gravel trails and hard-packed dirt trails
Elevation Change: Mostly flat, with a few short but steep ascents and descents

SAFETY

Usage ★★★☆☆
Visibility ★★★★☆
Upkeep ★★★★★
Parking ★★★★☆

HOURS

Dawn to dusk

DOGS

Leashed dogs allowed

FACILITIES

- Toilets located at Steeplechase Trailhead and near the Old Oak Tree Trailhead in the Horse Park at the RV lot
- Picnic areas and canoe/kayak launch; within the nearby Georgia International Horse Park are a water fountain, concessions, and additional amenities

FEES & PERMITS	None
LAND MANAGER	Georgia International Horse Park

Landmarks

WETLAND OVERLOOK

The views of the wetland will transport you to the swamps of south Georgia. Lily pads float on the surface of the water, where wading birds and turtles are abundant. Paddlers can explore the inner channels of the wetland, but fishing is not allowed.

OLD FARMHOUSE

At the edge of a meadow sits a small intact building with a circular stone fence—a replica of the type of house that might have stood here when this land was farmed. This structure can lead your mind to drift back in time and imagine the various human uses of this park over the years.

GRANITE OUTCROP

Granite outcrops are a common geological formation in the Piedmont region of Georgia. In fact, Rockdale County was named for this reason. Watch your step, if you choose to explore this outcrop. Though made of rock, it's home to an abundance of living organisms and plants. How many can you spot?

Hike Route

Begin your hike at the far left end of the parking area, at the map board and pollinator garden. In 50 feet, the trail reaches a junction with Blue and Purple Trails. Go right onto Purple Trail. In 50 yards, reach junction 109 and bear right to continue on Purple Trail. At junction 110, stay to the right and pass an outdoor classroom on the left at junction 111.

At junction 112, stay straight and hike along the edge of the wetland. When you reach junction 113 stay to the right, keeping the wetland to your right and passing a covered viewing platform. Turn right at junction 114, 50 feet past the covered platform, and walk onto the observation platform to get a great view of the expansive wetland. Wetlands like this one are important animal habitat, and you may see a variety of wildlife in the water, including birds, reptiles, fish, insects, and even mammals such as river otters and beavers.

After enjoying the wetland view, exit the platform and take an immediate right onto the dirt trail that skirts the edge of the wetland.

At junction 115 continue straight. The trail continues through the woods past groves of ferns and young trees. After junction 116 cross two small footbridges. Reach junction 035 just past the second footbridge and continue on the far right to stay on Purple Trail.

For 0.3 mile, hike along the edge of the wetland to come to junction 036, where Purple and Blue Trails intersect. Stay to the right and immediately cross a small footbridge. Keep right at the subsequent junctions (037, 118, 119) to continue on Purple Trail.

At junction 120, hike through a low, muddy section of trail to reach a junction where Purple and Blue Trails converge. Keep right at this and at junction 043 to stay on Purple Trail. In 0.1 mile at a T intersection with junction 121, take the trail to the right past a picnic table and trash cans onto the boardwalk for another viewpoint of the wetland.

After taking in the view, backtrack to junction 121 and continue straight onto Blue Trail. Go right at junction 045 and come to a large field and camping area. Take a sharp left to stay on Blue Trail at junction 047 and then stay to the right. Pass a large water oak on your right and hike a flat stretch of grassy understory for 0.1 mile. Keep right at the next three posts as the trail runs parallel to Big Haynes Creek.

In 0.15 mile, reach an unmarked junction with a fenceline in front of you. Curve left to reach junction 051, where you'll stay to the right. Hike a steady incline that opens to a large meadow at junction 052. Turn left and stay right at the next post (junction 157). In early fall, you'll likely encounter bright bursts of yellow from the abundant goldenrod flowers as you hike through the meadow.

In 100 yards at junction 156, the trail curves left past an old farmhouse. Hike uphill and around a large field on the right. At junction 155, continue straight to reach junction 154. Turn left here, and just before reaching the next post, turn left onto a wide gravel trail leading down into the forest. In 100 feet, come to a four-way junction on the right at the edge of the tree line, with trails leading into the forest. Turn right and continue straight and downhill into the forest, passing a dilapidated wooden structure on your right at the bottom of the hill.

Hike down into the floodplain before climbing steeply again. In 0.1 mile, reach the top of the hill and junction 152 as you exit the forest. Turn left at the marker and hike along the edge of the tree line with the field to your right. Stay straight at junction 151 and pass a remnant of the 1996 Olympic cross-country equestrian competition that was

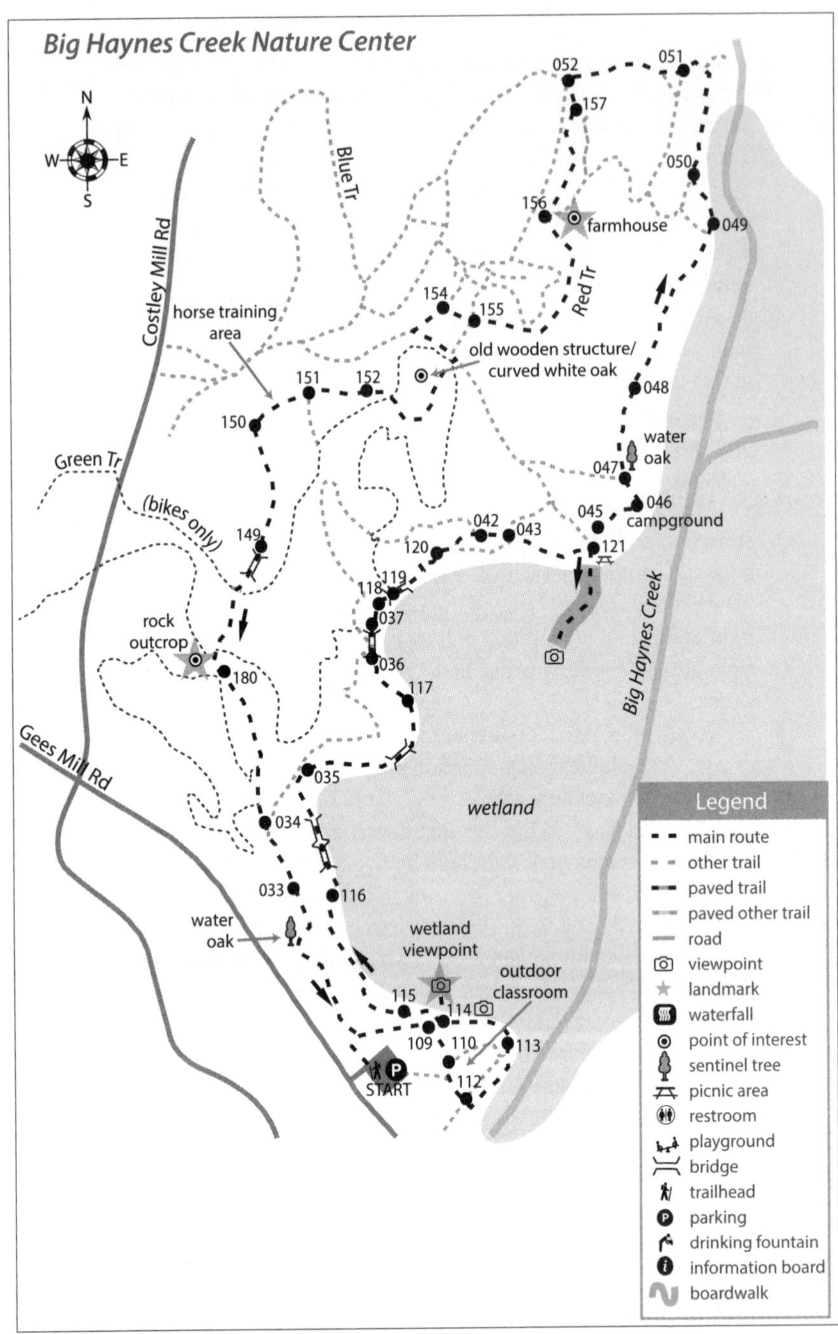
Big Haynes Creek Nature Center
N
W
E
S
Costley Mill Rd
Blue Tr
Red Tr
farmhouse
horse training area
old wooden structure/ curved white oak
Green Tr
(bikes only)
water oak
campground
Big Haynes Creek
rock outcrop
Gees Mill Rd
wetland
water oak
wetland viewpoint
outdoor classroom
START
052
051
157
050
156
049
154
155
151
152
150
048
047
046
045
042
043
120
121
149
118
119
037
036
180
117
035
034
033
116
115
114
109
110
113
112
Legend
main route
other trail
paved trail
paved other trail
road
viewpoint
landmark
waterfall
point of interest
sentinel tree
picnic area
restroom
playground
bridge
trailhead
parking
drinking fountain
information board
boardwalk

Lily pads and lotus flowers add a burst of color on the water's surface.

held here. Then arrive at junction 150 and hike left across the field for 0.1 mile to reach junction 149 and a bridge.

After crossing the bridge, pass the remnants of an old fence and come to a junction with an orange signpost. Take the far left trail. At an unmarked junction in 100 feet, take the far right trail and come to a spur on the right that leads out to the granite outcrop. Take a closer view of the outcrop, but if you walk out onto the rock, be careful to avoid stepping on sensitive plants, and be aware the rock may be slippery after a rain.

Return to the dirt trail and hike for 50 feet to junction 180, with a Bikes Only sign. Stay straight and hike downhill to junction 034 with Blue Trail. Keep right and hike uphill. The trail skirts the edge of the road at the top of the hill. In 0.1 mile, reach the junction where you began your hike. Turn right to exit the forest and return to the parking lot to end your hike.

US 78 EAST

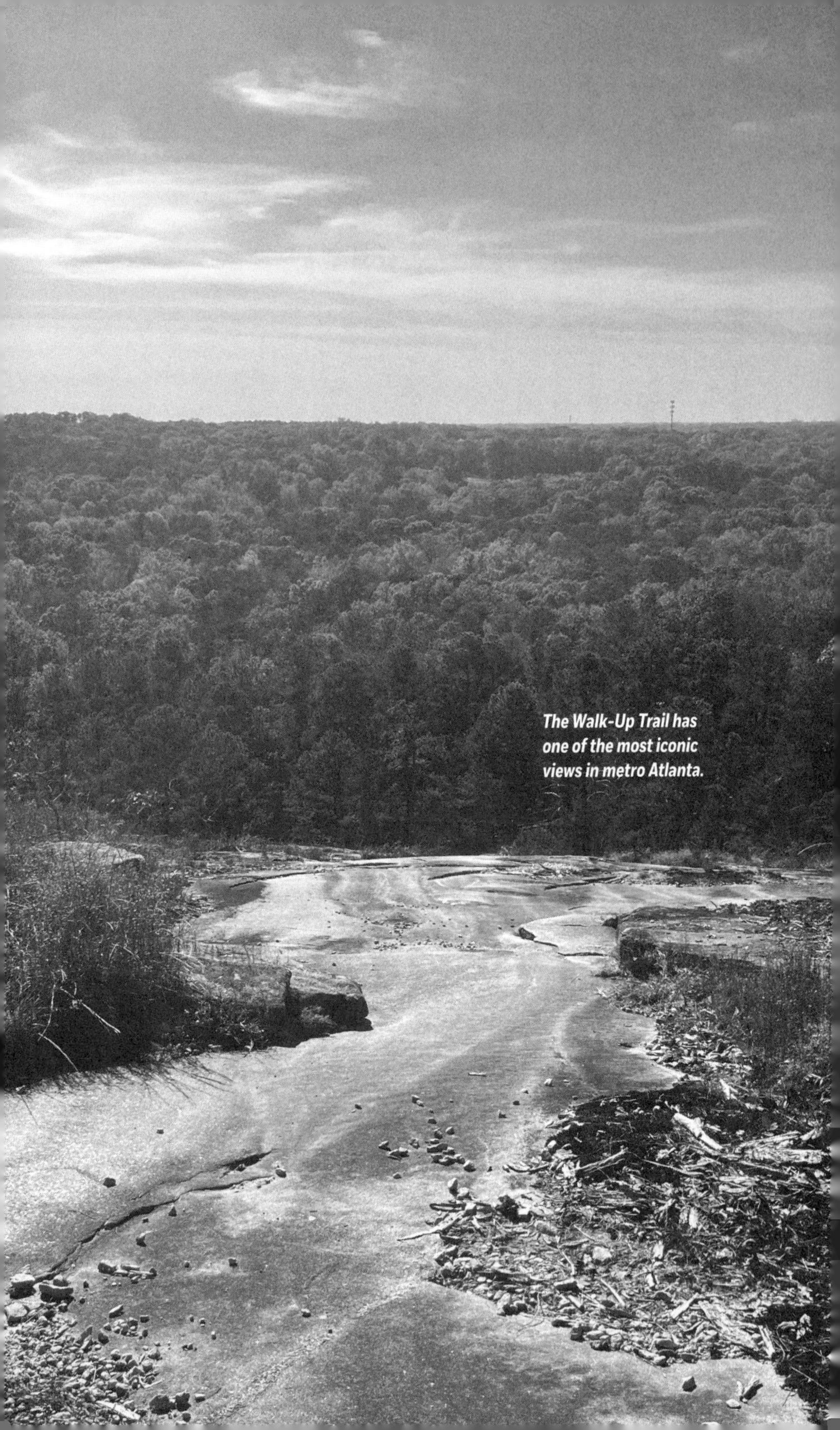

The Walk-Up Trail has one of the most iconic views in metro Atlanta.

Walk-Up Trail

STONE MOUNTAIN PARK

Stone Mountain is one of the icons of Atlanta hikes, and its Walk-Up Trail is the most used and has the best views in the metro area. Once the meeting location of the Ku Klux Klan, the mountain has been reclaimed as a premier hiking experience for a diversity of people from many cultures and nationalities. Though this is a strenuous route, you'll see an array of ages making the trek to the top. It will make you sweat, but the views make it worthwhile—on a clear day you can see as far as the Appalachian Mountains in north Georgia.

HOW TO GET THERE

Driving Distance from Downtown Atlanta: 20 miles

Address: 2003 Robert E. Lee Boulevard, Stone Mountain, GA 30083

Closest Highway: US 78

City, County: Stone Mountain, DeKalb

Parking: Large paved parking lot and overflow lot; look for signs for the Walk-Up Trail Lot

HIKE DISTANCE

2-mile out-and-back

DIFFICULTY

Overall: Strenuous

Navigation: Yellow blazes on ground

Terrain: Granite rock surface with many roots and large boulders. The granite can be very slippery in wet conditions.

Elevation Change: Very steep ascent and descent

SAFETY

Usage ★★★★★

Visibility ★★★★★

Upkeep ★★★★★

Parking ★★★★★

HOURS

5:00 am to 11:00 pm

DOGS

Dogs not allowed on Walk-Up Trail

FACILITIES

- Toilets near trailhead

- Water fountain, vending machine; many other amenities within the park

FEES & PERMITS $20 day use fee or $45 annual pass; purchase at entrance station

LAND MANAGER Stone Mountain Park

Landmarks

SENTINEL GEORGIA OAK

Georgia oaks only grow on rocky granite surfaces. Evolved to thrive on granite with very little soil, these trees look more like bushes, but with telltale oak-shaped leaves. You'll see many Georgia oaks along this trail. This one on the left of the path has multiple, thick, gnarled trunks.

FARKLEBERRY GROVE

Also called "sparkleberry," these shrubby trees produce a small dark fruit in the fall and through the winter. The plant grows on cliffs and rocky woodlands, which is why there are so many on the mountain. This grove is growing directly in front of the sentinel Georgia oak, but you're sure to spot many other plants of this species along your hike.

STONE MOUNTAIN SUMMIT

The view from the top of Stone Mountain is what makes this one of the most famous hikes in metro Atlanta. You'd usually have to travel to north Georgia for a view like this. See if you can find the metal United States Geological Survey marker for the highest point on the peak.

Hike Route

Start your hike near the restrooms and begin by crossing over the railroad tracks onto the granite outcrop. There is a large, green information sign that marks the start of the trail. Hike up the granite outcrop, following the yellow blazes on the ground that mark the trail to the summit.

Pass flagpoles on your right in 0.1 mile, then cross a service road in 100 feet. Continue hiking straight for another 0.1 mile to reach a junction with Cherokee Trail. Stay straight on the main path at this junction, then pass two poles covered in bubble gum (ew!).

In 0.25 mile, just before reaching call box 3, you'll come to a

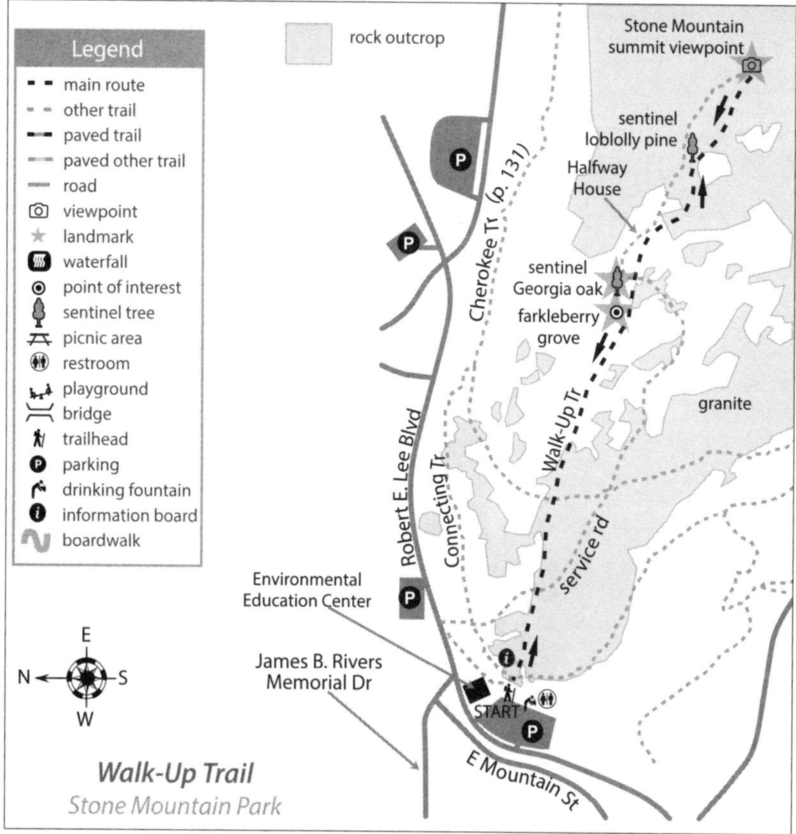

Georgia oak in the middle of the trail. Look to the left, just off the trail, for an even larger sentinel Georgia oak. In the fall, you may also see the deep-burgundy-colored leaves of farkleberry bushes lining the trail. Look closely for the small dark farkleberries (also called sparkleberries), which fruit in mid- to late fall. The taste and texture are like a wild blueberry.

Continue past the call box and cross a gravel road, continuing uphill for another 100 yards to reach Halfway House, a covered pavilion with benches that's a good place for a break. In 0.1 mile, reach the steepest section of the hike, where railings have been installed. Carefully ascend the hill, and 100 feet past the railings, look for a sentinel loblolly pine standing alone on your right, stunted by the stone and wind.

In another 0.1 mile, you'll reach the top of the mountain! Take in the view. On a clear day, you'll be able to see the skyscrapers of

The views from the summit are worth the challenging hike.

downtown, midtown, and Buckhead, as well as Kennesaw Mountain to the northwest. At the top is also the Top of the Mountain facility, which includes the Skyride gondola, a snack bar, and interpretive signs about the mountain's geological and ecological importance. After enjoying the summit, return down the mountain the way you came to finish your hike at the parking lot.

Enjoy views of the mountain and lake.

Cherokee Trail

STONE MOUNTAIN PARK

Stone Mountain was a landmark utilized by the Cherokee and Muscogee (Creek) people, and this trail, named after one of the important indigenous groups of Georgia, is one of the best ways to explore the diverse ecological features of Stone Mountain Park. You'll hike through old-growth forests, over the granite outcrop, and around the lake. And unlike the popular Walk-Up Trail, on this 5-mile loop you'll have plenty of stretches without encountering other hikers.

HOW TO GET THERE

Driving Distance from Downtown Atlanta: 20 miles

Address: Robert E. Lee Boulevard and Covered Bridge Lane, Stone Mountain, GA 30083; GPS for parking area: 33.805469, -84.135323

Closest Highway: US 78

City, County: Stone Mountain, DeKalb

Parking: Small paved parking lot near the historic gristmill off Robert E. Lee Boulevard

HIKE DISTANCE

5-mile loop

DIFFICULTY

Overall: Moderate to strenuous

Navigation: Blazes on trees, posts with arrows, and maps along route

Terrain: Hard-packed dirt trails, granite rock outcrop (the outcrop can be very slippery when wet)

Elevation Change: Mostly flat with an extended and very steep ascent and descent on the mountain

SAFETY

Usage ★★★☆☆

Visibility ★★★★☆

Upkeep ★★★★★

Parking ★★★★☆

HOURS

Dawn to dusk

DOGS

Leashed dogs allowed

FACILITIES	• Toilets near gristmill • Covered picnic pavilions, water fountain, trash cans, and many other amenities within the park
FEES & PERMITS	$20 day use fee or $45 annual pass; pay at entrance station
LAND MANAGER	Stone Mountain Park

Landmarks

GRISTMILL

At the beginning of the hike, explore the historic gristmill and the neighboring waterfall and creek that once would have powered the now inoperative mill. This century-old grain mill was originally located in Ellijay, Georgia, but was moved to Stone Mountain in 1965.

BEAUTYBERRY GROVE

About a mile into the hike, reach a dense grove of beautyberries. These native shrubs produce beautiful clusters of dark purple fruits in the early fall. In traditional Chinese medicine, the edible berries are used to treat inflammation.

PINE LODGE CHIMNEY

This site was once a retreat for students from Agnes Scott College in the early 1900s. A testament to the durability of granite, the large stone chimney is the last remnant of the Pine Lodge Camp cabin.

Hike Route

Exit the gristmill parking area at the far left end of the lot. Carefully cross the road and follow a trail on the left toward the bathrooms (a green building). Just before reaching the bathrooms, take a trail on the right down a flight of stairs that will bring you to the gristmill and a post with arrows marking the Cherokee Trail.

Stay straight onto the wooden bridge that leads you around the mill. At the next junction, marked with a post, go to the left. In 50 feet at a stone map legend, take the trail to the right to continue on Cherokee Trail. Hike along a stone embankment and the creek to your left. In 0.2 mile, carefully cross Robert E. Lee Boulevard and stay straight to hike into the forest. Just after entering the forest, in 100 feet on the left side of the trail is a large sweetgum tree. Cross two small footbridges, and in 0.1 mile the trail crosses the train tracks.

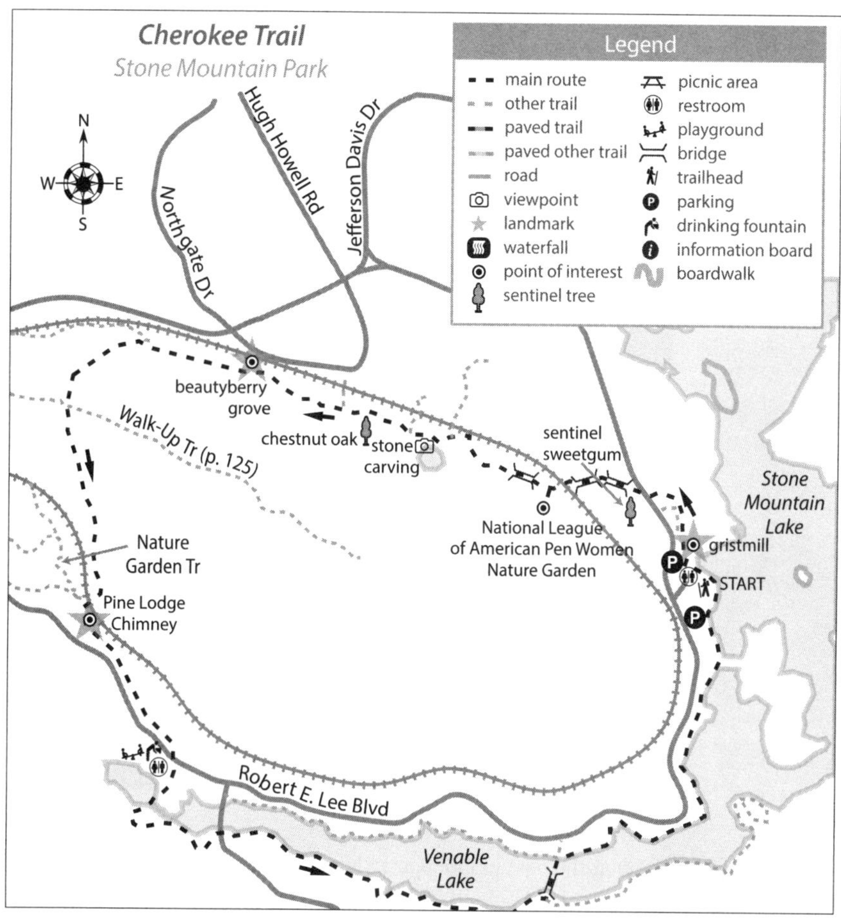

Reach a junction with the National League of American Pen Women nature garden on the left. Take the short loop through the garden or continue straight on the trail. Hike through the forest with the mountain and creek to your left. At the next junction, go right and in 100 feet, just before reaching the train tracks, go left. This trail brings you to a large field at the base of the mountain. Go left and immediately right to the small lake and viewpoint of the Confederate general carvings on the face of the mountain, one of the most recognized features of Stone Mountain.

Follow the paved trail around the lake as it turns right, away from the mountain, and curves immediately left and into the forest. Follow the white blazes on the trees. Hike through the forest for 0.2 mile to reach a sentinel double-trunked chestnut oak on the left side of the

The hike begins and ends at the gristmill.

trail. In 0.1 mile at the next junction, stay left, reaching a grove of beautyberries in 0.2 mile.

Hike for 0.3 mile to a clearing with the railroad tracks in view to your right and a post in front of you. Take the trail to the left to continue on Cherokee Trail over the mountain. Follow the white blazes on trees and marked on the rock beneath your feet to avoid getting lost as you begin a steep ascent up the granite outcrop. In 0.2 mile, reach a junction with the Walk-Up Trail. Continue straight, following the posts marking Cherokee Trail.

In 0.1 mile, cross a gravel path and stay straight on Cherokee Trail as it begins to descend down the mountain. Note that this steep section of trail can be slippery, especially when wet. You'll also need to pay close attention to the blazes to stay on the hike route. Hike downhill on the outcrop, following the white blazes for 0.4 mile until the trail exits the outcrop and reenters the forest.

Cross the train tracks, pass a post, and immediately come to a junction. Go left to stay on Cherokee Trail and come to the Agnes Scott retreat cabin chimney, a lone historic structure standing in the woods. After viewing the chimney, hike for 0.3 mile to where the trail crosses the street. At this crossing, there is a bathroom, water fountain, and picnic tables—a good place for a snack or break.

Continue your hike, following the trail into the forest where it parallels the fenceline on your right before coming to the lake. Keep an eye out for wildlife near the water. Cross a small stream and continue circling the lake. At the next junction, marked by two posts, go left and come to a road crossing and stone map legend. Cross the street, staying straight onto the trail. This is one of the most scenic sections of the hike. Enjoy the views as you hike along the edge of Venable Lake with the mountain in the background. In 0.8 mile, turn left across a bridge and stay left along the ridge between the lakes. At the opposite end of the lake, where the trail reaches a junction, turn right and continue on Cherokee Trail.

Hike with Stone Mountain Lake to your right and with views of Indian Island across the water. In 0.6 mile, cross a rock outcrop at the edge of the lake, another nice spot for a snack break or rest. In 0.15 mile, the trail comes to the road and covered bridge leading to Indian Island. Very carefully cross the road and look to the right for where the trail continues, just past the covered bridge. Hike carefully along the edge of the lake and along a narrow stone pathway before returning to the gristmill. Go left to take the stairs back up to the bathroom and parking area to end your hike.

Christmas ferns fan out along the trail.

Songbird Habitat Trail

STONE MOUNTAIN PARK

This beautiful hike within Stone Mountain Park is a great way to escape the crowds and connect with nature. The trail winds through open meadows, young pine forest, and mature hardwood forest. Bring your binoculars and bird-watch from the overlook platform, or just enjoy a peaceful walk through the woods.

HOW TO GET THERE

Driving Distance from Downtown Atlanta: 20 miles

Address: Take Robert E. Lee Boulevard to Stonewall Jackson Drive. Trailhead parking is 0.5 mile further on Stonewall Jackson Drive.; parking at GPS 33.793142, -84.146132

Closest Highway: US 78

City, County: Stone Mountain, DeKalb

Parking: Paved parking lot off Stonewall Jackson Drive

HIKE DISTANCE

1.5-mile figure-8 loop

DIFFICULTY

Overall: Easy

Navigation: Posts with directional arrows

Terrain: Hard-packed dirt and grass trails; one flight of stairs

Elevation Change: Mostly flat with a few rolling hills

SAFETY

Usage ★★★☆☆

Visibility ★★★★☆

Upkeep ★★★★★

Parking ★★★★☆

HOURS

5:00 am to 11:00 pm

DOGS

Leashed dogs allowed

FACILITIES

- Portable toilet
- Trash cans, benches

FEES & PERMITS

$20 day use fee or $45 annual pass; pay at entrance station

LAND MANAGER

Stone Mountain Park

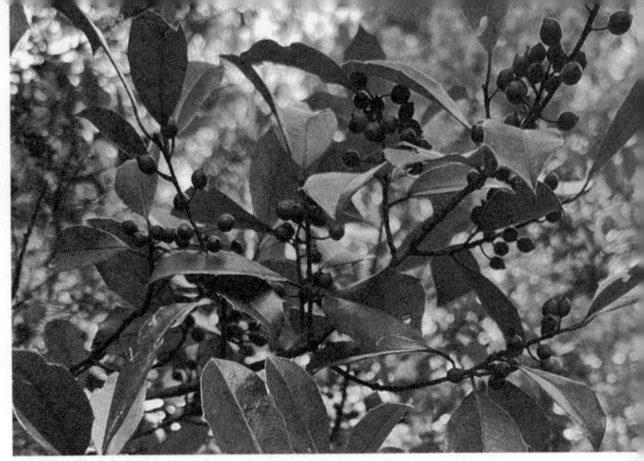

Holly berries make great snacks for the birds but not so much for humans.

Landmarks

MEADOW OVERLOOK

At the top of the ridge, the meadow overlook is a perfect spot for bird-watching. Songbirds favor transitional landscapes, which is why meadows along forests are preferred spots for birders.

BIGLEAF MAGNOLIA GROVE

As its name suggests, the bigleaf magnolia has the largest simple leaf of any native plant in North America. This magnolia species is a deciduous understory tree, so in the autumn, the giant fallen leaves cover the ground along the trail.

SENTINEL TULIP TREE

The largest in this area of forest, this tulip tree (commonly known as tulip poplar) is in remarkably good condition for its age. In leaf-free winter, you can locate older deciduous trees by looking up into the canopy and searching for thick upper limbs similar to the ones on this tree.

Hike Route

Start your hike at the map and information kiosk. Enter the trail and take an immediate right at a boulder and bench. Cross a small footbridge and hike 0.2 mile along the edge of the meadow, brimming with tall grasses and native plants, until you arrive at a junction. Go up the stairs and turn left along the ridge. Follow the fenceline to an overlook platform with nice views of the meadow. Pass the overlook and hike to the next junction. Follow the arrow straight ahead and cross a footbridge.

In 0.1 mile at a bench and signpost, the trail curves left through a grove of bigleaf magnolias. In 100 feet, at a junction with an unofficial

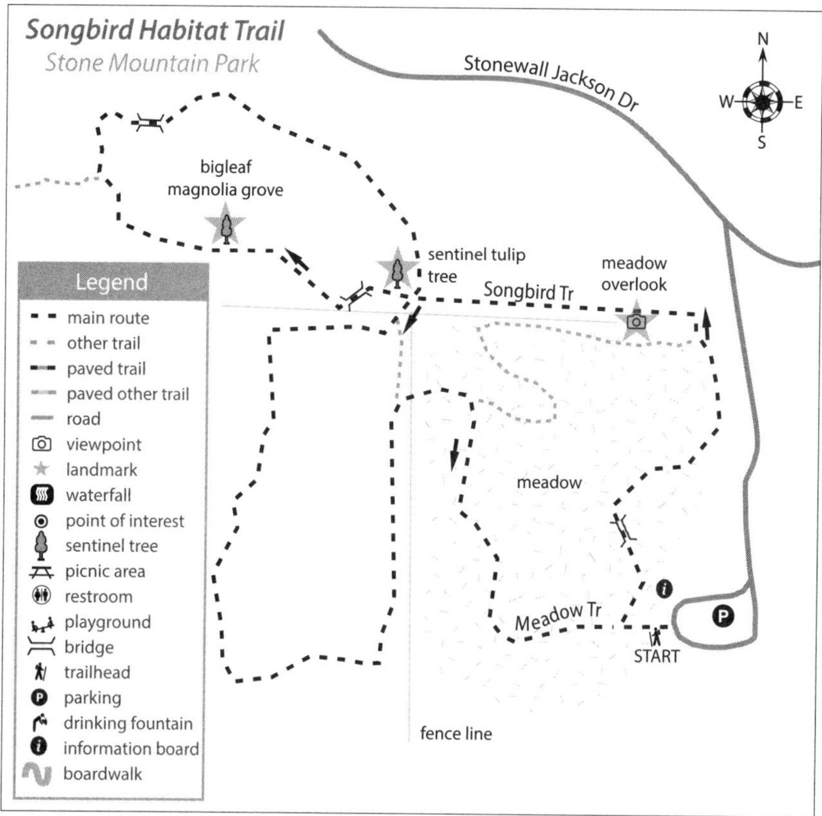

trail to a house on the left, look to the right for a large sentinel tulip tree. Hike downhill and cross a small footbridge. At the next junction, marked with a post, hike for 0.1 mile back to the previous trail junction where you first entered this loop.

Hike straight through the gate in the fence and cross some granite stepping stones on the right to reach another junction. Go right (on the left is a shortcut trail back to the Meadow Trail) and hike along the fenceline.

The trail curves away from the fence in 0.1 mile, then reaches another fenceline in 0.2 mile. Continue hiking through the forest, noticing how the forest changes the closer you get to the meadow. At a junction in 0.1 mile, turn right, walk through an opening in the fence, and go right immediately onto Meadow Trail, then pass a covered bench. The trail winds along the edge of the meadow. Proceed quietly, keeping your eye out for wildlife. In 0.3 mile, the trail loops back to the parking lot, where your hike ends.

Hike past a series of beautiful cascades on this trail.

North Loop

YELLOW RIVER PARK

The northern trails of Yellow River Park are shared with mountain bikers and equestrians, yet the trails still feel solitary and peaceful. The route traverses rolling hills through a healthy forest and leads to a beautiful creek with several cascading waterfalls. Wildlife, wildflowers, and interesting trees abound on this gorgeous trail.

HOW TO GET THERE

Driving Distance from Downtown Atlanta: 23 miles

Address: 3232 Juhan Road SW, Stone Mountain, GA 30087

Closest Highway: US 78

City, County: Rockbridge, Gwinnett

Parking: Access the trailhead from the equestrian parking entrance off Juhan Road. Park in the large gravel parking area.

HIKE DISTANCE

4.5-mile figure-8 loop

DIFFICULTY

Overall: Moderate to strenuous

Navigation: Map posted at trailhead, and equestrian, mountain bike, and pedestrian trail signs posted at many trail junctions

Terrain: Hard-packed dirt or gravel trails; several large bridges; and some rocky sections of trail

Elevation Change: Rolling hills with several steep ascents and descents

SAFETY

Usage ★★★☆☆

Visibility ★★★☆☆

Upkeep ★★★★☆

Parking ★★★★☆

HOURS

Sunrise to sunset

DOGS

Leashed dogs allowed

FACILITIES

- Restrooms at other trailheads
- Information board and portable toilet at this trailhead; playground, drinking fountain, and picnic areas at other trailheads

FEES & PERMITS	None
LAND MANAGER	Gwinnett County Parks & Recreation

Landmarks

SENTINEL BEECH GROVE

American beech trees have smooth gray bark and can be identified in the winter because they keep their brown leaves on their branches until the spring.

FIRST CASCADE

This cascade near where the trail crosses the creek is a bit off the trail. Listen for the rushing water and you'll find it.

SECOND CASCADE

The water falls over 10 feet across a series of cascading rocks. A small pool at the cascade is great for cooling off bare feet on a hot summer day.

Hike Route

The trails in Yellow River Park are shared with mountain bikers and equestrians. Hikers are welcome, but please be aware of and courteous to bicyclists and horses. Pay special attention while hiking uphill because bikes may be coming downhill toward you at fast speeds. Always keep your eyes open and listen while hiking on trails shared with mountain bikers. Pay attention to the map, as this park contains an extensive network of intersecting trails.

Start your hike to the left of the information board, behind the equestrian trail sign. After 0.1 mile, reach a junction in a clearing near the driveway, turn left, and hike downhill. In another 100 yards, stay straight at a junction with a bike trail on the right, then reach junction 1.

Stay straight on the wide trail, then bear left at a junction with a trail on the right that leads to a gate at Juhan Road. The trail begins to ascend slowly. Cross a bridge in 0.2 mile, then hike another 0.1 mile to reach a complicated series of junctions. Generally stay to the right, though the trail on the farthest right leads downhill to Juhan Road and the park's main entrance. When in doubt, follow the blue arrows.

In 0.1 mile, the trail enters a power line clearing. Take the first left off the clearing onto a single-track trail and hike uphill to a

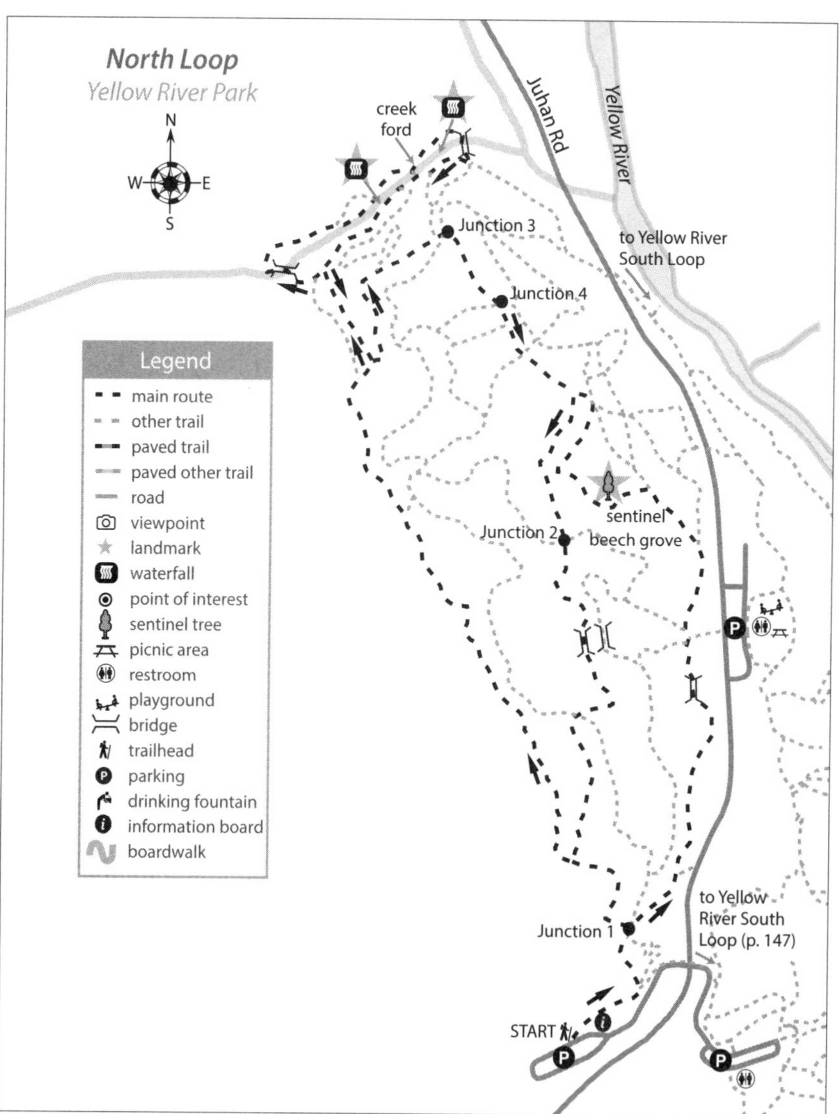
North Loop
Yellow River Park
N
W
E
S
creek
ford
Juhan Rd
Yellow River
Junction 3
to Yellow River
South Loop
Junction 4
Legend
main route
other trail
paved trail
paved other trail
road
viewpoint
landmark
waterfall
point of interest
sentinel tree
picnic area
restroom
playground
bridge
trailhead
parking
drinking fountain
information board
boardwalk
sentinel
beech grove
Junction 2
Junction 1
to Yellow
River South
Loop (p. 147)
START

Though designed for horseback riders, this trail is fantastic for hikers.

junction in a smaller clearing. Turn left and hike uphill. The trail slowly ascends through a beautiful beech forest.

At the next junction, go left to reach a junction with several signs. Go left, following the trail that leads slightly uphill and has a sign stating "0.8 Miles to Trailhead." Hike uphill to junction 2, stay straight, and descend to a bridge. After the bridge, the trail curves right and ascends 0.15 mile to another junction. Stay straight and hike until you reach a T-junction. Turn right, hike toward the sign that reads, "1.6 Miles to Trailhead," and stay right past a side trail that leads left to a lake on private property.

Hike this trail for 0.5 mile, keeping left at any junctions to stay on the main trail. In another 0.2 mile, pass a trail on the left and then reach a junction with a pedestrian sign. Turn left here and hike downhill. At the T-junction at the bottom of the hill, turn left and hike to a bridge over the creek. Cross the bridge and curve right. Stay right at the next junction and follow the creek to a ford and small picturesque cascade. Continue straight past another cascade before you reach a bridge.

At the junction just past the bridge, the trail on the left leads to the Yellow River South Loop. Go right here to parallel the creek for 0.25 mile. When you reach the pedestrian trail sign, turn left and hike back up the hill. At a junction with equestrian and pedestrian signs, turn left. In 0.2 mile, pass a junction with a pedestrian trail sign, then arrive at junction 3. Stay straight on the trail with an equestrian sign.

After another 0.1 mile of hiking, you'll continue straight at junction 4 and then continue straight until you reach a junction with two signs that read, "0.8 Miles to Trailhead." Either trail will lead back to your vehicle, and both are trails you've hiked already. This route turns right on the trail farther from the sounds of Juhan Road.

Stay straight at each junction and hike 0.6 mile to the T-junction with an equestrian trail sign. Turn left toward the "0.3 Miles to Trailhead" sign. The trail slopes downhill, reaches a small creek, curves left, then arrives at the four-way junction 1. Turn right, then stay straight on this wide trail as it climbs uphill through a clearing and then turns right at a sign that reads, "0.1 Miles to Trailhead." Your hike ends back at the equestrian parking area.

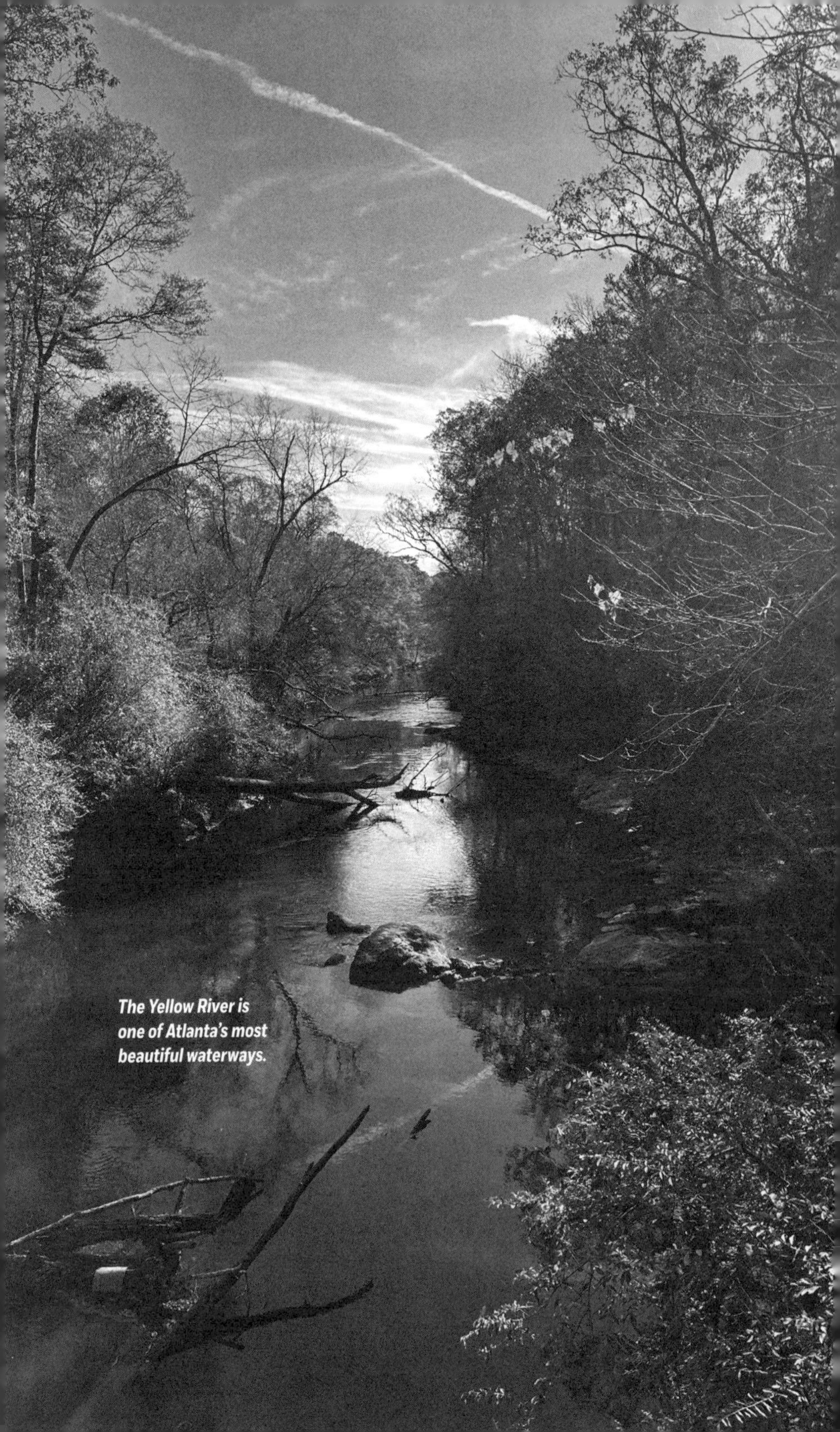

The Yellow River is one of Atlanta's most beautiful waterways.

South Loop

YELLOW RIVER PARK

Though Yellow River Park is best known by mountain bikers, hikers are welcome on all trails, and taking a walk there is highly recommended. The slower pace of hiking will allow you to more fully take in the beauty of the river and its surrounding forest. The best part of this loop is the views of the Yellow River. This park contains a maze of trails, so you'll have to pay attention to the map while you hike.

HOW TO GET THERE

Driving Distance from Downtown Atlanta: 23 miles

Address: 3232 Juhan Road SW, Stone Mountain, GA 30087

Closest Highway: US 78

City, County: Rockbridge, Gwinnett

Parking: Access the paved "passive area" parking lot off Juhan Road; the pavilion and playground are visible from the road

HIKE DISTANCE

3.75-mile figure-8 loop

DIFFICULTY

Overall: Moderate to strenuous

Navigation: Map posted at trailhead, and equestrian, mountain bike, and pedestrian trail signs posted at many trail junctions

Terrain: Hard-packed dirt or gravel trails; several large bridges; and some rocky sections of trail

Elevation Change: The first half of this hike is relatively flat, but there are a couple steep ascents and descents toward the end of the route

SAFETY

Usage ★★★★☆

Visibility ★★★☆☆

Upkeep ★★★★☆

Parking ★★★★★

HOURS

Sunrise to sunset

DOGS

Leashed dogs allowed

FACILITIES	• Restrooms near trailhead and at mountain bike parking area • Playground, picnic pavilion, water fountain, information boards, benches, and picnic tables
FEES & PERMITS	None
LAND MANAGER	Gwinnett County Parks & Recreation

Landmarks

YELLOW RIVER

The Yellow River is one of the important watersheds of the east metro area. This river flows south to Lake Jackson, where it joins the South and Alcovy Rivers to form the Ocmulgee River.

YELLOW RIVER OBSERVATION PLATFORM

The Yellow River Water Trail is a 53-mile paddling route that passes right through Yellow River Park. For more information about paddling the Yellow River, visit yellowriverwatertrail.org.

OUTCROP VIEWPOINT

Though this section of the Yellow River contains no rapids, there are several rock formations along the river, including this scenic spot where you can sit and observe the flowing water.

Hike Route

Start your hike facing the restrooms and picnic pavilion and walk the sidewalk to the left, around the playground. Turn left on the wide asphalt multiuse path. In less than 100 yards, you'll pass the 0.75-mile marker, which doesn't apply to this route. You'll pass several large water oak trees and picnic tables before reaching the far end of the multiuse trail loop near a picnic table and swinging bench. Go straight to visit an observation platform above the Yellow River.

Turn around, retrace your steps back to the multiuse path, and take the left fork to continue your hike. In 0.25 mile, once the path reenters the forest, you'll come to a small dirt trail leading to the left. This trail follows the bank of the Yellow River, parallel to the multiuse trail, if you're interested in exploring this unofficial trail. This route continues on the paved path, passing a 0.25-mile marker, before reaching a wide gravel trail on the left in another 0.25 mile.

Turn left and cross a bridge. Turn left at the next junction to visit another Yellow River observation platform, then back to the trail. Go

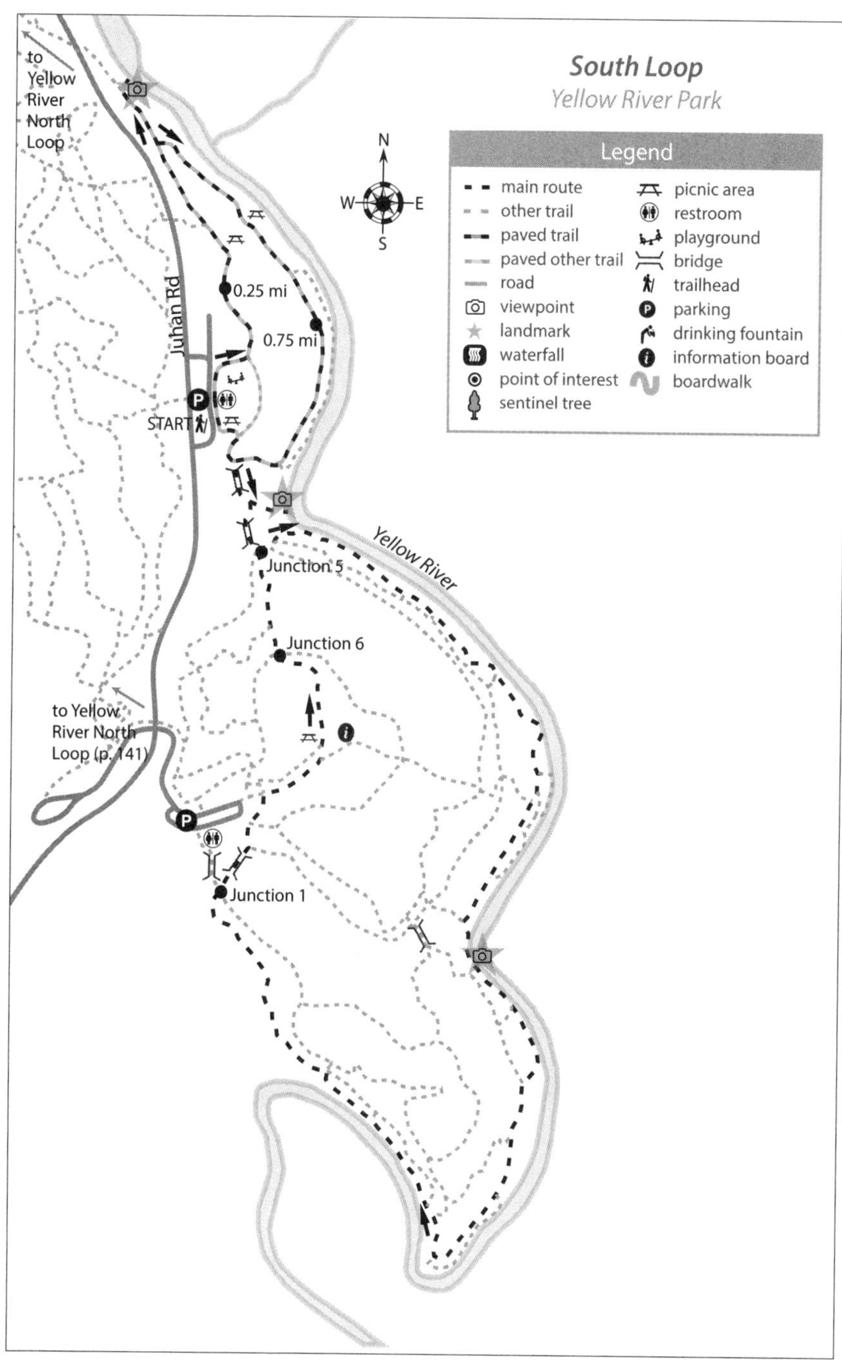
South Loop
Yellow River Park
Legend
main route
other trail
paved trail
paved other trail
road
viewpoint
landmark
waterfall
point of interest
sentinel tree
picnic area
restroom
playground
bridge
trailhead
parking
drinking fountain
information board
boardwalk
N
W
E
S
to Yellow River North Loop
Juhan Rd
0.25 mi
0.75 mi
START
Yellow River
Junction 5
Junction 6
to Yellow River North Loop (p. 141)
Junction 1

This rock outcrop is a great place to view the river.

left to cross another bridge. At the far side of this bridge, you'll arrive at a complicated junction labeled with the number 5. Stay on the farthest left trail, and you'll arrive at the edge of the river. There are many interconnecting trails in this park, but if you stay parallel to the river for this portion of the hike, you're going in the right direction.

After paralleling the river for 0.75 mile, the trail crosses a usually dry creekbed, then curves left, back toward the river. Stay left along the river, passing a beautiful rock outcrop and viewpoint. In 0.2 mile, this single-track trail meets the wider equestrian trail. Turn left and continue to parallel the river for another 0.75 mile. When you reach a four-way junction with equestrian and mountain bike signs, go left on the equestrian trail and ascend the hill, away from the river.

After a steep 0.2-mile ascent, crest the high point of this trail and hike downhill to junction 1. Stay straight and cross a bridge to reach a junction with several mileage signs. Bear left. The next junction is in a wide clearing from which you can see the mountain bike parking on the left. Take the middle trail, which leads to a wide gravel path. Turn right and follow this path to a pavilion in a large clearing. Turn left at the pavilion to cross the clearing and reenter the woods on the equestrian trail.

In 0.1 mile, reach junction 6 and stay straight on the equestrian trail. Continue straight for another 0.1 mile to reach junction 5 near the bridge. Cross the bridge, then follow this wide trail across one more bridge to arrive at the paved multiuse path. Turn left and hike back to the picnic area and playground, where you'll end your hike.

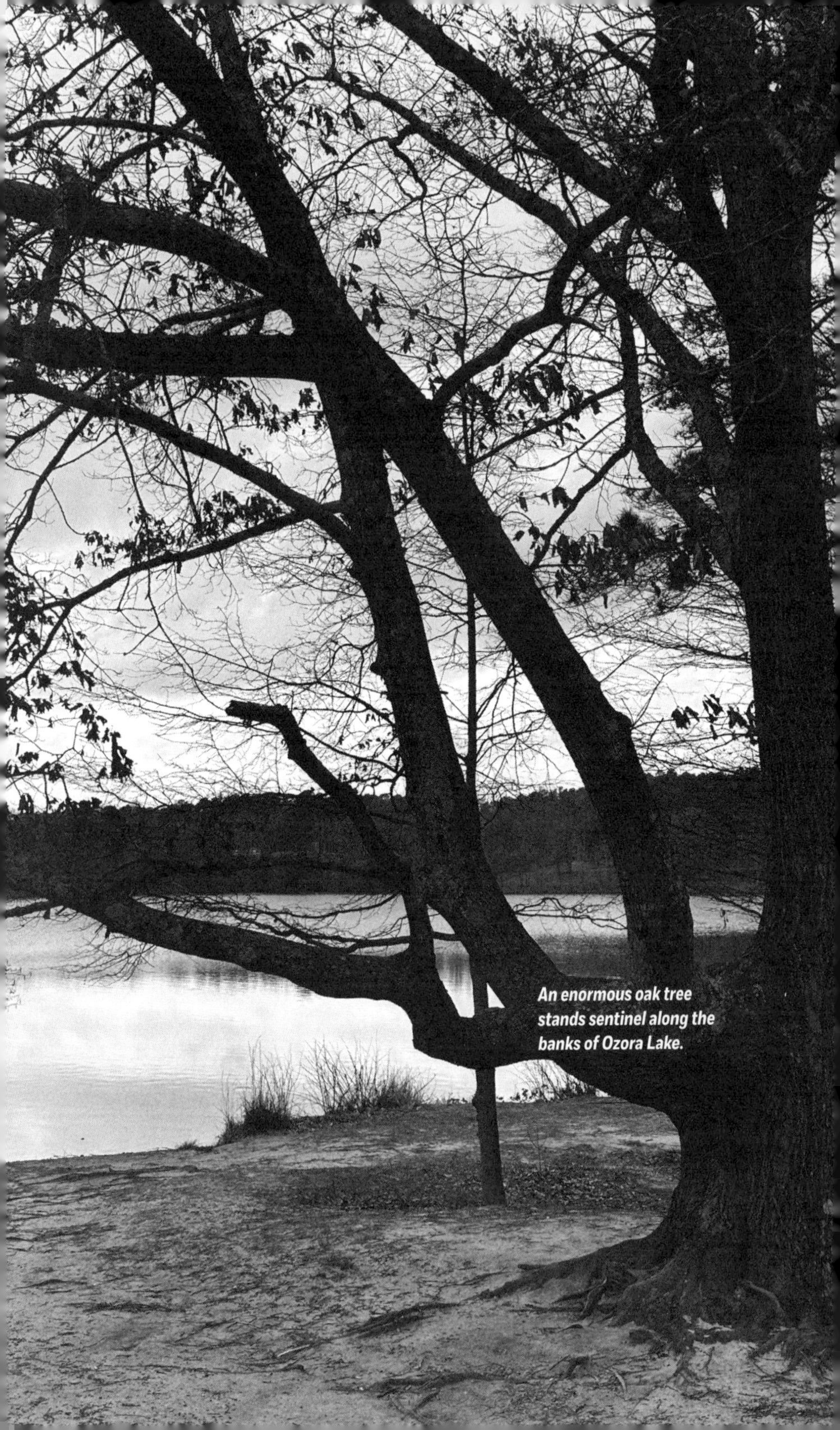

An enormous oak tree stands sentinel along the banks of Ozora Lake.

Tribble Mill Park

This giant county park in eastern Gwinnett County has trails for just about everyone—paved lakeside paths and dirt trails for hikers, bikers, and horses. You'll be captivated by the beauty of Ozora and Chandler Lakes, amazed by the waterfall, and fascinated by the flora and fauna of this greenspace. Want to stay on only paved paths? You can do that and still hike over 5 miles here. Want more dirt trails? There's a whole network to explore next time you visit Tribble Mill Park.

HOW TO GET THERE

Driving Distance from Downtown Atlanta: 42 miles
Address: 2125 Tribble Mill Parkway SE, Lawrenceville, GA 30045
Closest Highway: US 78
City, County: Grayson, Gwinnett
Parking: Large paved parking area

HIKE DISTANCE

6-mile double loop

DIFFICULTY

Overall: Moderate
Navigation: Trail maps posted in several places; mileage markers along paved trails; no navigation signs on dirt trails
Terrain: Main loop is paved and appropriate for bicycles, strollers, and wheelchairs; this route also includes a hard-packed dirt trail and a short trail across a rock outcrop
Elevation Change: Rolling hills, but no major ascents or descents

SAFETY

Usage ★★★★★
Visibility ★★★★★
Upkeep ★★★★★
Parking ★★★★★

HOURS

Sunrise to sunset

DOGS

Leashed dogs allowed

FACILITIES

- Toilets near playground
- Playground, picnic areas, water fountains, information boards, boat ramp, equestrian and mountain bike trails

FEES & PERMITS None

LAND MANAGER Gwinnett County Parks & Recreation

Landmarks

GRANITE SHOALS WATERFALL & MILL SITE

As the water flowing out of Ozora Lake crosses this large rock outcrop, it forms Granite Shoals waterfall near the ruins of the Tribble gristmill, which originally was used for refining corn and wheat. Ansley Tribble obtained the site in 1873, and it was known as a "flouring and corn mill."

CHANDLER LAKE VIEWPOINT

The 40-acre Chandler Lake is less well known than the other, larger lake (Ozora Lake) in this park, but here you can see water birds, hike paved and dirt trails, go fishing, and even paddle a kayak.

SENTINEL SOUTHERN RED OAK

Southern red oaks are one of the most common canopy trees in the Atlanta metro area, but this one is unique for its size and how its branches stretch low enough to the ground that you might even be able to climb.

Hike Route

Start your hike at the information board at the end of the farthest parking area from the park entrance, past the playground area. Facing the information board, take the paved path on the left downhill and into the woods. In 0.4 mile, the pavement ends near a bicycle rack, and the trail continues across a short bridge and onto the granite outcrop, where you get a view of Granite Shoals waterfall and mill ruins. Turn around and backtrack to the information board, then turn right on a paved path, then another right on an asphalt trail that leads 0.1 mile to Lloyd N. Harris Loop at a junction near the 0.25-mile marker.

Turn right and hike across the bridge over the Ozora Lake spillway. At a junction with Harris Greenway Trail on the right, turn left to continue along the lakeshore on Harris Loop.

In just over 0.5 mile, pass a circular stone viewpoint on the left and continue 0.15 mile until you reach a parking lot. The asphalt trail parallels the parking area before dipping back down into the woods. For the next 0.4 mile, the trail generally parallels Tribble Mill

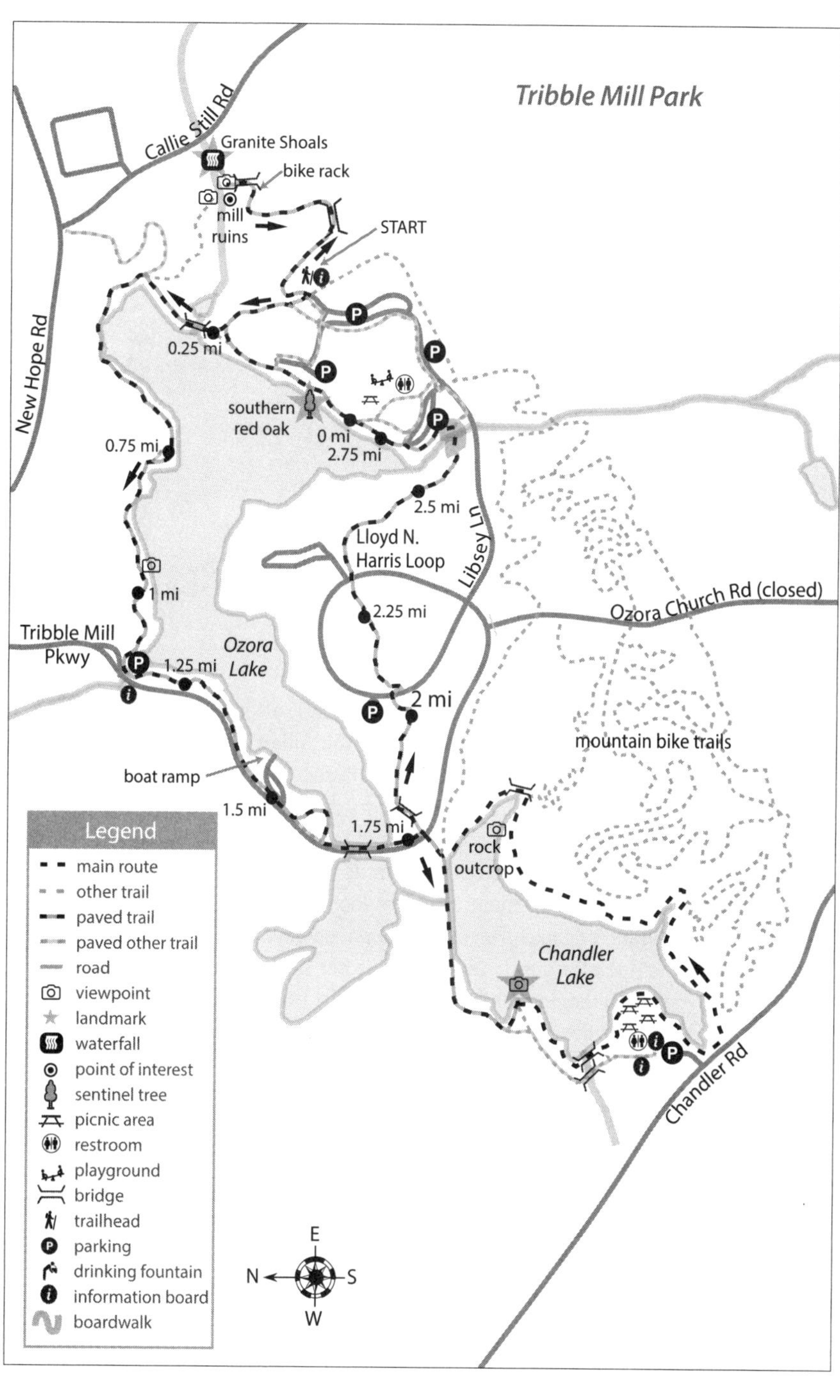

Tribble Mill Park
Callie Still Rd
Granite Shoals
bike rack
mill ruins
START
New Hope Rd
0.25 mi
southern red oak
0 mi
2.75 mi
0.75 mi
2.5 mi
Lloyd N. Harris Loop
Libsey Ln
Ozora Church Rd (closed)
1 mi
2.25 mi
Tribble Mill Pkwy
1.25 mi
Ozora Lake
2 mi
mountain bike trails
boat ramp
1.5 mi
1.75 mi
rock outcrop
Chandler Lake
Chandler Rd
Legend
main route
other trail
paved trail
paved other trail
road
viewpoint
landmark
waterfall
point of interest
sentinel tree
picnic area
restroom
playground
bridge
trailhead
parking
drinking fountain
information board
boardwalk
E
N
S
W

A peaceful paved trail circles the lakes of Tribble Mill Park.

Parkway. Take the left fork (away from the road) after passing the boat ramp parking area and then arrive at the Julian W. Archer Sr. Bridge, which is designed to look like the frame of a covered bridge. Cross the bridge and hike uphill to a junction near a crosswalk.

Turn right and carefully cross the road to begin the Chandler Lake loop. (This section has both dirt trails and paved trails—if you need to stay only on pavement, skip this loop.) Follow the paved path alongside Chandler Lake. Turn left on a paved side trail in 0.3 mile and visit the dock for great views of Chandler Lake. Turn around and as you leave the dock, hike left on the dirt trail on the lake's edge. This trail follows the water's edge around a picnic and parking area and near Chandler Road. Generally bear left and stay along the lakeshore.

You are now on trails shared with mountain bikes, so be aware of your surroundings. There are many trail junctions over the next mile, but this route stays on the edge of the lake. When in doubt, keep the lake on your left. When you arrive back at the paved path, turn right, cross the road, and continue straight on Harris Loop.

On Harris Loop, pass the 2-mile marker, then cross a park road. Pass the 2.25-mile marker and cross another park road near the equestrian overflow parking. From here, hike 0.3 mile before the paved trail becomes a boardwalk. Stay left on the boardwalk, and when it transitions into asphalt again near stairs, continue straight. Pass two side trails on the right. After passing the 0-mile marker, look on your left near the lake for a huge sentinel southern red oak with branches low enough for climbing. Hike 0.2 mile farther to a junction just before the spillway bridge. Turn right and hike back to the information board and parking lot to end your hike.

WESTSIDE

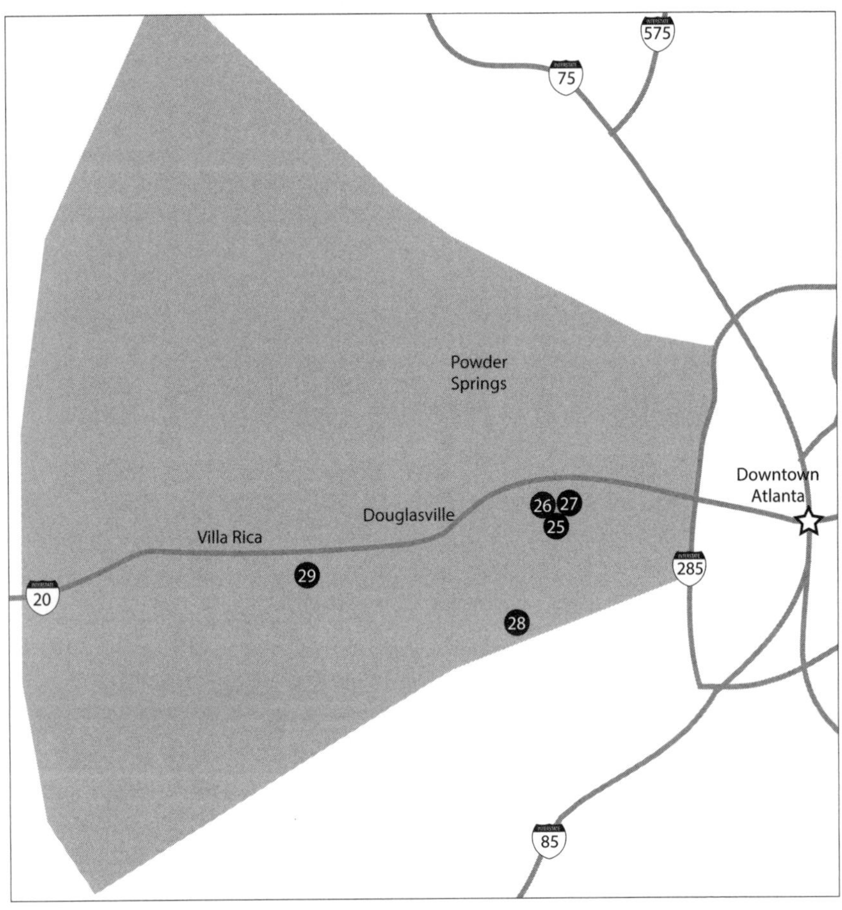

25 Sweetwater Creek Red Trail

26 Sweetwater Creek White Trail

27 Sweetwater Creek Yellow & Orange Trails

28 Boundary Waters Park

29 Clinton Nature Preserve

I-20 WEST

The New Manchester Mill ruins are a well-known site in the park.

Red Trail

SWEETWATER CREEK STATE PARK

The Red Trail is the most popular hike in Sweetwater Creek State Park because it provides a close-up view of the mill ruins and stunning views along the banks of Sweetwater Creek. This is a short and easy to moderate hike, but it can easily be combined with White Trail (p. 167) for a longer adventure through different parts of the park.

HOW TO GET THERE	**Driving Distance from Downtown Atlanta:** 19 miles **Address:** 1750 Mount Vernon Road, Lithia Springs, GA 30122; turn onto Factory Shoals Road to reach parking at GPS 33.753421, -84.628801 **Closest Interstate:** I-20 **City, County:** Lithia Springs, Douglas **Parking:** Large paved parking lot; follow signs for nature center at the end of the road
HIKE DISTANCE	2-mile out-and-back
DIFFICULTY	**Overall:** Easy to moderate **Navigation:** Blazes on trees along route **Terrain:** Wide, hard-packed dirt trails, wooden stairs, dirt trails with exposed roots and rocks **Elevation Change:** Flat sections for first half of trail; short but steep ascents over rock outcrops farther along trail
SAFETY	**Usage** ★★★★★ **Visibility** ★★★★☆ **Upkeep** ★★★★★ **Parking** ★★★★★
HOURS	7:00 am to sunset
DOGS	Leashed dogs allowed
FACILITIES	• Toilets in nature center and at top of parking lot • Nature center with concessions, water fountain, picnic pavilions

FEES & PERMITS	$5 daily ParkPass—purchase at gastateparks.org
LAND MANAGER	Georgia State Parks

Landmarks

MOUNTAIN LAUREL GROVE

Although the name mountain laurel suggests that it grows in alpine ecosystems, this flowering evergreen shrub can often be found in forests with well-drained, rich, acidic soil. In the spring, mountain laurels produce beautiful pink blooms.

MILL RUINS VIEWPOINT

The New Manchester Mill ruins are an iconic landmark in Sweetwater Creek State Park. The mill was once one of the largest mills in Georgia. From multiple viewpoints, you can see the outer foundation of the five-story textile mill, which was destroyed by Union soldiers in 1864.

SENTINEL CURVED AMERICAN BEECH

Halfway up a staircase and at a bench, look to your right to see a beech tree off the trail with a curiously curved trunk. It appears the trunk was once cut and then regrew at this awkward angle.

Hike Route

Begin your hike facing the information kiosk across from the nature center. Turn left and follow the red blazes for Red Trail. Immediately turn right at the first junction onto Red Trail. Shortly after, come to a forked junction and bear right, continuing to follow the red blazes downhill and parallel to a stream. Turn right at the next junction and cross a small culvert.

In 100 feet, take a short loop spur on the left that brings you past a large grove of mountain laurels on the bank of Sweetwater Creek before returning to the main trail. Hike past a rock outcrop on the right and a small viewing platform and bench on the left a few yards down. In 0.1 mile, hike past a bridge on the left. Stay straight on the main path. The bridge takes you to a small island on the edge of the water, but be aware that it does not reconnect to the main path.

Cross over a bridge in 0.1 mile and shortly come to a staircase on the left that leads down to a swinging bench and an overlook of Sweetwater Creek and the mill ruins. Take these stairs down to the seating area or continue past a junction with White Trail on the right

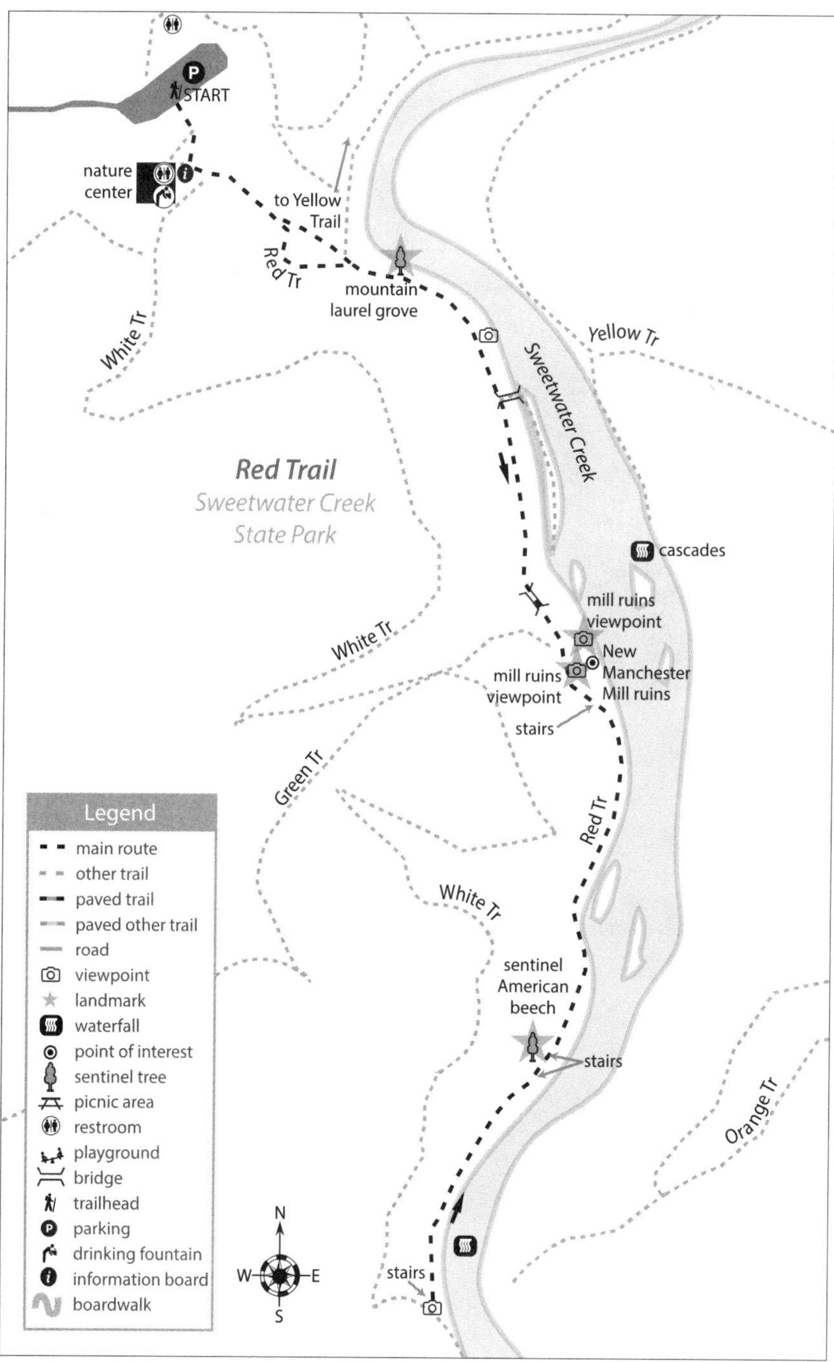
START
nature center
to Yellow Trail
Red Tr
mountain laurel grove
White Tr
Yellow Tr
Sweetwater Creek
Red Trail
Sweetwater Creek State Park
cascades
mill ruins viewpoint
New Manchester Mill ruins
mill ruins viewpoint
White Tr
stairs
Green Tr
Red Tr
White Tr
sentinel American beech
stairs
Orange Tr
stairs
N
W
E
S
Legend
main route
other trail
paved trail
paved other trail
road
viewpoint
landmark
waterfall
point of interest
sentinel tree
picnic area
restroom
playground
bridge
trailhead
parking
drinking fountain
information board
boardwalk

The Red Trail has several secluded spots to view the creek.

to a larger second overlook. After exiting the second overlook, on the left is a staircase leading down to the creek. This next section of Red Trail becomes moderate to difficult and requires you to cross over rocks and rough terrain.

Take the stairs to the bottom for a different angle of the ruins and exit onto the dirt trail that runs parallel to Sweetwater Creek. Hike along the edge of the water, and in 0.1 mile the trail ascends along a cliff at a railing. In another 0.1 mile, hike up another staircase, pausing halfway at a bench to find the sentinel curved beech tree on the right side of the trail. At the top of the stairs, pass a viewpoint platform and descend another flight of stairs. Carefully hike along the rock outcrop, pausing to take in the sweeping views of the creek. In 0.3 mile at a large rock outcrop, reach a set of ascending stairs. This is the turnaround point of the hike, or you can continue up the stairs where the trail connects with White Trail (p. 167) to extend your hike.

Turn around and retrace your steps back to the parking area to end your hike.

What messages will you receive while hiking on this trail?

One day
at a time.

White Trail

SWEETWATER CREEK STATE PARK

Sweetwater Creek's White Trail provides the park's most extensive hiking route. It will take you through stunning forests along the edge of Sweetwater Creek, and past the open meadows of a former farm. This hike follows the ridges overlooking Sweetwater Creek and offers a chance to experience the more remote areas of the park where native plants and wildlife flourish. This route even runs close enough to the famous New Manchester Mill ruins that you can easily access them at an intersection with Red Trail (p. 161).

HOW TO GET THERE

Driving Distance from Downtown Atlanta: 19 miles

Address: 1750 Mount Vernon Road, Lithia Springs, GA 30122; turn onto Factory Shoals Road to reach parking at GPS 33.753421, -84.628801

Closest Interstate: I-20

City, County: Lithia Springs, Douglas

Parking: Large paved parking lot

HIKE DISTANCE

5-mile loop

DIFFICULTY

Overall: Moderate to strenuous

Navigation: White blazes on trees and on posts

Terrain: Hard-packed dirt and gravel trails, stairs, trails with exposed rocks and roots

Elevation Change: Rolling hills with one major ascent

SAFETY

Usage ★★★★☆

Visibility ★★★☆☆

Upkeep ★★★★★

Parking ★★★★★

HOURS

7:00 am to sunset

DOGS

Leashed dogs allowed

FACILITIES

- Toilets in nature center and at top of parking lot
- Nature center with concessions, water fountain, picnic pavilions, playground

FEES & PERMITS $5 daily ParkPass—purchase at gastateparks.org

LAND MANAGER Georgia State Parks

Landmarks

SWEETWATER CREEK VIEWPOINT

Take a moment to enjoy the beauty of Sweetwater Creek from atop this large rock outcrop overlook, where you can easily forget you're less than 5 miles from a major highway.

SENTINEL AMERICAN BEECH

Just past the halfway point on the hike, look to the left of the trail for this sentinel American beech close to the water's edge. It has a cavernous hollow at the base of its trunk, giving the impression that it has legs.

WATERFALL AT JACK'S LAKE DAM

Although Sweetwater Creek is the most famous water feature in the park, you will also enjoy the quiet and serenity of Jack's Lake and the waterfall. This hidden oasis is a great location to spot wading birds or other wildlife.

Hike Route

From the parking area, walk toward the visitor center. Begin your hike facing the information kiosk directly across from the visitor center. Directly behind the information kiosk, look for white blazes on trees that signify the start of White Trail. The trail curves behind the visitor center and into the forest. At the junction with the signpost and white marker, stay straight and continue on White Trail.

Hike through the forest and past a fallen tree with a huge exposed root ball on the left. In 0.15 mile, cross several small footbridges. Pass a bench on the right and hike a slight incline. Continue 0.2 mile to the top of the ridge and a set of stairs. Go up the stairs, then soon hike down another set of stairs. Climb more stairs before the trail descends and runs parallel to the stream.

Cross a bridge in 0.1 mile and continue hiking along the upper ridge for 0.2 mile before coming to a four-way junction with Green Trail. If you'd like a quick detour to view the New Manchester Mill ruins, turn right and hike to the next junction. The mill will be directly in front of you. Otherwise, go straight to continue on White Trail. As you hike uphill, look to the left 50 yards off the trail for a large

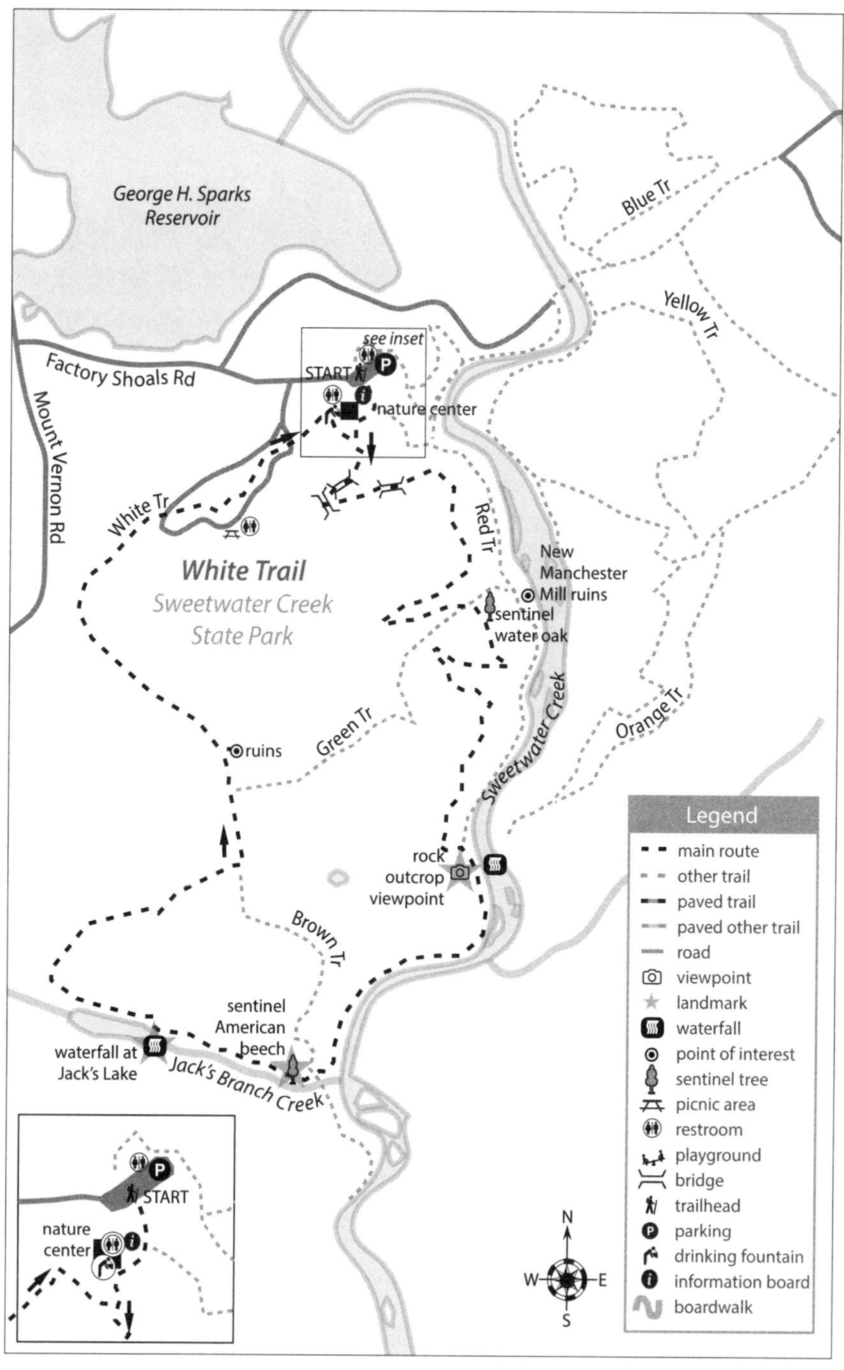
George H. Sparks Reservoir
Factory Shoals Rd
Mount Vernon Rd
see inset
START
nature center
White Tr
White Trail
Sweetwater Creek State Park
Red Tr
Blue Tr
Yellow Tr
New Manchester Mill ruins
sentinel water oak
Sweetwater Creek
Orange Tr
Green Tr
ruins
rock outcrop viewpoint
Brown Tr
sentinel American beech
waterfall at Jack's Lake
Jack's Branch Creek
Legend
main route
other trail
paved trail
paved other trail
road
viewpoint
landmark
waterfall
point of interest
sentinel tree
picnic area
restroom
playground
bridge
trailhead
parking
drinking fountain
information board
boardwalk
N
W
E
S

Sweetwater Creek's White Trail showcases the diverse habitats of the park.

sentinel white oak with many large limbs branching from the trunk. In 0.15 mile, reach a junction and go right, continuing to follow the white blazes.

Hike with the stream on your left and a grove of ferns on your right before climbing uphill. In 0.3 mile at an intersection with a service road, continue straight and hike at the top of the ridge with views and sounds of the running river below. Reach a four-way intersection in another 0.3 mile, continue straight, and hike down a very rocky, rooty path to reach an intersection with Red Trail (p. 161). Go right and take the stairs down to the river's edge for close-up views and access to the water.

Take in views of Sweetwater Creek as you hike along the bank. In half a mile, reach a rock outcrop with amazing views of the creek. This is a great spot for a snack break or chance to rest and enjoy the views. From here, continue hiking for 0.1 mile to a junction with Brown Trail. That marks the halfway point of this hike.

Stay straight to continue hiking on White Trail with Jack's Branch Creek to your left. Pass a junction, hike 50 yards, then look to the left for the sentinel beech tree with a large cavern at the base of the trunk. Cross a footbridge and hike up stairs shortly after. From here, go left and take a spur to a view of the dam waterfall. Return to the main trail as it curves to the left and around a wetland and then begins a long, steady uphill climb.

In 0.35 mile at the top of the hill, reach a junction and go left into the meadow. Hike through the meadow, keeping an eye out for wildlife that enjoys the transitional habitat. In 0.2 mile at a junction with a trash can and map post, go left and take the trail back into the forest. Reach a junction with Green Trail in 0.1 mile and continue straight. In 100 feet, look to the right for circular benches. Take the short spur behind the benches that leads to dilapidated ruins.

Return to the main trail and go right. At a junction with a gravel road that leads right to the park manager's house, stay to the left on a large gravel road. Hike for 0.3 mile to a junction and go right onto the dirt road, continuing on White Trail. Cross a park road in 0.2 mile, continuing to hike through the forest near a picnic area. In half a mile, reach the junction where you first began the White Trail loop. Go left and follow the trail back to the nature center and parking lot to end the hike.

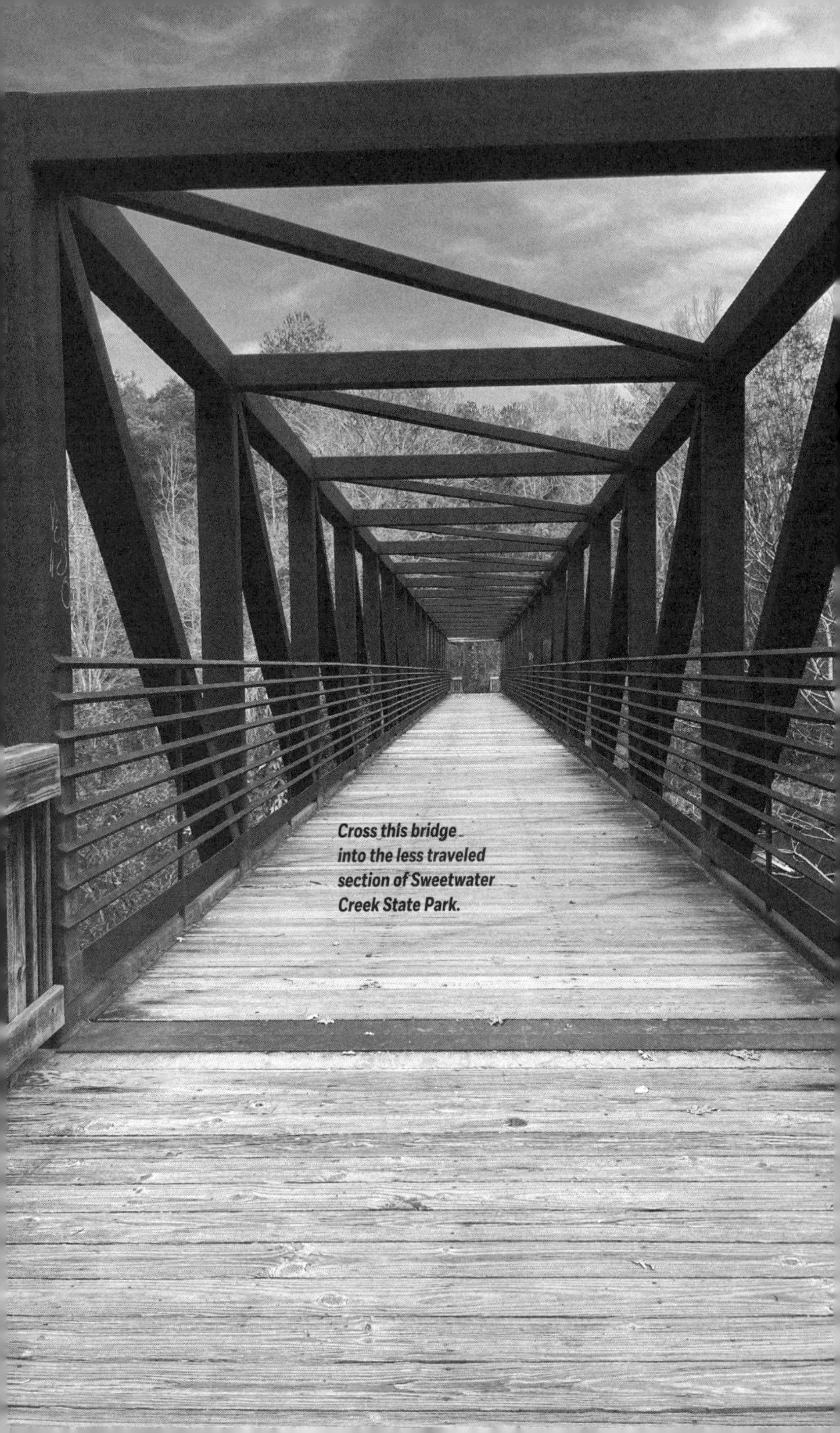

Cross this bridge into the less traveled section of Sweetwater Creek State Park.

Yellow & Orange Trails

SWEETWATER CREEK STATE PARK

This route combines the Yellow and Orange Trails on the east side of Sweetwater Creek, where you will enjoy hiking along the edge of Sweetwater Creek and through beautiful hardwood forests. This trail also brings you past a rock overhang archaeologists believe was a Native American shelter. In the winter, you can see extraction pits where bricks for the mill were made in the 1840s.

HOW TO GET THERE

Driving Distance from Downtown Atlanta: 19 miles

Address: 1750 Mount Vernon Road, Lithia Springs, GA 30122; turn onto Factory Shoals Road to reach parking at GPS 33.753421, -84.628801

Closest Interstate: I-20

City, County: Lithia Springs, Douglas

Parking: Large paved parking lot

HIKE DISTANCE

3-mile loop

DIFFICULTY

Overall: Moderate

Navigation: Blazes on trees and directional posts

Terrain: Hard-packed dirt trails

Elevation Change: Mostly flat with one major ascent and descent

SAFETY

Usage ★★★★☆

Visibility ★★★★☆

Upkeep ★★★★★

Parking ★★★★☆

HOURS

7:00 am to sunset

DOGS

Leashed dogs allowed

FACILITIES

- Toilets in nature center and at top of parking lot
- Nature center with concessions, water fountain, picnic pavilions

FEES & PERMITS

$5 daily ParkPass—purchase at gastateparks.org

LAND MANAGER Georgia State Parks

Landmarks

SENTINEL TULIP TREE

On the left side of the trail stands a huge tulip tree (also referred to as a tulip poplar). This tree is the largest in this area of the forest, and its trunk is nearly double the circumference of the trees surrounding it.

NATIVE AMERICAN CLIFF OVERHANG

As the trail descends through the ravine, look for the large rock overhang on the left. Based on artifacts found here, archaeologists estimate that Native Americans used this as shelter for several thousand years. To protect this area, do not climb on the slope or the rocks.

RUINS AND CREEK VIEWPOINT

Even if you've hiked Sweetwater Creek's Red Trail to the New Manchester Mill ruins before, this spur trail along the water's edge will allow you to see the ruins from a new angle—from across the creek.

Hike Route

From the parking area, hike toward the nature center. Begin your hike at the information board adjacent to the center. Facing the map board, look left for the red blazes on the trees for the start of the trail. Follow the red blazes into the forest, and at the first junction in 50 feet go left, following the purple blazes for the connector trail that will lead you to Yellow Trail.

Go left at the next junction and take an immediate right at a signpost. Hike on Yellow Trail for 0.2 mile before crossing a small bridge. Bear left and hike along the water's edge for 0.3 mile to reach the bottom of the tall bridge over the creek. Cross the bridge, taking in the grand views of Sweetwater Creek below. At the end of the bridge, stay straight on Orange Trail, following the orange blazes.

Hike past a post on the left marking Blue Trail and in 0.1 mile take the trail to the right, following the markers for Orange Trail deeper into the forest and past a cascading creek on the right. After a small creek crossing, walk through a dense grove of ferns along the forest floor. In 50 yards, begin a long, steady ascent uphill. In 0.2 mile, about three-fourths of the way uphill, look to the left of the

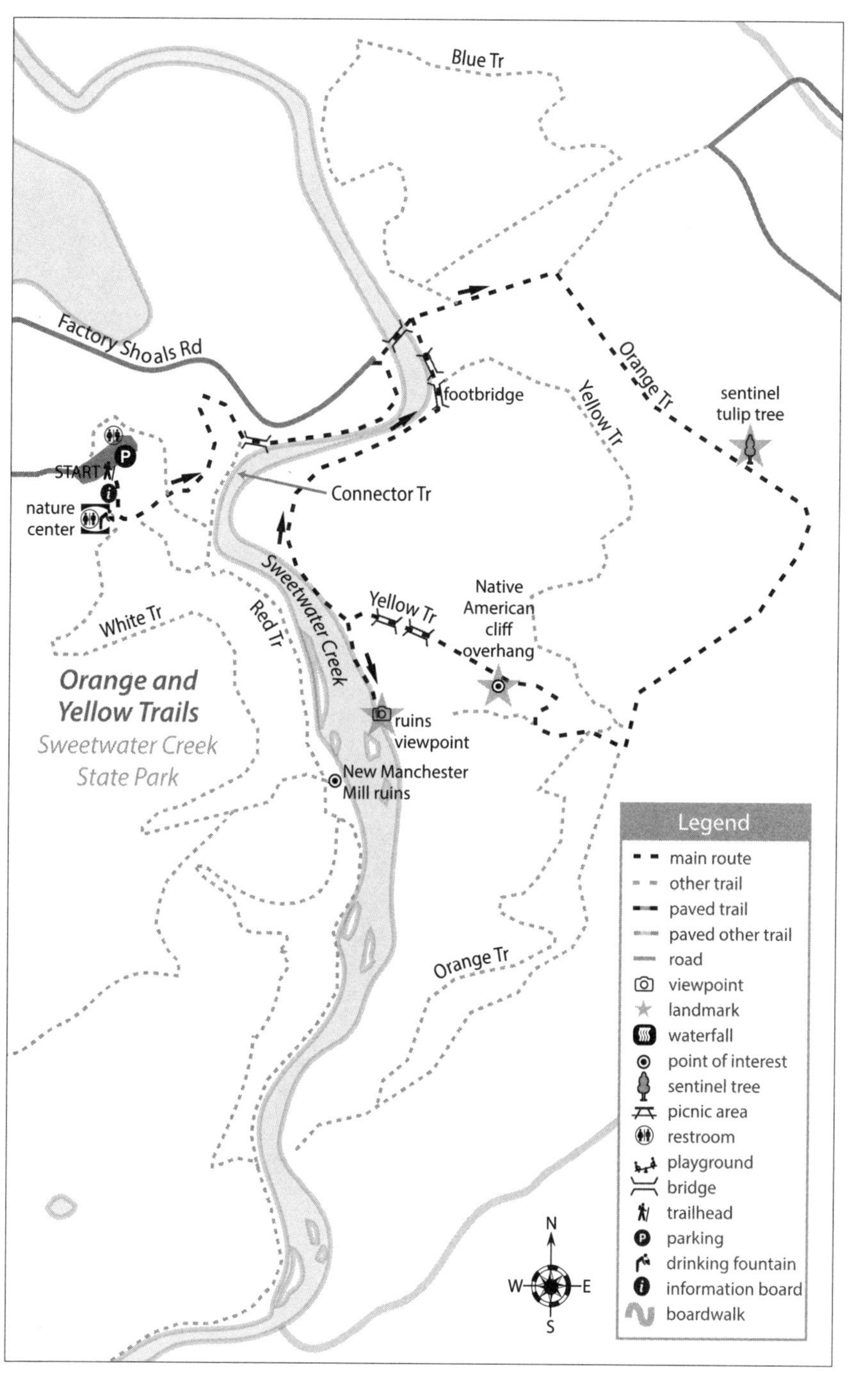
Blue Tr
Factory Shoals Rd
footbridge
Orange Tr
Yellow Tr
sentinel
tulip tree
START
nature
center
Connector Tr
Sweetwater Creek
Red Tr
White Tr
Yellow Tr
Native
American
cliff
overhang
Orange and
Yellow Trails
Sweetwater Creek
State Park
ruins
viewpoint
New Manchester
Mill ruins
Orange Tr
Legend
main route
other trail
paved trail
paved other trail
road
viewpoint
landmark
waterfall
point of interest
sentinel tree
picnic area
restroom
playground
bridge
trailhead
parking
drinking fountain
information board
boardwalk
N
W
E
S

Find serenity on the trail near Sweetwater Creek.

trail for a gargantuan tulip poplar. Hike uphill for another 0.1 mile to reach the top of the ridge.

Turn right, hiking under the power lines for 0.2 mile to reach a junction with a bench. Go right here, following the trail into the forest and coming to a junction with Yellow Trail. Stay straight at the first post, then continue straight at another post to merge onto Yellow Trail and begin hiking downhill.

Hike downhill into the valley. In 0.1 mile, toward the end of the descent, look to the left to see the Native American cliff overhang. Cross a small footbridge at the bottom of the hill and come to a junction with a yellow post. Take this spur 0.1 mile to the left for a scenic view of the New Manchester Mill ruins and creek. Return to the main trail and go left. Continue hiking along the water's edge past groves of lush mountain laurels on the right. Stay straight at the next junction, cross a bridge, and hike to the end of Yellow Trail at the bottom of the bridge. Go left across the bridge and retrace your steps, following the purple blazes back to the parking lot to end your hike.

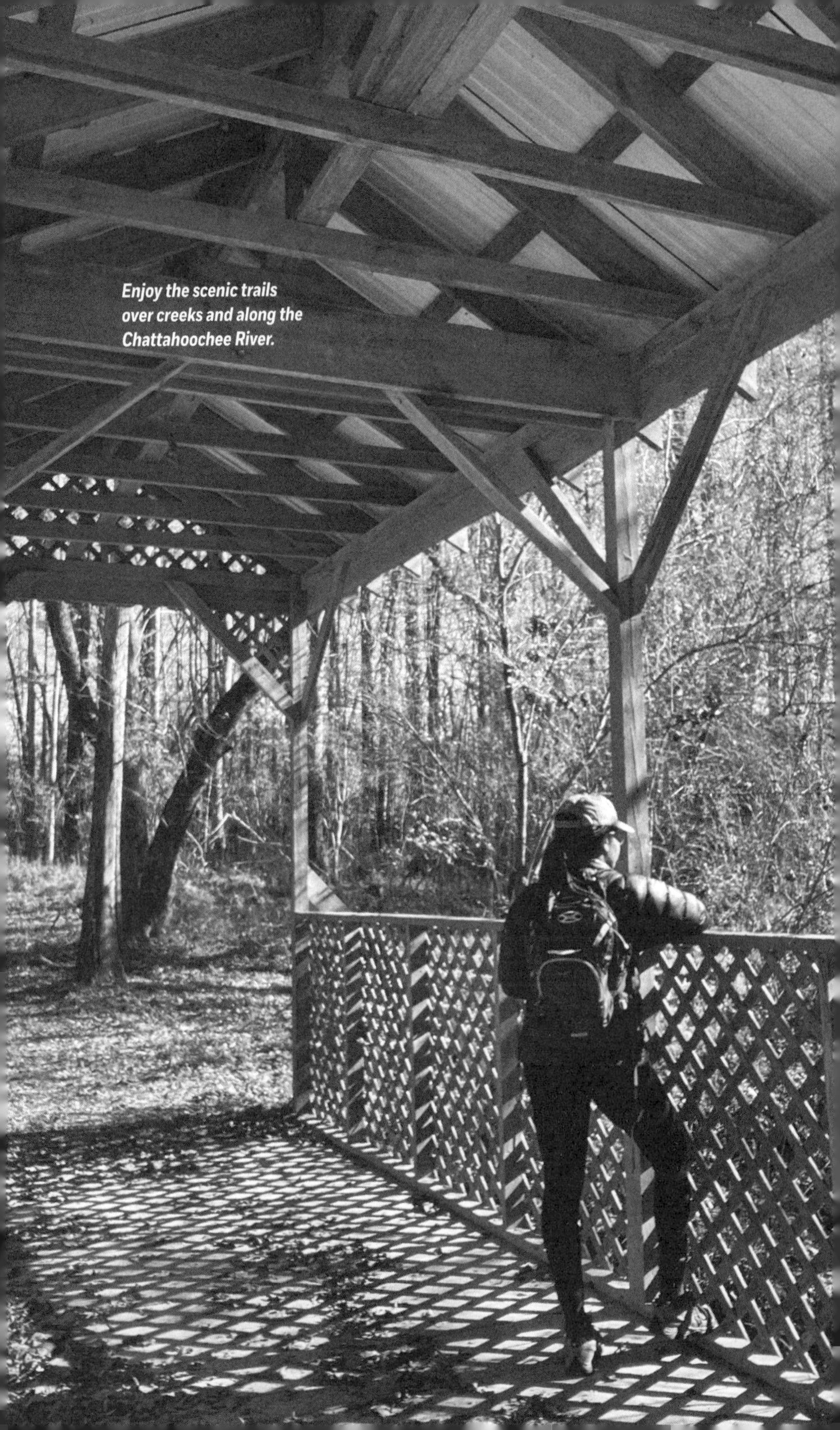

Enjoy the scenic trails over creeks and along the Chattahoochee River.

Boundary Waters Park

Known primarily for its sports fields and aquatic center, Boundary Waters Park is also a hiking gem in the Douglas County parks system. It contains over 12 miles of trails for hikers, bikers, runners, and equestrians, as well as two 18-hole disc golf courses. This strenuous and beautiful hike takes you along the Chattahoochee River and winds through healthy Piedmont forests.

HOW TO GET THERE

Driving Distance from Downtown Atlanta: 22 miles
Address: 5000 GA 154, Douglasville, GA 30135
Closest Interstate: I-20
City, County: Near South Fulton, in Douglas County
Parking: Large paved parking lot behind the aquatic center

HIKE DISTANCE

7-mile figure-8 loop

DIFFICULTY

Overall: Moderate to strenuous
Navigation: Posts marked with arrows
Terrain: Paved multiuse path and wide, hard-packed dirt trails
Elevation Change: Mostly flat with several short but steep ascents and descents

SAFETY

Usage ★★★☆☆
Visibility ★★★★☆
Upkeep ★★★★☆
Parking ★★★★★

HOURS

8:00 am to 8:00 pm

DOGS

Leashed dogs allowed

FACILITIES

- Toilets in recreation center
- Water fountains, picnic areas, playground, disc golf course, aquatic center, athletic fields

FEES & PERMITS

None

LAND MANAGER Douglas County Parks & Recreation

Landmarks

MOUNTAIN LAURELS AND RIVER VIEWPOINT

This clearing along the banks of the river provides an opportunity for unobstructed views of the Chattahoochee and a large grove of mountain laurels, a flowering shrub that's more commonly found in north Georgia.

SENTINEL SYCAMORE

This sentinel sycamore sits right on the trail and is one of the largest trees in this section of forest. Take a close look at this tree's bark, as it is a prime example of both the flaky lower bark and smooth white bark on the upper branches that are characteristic of these trees.

GROOVER LAKE

At the end of this strenuous hike, take a moment to sit and enjoy the scenic lakeside views. It's a perfect spot for photos or fishing, and you'll see visitors of varying interests congregate at this 10-acre lake.

Hike Route

Start your hike at the far right corner of the aquatic center (the building adjacent to the recreation center) parking lot at the trailhead sign. Hike on the paved path through the bollards and past a little free library. In 50 yards, look for the Blue Trail sign at a junction on the right side of the trail. Take the dirt Blue Trail into the woods, and at the post marked with a blue arrow continue left on Blue Trail through a pine forest. The trail skirts the edges of a private residence and road before coming to a junction in 0.25 mile.

At this junction with a post and large clearing for the disc golf course, go right toward the fence and disc golf hole number 7. Across the road you may see grazing horses on the private property near the park. Turn left at the fence and continue straight with the road and horse meadow to your right. Stay straight at a junction with Yellow Trail and go left at the next post marked with yellow arrows next to the power line pole.

Hike on Yellow Trail underneath the power lines for 0.1 mile to another post. Continue straight, hiking through the forest along the fenceline. Reach a junction in 0.4 mile with benches and stay to the right. In about 1 mile, the trail begins to curve away from the fence and deeper into the forest. Continue to follow the yellow marked

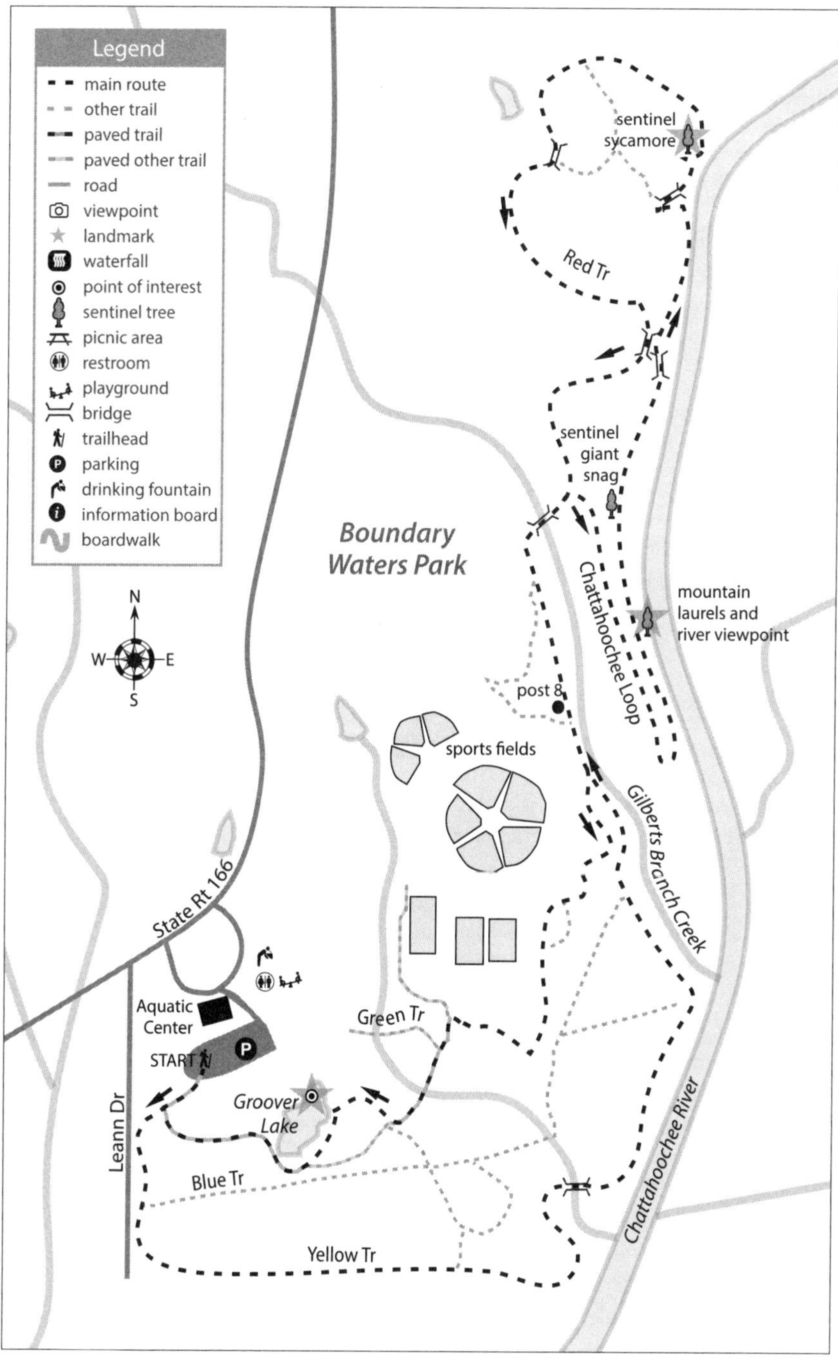

Legend
main route
other trail
paved trail
paved other trail
road
viewpoint
landmark
waterfall
point of interest
sentinel tree
picnic area
restroom
playground
bridge
trailhead
parking
drinking fountain
information board
boardwalk
N
W
E
S
Boundary Waters Park
sentinel sycamore
Red Tr
sentinel giant snag
mountain laurels and river viewpoint
Chattahoochee Loop
post 8
sports fields
Gilberts Branch Creek
State Rt 166
Aquatic Center
START
Green Tr
Groover Lake
Leann Dr
Blue Tr
Yellow Tr
Chattahoochee River

Disc golf is another way to enjoy time at this park.

posts for Yellow Trail. Hike through an intersection with the disc golf trail and come to a covered bridge. Past the bridge, the trail curves to the left past disc golf hole number 9 and arrives at a large clearing.

Hike across the clearing and back into the forest, taking a moment to view the Chattahoochee River at the far right edge of the clearing. Continue through the forest for 0.2 mile to reach a junction with a bench on the left. Stay to the right and hike for another 0.2 mile to reach a junction with Red Trail, marked with a post. Go right onto Red Trail.

Shortly into Red Trail, the path forks, but stay to the right and hike for 0.1 mile to a three-way junction. Turn right onto the wide trail. Pass a junction and post marked number 8, staying to the right, and hike along the lower ridge with a residential area up the hill on your left. In 0.1 mile at a bench and junction, stay right and go right again, crossing over a bridge.

Ascend a short hill to a three-way junction with a signpost. Go to the right to take the Chattahoochee Loop. Hike along the ridge.

In fall and winter you can view the Chattahoochee below. The trail descends into the floodplain and then makes a sharp left turn to parallel the bank of the river. In 0.15 mile, reach a clearing along the bank that gives unobstructed views of the Chattahoochee on the right and a grove of mountain laurels on the left. Hike along the river for another 0.3 mile to the debris of a large fallen tree close to the trail on the left. Up the hill 50 feet, you can see a giant snag from which the trunk fell. Even though it is dead, this is still one of the largest trees in this section of forest.

In 0.2 mile, stay to the right at a post and junction with a bench. Immediately cross a bridge to come to a four-way junction and green signpost. If you'd like a shorter and less strenuous hike, go left, following the sign for the exit. Otherwise, take a sharp right to continue the Red Trail loop along the banks of the Chattahoochee River. Hike for 0.3 mile to a bridge and go right. In 0.1 mile, as the trail curves right at the bottom of a hill, you'll find a large sentinel sycamore tree.

Begin a long, steady climb uphill. Reach the top of the incline in 0.2 mile. From here the trail continues to undulate along the ridge. Cross a bridge in 0.3 mile and stay right. Just before reaching a private property sign, veer left, continuing to hike uphill with the fence to your right. Reach the top of the hill and begin hiking downhill until you reach the four-way intersection where you began this loop. Stay to the far right and cross over a bridge.

Hike for 0.3 mile to reach the Red Trail loop intersection and go right, following the exit sign. Retrace your steps back over the bridge and to the left at the next junction. In 0.1 mile, stay straight at the three-way intersection you traversed previously. This section of forest is mostly pine. Continue following the red arrows until the trail dead-ends at a junction with a signpost. Go right, following the exit sign. Don't forget to look down occasionally through this section of trail to see the variety of mosses growing along the edge of the forest.

In 0.1 mile at a signpost, stay straight on the wide main trail. Just before reaching the athletic fields, take a sharp left. In 0.1 mile, go left onto the paved Green Trail. At an intersection with the disc golf course with a No Motor Vehicles sign, go right into the grassy clearing to reach Groover's Lake. Go left, hiking along the edge of the lake, and then reconnect with the paved trail. Go right and stay on the paved path for 0.2 mile to reach the parking area and end your hike.

Hike across granite landscapes at this park.

Clinton Nature Preserve

Originally donated to Douglas County by Annie Mae Clinton, Clinton Nature Preserve is now a popular spot for hikers, mountain bikers, equestrians, and runners in Douglas County. With over 200 protected acres to explore, you can hike for miles in solitude, even on a busy weekend. At the request of Ms. Clinton, the preserve's natural state is protected, and this hike will take you through forests, across meadows, and over granite outcrops with opportunities to view several well-preserved structures from the 1800s.

HOW TO GET THERE

Driving Distance from Downtown Atlanta: 30 miles
Address: 8720 Ephesus Church Road, Villa Rica, GA 30180
Closest Interstate: I-20
City, County: Near Villa Rica, in Douglas County
Parking: Large gravel parking lot; last parking area on the right is closest to the trailhead

HIKE DISTANCE

5-mile figure-8 loop

DIFFICULTY

Overall: Moderate to strenuous
Navigation: Map posts at several junctions, trailheads marked with signposts, arrows on ground
Terrain: Wide gravel trails, hard-packed dirt trails, wide sandy trails, granite rock outcrop
Elevation Change: Rolling hills

SAFETY

Usage ★★★★☆
Visibility ★★★★☆
Upkeep ★★★★★
Parking ★★★★☆

HOURS

8:30 am to sunset

DOGS

Leashed dogs allowed

FACILITIES

- Toilets at both parking areas
- Water fountains, picnic pavilions, outdoor exercise equipment, playground, trash cans, benches

FEES & PERMITS	None
LAND MANAGER	Douglas County Parks & Recreation

Landmarks

JOHN THOMAS CARNES LOG CABIN

A piece of history hidden in the forest, this log cabin is listed on the National Register of Historic Places and dates back to the early 1800s. From the trail, you can see into the rooms of the well-preserved log cabin and imagine pioneer life.

LAKE

You'll have multiple opportunities to pass by the major water feature of this park. You'll pass the lake at the beginning of your hike, and it is a great spot to eat lunch or a snack or look for turtles in the water.

CLINTON BUNKHOUSE

Across from the parking area, you will find the Clinton bunkhouse, which housed the ranch hands who managed the property back when it was farmland. Notice how it sits on large rocks to keep it raised off the ground—a common design to keep homes cool in summer and warm in winter.

Hike Route

The trails in Clinton Nature Preserve are shared with mountain bikers. Hikers are welcome, but please be aware and courteous to bicyclists. Pay special attention while hiking uphill, because bikes may be coming downhill toward you at fast speeds. Always keep your eyes open and listen while hiking on trails shared with mountain bikers.

Begin your hike by turning right onto the wide gravel trail at the far left end of the parking lot near the picnic pavilion. Shortly, in 0.1 mile, come to a junction with Blue, Red, and Yellow Trails and a map post. Stay left and hike Yellow and Red Trails past the lake on your left. At the next junction, marked with a post, go right onto Red Trail and take a left at the next junction, marked Nature Trail.

The trail leads you along a streambed and switches back to a bridge in 0.3 mile. Cross a small footbridge shortly after in 0.1 mile, then stay right at the following junction. Notice the subtle change in tree species on this side of the forest, which has more hardwoods and less dense understory. Cross a bridge and continue hiking on Nature

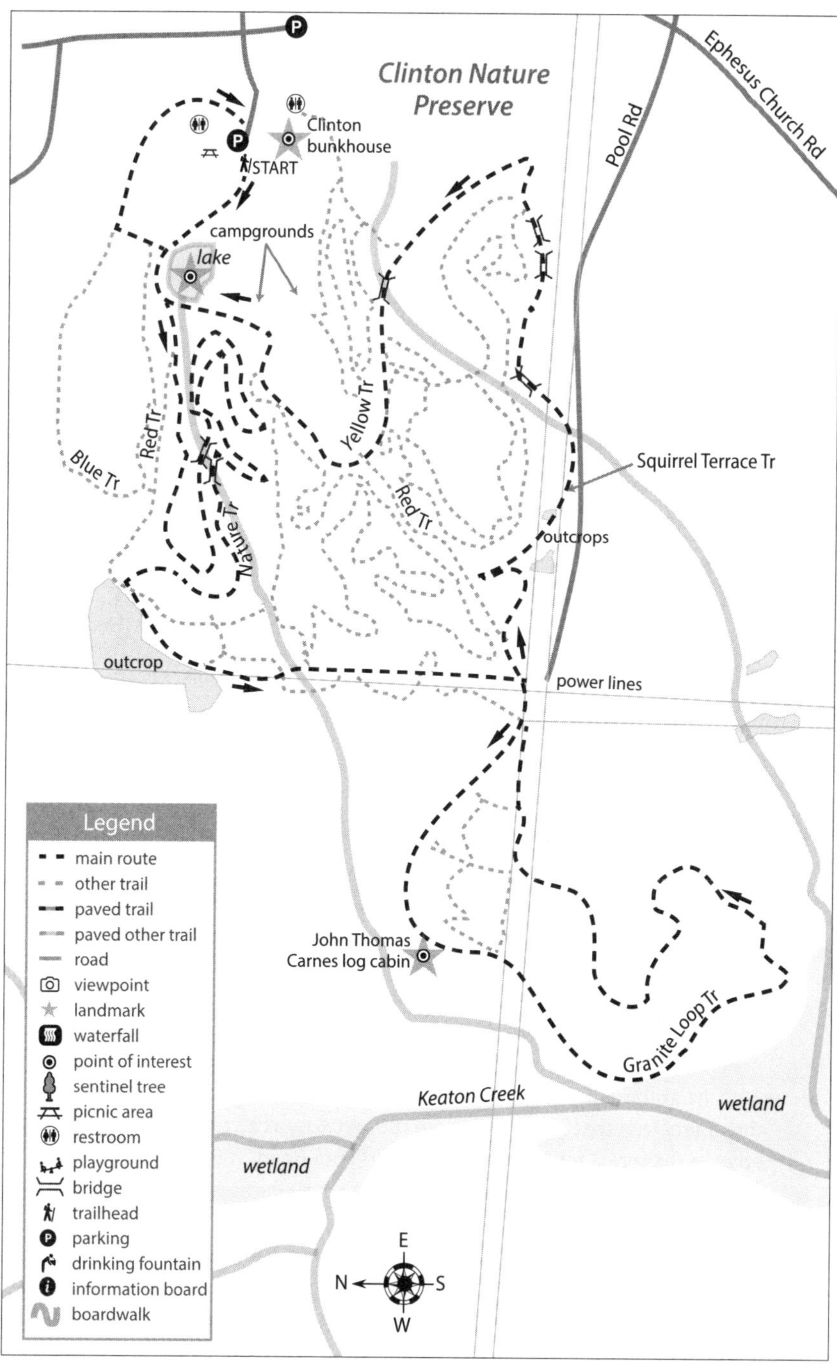

Clinton Nature Preserve
Ephesus Church Rd
Pool Rd
Clinton bunkhouse
START
campgrounds
lake
Red Tr
Blue Tr
Yellow Tr
Nature Tr
Red Tr
Squirrel Terrace Tr
outcrops
outcrop
power lines
John Thomas Carnes log cabin
Granite Loop Tr
Keaton Creek
wetland
wetland
E
N
S
W
Legend
main route
other trail
paved trail
paved other trail
road
viewpoint
landmark
waterfall
point of interest
sentinel tree
picnic area
restroom
playground
bridge
trailhead
parking
drinking fountain
information board
boardwalk

View the historic Carnes family log cabin from the trail.

Trail through the forest for 0.3 mile until the path ends at a granite outcrop.

Step out onto the outcrop and go left toward the power lines. Ample reindeer moss and haircap moss grow on the edges of the outcrop. Continue hiking on the outcrop to where the trail opens up to a large clearing under the power lines. Go left here, pass a blue trash can, and take the trail underneath the power lines. Reach a post marked Red Trail and follow this path, continuing under the power lines for 0.3 mile to where the trail reaches a fence and another set of power lines running perpendicular.

Turn right, following the orange signs marked Log Cabin. Stay off the gravel trail that leads to private property. Look to the right at the edge of the forest for a sign marking Old Pool Road Trail. Take that path into the forest and hike downhill. Stay straight past two junctions with Granite Loop Trail on your left. When you reach a junction at the bottom of the hill, bear left and come to the John Thomas Carnes log cabin. Admire the rooms and structure of this well-preserved cabin from the trail, but as the No Trespassing sign reminds, do not enter the cabin.

Continue on this trail past more remnants of the old homestead. Just past the historic structures, exit the forest into the power line clearing. Hike across the clearing and enter the opposite side of the forest onto Granite Loop Trail. Follow the trail into the floodplain and past a wetland and fence on your right. When the trail emerges from the forest onto a granite outcrop, take a left and hike along the edge of the forest line. Look for red arrows on the ground to direct you. In 50 yards at an unmarked white post, take the far left trail and continue hiking back into the forest. Past a large pile of rocks in 0.3 mile, the trail once again crosses the granite outcrop. Stay straight to reach the power line clearing, where you'll go right and hike uphill underneath the power lines.

When you reach the top of the hill, continue straight, passing the marked post on your left where you first entered the loop. Hike straight past the green No Motor Vehicles sign on your left and look for the post marked Exit on the left edge of the forest. Take this trail and come to an intersection with a map post. Take the farthest right Squirrel Terrace Trail and stay to the right at the next junction.

In 0.2 mile, the trail emerges into the power line clearing and crosses to the right side of the meadow. Be careful to stay on the path that is underneath the power lines and not the gravel access road trail. Squirrel Terrace Trail switches back underneath the power lines and reenters the forest at a marked signpost. Once back in the forest, cross two footbridges and reach a junction. Stay to the right. Go right again immediately at the next junction. Hike for 0.2 mile to another junction and go left.

Cross a bridge and come to a four-way junction with Yellow Trail. Go left onto Yellow Trail and stay right at all subsequent junctions until the trail comes to an open field by the lake. Cross the field and hike around the left edge of the lake. Go right on Yellow Trail and at the next junction, marked with signposts, go left onto Blue Trail. Reach a three-way junction and go right toward the clearing. Follow Blue Trail along the edge of the forest and back into the developed area of the park. Before returning to your vehicle, carefully cross the gravel park road and take a moment to explore the historic Clinton bunkhouse to end your hike.

NORTHSIDE

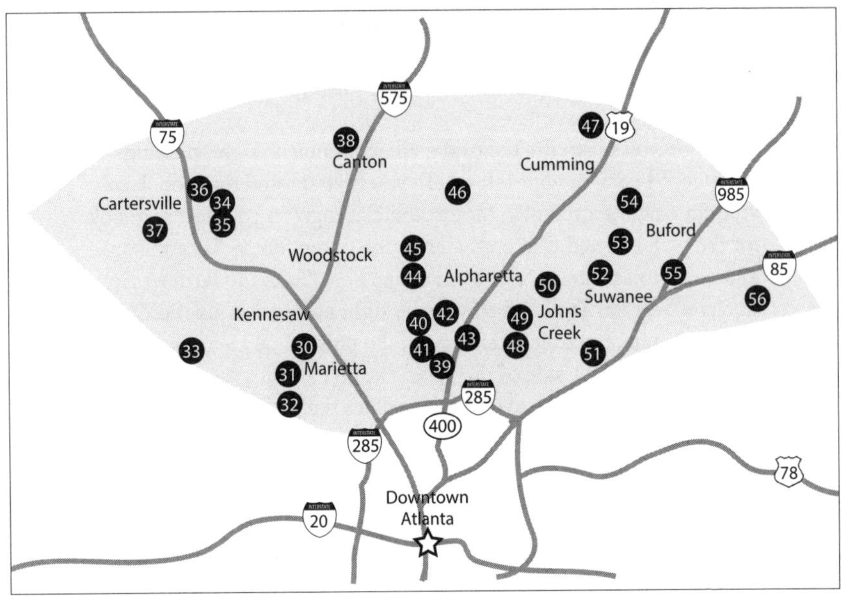

- 30 Summit Trail
- 31 Cheatham Hill Loop
- 32 Kolb Farm Loop
- 33 Pickett's Mill Battlefield State Historic Site
- 34 Homestead & Sweet Gum Trails
- 35 Iron Hill Trail
- 36 Pine Mountain Recreation Area
- 37 Etowah Indian Mounds State Historic Site
- 38 Etowah Hiking Trails
- 39 Big Trees Forest Preserve
- 40 Chattahoochee Nature Center
- 41 Gold Branch
- 42 Vickery Creek
- 43 Island Ford
- 44 Leita Thompson Memorial Park
- 45 Lakhapani Preserve
- 46 Birmingham Park
- 47 Sawnee Mountain Preserve
- 48 Simpsonwood Park
- 49 Jones Bridge
- 50 Medlock Bridge
- 51 McDaniel Farm Park
- 52 Chattahoochee Pointe Park
- 53 Settles Bridge Park
- 54 Bowmans Island & Laurel Ridge Trail
- 55 Gwinnett Environmental and Heritage Center & Ivy Creek Greenway
- 56 Little Mulberry Park

I-75 NORTH

Enjoy iconic views from the Kennesaw Mountain summit.

Summit Trail

KENNESAW MOUNTAIN NATIONAL BATTLEFIELD PARK

This route follows one of the best-known and most well used trails in the Atlanta area. On warm weekends thousands of people walk up and down the mountain for exercise and the sweeping skyline views. Of the four other granite mountains in the metro area, Kennesaw Mountain is the tallest, with an elevation of 1,808 feet. Enjoy the history museum in the visitor center for background on the Civil War battles that took place within the park.

HOW TO GET THERE

Driving Distance from Downtown Atlanta: 25 miles

Address: 900 Kennesaw Mountain Drive, Kennesaw, GA 30152

Closest Interstate: I-75

City, County: Marietta, Cobb

Public Transit: MARTA 45 bus stops at Cobb Parkway and White Circle; 0.8-mile walk to the visitor center

Parking: Paved parking lot; overflow lot at 1200 Old 41 Hwy NW, Kennesaw, GA 30152

HIKE DISTANCE

2-mile out-and-back or 6-mile loop

DIFFICULTY

Overall: Strenuous

Navigation: Signposts along the trail

Terrain: Hard-packed dirt trails with exposed roots and large rocks, paved sections

Elevation Change: Extended ascent and descent

SAFETY

Usage ★★★★★

Visibility ★★★★★

Upkeep ★★★★★

Parking ★★★★★

HOURS

6:30 am to 6:30 pm (standard time); 6:30 am to 8:00 pm (daylight saving time); visitor center open daily 9:00 am to 5:00 pm except Thanksgiving, Christmas Day, and New Year's Day

DOGS

Leashed dogs allowed

FACILITIES	• Toilets in visitor center • Water fountain, picnic area, trash can, dog waste station
FEES & PERMITS	$5 daily fee or $40 annual pass—purchase at the ticket kiosk or at recreation.gov
LAND MANAGER	Kennesaw Mountain National Battlefield Park—National Park Service

Landmarks

GEORGIA MONUMENT

Before beginning your ascent to the summit, take a spur on the left to view the Georgia Monument. This monument is one of many reminders of the battles that took place at Kennesaw Mountain and in the surrounding park area.

DUELING CANNONS

Pass two replica cannons on your way to the summit. Confederate troops positioned cannons at the top of the mountain to return fire to the Union army. The two armies fired back and forth day and night for weeks.

SUMMIT VIEWPOINT

The strenuous hike to the top of Kennesaw is well worth the view. On clear days, you can see Stone Mountain, Buckhead, midtown, and downtown.

Hike Route

Start your hike at the visitor center. (If you're walking from the overflow lot, just follow the paved path to the visitor center.) Take the paved path to the right of the building toward the woods beyond the building and road. Cross the road and enter the woods on a hard-packed dirt trail.

This section of trail is very popular, and you can generally follow the crowds to the top of the mountain. But take a slight detour first. In 100 feet, go left at the first junction and walk 100 yards to the Georgia Monument, one of many monuments dedicated to the Civil War battles at this park. If you'd like a slightly less steep ascent, you can continue on this trail, taking the Pickett Line Trail and turning right where it reconnects with the summit trail. Otherwise, return to the main path, turn left, and hike uphill for 0.3 mile to a junction. Go to the right onto a wider trail.

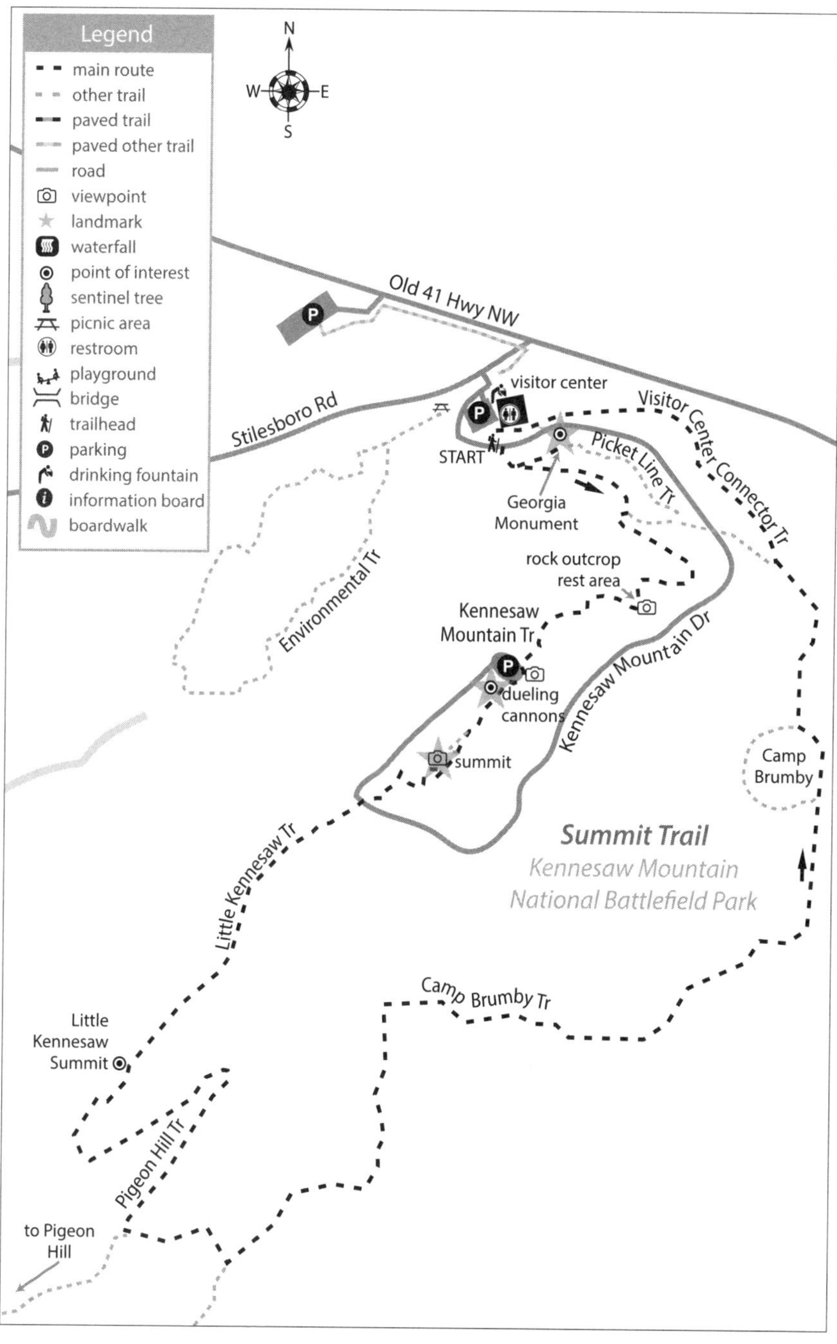
Legend
main route
other trail
paved trail
paved other trail
road
viewpoint
landmark
waterfall
point of interest
sentinel tree
picnic area
restroom
playground
bridge
trailhead
parking
drinking fountain
information board
boardwalk
N
W
E
S
Old 41 Hwy NW
visitor center
Stilesboro Rd
Visitor Center Connector Tr
START
Picket Line Tr
Georgia Monument
Environmental Tr
rock outcrop rest area
Kennesaw Mountain Tr
Kennesaw Mountain Dr
dueling cannons
summit
Camp Brumby
Summit Trail
Kennesaw Mountain National Battlefield Park
Little Kennesaw Tr
Camp Brumby Tr
Little Kennesaw Summit
Pigeon Hill Tr
to Pigeon Hill

Pass replica cannons on the mountain.

After another 0.2 mile of ascent, bear right and climb a set of steps. You'll pass overlooks on the left that are good places to take a breather. After another steep 0.4 mile over large roots and rocks, walk up a short paved section to the Mountain Road parking area and your first fantastic viewpoint. Stop for a view of the city, then continue on the paved path around the parking area to climb a set of stairs.

Hike past the dueling cannons on the right side of the trail and in 0.15 mile, reach the top of the mountain. Enjoy a well-deserved break and take in the surrounding views. Turn around and retrace your steps down the mountain to return to the parking area and end your hike. If you'd like to extend your hike and explore the other side of the mountain, the trail continues from the summit to connect to

Little Kennesaw Mountain summit and a loop trail that connects with Pigeon Hill for a challenging 6-mile round-trip hike.

SUMMIT LOOP EXTENSION

From the peak continue on the main trail down the other side of the mountain. Cross Kennesaw Mountain Road and follow the trail to reach the peak of Little Kennesaw Mountain in half a mile. Continue on Little Kennesaw Trail as it becomes Pigeon Hill Trail and descends steeply for 0.7 mile. Stay to the left at the next two junctions, turning onto Camp Brumby Trail.

Take this trail 1.5 mile to reach the site of Camp Brumby, a Civilian Conservation Corps camp from the 1940s. The short 0.3-mile loop around the camp provides an interesting history tour should you choose to take it. On the main trail, in 0.15 mile, turn left, following the sign for the visitor center. When you come to another junction in 0.15 mile, stay right onto Visitor Center Connector Trail and follow this path around a field and back to the visitor center to end your hike.

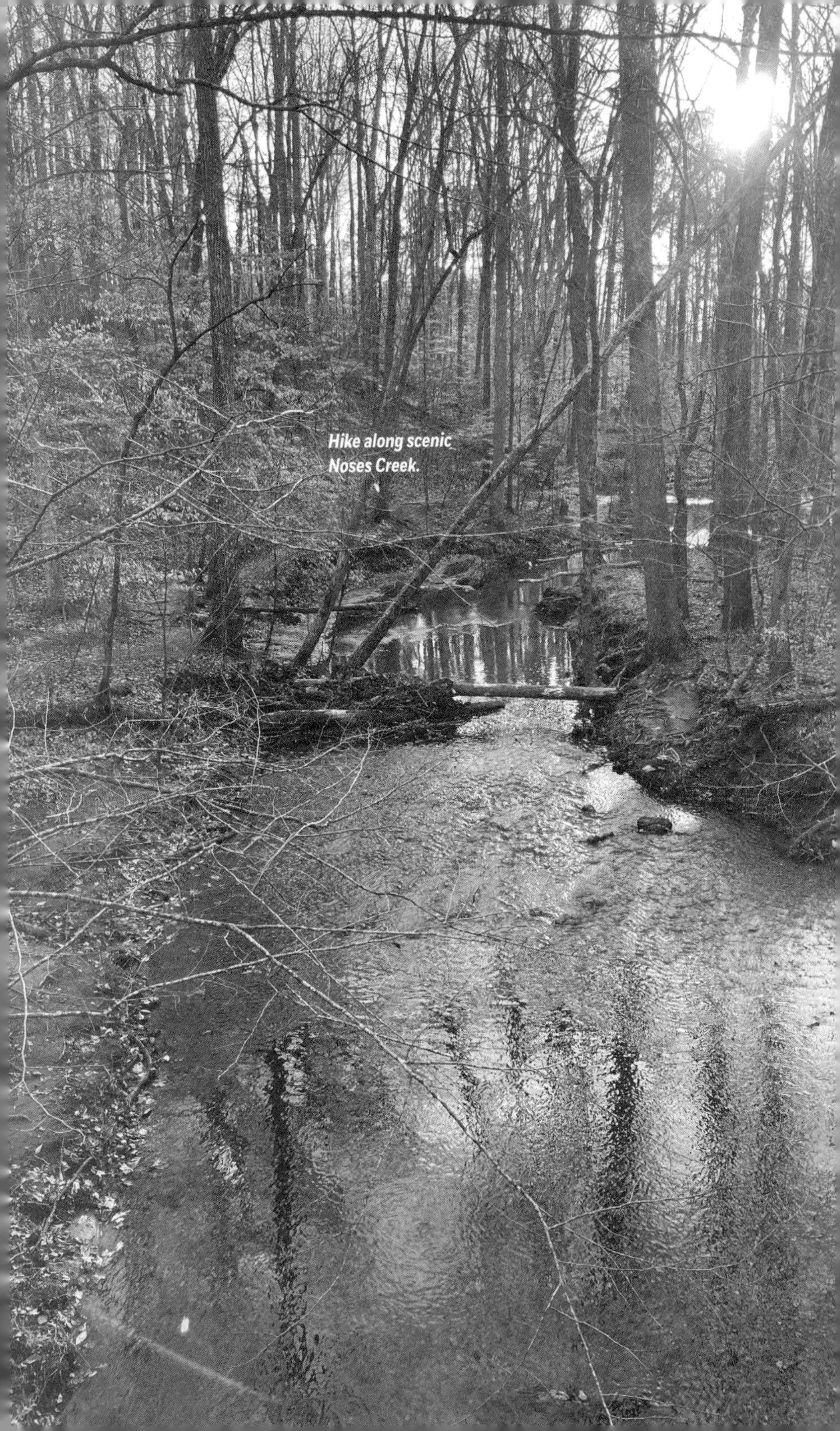

Hike along scenic Noses Creek.

Cheatham Hill Loop

KENNESAW MOUNTAIN NATIONAL BATTLEFIELD PARK

This is an excellent hike for those wanting to escape the crowds of the Summit Trail (p. 193). The route is split into two sections, West Trail and Noses Creek Trail. You'll wind through some of the nicest Piedmont forests in the national battlefield park. As you pass several creeks near Civil War–era earthworks, West Trail offers peace and solitude. The second half of the loop is on a wide gravel roadbed with an easy grade where hikers can cool off from the more challenging West Trail.

HOW TO GET THERE	**Driving Distance from Downtown Atlanta:** 24 miles **Address:** 1520 Burnt Hickory Road NW, Marietta, GA 30064 **Closest Interstate:** I-75 **City, County:** Marietta, Cobb **Parking:** Paved parking lot on Burnt Hickory Road
HIKE DISTANCE	3.75-mile figure-8 loop
DIFFICULTY	**Overall:** Moderate **Navigation:** Signposts at many junctions **Terrain:** Hard-packed dirt trail, wide gravel trail **Elevation Change:** Rolling hills, with few short but steep ascents and descents
SAFETY	**Usage** ★★★★☆ **Visibility** ★★★★☆ **Upkeep** ★★★★★ **Parking** ★★★★★
HOURS	6:30 am to 6:30 pm (standard time); 6:30 am to 8:30 pm (daylight saving time)
DOGS	Leashed dogs allowed
FACILITIES	• No toilets • Water fountain, bike rack, bench

FEES & PERMITS $5 daily fee or $40 annual pass—purchase at the parking kiosk or at recreation.gov

LAND MANAGER Kennesaw Mountain National Battlefield Park—National Park Service

Landmarks

FOUR-TRUNKED TULIP TREE

Look for this unusual tree on your right after the trail descends and turns left. It's made up of four separate trees that have fused together. At the seams where the trunks meet, the wood has grown outward very slowly over many years.

SENTINEL CHESTNUT OAK

A relic of the Civil War era, this is one of two trees of its age and size in this area of the park. In fact, it's one of the largest chestnut oaks in Atlanta. Its small, lobed leaves resemble those of the American chestnut, hence its name.

SENTINEL WHITE OAK

Down a short hill on the left of the trail is a white oak of similar age to the nearby sentinel chestnut oak. White oaks are more common to Atlanta and are identified by extremely flaky bark on their upper limbs.

Hike Route

Start your hike near the information kiosk and water fountain at the far end of the parking lot. Immediately turn right onto the wide gravel trail to hike past the field and enter the forest after 0.1 mile.

At the bottom of the hill cross a small creek and then hike up a steep grade past a small trail leading through a field on your left. Hike uphill past a dog waste station and turn right onto West Trail at the first junction after you crest the hill.

In 0.25 mile at a junction with the field to your left, continue straight, then hike 0.65 mile, passing the Civil War earthworks and signage of brigade lines at the top of the ridge. After the trail descends and curves left, stay to the left at a junction with an unofficial trail that leads to a view of Noses Creek, then pass a sentinel tulip tree with four trunks on the right side of the trail. In 0.15 mile, reach Noses Creek. The creek is a great place for kids (or adults) to play.

Follow the trail left along the bank of the creek to intersect with

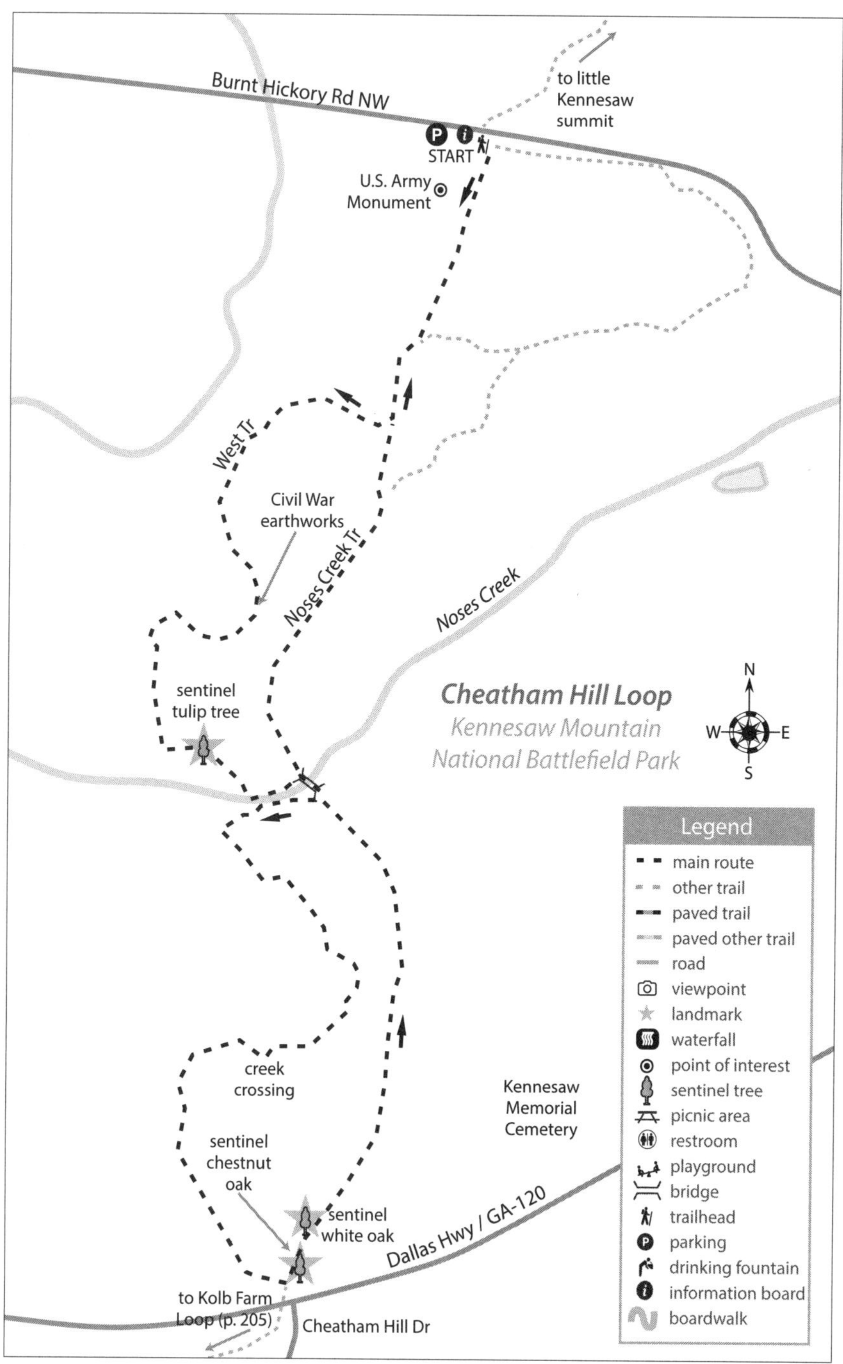
Burnt Hickory Rd NW
to little
Kennesaw
summit
START
U.S. Army
Monument
West Tr
Civil War
earthworks
Noses Creek Tr
Noses Creek
sentinel
tulip tree
Cheatham Hill Loop
Kennesaw Mountain
National Battlefield Park
N
W
E
S
Legend
main route
other trail
paved trail
paved other trail
road
viewpoint
landmark
waterfall
point of interest
sentinel tree
picnic area
restroom
playground
bridge
trailhead
parking
drinking fountain
information board
boardwalk
creek
crossing
Kennesaw
Memorial
Cemetery
sentinel
chestnut
oak
sentinel
white oak
Dallas Hwy / GA-120
to Kolb Farm
Loop (p. 205)
Cheatham Hill Dr

Civil War history abounds along this trail.

Noses Creek Trail at a large bridge. Turn right, crossing the bridge, and immediately turn right again onto West Trail. Walk along the opposite bank of the creek, then follow the trail as it curves uphill to the left. Do not take the small unofficial side trail along the creek's bank.

Hike past more earthworks on your left. For half a mile, hike uphill and along the ridge before reaching a small creek crossing near a bench. After crossing the creek, the trail switchbacks up the hill. In 0.5 mile, you'll reach a junction with Noses Creek Trail at Whitlock Avenue NW. Take a sharp left onto the wide gravel trail past the metal gate. Immediately on your right at a junction leading to the crosswalk is the sentinel chestnut oak. In less than 100 yards, look to the left of the trail for the sentinel white oak at the bottom of the floodplain.

Enjoy this wide, gently sloping trail through quiet forest. In half a mile, reach the bridge over Noses Creek. Cross and continue straight for 0.4 mile to reach a junction with East Trail. Stay left on the main trail, pass a small side trail that leads across a field on the left, and hike 0.1 mile farther past the junction with West Trail on the left.

Continue straight and hike for 0.4 mile back to the parking lot to finish your hike.

Avoid the crowds by hiking at Kolb Farm.

Kolb Farm Loop

KENNESAW MOUNTAIN NATIONAL BATTLEFIELD PARK

The 6-mile Kolb Farm Loop is less known than the Summit Trail (p. 193), but it still provides natural beauty and challenge. This is where Union commander William T. Sherman's troops eventually outmaneuvered Confederate general Joseph E. Johnston's forces to win the explosive Battle of Kennesaw Mountain during the Civil War. Today the peaceful forest and meandering streams of this hike offer respite from the noise of the bustling city. This route is shared with horses, so be aware of your surroundings and remember to give equestrians right-of-way on the trail.

HOW TO GET THERE

Driving Distance from Downtown Atlanta: 24 miles
Address: 1544 Whitlock Avenue NW, Marietta, GA 30064
Closest Interstate: I-75
City, County: Marietta, Cobb
Parking: Paved parking lot

HIKE DISTANCE

6-mile loop

DIFFICULTY

Overall: Moderate
Navigation: Signs at many junctions
Terrain: Hard-packed dirt and gravel trails
Elevation: Rolling hills, with few short but steep ascents

SAFETY

Usage ★★★★☆
Visibility ★★★★☆
Upkeep ★★★★★
Parking ★★★★☆

HOURS

8:00 am to 5:30 pm (standard time); 8:00 am to 7:30 pm (daylight saving time)

DOGS

Leashed dogs allowed

FACILITIES

- Toilets at parking lot
- Water fountain, dog waste station, trash cans, benches

FEES & PERMITS $5 daily fee or $40 annual pass—purchase at the parking kiosk or at recreation.gov

LAND MANAGER Kennesaw Mountain National Battlefield Park—National Park Service

Landmarks

CIVIL WAR EARTHWORKS

Just before beginning your hike, view the historic earthworks. These mounds and shallow ditches were dug by Confederate soldiers on the front lines in 1864.

ILLINOIS MONUMENT

The massive monument overlooks the "Dead Angle," the site of the most hard fought battle at Kennesaw Mountain. This monument is a tribute to the large number of Union soldiers killed in battle, many of whom were from Illinois.

SENTINEL POST OAK

This relic of the Civil War era is one of the largest of its species in Atlanta. Its cross-shaped leaves identify it as a post oak.

Hike Route

Start your hike by the information kiosk and water fountain. Before beginning the hike, take a moment to explore the historic earthworks, mounds, and cannons. Exit the earthworks and turn left onto the main trail.

In 0.2 mile, you'll reach the Illinois Monument. Go to the far right, circling around to the front of the monument and a viewpoint overlooking the Dead Angle. Facing the field of the Dead Angle, go right to take the trail to a junction and bear left. Hike the high trail at the top of the field and enter the forest. At a junction with a signpost, stay to the right.

At a junction on the right side of the trail, continue straight and cross a bridge. For 0.2 mile the trail runs behind a residential area before connecting to a paved section of path. Turn right onto the path and cross the street to the left at the pedestrian walkway. Turn left and carefully make your way to the far end of the parking area. Hike along the fenceline and the road to reach a metal gate and signpost.

Go right into the forest and hike past an information kiosk. Then hike for 0.25 mile downhill and through a pine forest. In another half

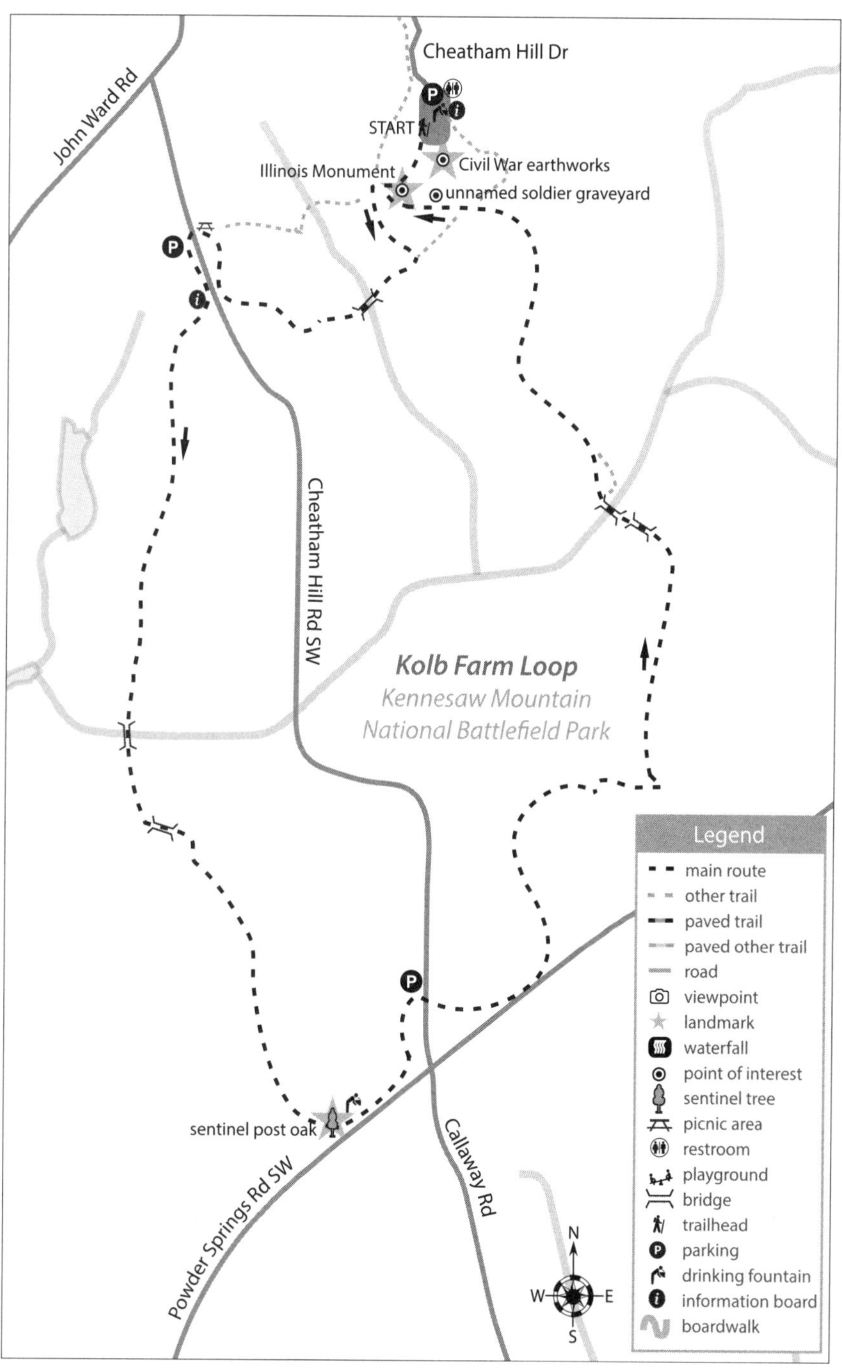
Cheatham Hill Dr
John Ward Rd
START
Civil War earthworks
Illinois Monument
unnamed soldier graveyard
Cheatham Hill Rd SW
Kolb Farm Loop
Kennesaw Mountain
National Battlefield Park
Legend
main route
other trail
paved trail
paved other trail
road
viewpoint
landmark
waterfall
point of interest
sentinel tree
picnic area
restroom
playground
bridge
trailhead
parking
drinking fountain
information board
boardwalk
sentinel post oak
Powder Springs Rd SW
Callaway Rd
N
W
E
S

The Illinois Monument is a remembrance of the bloody battle of Dead Angle.

mile, reach a junction at a post, stay to the left, and follow the trail through a wetland. Cross a bridge over John Ward Creek.

The trail again runs behind a residential area. After crossing a small footbridge, hike for 0.7 mile along the trail, passing several places where the trail splits and reconnects. Stay on the main trail until it curves to the left, coming to an opening in the tree canopy and parallel to Powder Springs Road. Just before passing a metal gate, pass the sentinel post oak on the right edge of the trail.

Continue on the trail, passing a water fountain and a view of Kolb Farm cabin across the road to the right. Hike 0.2 mile to reach a junction, stay to the left, and reach the horse trailer parking lot. Look to the right of the parking lot for a signpost for the hiking trail. Take this trail and carefully cross the street at the pedestrian crosswalk.

On the opposite side of the street turn right and then immediately go left into the forest at the signpost. At a marked junction in 0.2 mile, bear left. For the next 0.5 mile, the trail winds through a forest adjacent to a residential area. After passing the houses you'll come to a bench on your right. Cross the creek and follow the arrows to turn right at a junction.

Hike along the creek for 0.5 mile. The trail splits near a double trunked tulip tree on your left; take either fork, as the trail reconnects in 50 yards. In 0.2 mile, turn right, following a hiker sign, and cross two bridges. From here, stay left at the next junctions for 0.7 mile until you reach a major junction marked with signposts. Go left and take a right at the next junction, hiking uphill and past an unnamed soldier's grave to reach the Illinois Monument. Follow the trail back to the parking area to end your hike.

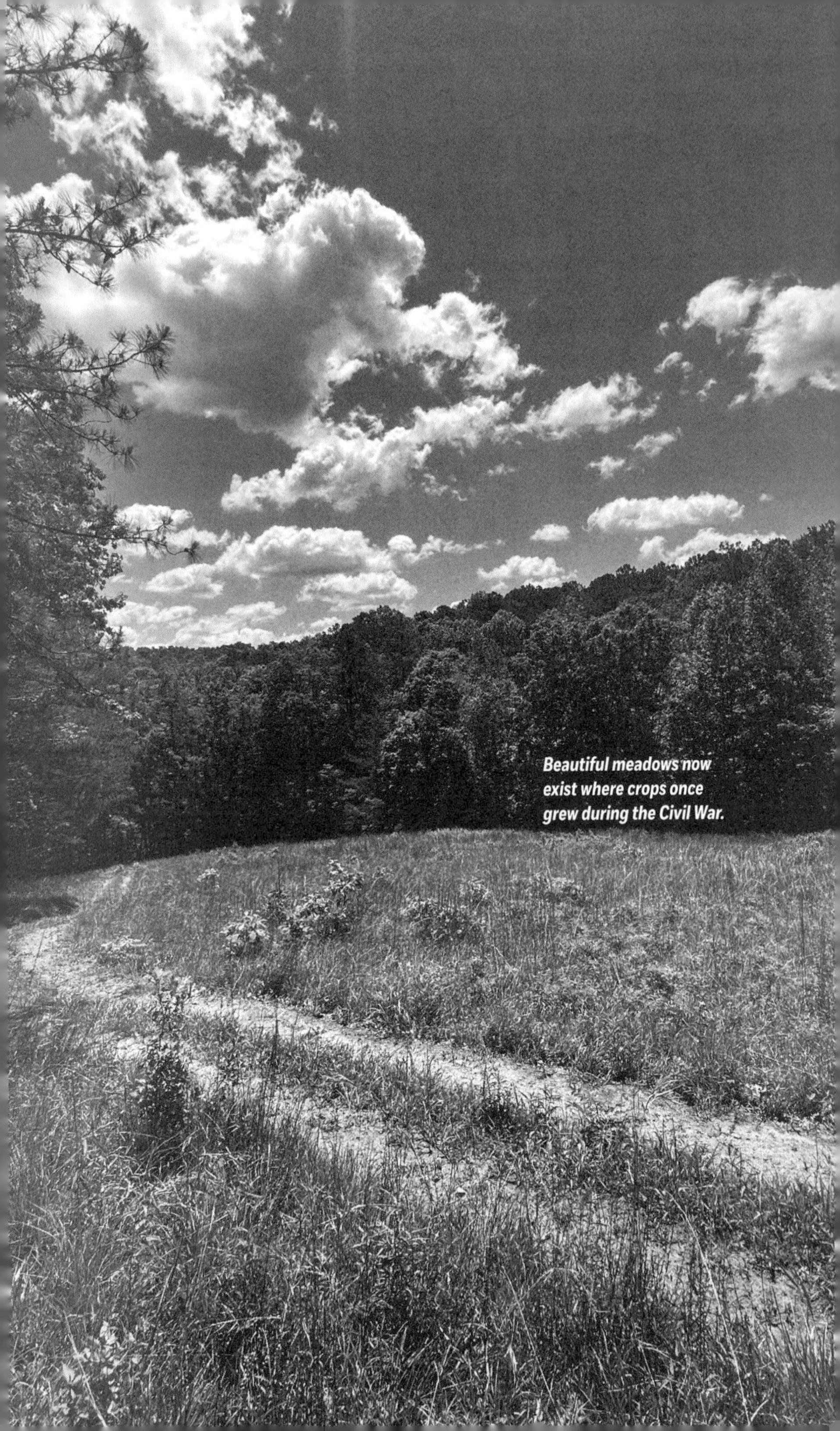

Beautiful meadows now exist where crops once grew during the Civil War.

Pickett's Mill Battlefield State Historic Site

This beautiful tract of land was originally purchased by historians in the 1970s and became a state historic site in the 1980s. This 765-acre park in Paulding County was the site of a bloody Civil War battle on May 27, 1864. Today it is an oasis for nature and a destination for hiking. The ravine, ridges, and creek that influenced the outcome of the battle now provide a peaceful habitat for animals and a haven for hikers. Along the trails and in the visitor center museum, you can learn the story of the battle and complete a pleasurable hike.

HOW TO GET THERE

Driving Distance from Downtown Atlanta: 34 miles

Address: 4432 Mount Tabor Church Road, Dallas, GA 30157

Closest Interstate: I-75

City, County: Dallas, Paulding

Parking: Paved parking lot near the visitor center at the end of a 0.6-mile park road

HIKE DISTANCE

3.75-mile double figure-8 loop

DIFFICULTY

Overall: Moderate

Navigation: Trail map available at visitor center; color-coded diamond blazes

Terrain: Hard-packed dirt trails with roots and rocks; can be muddy and slippery after rain

Elevation Change: Rolling hills with several short but steep ascents and descents

SAFETY

Usage ★★★★★

Visibility ★★★★☆

Upkeep ★★★★☆

Parking ★★★★★

HOURS

9:00 am to 5:00 pm daily except Thanksgiving, Christmas, and New Year's Day

DOGS

Leashed dogs allowed

FACILITIES	• Toilets at visitor center • Drinking fountain, picnic tables, interpretive signs, benches, history museum
FEES & PERMITS	Adults (18-61): $6.00; seniors (62+): $4.50; youth (6-17): $3.50
LAND MANAGER	Georgia State Parks & Historic Sites

Landmarks

FEDERALS IN THE RAVINE

The steep walls of this ravine trapped Federal troops in what they called a "hell hole." Injured soldiers were stuck in the ravine with Confederate bullets raining down on them. Afterward, writer Ambrose Bierce called the battle "The Crime at Pickett's Mill."

SITE OF PICKETT'S MILL

Before the Civil War, the Pickett family built a gristmill on what used to be called Little Pumpkinvine Creek. During the battle, Union troops destroyed the mill dam and burned down the wood frame mill house.

WILDCAT FALLS

Though it is only 4 feet tall, this waterfall is particularly beautiful. The water of Pickett's Mill Creek cascades over a rock ledge covered in moss and other plants. Sit on the nearby bench and listen to the peaceful sound of flowing water.

Hike Route

Check in and pay the entrance fee inside the visitor center. Pick up a trail map and consider a stop at the museum. Start your hike through the back doors of the visitor center and hike left on the sidewalk to the wooden ravine overlook platform. Hike down the stairs and go straight on Red, White, and Blue Trails, blazed with diamonds of each color.

This trail slowly descends into the ravine that was the bloodiest place in the battle of Pickett's Mill. Federal troops were trapped in this ravine with Confederate fire raining down on them. Over 2,000 soldiers were killed in this battle. Read about it on the Federals in the Ravine interpretive sign that you'll pass on your right.

The trail continues descending along a small creek. Cross a small bridge at the bottom of the ravine and then hike uphill 0.15 mile to a

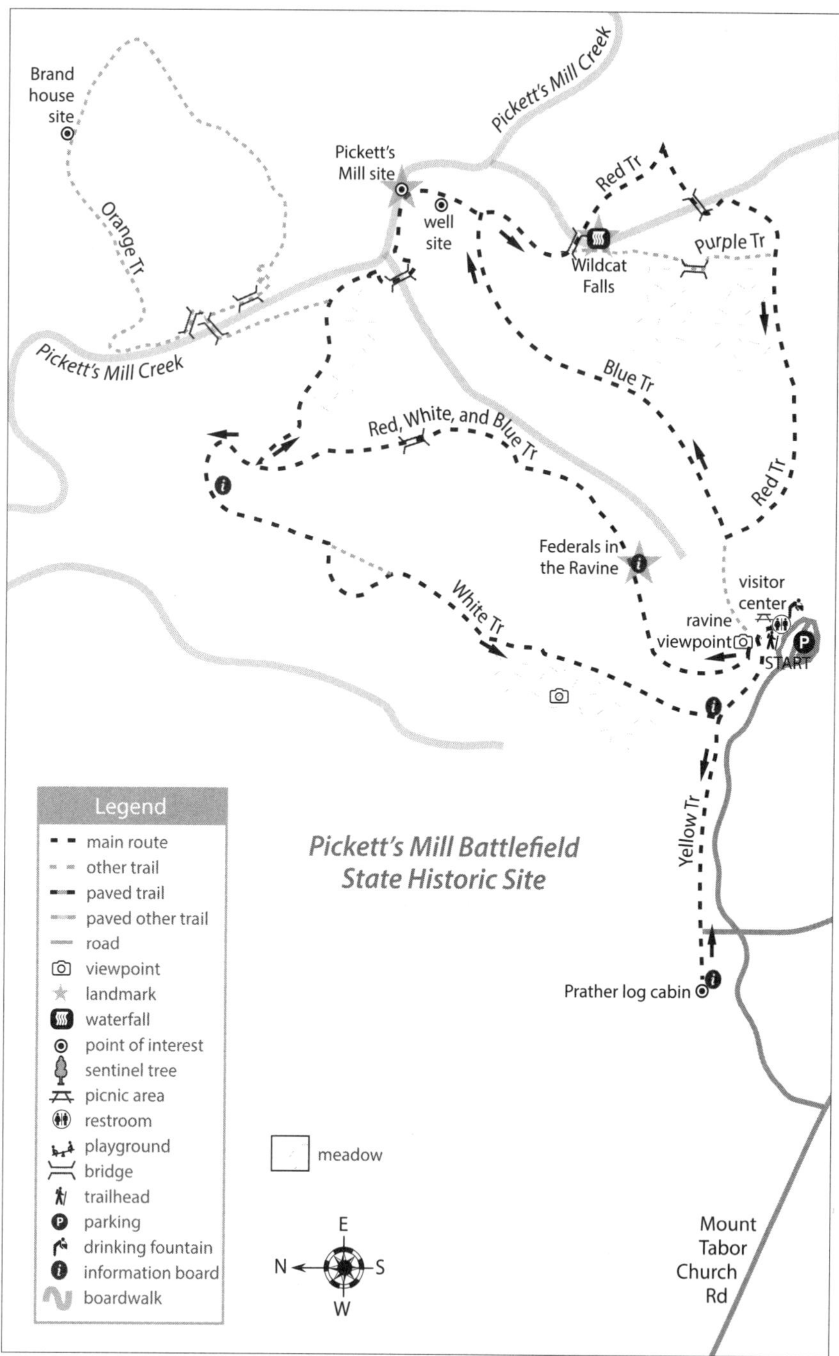

Brand house site
Orange Tr
Pickett's Mill Creek
Pickett's Mill site
well site
Red Tr
Wildcat Falls
Purple Tr
Pickett's Mill Creek
Blue Tr
Red, White, and Blue Tr
Red Tr
Federals in the Ravine
visitor center
ravine viewpoint
START
White Tr
Yellow Tr
Prather log cabin
Pickett's Mill Battlefield State Historic Site
Legend
main route
other trail
paved trail
paved other trail
road
viewpoint
landmark
waterfall
point of interest
sentinel tree
picnic area
restroom
playground
bridge
trailhead
parking
drinking fountain
information board
boardwalk
meadow
E
N
S
W
Mount Tabor Church Rd

Wildcat Falls is a particularly peaceful spot in this 750-acre forest.

junction with a wide forest road. Turn right and follow red and blue diamonds. Pay attention, because in 100 yards the trail turns sharply left, leaving the forest road. Once on the single-track trail, hike steeply downhill past several benches and a meadow viewpoint.

Turn right at a junction with Orange Trail and stay on Red and Blue Trails. Cross a bridge and then hike along Pickett's Mill Creek to an interpretive sign at the historic site of Pickett's Mill. From the mill site, the trail curves right and ascends a steep hill past a covered well site. In 0.1 mile, reach the junction where Blue and Red Trails split. Go left on Red Trail and hike 0.1 mile to a junction with Purple Trail. This is the site of Wildcat Falls, a small but picturesque water feature. You can view it from the bridge or a bench.

Cross the bridge on your left to stay on Red Trail and hike steeply uphill to the ridge that was once the site of a homestead. Then hike back downhill to another junction with Purple Trail. (If you want to avoid this steep ascent and descent, Purple Trail offers a more moderate grade.) Stay straight on Red Trail to continue your hike on this wide trail.

Hike 0.3 mile to a junction with Blue Trail. Turn right and hike almost 0.4 mile to reconnect with Red and Blue Trails. Turn left and hike back past the Pickett's Mill site, along the creek, and back to the junction with Orange Trail. This optional side trail offers a 1-mile lollipop loop with a scenic bridge over Pickett's Mill Creek and a steep ascent to the historic site of the Brand family's house, which was destroyed during the battle.

After the Orange Trail junction, continue uphill on Red and Blue Trails. This is the steepest trail on this route, so take your time and rest at benches if you need to. In 0.1 mile, turn right onto a wide trail that doubles as a forest road. Pay close attention, looking for a junction with the single-track White Trail on the right in 100 yards. Turn onto White Trail and follow white diamonds past an interpretive sign, then bear right to reconnect with the forest road. Follow this wide trail for 0.5 mile. Along the way, White Trail makes a steep right-hand turn off the forest road, crests a small ridge, then rejoins the forest road. You'll also pass another interpretive sign and parallel a large meadow that was once a wheat field.

At a junction with Yellow Trail, turn right and hike 0.25 mile to the Prather log cabin, which was relocated to this park but was originally built in 1853. After visiting the cabin, retrace your steps on Yellow Trail, then stay straight at the junction with White Trail to return to the visitor center and end your hike.

The rolling hills of Red Top Mountain State Park are peaceful.

Homestead & Sweet Gum Trails

RED TOP MOUNTAIN STATE PARK

Often known as the Red Top Loop, this hike combines two beautiful woodland trails into a peaceful but moderately strenuous day hike. Quiet mountain hollows, lakeside views, historic ruins, and bubbling streams provide beautiful scenery while you get some exercise. Want more miles? You can walk an additional 1.5 miles by adding White Tail Trail and Osprey Loop Trail to this hike. Plus, Iron Hill Trail (p. 223) is just a mile down the road.

HOW TO GET THERE	**Driving Distance from Downtown Atlanta:** 38 miles **Address:** 659 Red Top Mountain Road SE, Acworth, GA 30102 **Closest Interstate:** I-75 **City, County:** Emerson, Bartow **Parking:** Paved and gravel parking areas near the trading post
HIKE DISTANCE	5.5-mile loop
DIFFICULTY	**Overall:** Moderate to strenuous **Navigation:** Maps at trailheads, blazes along trail, and mileage markers **Terrain:** Hard-packed dirt trails with roots and rocks **Elevation Change:** Rolling hills with several short, steep ascents and descents
SAFETY	**Usage** ★★★★★ **Visibility** ★★★★☆ **Upkeep** ★★★★★ **Parking** ★★★★★
HOURS	7:00 am to dark
DOGS	Leashed dogs allowed
FACILITIES	• Toilets at trading post and visitor center • Information boards, benches, picnic areas, tennis courts, campground, playground, historic sites

FEES & PERMITS $5 daily ParkPass—purchase at gastateparks.org

LAND MANAGER Georgia State Parks

Landmarks

HOMESTEAD CHIMNEY

In the 19th century, before the Etowah River was dammed to form Lake Allatoona, these hills were the site of several homesteads. A ruined chimney stands 100 feet off the Homestead Trail and can help you picture how families once lived here.

DAM VIEWPOINT

From this point at the end of a peninsula you can view Allatoona Dam, which was completed in 1950 and holds over 100 billion gallons of water in the resulting reservoir. You are seeing the dam from the lake side, so it doesn't look very tall from here. But from the other side, you would see that it stands 190 feet high.

RED TOP MOUNTAIN

Red Top Mountain got its name and fame from the iron ore content of its red soil. Though Homestead Trail doesn't cross the mountain's 1,060-foot peak, you can see from below how this high point looms over the surrounding land. It seemed even taller when the valley was 200 feet lower, before Lake Allatoona was filled.

Hike Route

Facing the front porch of the trading post, start your hike on Homestead Trail to the left. Follow yellow blazes and hike downhill. In 0.45 mile, continue straight where Sweet Gum Trail joins Homestead Trail, then turn left on Homestead Trail at the next junction. This trail winds through several mountain hollows, then reconnects with Sweet Gum Trail in 0.5 mile.

Turn left, following a sign and yellow blazes on Homestead Trail. In 0.2 mile, cross a wooden bridge, then cross paved Lodge Road to reach another junction with Sweet Gum Trail. Stay straight on Homestead Trail and hike downhill to a T-junction. Turn right to hike Homestead Trail loop counterclockwise.

Pass a very large, double-trunked sycamore tree in 0.2 mile, then continue for another 0.5 mile. About 100 yards after passing the 2-mile marker, look for an unofficial trail on the left that leads to a chimney from one of the historic homesteads for which this trail is named. Continue on Homestead Trail after visiting the chimney.

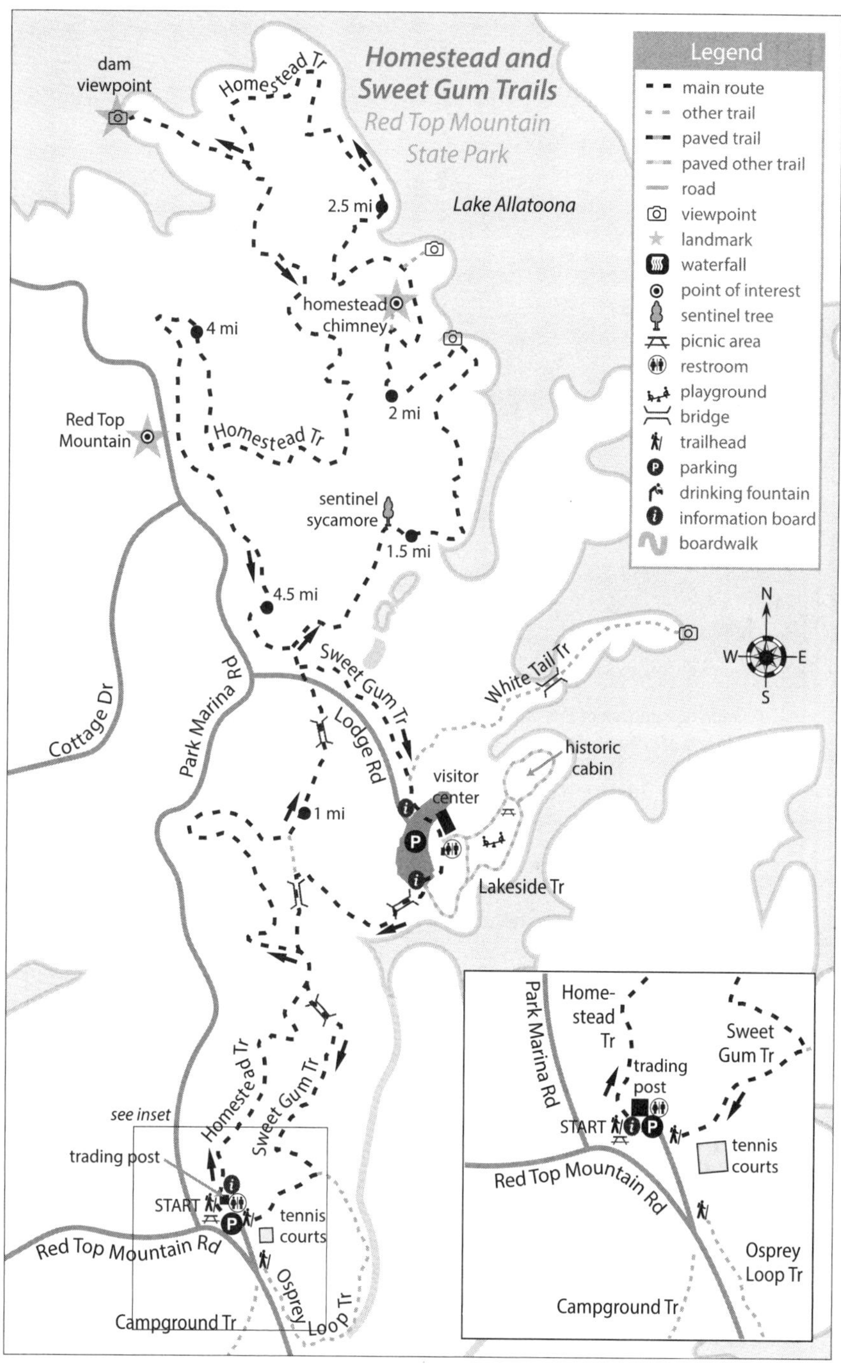
Homestead and Sweet Gum Trails
Red Top Mountain State Park
Legend
main route
other trail
paved trail
paved other trail
road
viewpoint
landmark
waterfall
point of interest
sentinel tree
picnic area
restroom
playground
bridge
trailhead
parking
drinking fountain
information board
boardwalk
N
W
E
S
Lake Allatoona
dam viewpoint
Homestead Tr
2.5 mi
homestead chimney
4 mi
2 mi
Red Top Mountain
Homestead Tr
sentinel sycamore
1.5 mi
4.5 mi
Sweet Gum Tr
White Tail Tr
Park Marina Rd
Cottage Dr
Lodge Rd
historic cabin
visitor center
1 mi
Lakeside Tr
see inset
trading post
Homestead Tr
Sweet Gum Tr
START
tennis courts
Red Top Mountain Rd
Osprey Loop Tr
Campground Tr
Park Marina Rd
Homestead Tr
trading post
Sweet Gum Tr
START
tennis courts
Red Top Mountain Rd
Osprey Loop Tr
Campground Tr

A significant portion of this hike is along the shores of Lake Allatoona.

This next portion of the trail parallels the lakeshore and has many viewpoints. In almost a mile, come to a junction with wooden railings and a trail that leads to the right, downhill along a peninsula. Hike this trail to a bench near the lake's edge, where you can find a view of the Allatoona Dam. Then hike 0.2 mile back uphill and turn right on Homestead Trail to continue the loop. From here, the trail turns inland, away from the lake.

After 0.9 mile and several extended ascents and descents, pass the 4-mile marker, then hike uphill some more. You are now ascending Red Top Mountain. Though this trail will not go across the mountain's 1,060-foot peak, you can tell this is near the highest point in the park. Then the trail descends, passing the 4.5-mile marker and then arriving back at the Homestead Trail loop junction. Turn right, hike up a short hill, then meet Sweet Gum Trail near Lodge Road. Turn left on Sweet Gum Trail and hike 0.25 mile to a junction with White Tail Trail. This side trail leads to a beautiful view of Lake Allatoona and adds 1 mile to your hike, if you want to hike this out-and-back trail. Otherwise, continue straight on Sweet Gum

Trail for 100 feet to reach an information board and the large visitor center parking lot. Look across the parking lot in the direction of the security kiosk. There you can see another information board where this trail continues. You can carefully cut across the parking lot or stop by the visitor center on your way.

At the information board that serves as a trailhead for Sweet Gum Trail and the paved Lakeside Trail, take the right fork to follow red blazes. Cross a bridge, then curve left and hike 0.15 mile to a Sweet Gum Trail junction. Turn left, cross a bridge, and hike 0.1 mile to a junction with Homestead Trail. Continue straight. At the next junction, stay left on Sweet Gum Trail, then cross a bridge.

In 0.3 mile, you'll reach a junction with Osprey Loop Trail. From here, turn right and hike 0.1 mile to return to the trading post and finish your hike. Or if you want a little more mileage, you can turn left and hike Osprey Loop Trail 0.4 mile to the trading post.

Take in views of Allatoona Lake from the site of a historic campground.

Iron Hill Trail

RED TOP MOUNTAIN STATE PARK

The Iron Hill Trail is one of the newer routes within Red Top Mountain State Park, but it has a long history. This ridge was an iron mine from the late 1800s to the early 1900s. When Allatoona Dam was completed in 1950, the water rose and the ridge turned into a lakeside peninsula. A popular campground opened, and Iron Hill became a recreation site. Today, you can see signs of the iron mines and abandoned campground, but the beauty of the lake is what is most memorable. Because the trail is built for shared use between hikers and bikers, the grade is mild and the trails are wide.

HOW TO GET THERE

Driving Distance from Downtown Atlanta: 37 miles

Address: 1 mile south of the Red Top Mountain State Park trading post (659 Red Top Mountain Road SE, Acworth, GA 30102); parking at GPS 34.139639, -84.699972

Closest Interstate: I-75

City, County: Emerson, Bartow

Parking: Gravel parking area off Red Top Mountain Road

HIKE DISTANCE

4.5-mile loop

DIFFICULTY

Overall: Moderate

Navigation: Map at trailhead; blue blazes along trail

Terrain: Gravel and hard-packed dirt trails

Elevation Change: Rolling hills, but no major ascents or descents

SAFETY

Usage ★★★★★

Visibility ★★★★☆

Upkeep ★★★★★

Parking ★★★★★

HOURS

7:00 am to dark

DOGS

Leashed dogs allowed

FACILITIES

- Toilets available at trading post and visitor center; portable toilet at trailhead
- Information board, benches along trail

FEES & PERMITS	$5 daily ParkPass—purchase at gastateparks.org
LAND MANAGER	Georgia State Parks

Landmarks

ABANDONED CAMPGROUND

From the 1940s through the 1970s, this was a popular campground. On this peninsula and at many other spots along Iron Hill Trail, you'll see broken picnic tables, old grills, and abandoned bathhouses.

LAKE ALLATOONA VIEWPOINT

Lake Allatoona covers 12,000 acres and provides hydroelectric power and drinking water for Cartersville, Marietta, and Cobb County. It is also a popular destination for water recreation. This beautiful lake is formed from the Etowah and Little Rivers, as well as many other creeks.

IRON MINE

From the late 1800s until the early 1900s, two iron mines operated in this area: Crowe Ore Bank and Iron Hill Ore Bank. The canyon adjacent to Iron Hill Trail is a remnant of this mining operation. Notice the iron-rich red soil.

Hike Route

Start your hike at the information board and follow trailhead signs to the right to reach the blue-blazed Iron Hill Trail. At a large field, bear left and then turn right to hike this loop counterclockwise. In 0.1 mile, stay straight at a junction with Campground Connector Trail. After another 0.1 mile, walk a short boardwalk to reach the lake. Hike along a ridge above the lake for 0.2 mile before reaching a trail that leads right, down to the lakeshore.

Continue straight, then stay right at a junction, cross a wooden bridge, and pass a 3-mile marker. Hike 0.3 mile across two more bridges to reach a junction with a wide trail on the right that leads to the end of a small peninsula with nice views of the lake. This is the first place you'll see signs of the campground that used to be on this site. Continue straight on Iron Hill Trail, following blue blazes. The trail continues to wind along the edge of the lake for 1 mile.

When you reach an old picnic table and a junction, take the trail on the right to hike a short loop around the end of a peninsula, where you'll see signs of old campsites and a defunct bathhouse. Back at the picnic table junction, turn right to continue on Iron Hill Trail.

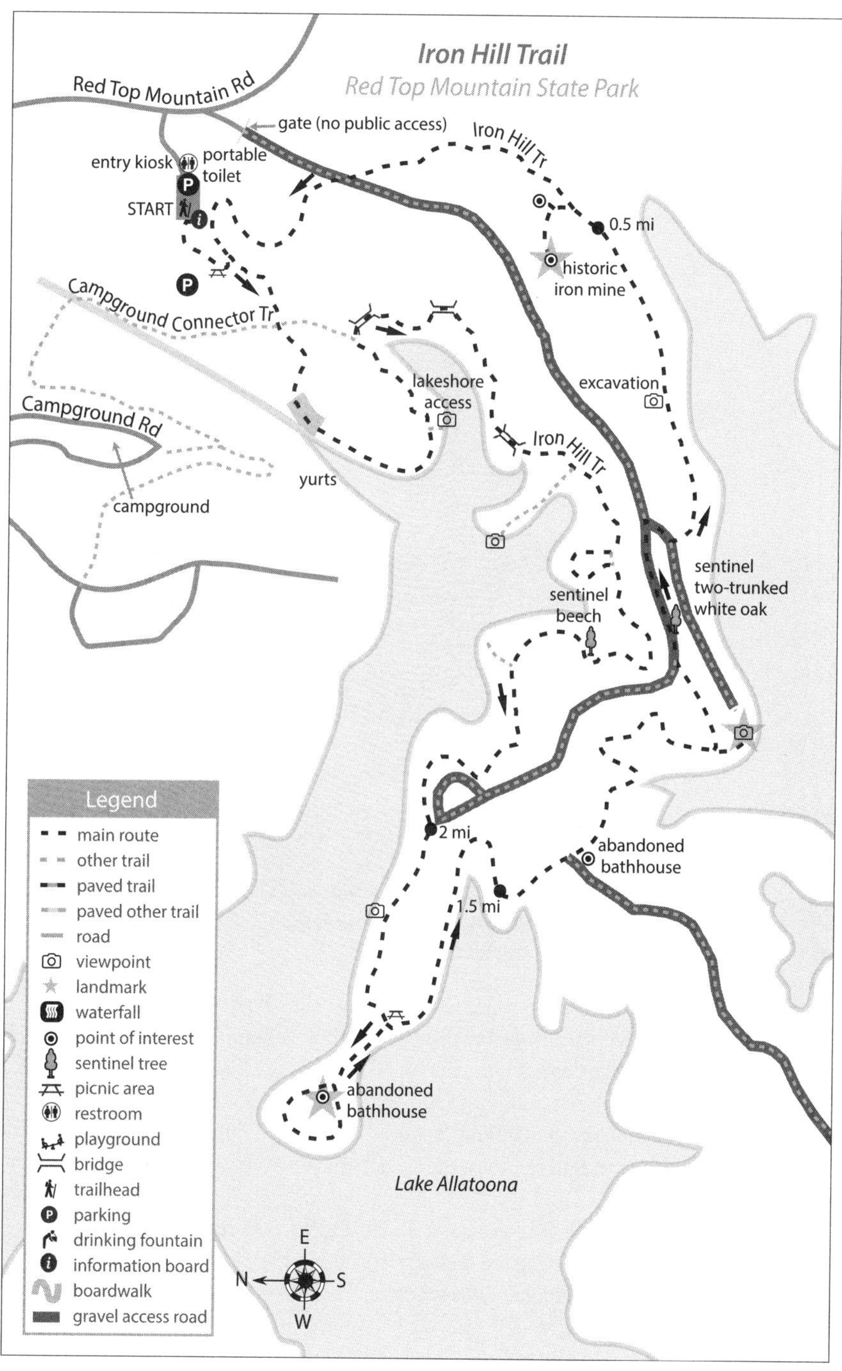
Iron Hill Trail
Red Top Mountain State Park
Red Top Mountain Rd
gate (no public access)
Iron Hill Tr
entry kiosk
portable toilet
START
0.5 mi
historic iron mine
Campground Connector Tr
lakeshore access
excavation
Campground Rd
Iron Hill Tr
yurts
campground
sentinel two-trunked white oak
sentinel beech
2 mi
abandoned bathhouse
1.5 mi
abandoned bathhouse
Lake Allatoona
Legend
main route
other trail
paved trail
paved other trail
road
viewpoint
landmark
waterfall
point of interest
sentinel tree
picnic area
restroom
playground
bridge
trailhead
parking
drinking fountain
information board
boardwalk
gravel access road
E
N
S
W

The steep cliffs of a canyon created by iron mining are visible from this trail.

Pass a bench and 1.5-mile marker in 0.3 mile. Then stay straight at a junction with an access road near another defunct bathhouse. Follow blue blazes to stay on Iron Hill Trail. In 0.3 mile, take a short right turn to visit a viewpoint of the lake that provides panoramic views, especially in the winter. Return to Iron Hill Trail, turn right, and follow the trail uphill to reach a wide access road where the trail turns right.

In 0.15 mile, follow blue blazes as the trail curves right on another old access road, then makes a sharp left near a bench. From here, the trail parallels the lake, with many unofficial trails leading down to the lake's edge. This part of the park was once an iron-mining community. You'll pass an excavated area on the left where you can see layers of soil. After passing the 0.5-mile marker, take the unofficial trail that leads left into a miniature canyon with steep walls created by the historic mining operation.

After marveling at the mine site, continue on Iron Hill Trail for 0.2 mile to cross a gravel access road and continue straight, following a large exit sign.

After 0.25 mile, reach a junction with the spur trail that leads back to the parking lot. Turn right and hike 0.1 mile back to your vehicle to end your hike.

The summit of Pine Mountain will make you jump for joy!

Pine Mountain Recreation Area

Though you may have visited the southwestern Georgia town of Pine Mountain on a trip to Callaway Gardens, the similarly named Pine Mountain Recreation Area in Cartersville is much closer to Atlanta and might even be more beautiful. Rocky trails, steep ascents, and fantastic views await you on Pine Mountain. Though most visitors only hike one trail, the City of Cartersville has developed a whole network of trails that provide an inspiring (and tiring) 5-mile loop across this beautiful mountain ridge. A spur trail on the east side of the mountain leads to Cooper's Furnace, where you can find even more trails near the Allatoona Dam.

HOW TO GET THERE	**Driving Distance from Downtown Atlanta:** 42 miles **Address:** 30 Komatsu Drive SE, Cartersville, GA 30121 **Closest Interstate:** I-75 **City, County:** Cartersville, Bartow **Parking:** Gravel parking area on the left, just before the entrance to the Komatsu facility
HIKE DISTANCE	5-mile figure-8 loop
DIFFICULTY	**Overall:** Strenuous **Navigation:** Map at trailhead, color-coded blazes, and signs at most junctions **Terrain:** Hard-packed dirt trails with lots of roots and rocks **Elevation Change:** Almost all steep ascents and descents
SAFETY	**Usage** ★★★★★ **Visibility** ★★★★☆ **Upkeep** ★★★★★ **Parking** ★★★★☆
HOURS	Dawn to dusk
DOGS	Leashed dogs allowed
FACILITIES	• Portable toilet in parking area • Fitness area, trail signs

FEES & PERMITS None

LAND MANAGER City of Cartersville Parks & Recreation

Landmarks

DAVID ARCHER OVERLOOK AT PINE MOUNTAIN SUMMIT

Though this summit is only 1,512 feet above sea level, the peak towers over 750 feet above much of the surrounding land. From here, you can see Sawnee Mountain to the east and Kennesaw Mountain to the south. The overlook is named for a Cartersville city attorney who was instrumental in helping the city acquire this recreation area.

SENTINEL CHESTNUT OAK

Chestnut oaks are a common tree species on rocky mountain slopes in north Georgia. This one is particularly gnarled and is an inviting climbing tree. Find the tree near a large rock cairn.

SENTINEL BEECH & LAUREL VALLEY

Pine Mountain is in a transitional area between the Blue Ridge Mountains and Atlanta's Piedmont region. This small cove contains many American beech trees, which are common in the Piedmont, and a large thicket of mountain laurels, which are more often found in the Appalachian Mountains. Look for the smooth gray bark of the beech and the twisted trunks and evergreen leaves of the laurels.

Hike Route

Start your hike near the information sign at the Main Street parking area and hike into the woods. Stay right and hike downhill to reach a bridge. Cross the bridge and hike 0.1 mile to reach a junction with Boot and Hiking Poles Trails.

Boot Trail is the popular and traditional route to the Pine Mountain summit, but we recommend using the less traveled Hiking Poles Trail to reach the summit for more solitude and natural beauty. Turn left on Hiking Poles Trail and follow blue blazes. In 0.25 mile, reach a series of switchbacks. Pass a rock viewpoint, maneuver past a small rock formation called "the squeeze," and continue the ascent. When the trail meets a wide junction, go left to continue hiking uphill, then make a sharp right at a metal sign that signifies the park boundary. In 0.15 mile, arrive at a junction with Boot Trail.

Turn left and hike 0.1 mile to a junction with David Archer Overlook Trail on the right. Turn right and hike 0.15 mile to the

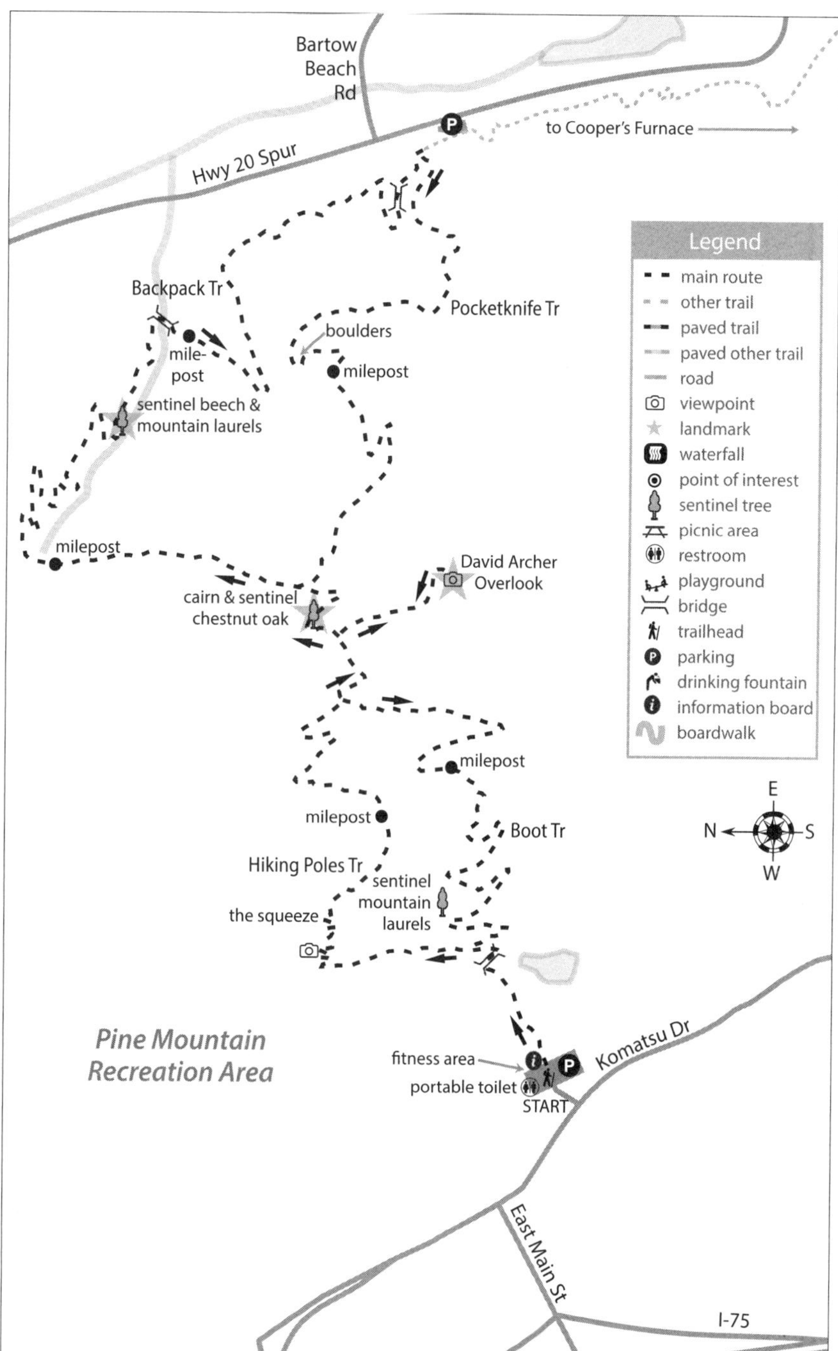
Bartow
Beach
Rd
to Cooper's Furnace
Hwy 20 Spur
Legend
main route
other trail
paved trail
paved other trail
road
viewpoint
landmark
waterfall
point of interest
sentinel tree
picnic area
restroom
playground
bridge
trailhead
parking
drinking fountain
information board
boardwalk
Backpack Tr
Pocketknife Tr
boulders
mile-
post
milepost
sentinel beech &
mountain laurels
milepost
David Archer
Overlook
cairn & sentinel
chestnut oak
milepost
E
N
S
W
milepost
Boot Tr
Hiking Poles Tr
sentinel
mountain
laurels
the squeeze
Pine Mountain
Recreation Area
fitness area
portable toilet
START
Komatsu Dr
East Main St
I-75

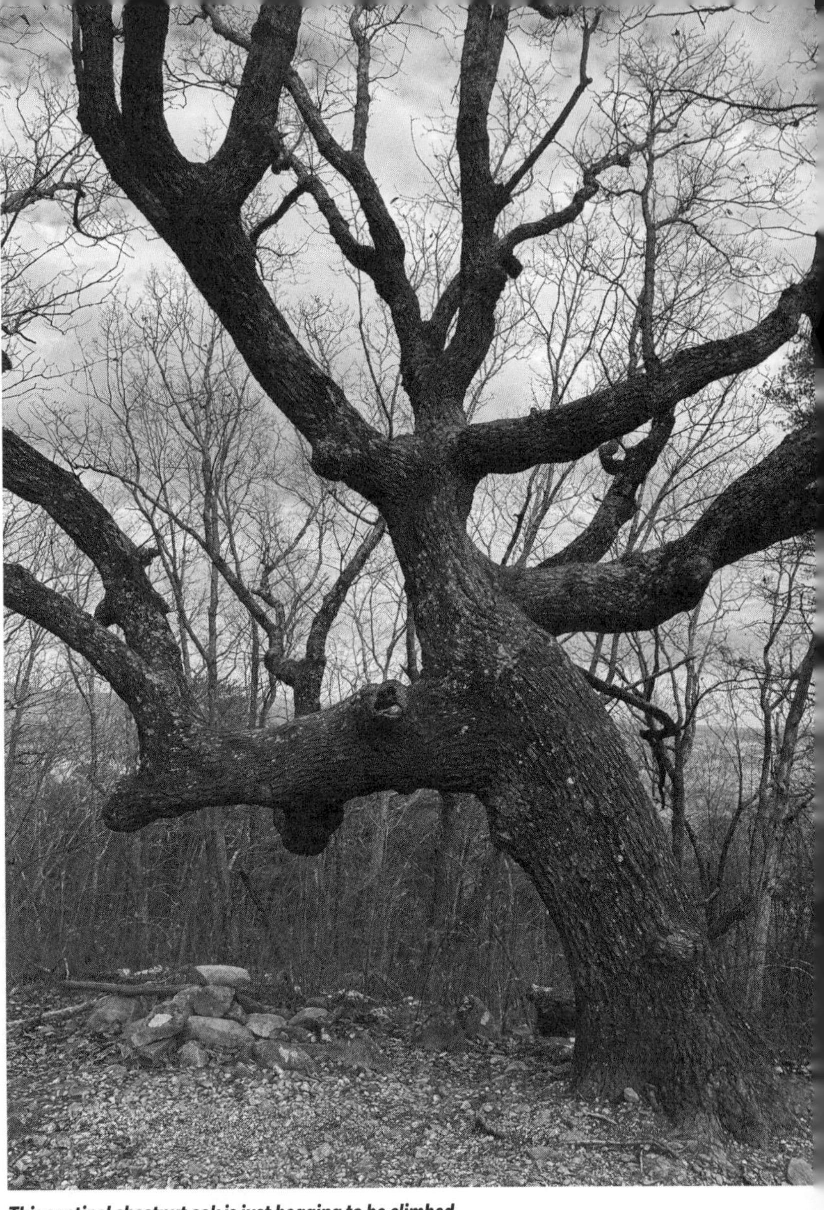

This sentinel chestnut oak is just begging to be climbed.

summit, where you'll find views of Sawnee Mountain (p. 299) and Kennesaw Mountain (p. 193) in the distance.

Return to the junction and turn right to hike the eastern loop, with white and yellow blazes. Arrive at a giant cairn (pile of rocks) near a sentinel chestnut oak tree, which is gnarled and great for climbing. Continue on the trail, staying right, to reach the Backpack and Pocketknife Trails junction. Turn left on Backpack Trail and hike downhill, following yellow blazes.

In 0.35 mile, the descent steepens and the trail switchbacks. Please stay on the trail and do not cut the switchbacks. After almost 0.5 mile of hiking, the trail begins to parallel a seasonal creek in a beautiful cove filled with young American beech trees and mountain laurel shrubs. Cross two bridges, then the trail ascends for a bit, then descends again. In another 0.5 mile, cross a small bridge, then reach a junction with Pocketknife Trail and the Spur 20 parking area near an emergency call box. Turn sharply right to hike uphill on Pocketknife Trail, following white blazes.

In 0.4 mile, the trail makes a hard left near some interesting boulders. Continue hiking uphill for another 0.4 mile to reach the junction with Backpack Trail. Go left and hike uphill toward the David Archer Overlook junction. Pass the chestnut oak and cairn again, then go straight at the junction with David Archer Overlook Trail. In 0.1 mile, reach the junction with Boot Trail, turn left, and follow the red blazes.

Boot Trail is very eroded, with many roots and rocks. Switchback down the mountain for 0.75 mile, passing through several thickets of mountain laurels. At the junction with Hiking Poles Trail, turn left to hike 0.2 mile to the Main Street parking area to end your hike.

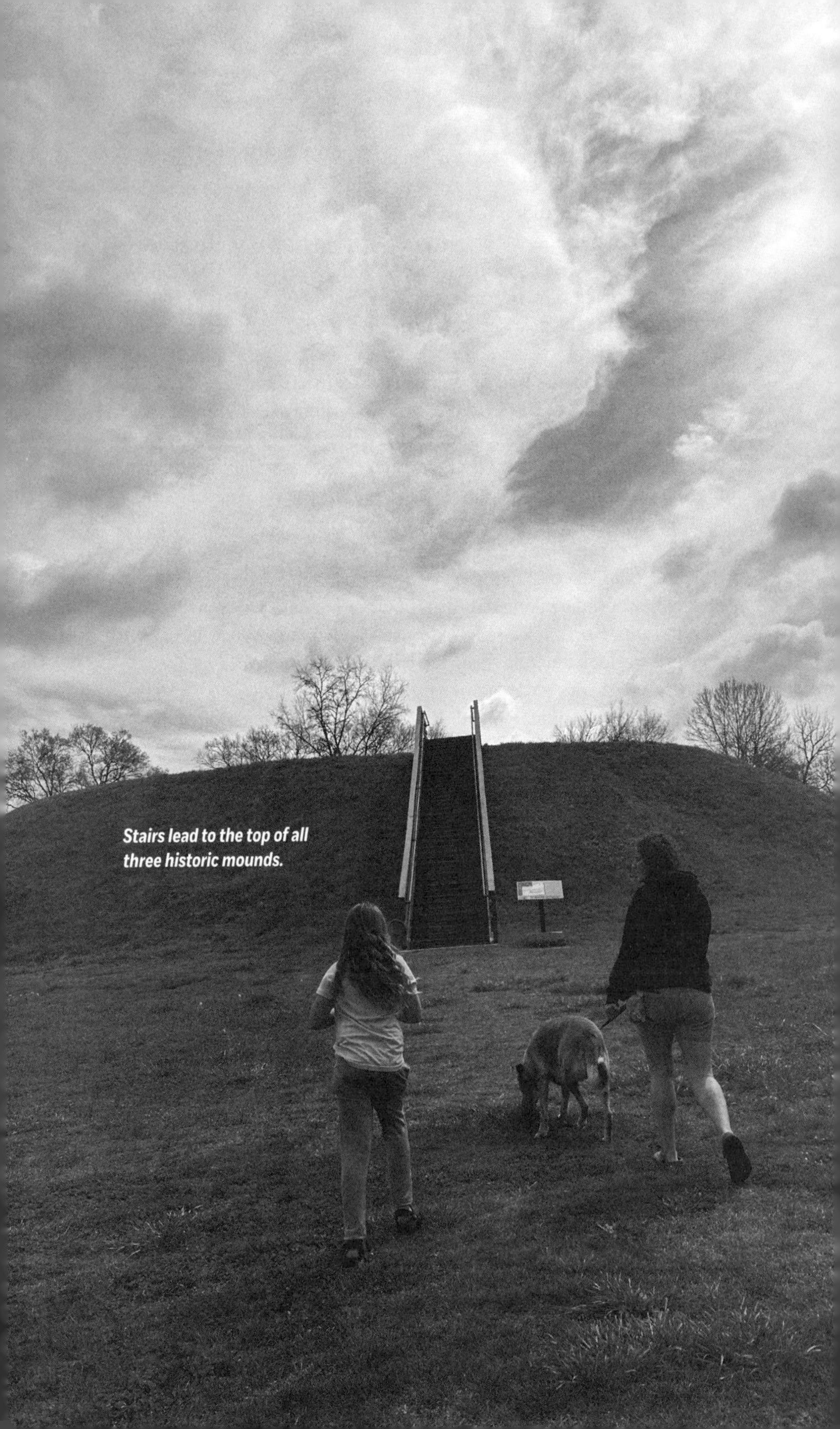

Stairs lead to the top of all three historic mounds.

Etowah Indian Mounds State Historic Site

Though not as forested as most other hikes in this book, this state historic site is absolutely worth a visit to experience the intersection of hiking, nature, and history. One unique thing about this hike is that the trails are flat and easy, but the mounds offer heart-pumping stair climbs. On this figure-8 loop, you'll visit a six-story-tall, 1,000-year-old mound, several smaller mounds, the pits from which mound builders excavated the dirt, a re-created fish weir, and breathtaking views at every turn.

HOW TO GET THERE

Driving Distance from Downtown Atlanta: 44 miles
Address: 813 Indian Mound Road SE, Cartersville, GA 30120
Closest Interstate: I-75
City, County: Cartersville, Bartow
Parking: Paved, gated parking area

HIKE DISTANCE

2.25-mile figure-8 loop

DIFFICULTY

Overall: Easy to moderate
Navigation: No blazes or navigation markers, but trails are wide and relatively easy to follow
Terrain: Grass, mulch, and boardwalk trails, with steep stairs leading up onto mounds
Elevation Change: Minimal elevation change except for steep stairs leading to the top of each mound

SAFETY

Usage ★★★★★
Visibility ★★★★★
Upkeep ★★★★★
Parking ★★★★★

HOURS

Museum open 9:00 am to 5:00 pm daily except Thanksgiving, Christmas, and New Year's Day; trails close at 4:30 pm

DOGS

Leashed dogs allowed on trails

FACILITIES	• Toilets in museum • Interpretive signs, artifacts, museum, picnic tables, and benches
FEES & PERMITS	Adults (18-61): $6.00; seniors (62+): $4.50; youth (6-17): $4.00; children (under 6): $2.00
LAND MANAGER	Georgia State Parks & Historic Sites

Landmarks

MOUND A

This 63-foot-tall, flat-topped mound was where the community's chief once lived. It was also a ceremonial site. From here, you can see other mounds, the river, and surrounding farmlands and houses. It's a fantastic spot.

FISHING WEIR

For millennia, humans have used rock weirs (usually shaped like a U, V, or W) to funnel fish in the river into traps they have placed. The rocks of this re-created weir are visible in low water conditions, but you can see the V-shaped ripples in the water at other times.

BORROW PIT

In order to build these giant mounds, people had to excavate dirt from somewhere else. The defensive ditches and borrow pits through which you hike are a historical feature almost as intriguing as the mounds themselves.

Hike Route

Before your hike, visit the museum to view artifacts, models of the mounds, and a short video presentation about the history of southeastern indigenous groups. After exploring the museum, start your hike at the rear doors and hike across the bridge over the defensive ditch. Walk straight across the field along the grassy trail toward the towering Mound A.

Pass several interpretive signs before arriving at the base of Mound A, where the community's leader would have lived. Climb the long staircase to the flat top of the mound and circle around the top, taking in views from all directions. You can see why someone would want to live up here.

Descend the stairs, then turn right and hike to Mound B. After using the stairs to visit the top of this smaller mound, hike left

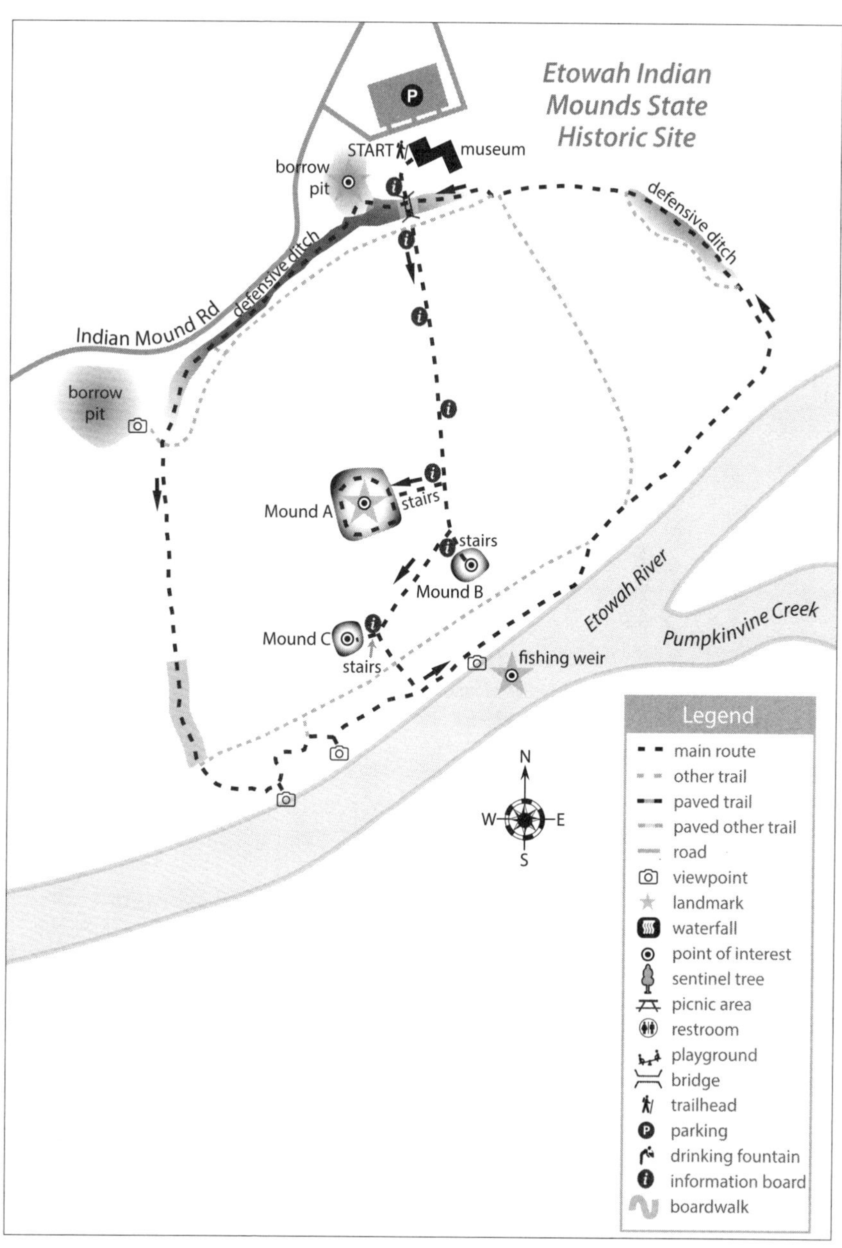
Etowah Indian Mounds State Historic Site
START
museum
borrow pit
defensive ditch
Indian Mound Rd
defensive ditch
borrow pit
Mound A
stairs
stairs
Mound B
Mound C
stairs
Etowah River
Pumpkinvine Creek
fishing weir
N
W
E
S
Legend
main route
other trail
paved trail
paved other trail
road
viewpoint
landmark
waterfall
point of interest
sentinel tree
picnic area
restroom
playground
bridge
trailhead
parking
drinking fountain
information board
boardwalk

The open fields of Etowah Indian Mounds provide a hiking environment different from any other place in this book.

to Mound C, which is a reconstruction of a burial mound. After ascending and descending this final mound, turn right and hike directly toward the Etowah River.

At the water's edge, turn left and hike among many big trees to a spot just before a leaning sycamore tree, where you get a view of the V-shaped ripples in the river caused by a fish weir. Then continue straight along the river until passing the last set of benches. Bear left toward a small utility building and then turn right onto a wide grass and gravel path that doubles as a service road. The gravel service road curves left, but this route stays straight, parallel to the tree line, on a grassy trail.

Curve left when the trail reaches a chain-link fence. The trail then dips into a depression that was dug for defensive purposes. In 0.1 mile, emerge from the defensive ditch and continue hiking along the fenceline until you reach the service road and a gate near the museum. You can end your hike here, but we highly recommend completing the final leg of this hike.

Bear right and hike downhill into the defensive ditch, under the bridge, and through a wide borrow pit where dirt was excavated to build the mounds. Generally curve left and continue hiking through the narrow defensive ditch for 0.1 mile, where you'll reach a junction and great view of Mound A. Continue straight through another wooden depression before reaching a wooden observation deck over the largest borrow pit.

Continue straight between trees and then onto a 100-yard boardwalk. When the boardwalk ends, the trail curves left through the woods. Pass two nice views of the river on your right before reaching a sign for Etowah River Walk Nature Trail. Turn left and hike into the grassy field to Mound C. Retrace your original route from Mound C to Mound B to Mound A, then back to the museum to end your hike.

I-575 NORTH

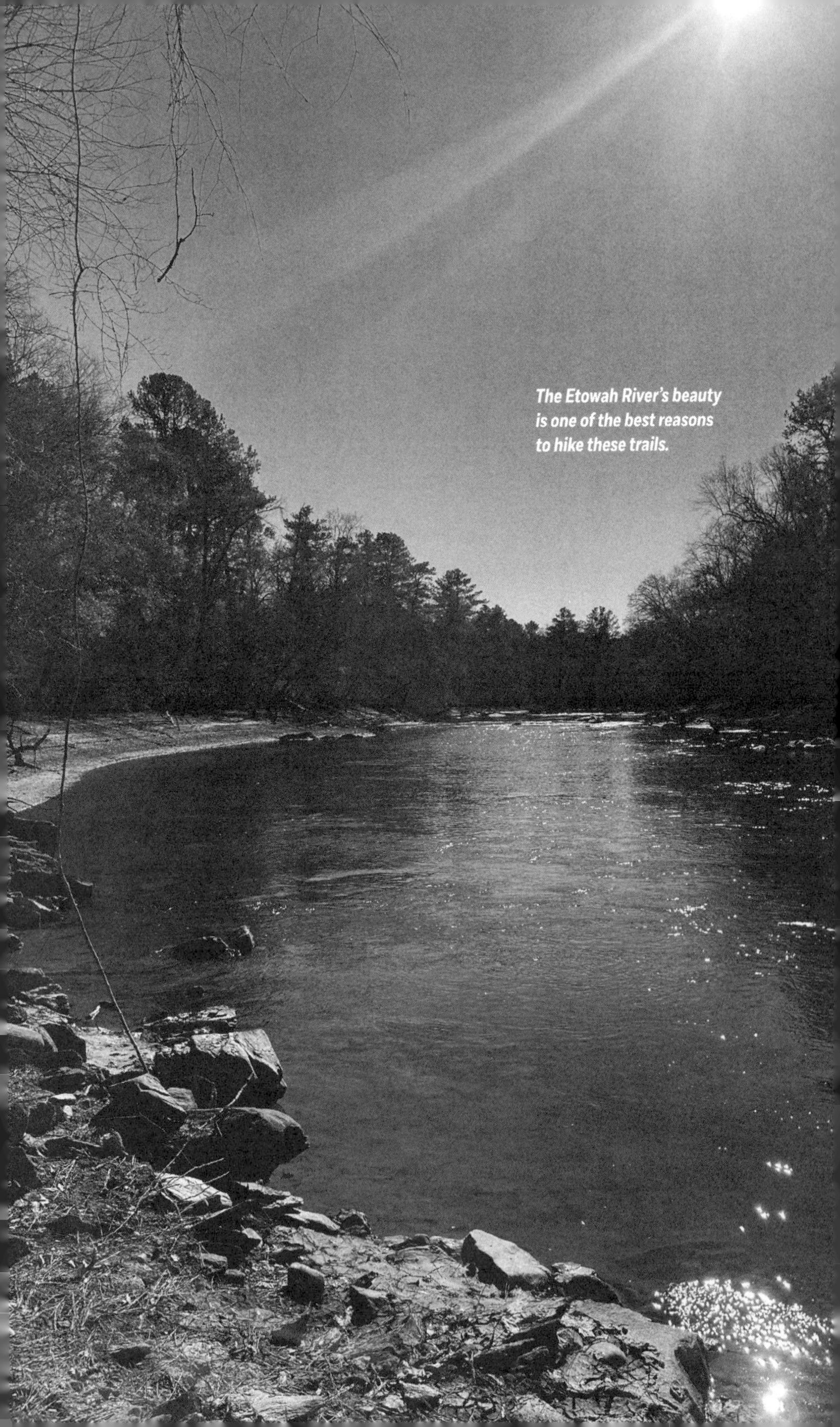

The Etowah River's beauty is one of the best reasons to hike these trails.

Etowah Hiking Trails

This extensive network of trails in the Appalachian foothills provides everything a hiker could ask for: over 14 miles of well-marked trails, natural beauty, unique landmarks, and historical intrigue. The trailhead is located behind Cherokee High School, tucked into a corner of Boling Park, but don't let the entrance fool you—this greenspace along the Etowah River is one of the most beautiful hikes in the Atlanta metro area.

HOW TO GET THERE

Driving Distance from Downtown Atlanta: 41 miles

Address: Boling Park, 1200 Marietta Highway, Canton, GA 30114

Closest Interstate: I-575

City, County: Canton, Cherokee

Parking: Paved parking area in Boling Park behind Cherokee High School; parking closest to the trailhead is near the picnic pavilion

HIKE DISTANCE

7.3-mile loop

DIFFICULTY

Overall: Strenuous

Navigation: Map at trailhead, color-coded blazes for each trail, and signs at most junctions

Terrain: Hard-packed dirt or gravel trails with bridges over creeks; some areas can be muddy

Elevation Change: Rolling hills with short but steep ascents and descents

SAFETY

Usage ★★★☆☆

Visibility ★★★☆☆

Upkeep ★★★★☆

Parking ★★★★☆

HOURS

Dawn to dusk

DOGS

No dogs allowed in Boling Park; leashed dogs allowed on Etowah Hiking Trails

FACILITIES
- Portable toilet near parking
- Drinking fountain, picnic pavilion

FEES & PERMITS None

LAND MANAGER Boling Park managed by City of Canton Parks & Recreation; Etowah Trails land managed by Cherokee County Water & Sewer and U.S. Army Corps of Engineers

Landmarks

NEW HIGHTOWER BAPTIST CHURCH

Hightower Baptist Church was first built in the 1880s but was destroyed by vandals and then rebuilt in 1991 in the spot you now see it. The church got the undeserving nickname "Hell's Church" by local teens who told stories of hauntings and drownings in the church's baptismal pool.

SUTALLEE TRACE

The first settlement in north Georgia by European colonizers was centered around a road called Sutallee Trace along the Etowah River. As you walk this section of the trail, you can see the engineering that went into building and maintaining the road.

ETOWAH RIVER AND ROCK CARVINGS

This sloping stone along the Etowah River has many carvings, some dating as far back as the 1890s. This is a great place to view the river and marvel at the long history of human interaction with the land.

Hike Route

Begin your hike at the information board adjacent to the parking lot nearest to the picnic pavilion in Boling Park. Take the white blazed hiking trail to your left when facing the info board. This is Trace Trail, and it parallels the open fields of Boling Park for 0.7 mile, when you'll arrive at the unusually engineered Frank Stone Bridge over Pucket Creek.

Cross the bridge, and you'll see an unofficial trail on the left that leads to the banks of the Etowah River. This is a nice spot to get your first view of the river. Continue on the white-blazed Trace Trail for 50 feet before arriving at a junction with Yellow Trail on your right.

Turn right and hike uphill on Yellow Trail. This trail winds

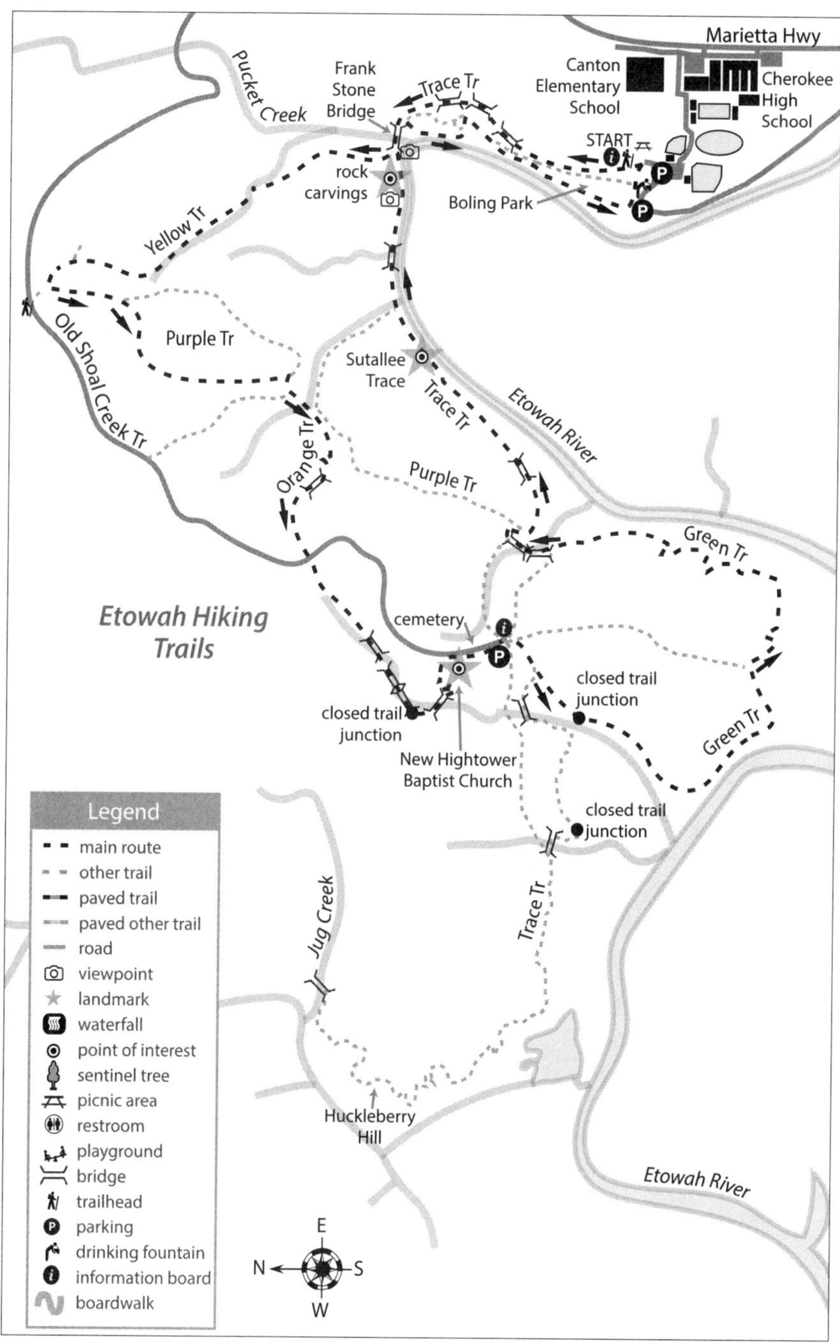

Marietta Hwy
Canton Elementary School
Cherokee High School
START
Boling Park
Frank Stone Bridge
Trace Tr
Pucket Creek
rock carvings
Yellow Tr
Purple Tr
Old Shoal Creek Tr
Sutallee Trace
Trace Tr
Etowah River
Orange Tr
Purple Tr
Green Tr
Etowah Hiking Trails
cemetery
closed trail junction
closed trail junction
New Hightower Baptist Church
Green Tr
closed trail junction
Trace Tr
Jug Creek
Huckleberry Hill
Etowah River
Legend
main route
other trail
paved trail
paved other trail
road
viewpoint
landmark
waterfall
point of interest
sentinel tree
picnic area
restroom
playground
bridge
trailhead
parking
drinking fountain
information board
boardwalk
E
N
S
W

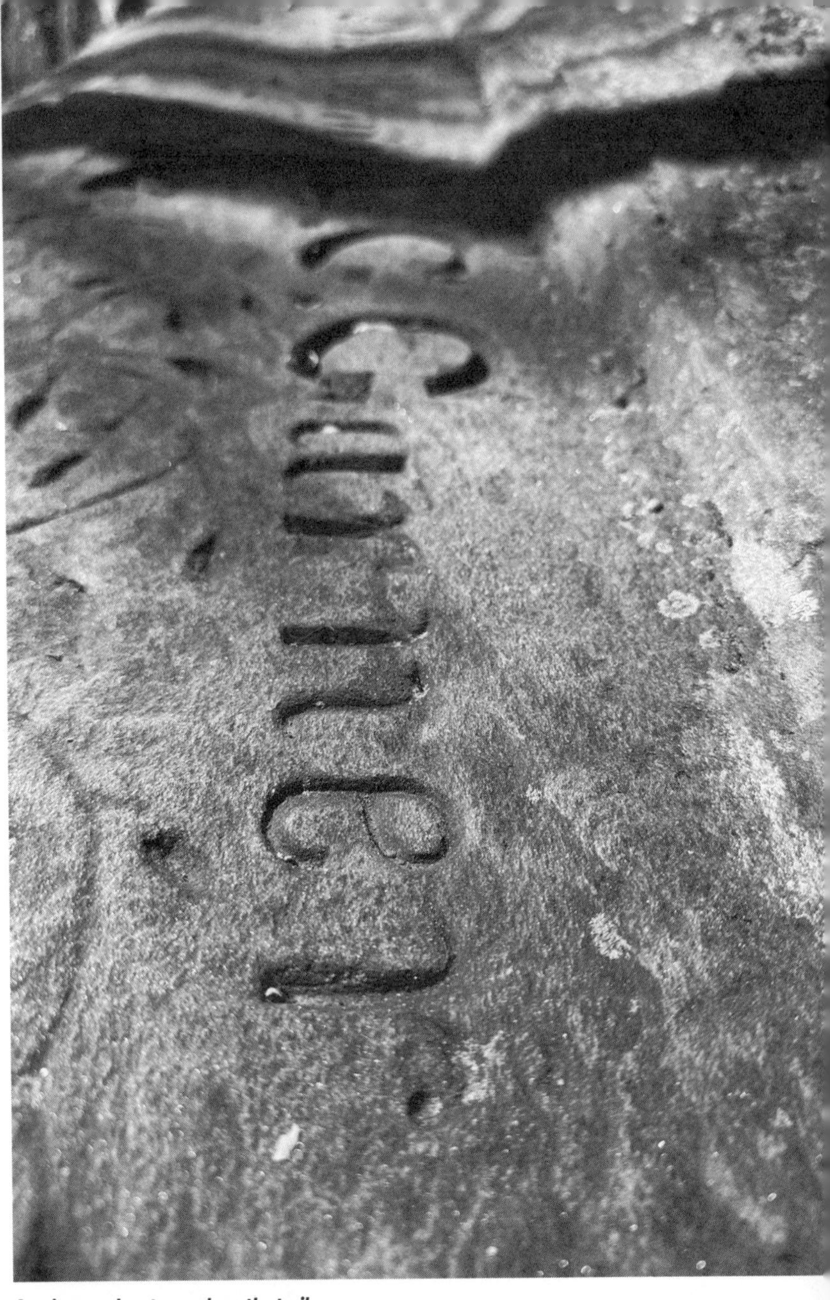

A unique rock outcrop along the trail has carvings from the 1890s.

through a mature forest with a small creek and past some areas of clearcut forest for 1 mile. There are a few unofficial trails on the right, so be sure to follow the yellow blazes. When you reach a junction with Purple Trail, turn left.

In 0.15 mile, Purple Trail splits. Take the right fork and hike downhill. Enter a clearcut section of forest as the trail generally follows a small creek. This part of the hike can be sunny and hot. In 0.3 mile, reach a logging road and turn right. Then, in 100 yards, turn left off the logging road to stay on Purple Trail for 100 more yards, when you'll reach a junction with Orange Trail.

Turn right on Orange Trail and hike 0.4 mile to reach Johnson Trail road. Cross this paved road and continue on Orange Trail through another clearcut section. In another 0.4 mile, reach a trail junction sign with the former route of Orange Trail (now closed) on the right. Stay straight on Orange Trail; a sign is marked N'H'Tower Church. The trail crosses a creek and then switchbacks up the ridge to arrive at the paved road near New Hightower Baptist Church. Turn right and hike on the asphalt between the church and the cemetery, past a gravel parking area, and then around a white metal fence to arrive at an information board and junction with Trace Trail and Green Trail.

Facing this information board, you'll see three trails on your right. Take the middle trail, labeled with green and white blazes. In 0.1 mile, come to another junction and go left on Green Trail. (If you want to add 4 more miles to your hike, you can take a right to continue 2 miles on Trace Trail to reach Jug Creek, then backtrack to this junction.)

In 0.5 mile, Green Trail curves left along a bluff above the Etowah River. In winter and spring, the gorgeous river is visible through the leafless trees. If you look to your right, you might find an unofficial trail that can lead you closer to the river.

Ascend the ridge and come to a forest road in 0.5 mile. Cross to continue on Green Trail for another 0.8 mile, then reach a junction with white-blazed Trace Trail. Turn right and hike 0.1 mile to reach the historic Sutallee Trace. Turn right and then cross an old forest road, staying straight on Trace Trail, which parallels the old Sutallee Trace just below you. In 0.15 mile, stay straight at a junction with Purple Trail.

This next section of trail is very scenic, as the trail follows the route of the Sutallee Trace on the banks of the Etowah River. In 0.4 mile, reach a junction with Orange Trail near a rocky creek. There is a small cascade here, and you can see the stonework remains of a historic bridge foundation. Cross the creek and curve right to stay on Trace Trail. In 0.3 mile, reach a great view of the river and a sloping rock with names from the 1800s etched into it.

Beyond the rock 100 yards, pass Yellow Trail junction, then cross Frank Stone Bridge again. Turn right at the first trail after the bridge to enter Boling Park and walk the wide path back to the parking lot to end your hike. Alternatively (particularly if you have a dog with you), you can also hike Trace Trail parallel to Boling Park to return to the parking lot.

GA 400 NORTH

Big Trees Forest Preserve really lives up to its name.

Big Trees Forest Preserve

Just off the busy thoroughfare of Roswell Road you can get a glimpse of how Atlanta looked before white settlers arrived—rolling hills, steep-banked creeks, and big trees. Unfortunately, this area of Sandy Springs was quickly urbanizing, and this land was slated to become a car dealership in the 1980s. Luckily, John Ripley Forbes (who also helped establish the Outdoor Activity Center and the Chattahoochee Nature Center [p. 257]) led a push to save this forest. Today it stands as a testament to Forbes's memory, and the park's official full name is John Ripley Forbes Big Trees Forest Preserve.

HOW TO GET THERE

Driving Distance from Downtown Atlanta: 19 miles

Address: 7645 Roswell Road NE, Sandy Springs, GA 30350

Closest Highway: GA 400

City, County: Sandy Springs, Fulton

Public Transit: MARTA 87 bus stops one block from the park entrance

Parking: Large paved parking area shared with the North Fulton Government Service Center

HIKE DISTANCE

1.25-mile loop

DIFFICULTY

Overall: Easy

Navigation: Posts at most junctions

Terrain: Some paved trail, but mostly hard-packed dirt trail

Elevation Change: Rolling hills with an extended ascent and descent on Backcountry Trail

SAFETY

Usage ★★★★☆

Visibility ★★★★☆

Upkeep ★★★★★

Parking ★★★★★

HOURS

Dawn to dusk

DOGS

Leashed dogs allowed

FACILITIES

- Toilets at trailhead near information board
- Water fountain, dog waste station, benches

FEES & PERMITS

None

LAND MANAGER Sandy Springs Parks & Recreation in partnership with Big Trees Forest Preserve, Inc.

Landmarks

SENTINEL WHITE OAK

This white oak stands alone next to the trail and is the first truly big tree you'll pass after leaving the pavement.

SENTINEL BEECH GROVE

Pass by several large sentinel beech trees along the creek. Beech trees can live for several hundred years, and based on the size of these trees, you can estimate they've lived a long life.

SENTINEL WHITE OAK

This tree is interesting because of the resurrection ferns, which live symbiotically with white oaks, growing on its branches. These ferns look dry and dead during times of little precipitation but become green and lush after rain.

Hike Route

Start your hike on the paved path next to the restrooms and information kiosk, passing a seating area on your right. Once the paved trail reaches the mulch path, go right and pass the large sentinel white oak on your right.

In 100 feet, come to a four-way junction. Stay straight and hike downhill and along the creek, reaching a section with three incredibly large beech trees on your right. When this trail reconnects with Big Trees Loop, look to the left for a large sentinel white oak whose branches are covered in resurrection ferns.

Turn right onto Powers Branch Trail. At the junction with Back 20 Connector Trail, go right again over a bridge. Turn right onto Backcountry Trail. Over the next 0.3 mile, the trail curves left and then ascends, passing young hemlock trees and buckeyes to reach the highest point in the park. As the trail begins to descend from the ridge, it switches back once before reaching a junction with Spring Hollow Trail in 0.2 mile. Continue straight for another 0.1 mile to a junction signed To Entrance with a seating area. Continue straight past this trail for 0.1 mile to once again reach

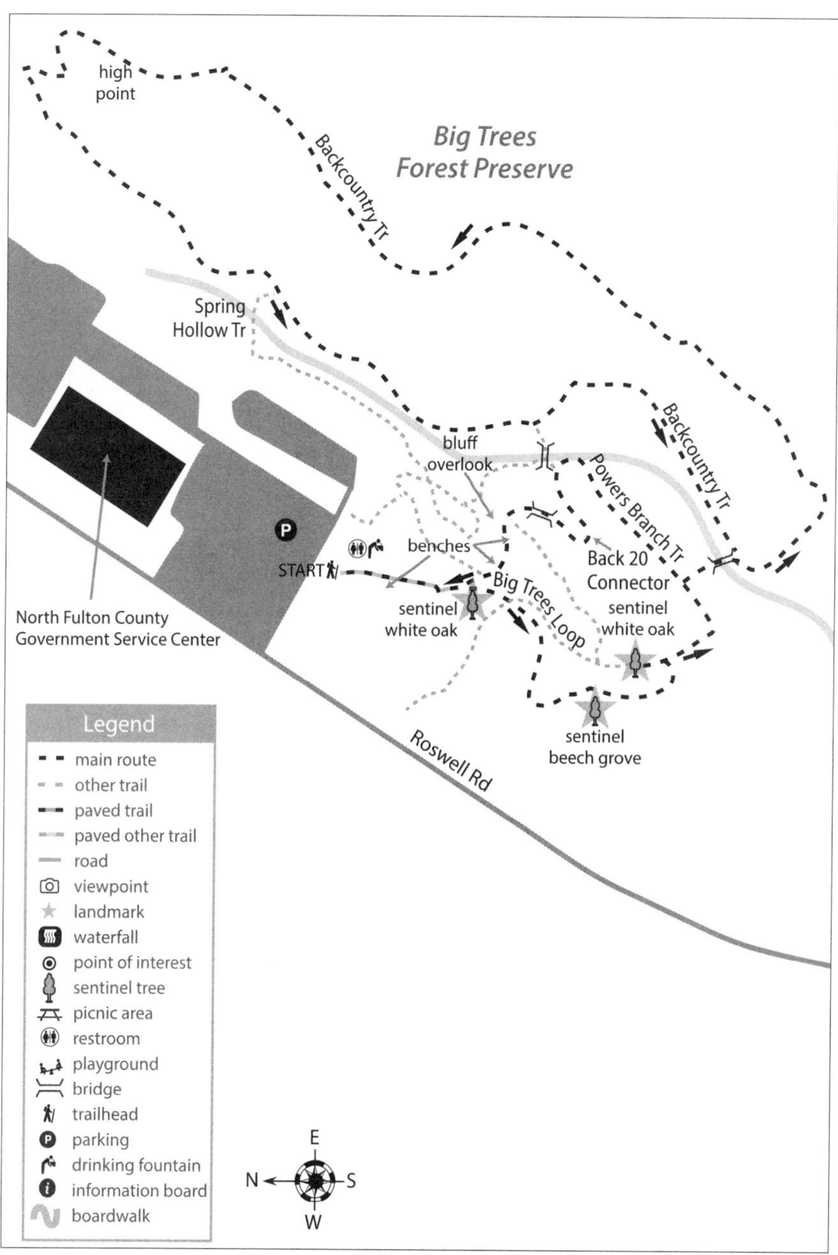
high point
Big Trees Forest Preserve
Backcountry Tr
Spring Hollow Tr
bluff overlook
Powers Branch Tr
Backcountry Tr
benches
Back 20 Connector
START
Big Trees Loop
sentinel white oak
sentinel white oak
North Fulton County Government Service Center
sentinel beech grove
Roswell Rd
Legend
main route
other trail
paved trail
paved other trail
road
viewpoint
landmark
waterfall
point of interest
sentinel tree
picnic area
restroom
playground
bridge
trailhead
parking
drinking fountain
information board
boardwalk
E
N
S
W

Backcountry Loop traverses the highest point of the forest.

the Backcountry Connector Trail junction. Turn right, cross the bridge, and turn right onto Powers Branch Trail.

In 100 yards at a junction with Back 20 Connector Trail near a bridge, go left and wind uphill. Cross a small boardwalk, then reach the Big Trees Loop and a bluff overlook. Go right, regain the paved path, and finish your hike at the parking lot in 0.1 mile.

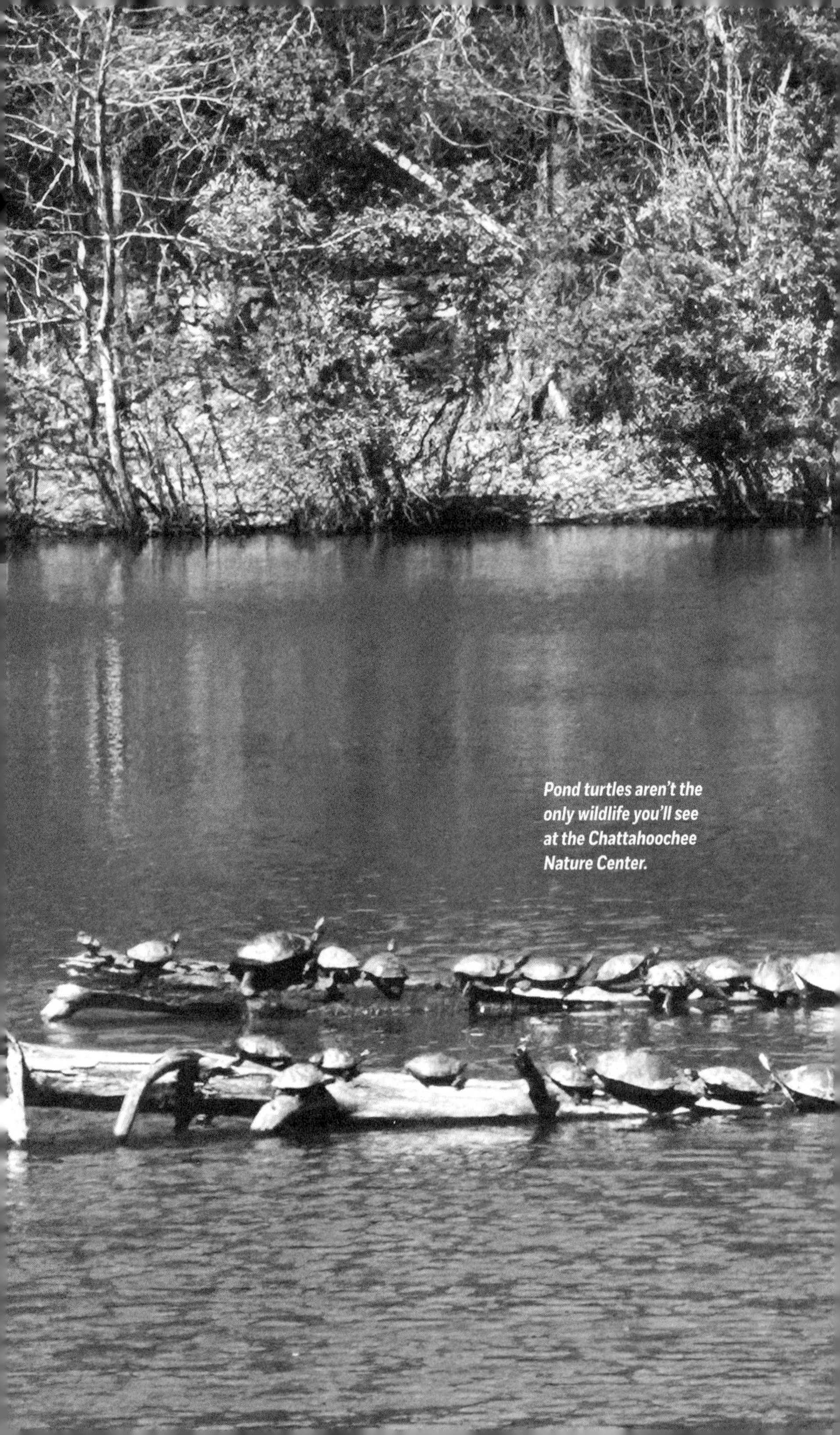

Pond turtles aren't the only wildlife you'll see at the Chattahoochee Nature Center.

Chattahoochee Nature Center

This is one of the most visited environmental facilities for school field trips, but it is also a fantastic hiking destination. You'll be excited to rediscover the Chattahoochee Nature Center, which has more than 2 miles of trails and a memorable boardwalk along the river. Along the route, you'll pass birds of prey, a live beaver, ponds, and historic sites. If you want to extend your hike, the Willeo Road Trail is just outside the gates of the center.

HOW TO GET THERE

Driving Distance from Downtown Atlanta: 24 miles
Address: 9135 Willeo Road, Roswell, GA 30075
Closest Highway: GA 400
City, County: Roswell, Fulton
Parking: Large paved parking area

HIKE DISTANCE

2.25-mile double figure-8 loop

DIFFICULTY

Overall: Easy to moderate
Navigation: Trail markers at most junctions; some painted blazes; trails are generally wide and easy to follow
Terrain: Paved, boardwalk, and dirt trails
Elevation Change: Mostly flat with a few minor hills on Forest and Homestead Trails

SAFETY

Usage ★★★★★
Visibility ★★★★★
Upkeep ★★★★★
Parking ★★★★★

HOURS

Monday through Saturday, 10:00 am to 5:00 pm; Sunday, 12:00 pm to 5:00 pm (see website for extended hours during certain school breaks)

DOGS

Dogs not allowed

FACILITIES

- Toilets in discovery center and at pavilion near Kingfisher Pond
- Picnic tables, water fountain, interpretive signs, animal exhibits, outdoor classrooms

FEES & PERMITS	Adults: $20; seniors (65+) and students (13-18): $16; children (3-12): $14; children (under 2): free
LAND MANAGER	Chattahoochee Nature Center

Landmarks

RAPTOR AVIARIES

Getting to see birds of prey up close is thrilling. Because the Chattahoochee Nature Center rehabs wild animals, you have the opportunity to view nonreleasable eagles, hawks, owls, and vultures on this trail.

HOMESTEAD RUINS

The stone chimney and grave on Forest Trail are two of the only remaining signs of human use of this land, which was initially stewarded by Muscogee people, then became home to the Kelpin family, and later became a vacation getaway.

RIVER BOARDWALK

One of the newest trails at the Chattahoochee Nature Center, this boardwalk is a fantastic amenity. Gaze down at the river, pond, and marsh from the highest point of the boardwalk, then continue your walk through the marsh and along the riverbank on this amazing trail.

Hike Route

Start your hike from the discovery center, where you'll pay the entry fee. Be sure to get the gate code from the staff member who checks you in. Exit the building on the lower level and follow a sign for Wildlife Walk to the left on a curving path that leads slightly downhill. Pass two raptor enclosures, then follow this paved path as it curves downhill and passes stairs twice before arriving at a large pavilion.

Stay left at the pavilion to continue hiking through the raptor aviaries. Pass bald eagles, vultures, owls, and hawks before arriving at a side trail to the beaver habitat. Take this short out-and-back trail to see this amazing animal, then continue straight when you return to this junction.

The paved path ends near a dirt trail on the edge of Beaver Pond. Turn right and hike along the dam and across a wooden bridge to reach a junction with Beaver Pond Trail. Turn left and hike this out-and-back trail to read the book posted on the Story Stroll and

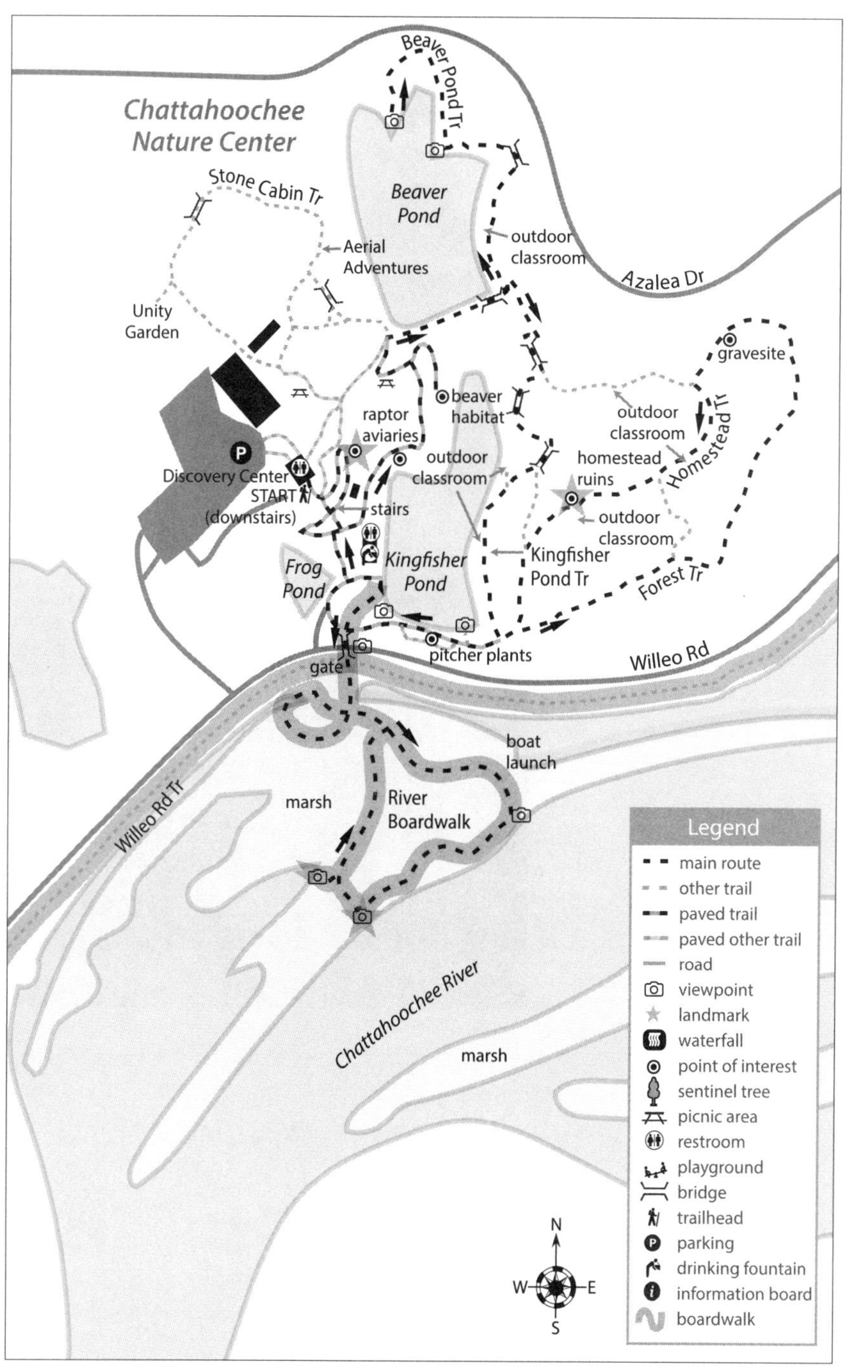

Chattahoochee Nature Center
Beaver Pond Tr
Stone Cabin Tr
Beaver Pond
Aerial Adventures
outdoor classroom
Azalea Dr
Unity Garden
gravesite
beaver habitat
raptor aviaries
outdoor classroom
homestead ruins
Homestead Tr
outdoor classroom
Discovery Center
START
(downstairs)
stairs
outdoor classroom
Frog Pond
Kingfisher Pond
Kingfisher Pond Tr
Forest Tr
pitcher plants
gate
Willeo Rd
boat launch
marsh
River Boardwalk
Willeo Rd Tr
Chattahoochee River
marsh
Legend
main route
other trail
paved trail
paved other trail
road
viewpoint
landmark
waterfall
point of interest
sentinel tree
picnic area
restroom
playground
bridge
trailhead
parking
drinking fountain
information board
boardwalk
N
W
E
S

A Cooper's hawk is one of the birds of prey you'll see in the raptor aviaries.

see several scenic views of the pond. Turn back at the bench and viewpoint at the far end of the pond.

Back at the junction with Kingfisher Pond Trail, turn left and cross a power line clearing before hiking downhill. Stay right at each trail junction until the trail begins to parallel the water's edge. Walk through a large outdoor classroom area and finally arrive at a junction with Forest Trail on the left and a paved path on the right.

Turn left and hike uphill on Forest Trail, bearing right at an immediate junction. Hike 0.3 mile on Forest Trail, staying right at the one junction you pass. After passing a historic gravesite and interpretive sign, turn left at a junction with Homestead Trail. In only 100 yards, pass a two-story chimney from a house that used to stand here. Continue downhill, back to the junction with Forest Trail.

Turn right and continue onto the paved path at the edge of Kingfisher Pond. Pass a pitcher plant bog. The trail then curves under a bridge and meets a service road near Frog Pond and a large pavilion. Turn right, then right again to access the elevated boardwalk. Follow the boardwalk ramp up and over Willeo Road to the high point, where there's a bench and viewpoint of the river and wetlands. Continue on the boardwalk as it curves down to a gate near Willeo Road. You'll have to punch in the gate code to access River Boardwalk Trail. Turn right after the gate and hike the boardwalk loop, passing several fantastic viewpoints on the Chattahoochee River.

Back at the gate, you can exit Chattahoochee Nature Center property and hike the Willeo Road Trail along the Chattahoochee, if you want to extend your hike. Otherwise, use the code to enter the gate on the left to ramp back up and over Willeo Road and back to the pavilion. Walk the painted stairs back up to the discovery center, where you'll end your hike.

Spring ephemerals like this mayapple thrive in this healthy forest.

Gold Branch

CHATTAHOOCHEE RIVER NATIONAL RECREATION AREA

Though it is not as popular as some of the other units of the Chattahoochee River National Recreation Area, Gold Branch is one of the best. Nestled in a relatively undeveloped area of Roswell, Gold Branch contains rolling hills covered with hardwood forest and waterside trails teeming with birds and other wildlife. This stretch of the river is just upstream from Morgan Falls Dam, so the river is wide, the water is still, marsh grasses flourish, and ducks, geese, herons, and kingfishers abound. It is unusual to see such natural diversity in a 3.5-mile hike.

HOW TO GET THERE

Driving Distance from Downtown Atlanta: 22 miles
Address: 6156 Lower Roswell Road, Marietta, GA 30068
Closest Highway: GA 400
City, County: Near Roswell, in Cobb County
Parking: Paved parking area at the end of a short access road off Lower Roswell Road

HIKE DISTANCE

3.5-mile loop

DIFFICULTY

Overall: Moderate
Navigation: Trail maps posted at each junction
Terrain: Hard-packed dirt trails with lots of roots and rocks
Elevation Change: Rolling hills with a few short but steep ascents and descents

SAFETY

Usage ★★★★☆
Visibility ★★★★☆
Upkeep ★★★★★
Parking ★★★★☆

HOURS

Dawn to dusk

DOGS

Leashed dogs allowed

FACILITIES

- No toilets
- Information board, one picnic table

FEES & PERMITS $5 daily fee—purchase at recreation.gov

LAND MANAGER Chattahoochee River National Recreation Area—National Park Service

Landmarks

RIVER MARSH VIEWPOINT

A series of islands and channels produce a haven for water birds on the marshy edge of the river. If you're lucky, you might see herons, ospreys, cormorants, mergansers, mallards, and many songbirds from this viewpoint.

MORGAN FALLS DAM

One of the reasons this trail is so beautiful is because the river slows and widens here, just above Morgan Falls Dam. From this spot on the trail, you can see the top of the dam as well as beautiful views of the Morgan Falls Reservoir.

SENTINEL TULIP TREE

This tulip tree (commonly known as tulip poplar) has been through a lot! Its lower trunk is significantly larger (12 feet around) than the upper trunk due to past damage. Walk up the hill from the trail 30 feet to visit this tree, and you'll find that the back side is burned out and hollow.

Hike Route

Begin your hike by entering the woods near the information board at the far end of the parking area. The path descends quickly over 0.1 mile to a bridge over a quiet creek. After crossing the bridge, turn to the left at junction GB 2. Hike this trail up and down small hills through a beech grove next to a creek and wetlands. In 0.25 mile, after crossing a wooden bridge, bear right and up a short hill to reach a map post at GB 6.

From here, take the trail to the left to continue hiking along the edge of the water. Keep an eye out for birds, including great blue herons, as you hike this section of the trail. In 0.2 mile, you'll come to another junction (GB 7). Stay left to continue your hike along the water's edge. The trail becomes very steep and narrow before dropping back down to the water's edge in 0.2 mile. Look for cattails and other marsh grasses on the far bank.

In another 0.2 mile, pass a viewpoint on the left with great views of the riverside wetland area. At the next trail junction (GB 8), take

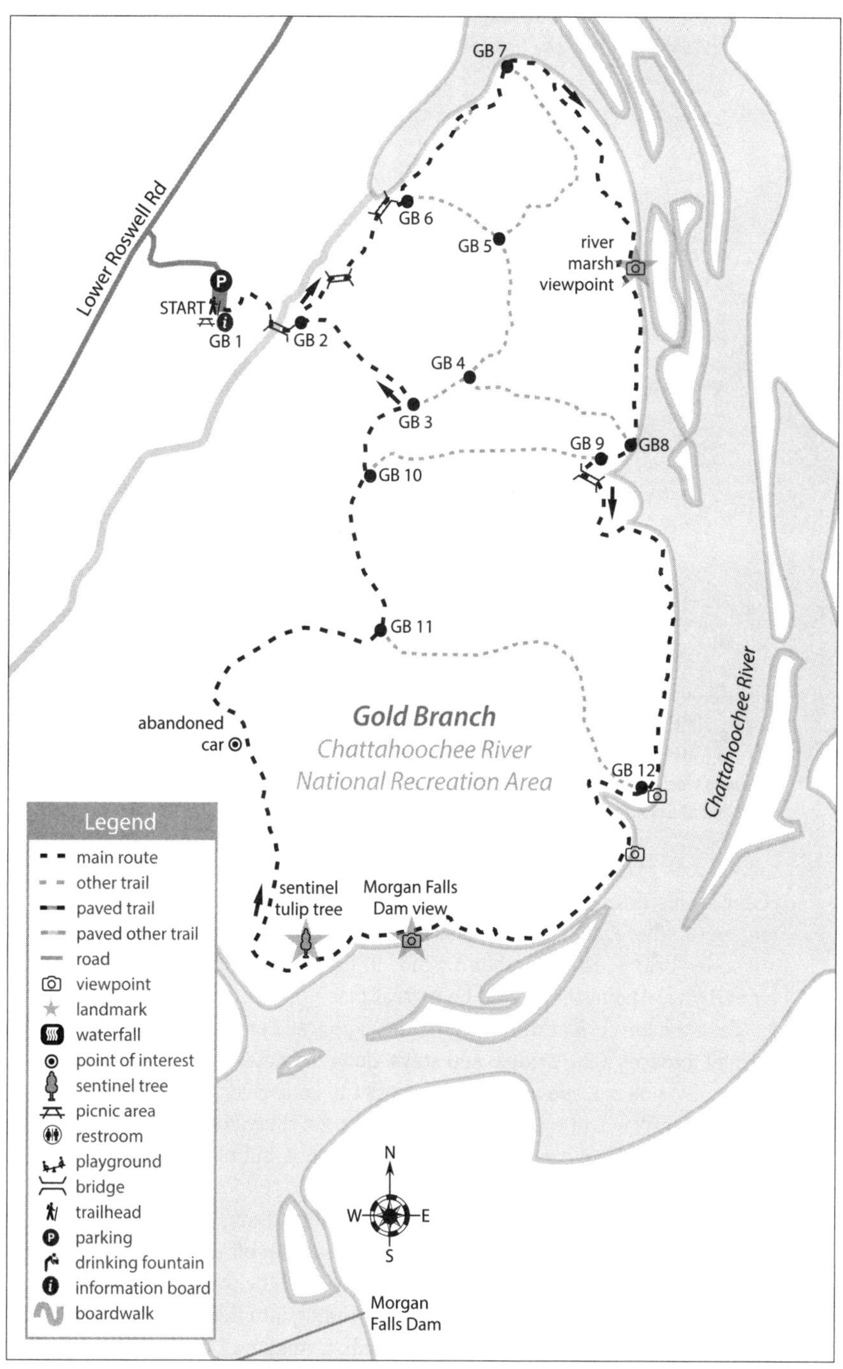
Lower Roswell Rd
GB 7
GB 6
GB 5
river
marsh
viewpoint
START
GB 1
GB 2
GB 4
GB 3
GB 9
GB8
GB 10
GB 11
abandoned
car
Gold Branch
Chattahoochee River
National Recreation Area
GB 12
Chattahoochee River
sentinel
tulip tree
Morgan Falls
Dam view
Legend
main route
other trail
paved trail
paved other trail
road
viewpoint
landmark
waterfall
point of interest
sentinel tree
picnic area
restroom
playground
bridge
trailhead
parking
drinking fountain
information board
boardwalk
N
W
E
S
Morgan
Falls Dam

Stunning views of Morgan Falls Reservoir await you at Gold Branch.

the left fork and hike 50 yards to reach another junction and map post (GB 9). This is an easy turn to miss, so keep your eyes peeled for the map post, where you'll make a sharp left turn downhill and then over a wooden bridge. Hike another 0.5 mile to junction GB 12, which has a nearby viewpoint that would be a great place to take a snack break.

Take the left fork at the trail junction. The trail curves around an inlet, crosses a log bridge, and stays along the edge of the water. In 0.1 mile, you can see all the way across the wide river. The trail becomes narrow and rocky. Keep an eye out for spiny yucca plants along the trail. Soap can be made from yucca root, but please don't disturb the plants, even if you're feeling dirty.

After 0.5 mile, you gain a view of Morgan Falls Dam, and then the trail begins to ascend. On the right about 30 feet off the trail is a sentinel tulip tree—the largest tree in this park. The trail curves right after passing the tree and begins ascending into the hills. A third of a mile after the trail begins to climb, a small trail leads 50 feet to an abandoned car riddled with bullet holes. It is intriguing (and sometimes disturbing) to come upon the ruins of human technology after spending time hiking in a pristine nature preserve.

A quarter mile past the abandoned car, you'll reach junction GB 11. Bear left and hike 0.2 mile to junction GB 10. Stay left again to junction GB 3. Make one more left turn and hike steeply downhill for almost 0.2 mile. The final junction you'll come to is GB 2. Continue straight across the bridge, then back uphill on the trail to the parking area to end your hike.

The rushing falls at Roswell Mill are the centerpiece of this hike.

Vickery Creek

CHATTAHOOCHEE RIVER NATIONAL RECREATION AREA

The trails of Vickery Creek offer an excellent loop hike, scenic views, waterfalls, and historic ruins, all within the heart of Roswell, Georgia. Accessible from Waller Park and the Roswell Mill Shopping Center, these trails are well used and provide many routes for exploration. Though this greenspace is a young forest, the steep banks of Big Creek and the rolling Piedmont hills make for a fantastic hike.

HOW TO GET THERE

Driving Distance from Downtown Atlanta: 21 miles

Address: 400 Riverside Road, Roswell, GA 30075

Closest Highway: GA 400

City, County: Roswell, Fulton

Public Transit: Take the 85 bus to Atlanta Street & Riverside Road. Turn right onto Riverside Road; the entrance to the parking area is 500 feet on the left

Parking: Gravel parking lot; alternative parking at Roswell Mill Shopping Center

HIKE DISTANCE

4.5-mile loop

DIFFICULTY

Overall: Moderate

Navigation: Maps at each junction, occasional blazes on trees

Terrain: Hard-packed dirt trail, paved trail

Elevation Change: Rolling hills with a few short ascents or descents

SAFETY

Usage ★★★★★

Visibility ★★★★☆

Upkeep ★★★★★

Parking ★★★☆☆

HOURS

Dawn to dusk

DOGS

Leashed dogs allowed

FACILITIES

- Toilets at Oxbo Road parking area
- Water fountain, dog waste station, picnic area

FEES & PERMITS $5 daily fee—purchase at recreation.gov

LAND MANAGER Chattahoochee River National Recreation Area—National Park Service

Landmarks

ROSWELL MILL DAM WATERFALL VIEWPOINT

The falls created by the dam at Big Creek are the largest in Roswell and for good reason attract many people to this scenic spot to enjoy waterfall views without traveling to north Georgia.

SENTINEL AMERICAN BEECH

On the right of the trail at the bottom of the ridge is a large sentinel American beech with a circumference of nearly 7 feet.

SIX-TRUNKED BIGLEAF MAGNOLIA

Though none of its trunks are that large, this tree is notable for the large number of trunks growing from the same node. This species of magnolia has the largest simple leaves of any tree native to North America.

Hike Route

Start your hike at the far end of the parking area next to the information board. Reach a junction (VC 2) in less than 75 yards. Turn right, climb up the stairs, and follow the trail as it switchbacks up onto the ridge, passing unofficial junctions on the left and then on the right. Reach a bench where the trail flattens out on the ridgetop in 0.15 mile. Bear right and walk 0.3 mile farther, passing another bench, and go left at junction VC 4.

Stay straight at junction VC 8 in 0.1 mile, then go left at junction VC 9 in another 0.1 mile. At junction VC 10, continue straight and then left at junction VC11. Hike steadily downhill for 0.2 mile to junction VC 12.

Turn right and hike along the bank of Big Creek. Pass a sewer pipe crossing the creek in 0.15 mile. In 0.1 mile at a junction across from a rock outcrop, turn left. This will take you closer to the creek near some large flat rocks at the water's edge and some small sandy areas. The paths reconnect in 0.1 mile near a sewer pipe and map kiosk (VC 14). Follow a small trail alongside the pipe that parallels the creek to reach a large covered bridge.

After passing under the bridge, turn right and climb the stairs. Cross the covered bridge to reach a boardwalk with picnic tables

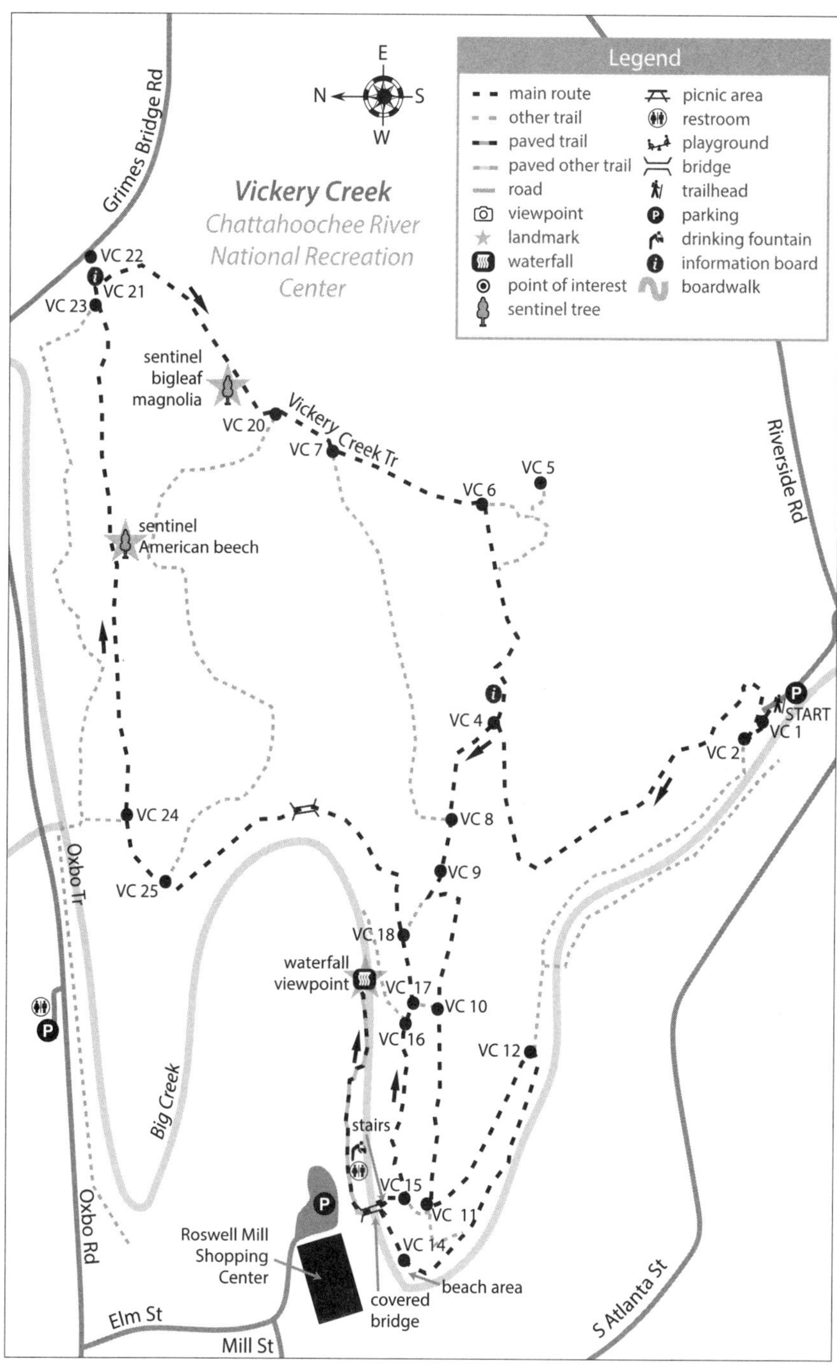

Legend
main route
other trail
paved trail
paved other trail
road
viewpoint
landmark
waterfall
point of interest
sentinel tree
picnic area
restroom
playground
bridge
trailhead
parking
drinking fountain
information board
boardwalk
E
N
S
W
Vickery Creek
Chattahoochee River
National Recreation
Center
Grimes Bridge Rd
Riverside Rd
Vickery Creek Tr
Oxbo Tr
Oxbo Rd
Big Creek
Elm St
Mill St
S Atlanta St
VC 1
VC 2
VC 4
VC 5
VC 6
VC 7
VC 8
VC 9
VC 10
VC 11
VC 12
VC 14
VC 15
VC 16
VC 17
VC 18
VC 20
VC 21
VC 22
VC 23
VC 24
VC 25
START
sentinel bigleaf magnolia
sentinel American beech
waterfall viewpoint
stairs
Roswell Mill Shopping Center
covered bridge
beach area

The historic mill machinery is still intact and is worth viewing.

and read signs explaining the history of Roswell Mill. Turn right after exiting the bridge and follow the lower paved path past the restroom and water fountain. Follow the trail up the ramp and turn right onto a wide paved path.

Pass a picnic area on the right and take a wooden wheelchair-accessible ramp down to the historic mill, where you'll also find interpretive signage. Exit the platform onto a wide sandbar next to the creek, then cross under the pipe and turn left onto a wide compact gravel trail. Hike uphill to the dam viewpoint platform. After enjoying your time at the falls, retrace your steps back to the bridge. Cross the bridge and take the stairs uphill, passing a large grove of rhododendrons. Turn left at the top of the stairs (VC 15). At junction VC 16, go right, and at junction VC 17, bear left.

Stay straight at junction VC 18, cross a small footbridge in 0.2 mile, then hike another 0.15 mile to a four-way junction at VC 25. Go straight here and then straight again at junction VC 24 in about 100 yards. In 0.25 mile, at the bottom of the hill where a stream runs between the two hills, look to the right for a large sentinel beech tree 50 feet off the trail.

Hike uphill for 0.25 mile to junction VC 23 and take the trail on the right. Reach junction VC 21 at a map kiosk and turn right. Hike 0.2 mile to reach a multitrunked bigleaf magnolia as the trail ascends a small hill.

At junction VC 20, just after the sentinel magnolia tree, stay straight. In about 100 yards, turn left at junction VC 7. Turn right at junction VC 6 in 0.2 mile and hike for 0.2 mile to reach junction VC 4, near an information board.

Turn left and follow this trail 0.5 mile back to the parking area to end your hike.

Several large outcrops are tempting to climb.

Island Ford

CHATTAHOOCHEE RIVER NATIONAL RECREATION AREA

Island Ford is one of the largest and most beautiful units of the Chattahoochee River National Recreation Area. Trails extend for several miles along the banks of the Chattahoochee, which widens and rolls over shoals here. Hikers also get to walk through scenic Piedmont forests, beside creeks, and past large granite outcrops. Many visitors stay close to the river, but this route will also take you through some of the more remote sections of the park.

HOW TO GET THERE

Driving Distance from Downtown Atlanta: 22 miles

Address: 1978 Island Ford Parkway, Atlanta, GA 30350

Closest Highway: GA 400

City, County: Roswell, Fulton

Parking: Large paved parking area near the visitor center; two additional parking areas along Island Ford Parkway

HIKE DISTANCE

6-mile triple loop

DIFFICULTY

Overall: Moderate

Navigation: Maps at trail junctions, some blazes along the route

Terrain: Hard-packed dirt trail; some sections have large rocks and roots

Elevation Change: Rolling hills with several short but steep ascents and descents

SAFETY

Usage ★★★★★

Visibility ★★★★☆

Upkeep ★★★★★

Parking ★★★★★

HOURS

Dawn to dusk

DOGS

Leashed dogs allowed

FACILITIES

- Toilet inside visitor center
- Water fountain, picnic area, dog waste station

FEES & PERMITS $5 daily fee—purchase at recreation.gov

LAND MANAGER Chattahoochee River National Recreation Area—National Park Service

Landmarks

SENTINEL WHITE OAK

Viewed from afar, trees don't always appear very large. But as you approach this white oak, you will be impressed by its size. See if you can wrap your arms around it—don't be ashamed to be a tree hugger!

SENTINEL NORTHERN RED OAK

This northern red oak has a trunk that was crooked from the start. Growing on a steep hillside near the creek, it had to compensate for the slope of the land by bending and growing wider at its base.

SENTINEL AMERICAN BEECH TREE

Located along the edge of a rushing stream, this large beech is at the bottom of a short spur trail. On this more quiet section of trail, its trunk has begun to tint green from moss.

Hike Route

This hike starts at the large paved parking area near the visitor center. You will pass two other parking areas on the way to this parking lot. Begin at the far end of the parking lot at map post IF 1. Soon after, at junction IF 7, turn left and cross the park road.

Turn left at the pond overlook and IF 6 to take the short loop around the pond. On a sunny day, look for turtles sunbathing on logs. At a parking area near map post IF 5, bear right. Finish the pond loop at junction IF 8. Turn left and hike upstairs to another parking area. Go right at the top of the stairs and reenter the woods next to a map kiosk (IF 10).

Hike this trail to junction IF 11 and turn left. In 0.1 mile, pass a large rock outcrop on the left before reaching junction IF 14. Go left and hike uphill along Summerbrook Creek. Just after the path crosses the creek, the large sentinel white oak is on the right in 100 yards.

You will reach junction IF 19 in 0.3 mile. Go right here and walk down the ridge through a much younger forest until you reach junction IF 18 in another 0.3 mile. Turn left and immediately left again at junction IF 17. The trail soon crosses another creek and then passes the sentinel northern red oak below the trail on your right. Hike another 0.2 mile to reach a parking area and junction IF 21.

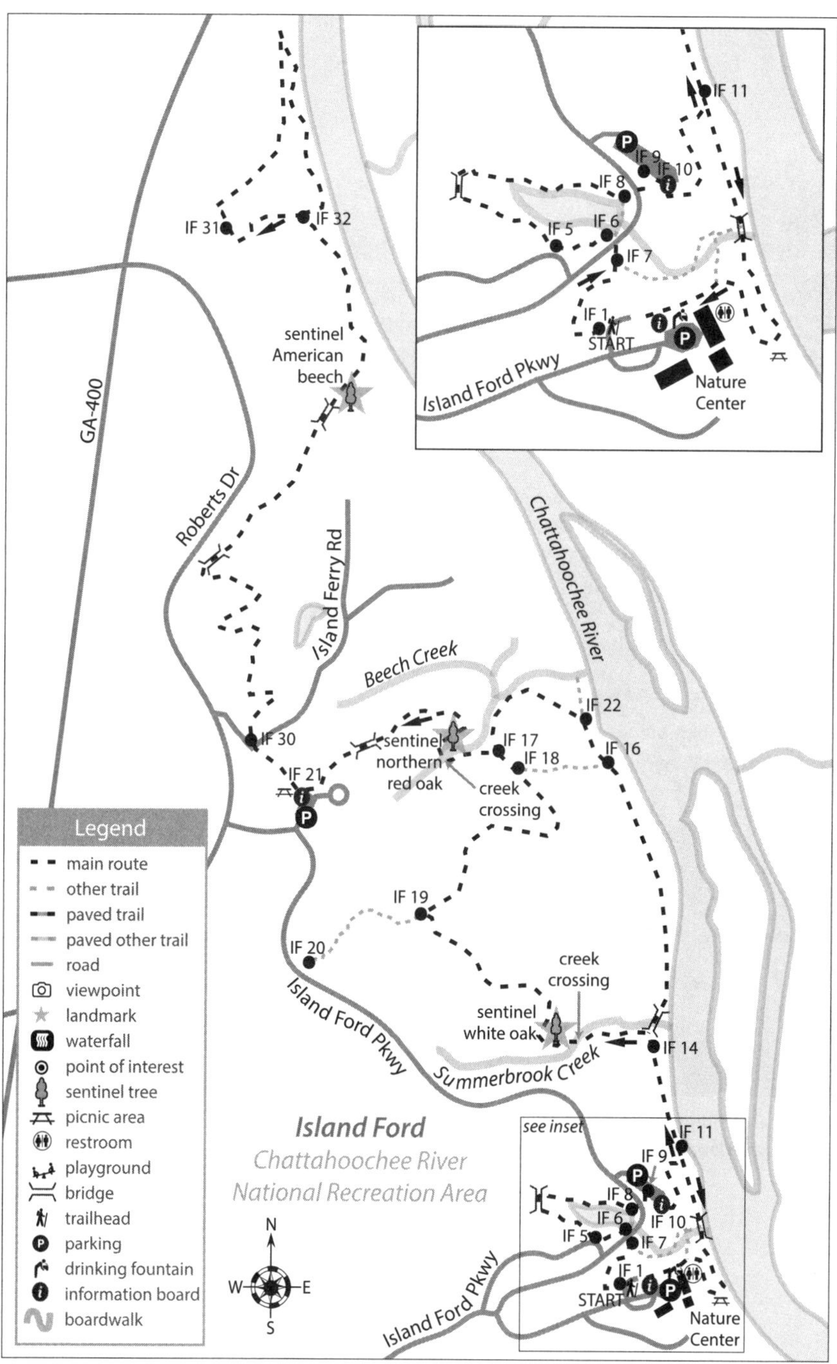

IF 11
IF 9
IF 10
IF 8
IF 5
IF 6
IF 7
IF 1
START
Island Ford Pkwy
Nature Center
IF 31
IF 32
sentinel American beech
GA-400
Roberts Dr
Island Ferry Rd
Chattahoochee River
Beech Creek
IF 22
IF 30
sentinel northern red oak
IF 17
IF 18
IF 16
IF 21
creek crossing
IF 19
IF 20
Island Ford Pkwy
creek crossing
sentinel white oak
IF 14
Summerbrook Creek
Legend
main route
other trail
paved trail
paved other trail
road
viewpoint
landmark
waterfall
point of interest
sentinel tree
picnic area
restroom
playground
bridge
trailhead
parking
drinking fountain
information board
boardwalk
Island Ford
Chattahoochee River National Recreation Area
see inset
N
W
E
S
Island Ford Pkwy
Nature Center

Don't forget to look down as you hike—wildflowers are everywhere!

Turn right immediately to begin the northern section of this hike: a 2.75-mile lollipop loop. In 0.1 mile, cross Island Ferry Road and continue straight. The trail generally descends for the next 0.9 mile, crossing a bridge after 0.4 mile. In another 0.2 mile, cross a second bridge and look to the right at the bottom of a short spur trail for the large sentinel beech tree.

At junction IF 32, turn left and stay to the right at junction IF 31. The trail curves to the right and downhill toward the Chattahoochee River. Stay right and hike along the lower section along the river before reaching the beginning of the loop. Turn left and hike 1 mile back to the parking area.

Turn left at the parking area, retracing your steps back to junction IF 17. Go left, and in 0.1 mile this trail arrives at Beech Creek and becomes significantly wider and flatter. Hike another 0.1 mile past junction IF 22, bearing right here. From here, stay straight at all subsequent junctions, following the trail parallel to the river, past several large rock outcrops, until you reach a large field and picnic areas below the visitor center. Turn right up the paved path to reach the visitor center parking lot and end your hike.

It's nice to pause and reflect on your hike around the pond.

Leita Thompson Memorial Park

One of the best-kept secrets in Roswell, Leita Thompson Memorial Park contains several creeks, many mature trees, and a well-maintained 2.5-mile loop trail. The trails are surfaced with crushed gravel and are well signed, making both the hiking and navigation easy. This is an excellent destination for trail running and for walking with children and seniors. Yet despite the ease of its footpath, the trail's length makes this hike enjoyable and even challenging for a hiker of any skill level.

HOW TO GET THERE

Driving Distance from Downtown Atlanta: 28 miles
Address: 1200 Woodstock Road, Roswell, GA 30075
Closest Highway: GA 400
City, County: Roswell, Fulton
Parking: Small paved parking lot near an apartment complex and overflow parking near Roswell's Art Center West entrance on Woodstock Road

HIKE DISTANCE

2.5-mile loop

DIFFICULTY

Overall: Easy to moderate
Navigation: Signposts at most junctions
Terrain: Wide crushed gravel trails
Elevation Change: Rolling hills with a few short ascents

SAFETY

Usage ★★★★★
Visibility ★★★★☆
Upkeep ★★★★★
Parking ★★★★★

HOURS

Dawn to dusk

DOGS

Leashed dogs allowed; dog park at far east side of park near a third parking area

FACILITIES

- Portable toilet at parking area and near pond
- Water fountain, dog waste station, benches

FEES & PERMITS None

LAND MANAGER City of Roswell Parks & Recreation

Landmarks

SENTINEL TULIP TREE

This is a tree worth stopping for. It's on the left side of the trail and is several feet larger in circumference than any tree around it. Tulip trees (commonly known as tulip poplars) are among the largest trees in Atlanta: this one survives from a time before the forest was clearcut.

SENTINEL RHODODENDRON GROVE

Just past a bridge over the pond is a large grove of rhododendrons. These native bushes are popular in ornamental gardens for their vibrant summer blooms.

SENTINEL WHITE OAK

This is the largest tree in Leita Thompson Memorial Park. Growing near Woodstock Road to the left of the trail about 50 feet, this tree was protected from axes and saws by its proximity to people's homes.

Hike Route

Start at the map kiosk on the southeast side of the parking lot (next to the driveway) and begin your hike on Yellow Loop. After 0.25 mile, pass a map kiosk near Roswell's Art Center West and the overflow parking lot. In another 0.1 mile, reach a junction at the edge of the field. Take the farthest right trail, skirting the outside of the open field. Continue for 0.2 mile over a bridge, reaching a junction with a bridge on the left and a trail leading to the dog park on the right.

Take a sharp left turn and cross the bridge. Cross a few more bridges and come to a junction with a map and bench. Bear right and hike downhill across two bridges. In 0.2 mile, pass the sentinel tulip tree on the left side of the trail.

Just after the tulip tree you'll pass a cabin on your right and come to a junction with a paved maintenance road. Cross the road and go straight on the gravel path along the left bank of the pond. Immediately after crossing a bridge, look to the left for a sentinel grove of rhododendrons.

Just after the end of the pond, pass a portable toilet, then cross the maintenance road and go straight and downhill past a map kiosk

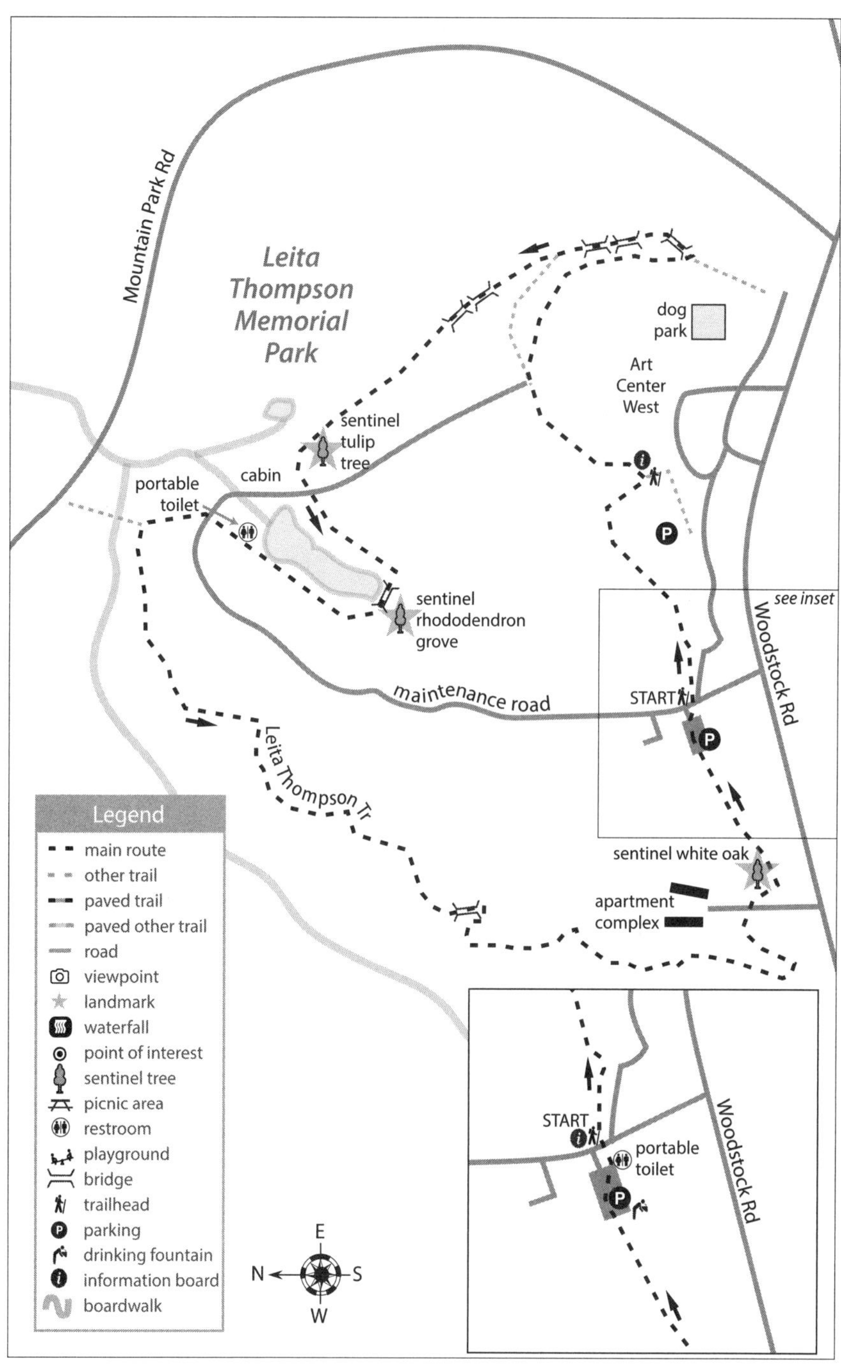
Mountain Park Rd
Leita Thompson Memorial Park
dog park
Art Center West
sentinel tulip tree
cabin
portable toilet
sentinel rhododendron grove
maintenance road
START
see inset
Woodstock Rd
Leita Thompson Tr
sentinel white oak
apartment complex
Legend
main route
other trail
paved trail
paved other trail
road
viewpoint
landmark
waterfall
point of interest
sentinel tree
picnic area
restroom
playground
bridge
trailhead
parking
drinking fountain
information board
boardwalk
E
N
S
W
START
portable toilet
Woodstock Rd

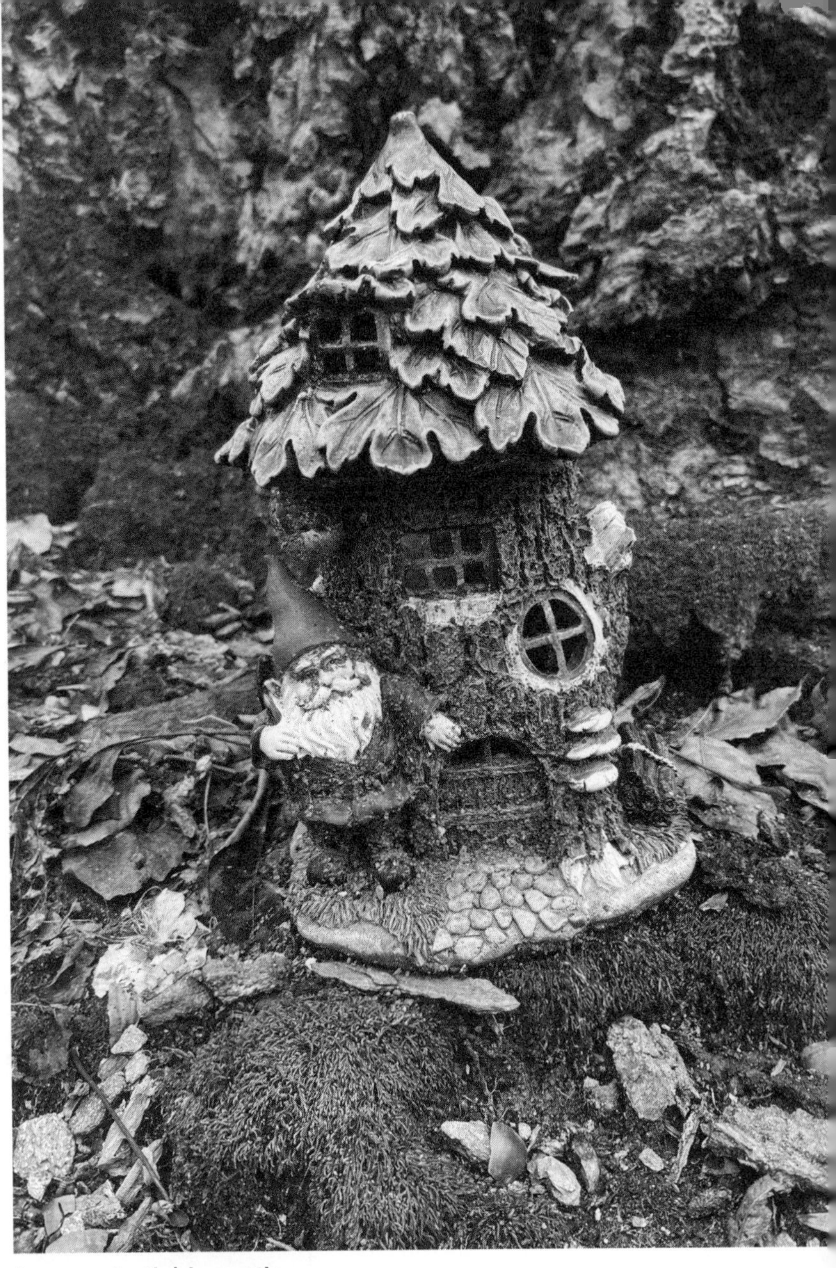

A gnome makes their home at the base of the sentinel tulip tree.

and mile marker. Pass two dilapidated metal sheds on your right, then pass a side trail to an elementary school on your right. Bear left and stay on the high ground.

In 0.1 mile at the top of the hill, pass a bench and small overlook, then continue on the main trail for 1 mile, past two junctions with maintenance roads. The trail winds and switchbacks in and out of several hollows to reach an apartment complex.

Cross the apartment complex driveway and reenter the woods. At the bottom of the hill, look to the left for the sentinel white oak, the largest tree in the park. From here it is 0.1 mile back to the parking lot to finish your hike.

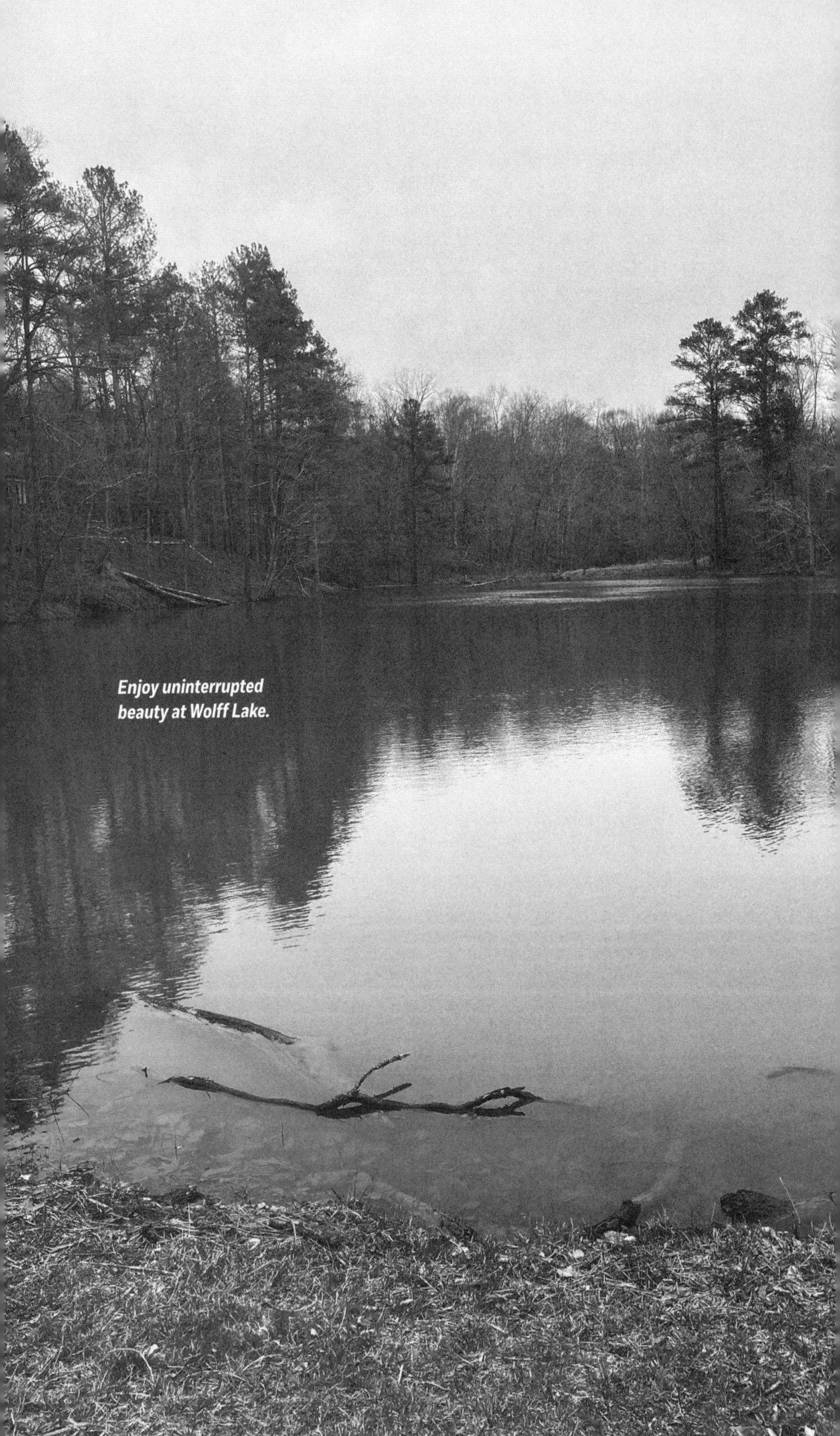

Enjoy uninterrupted beauty at Wolff Lake.

Lakhapani Preserve

Lakhapani Preserve (formerly Lackey Road Greenspace) is a developing park in Milton, Georgia, where you can truly escape into the solitude of nature. The 106-acre preserve was previously owned by the Wolff family. The park's current name was first suggested by Woolley Smith, a family friend and Indian tea plantation owner who combined two Hindi words—*lakh*, "100,000," and *pani*, "waters"—to call the property Lakhapani. After public input, the City of Milton adopted the name when it acquired the greenspace in 2018. Today this public greenspace offers a short, easy hike past meadows, through old-growth forests, and around a lake.

HOW TO GET THERE

Driving Distance from Downtown Atlanta: 30 miles
Address: 990 Lackey Road, Roswell, GA 30075
Closest Highway: GA 400
City, County: Milton, Fulton
Parking: Small gravel parking lot

HIKE DISTANCE

1.5-mile loop

DIFFICULTY

Overall: Easy to moderate
Navigation: Blazes on trees, occasional signage along route
Terrain: Hard-packed dirt trail
Elevation Change: Rolling hills with a few short but steep ascents

SAFETY

Usage ★★★★☆
Visibility ★★★☆☆
Upkeep ★★★★☆
Parking ★★★☆☆

HOURS

Dawn to dusk

DOGS

Leashed dogs allowed

FACILITIES

- No toilets
- Trash can

FEES & PERMITS	None
LAND MANAGER	City of Milton Parks & Recreation

Landmarks

SENTINEL AMERICAN BEECH

Beech trees are often found near sources of water. This large sentinel beech is growing out of the bank over a creek. You can see its exposed roots where the soil has eroded.

SENTINEL WHITE OAK

This white oak is among the largest trees in this section of forest. Its massive trunk splits halfway up.

WOLFF LAKE

The lake sits just below the home of the Wolff family, who previously owned this land. The easily accessible bank makes it a nice spot to watch for wildlife in the water, but fishing is not allowed.

Hike Route

Begin your hike by exiting the parking lot by the trash can and map sign. Carefully cross Lackey Road and enter the trail near the blue blazes, which signify the trailhead. Take the trail to the bottom of the hill and then go left, passing a large magnolia on your left.

In 100 feet, at the former residence, bear left and pass an old shed and barn. At the bottom of the hill, just past a small stream, there is a large beech tree on the right side of the trail. Hike over a small culvert and pass a grove of rhododendrons on the left side of the trail. Continue up the steep hill as it curves to the right and runs along a fence.

For 0.4 mile, the trail parallels the fence at the edge of a pasture and switches back and forth into the forest. At a post at the end of the fenceline, go right, following the trail back into the forest. In 0.1 mile, cross a creek and look to the left for a large sentinel American beech on the edge of the bank.

Hike uphill and reach a junction with a trail on the left that leads 0.25 mile to Sweetapple Road. Bear right and hike for 0.1 mile to a large sentinel white oak on the right side of the trail, just after a small creek crossing. Hike along the ridge with a larger creek below you to your right.

The trail continues to run parallel to the creek and through

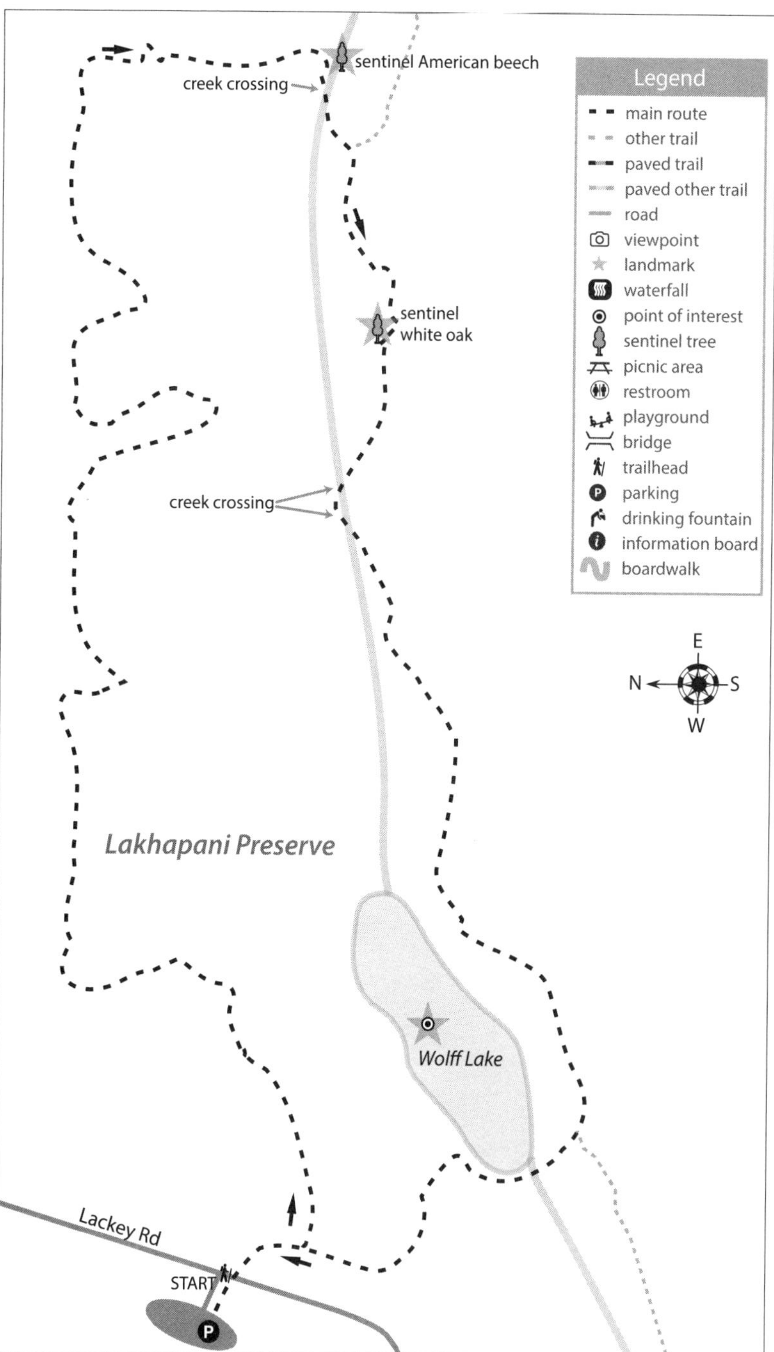
sentinel American beech
creek crossing
Legend
main route
other trail
paved trail
paved other trail
road
viewpoint
landmark
waterfall
point of interest
sentinel tree
picnic area
restroom
playground
bridge
trailhead
parking
drinking fountain
information board
boardwalk
sentinel
white oak
creek crossing
E
N
S
W
Lakhapani Preserve
Wolff Lake
Lackey Rd
START
P

Hike the peaceful coves of Lakhapani Preserve.

young beech trees growing on the hillside to your left. Enter a clearing and young pine forest just before reaching the lake. Take the trail around the left edge of the lake, staying to the right at any junctions, then crossing over the dam.

Follow the trail uphill and away from the lake to reach the junction where you first began the loop. Stay straight, then left across Lackey Road to reach the parking area and end your hike.

This park used to
be farmland.

Birmingham Park

Hidden down a gravel road behind the local fire station, Birmingham Park is an unexpected but great place to hike in Milton, Georgia. The trails transport you to a quiet escape into nature and are used by equestrians and hikers. With many trails to choose from, anyone can have an enjoyable experience hiking here. You can find a new adventure every time you visit this park. This route takes you past the best features of the park, through old-growth forests and meadows and along streams.

HOW TO GET THERE

Driving Distance from Downtown Atlanta: 36 miles
Address: 750 Hickory Flat Road, Milton, GA 30004
Closest Highway: GA 400
City, County: Milton, Fulton
Parking: Small paved parking area

HIKE DISTANCE

2-mile loop

DIFFICULTY

Overall: Easy to moderate
Navigation: Trail markers at many junctions, occasional maps at junctions, blazes throughout
Terrain: Wide gravel trail, hard-packed dirt trails
Elevation Change: Rolling hills with no major ascents or descents

SAFETY

Usage ★★★★☆
Visibility ★★★★☆
Upkeep ★★★★☆
Parking ★★★☆☆

HOURS

Dawn to dusk

DOGS

Leashed dogs allowed

FACILITIES

- No toilets
- Dog waste station, trash can

FEES & PERMITS

None

LAND MANAGER City of Milton Parks & Recreation

Landmarks

TRILLIUM PATCH

Just after crossing a junction and entering the Blue Trail, look down and to the left for a hearty patch of trilliums on the side of the trail. Several species of trillium are native to the southeastern United States. This flower blooms only in the spring, and the spotted leaves and purple flowers indicate that this is the Little Sweet Betsy (*Trillium cuneatum*) species.

BLACKBERRY PATCH

This patch of wild blackberries grows abundantly in the sunny meadow along Blue Trail. Wild blackberries grow best in sunny areas created by human disturbance and along forest edges.

SENTINEL AMERICAN BEECH

Most beech trees grow tall and straight. This beech at the edge of the stream is interesting for its wide crown and many branches that extend from its trunk. Look for smooth gray bark and serrated leaves.

Hike Route

All trails in Birmingham Park are shared with equestrians, so watch your step and remember to give horses the right-of-way. Begin your hike through the fence at the information board on the far right end of the parking lot. Hike to a post marked with a purple arrow and turn right onto the Purple Trail, passing the frame of an old building.

In 0.1 mile, reach a junction marked Percheron Pass and go left. Hike parallel to New Bull Pen Road for 0.2 mile to the next junction and turn left onto Pink Trail.

Hike uphill and past a bench. When you come to the next junction with a wide trail, you will turn right. But first, go straight across the trail for a quick detour to view an abandoned barn in the field. Then continue your hike on the wide path to a three-way junction where you'll turn left and continue circling the meadow on your left.

Just past a bench, come to a junction with Red Trail in 0.1 mile. Turn right onto Red Trail and pass a junction with Yellow Trail on your left. Then go right onto Orange Trail when the trail forks. At the next junction at the top of the hill bear left and continue hiking downhill to where Orange Trail reconnects with Red Trail.

Turn right onto Red Trail and hike along a ridge through a

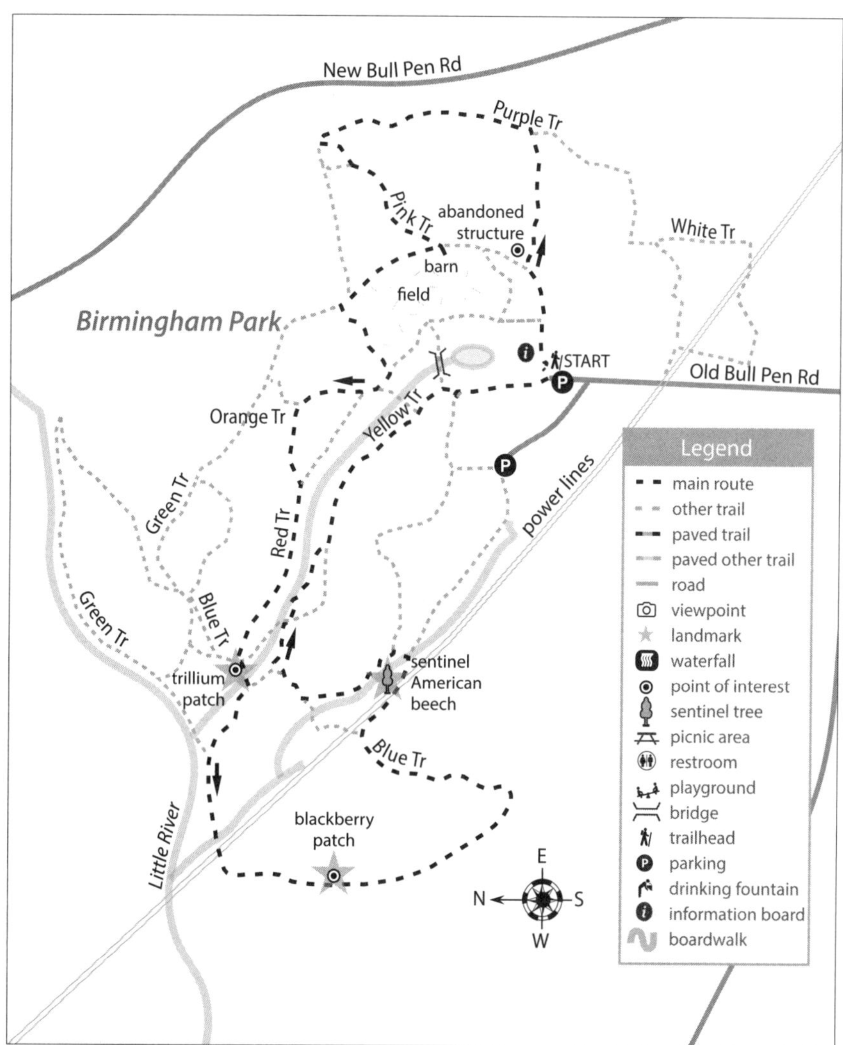

New Bull Pen Rd
Purple Tr
Pink Tr
abandoned structure
White Tr
barn
field
Birmingham Park
START
Old Bull Pen Rd
Orange Tr
Yellow Tr
Green Tr
Red Tr
power lines
Green Tr
Blue Tr
trillium patch
sentinel American beech
Blue Tr
Little River
blackberry patch
E
N
S
W
Legend
main route
other trail
paved trail
paved other trail
road
viewpoint
landmark
waterfall
point of interest
sentinel tree
picnic area
restroom
playground
bridge
trailhead
parking
drinking fountain
information board
boardwalk

Look for small treasures along the trail.

mature forest. At a four-way junction, go straight onto Blue Trail and immediately look down and to the left for a large patch of trillium flowers, which flourish in the spring. Pass a junction on the left and hike straight through this low section of forest. In 0.1 mile, reach a junction with Green Trail on the right and continue straight onto Blue Trail.

The trail briefly exits the forest into a power line clearing before reentering the forest. After 0.1 mile at the top of the hill, go left and hike out into a meadow and through a large patch of wild blackberries. Hike for 0.4 mile, walking through the clearing parallel to the power lines.

At a junction near a small stream, turn left into the forest, go left again immediately at the next junction onto Yellow Trail, and hike downhill. In 100 yards, look left for a large gray-barked beech tree on the hillside. Then at the bottom of the hill, turn right at the junction and right again at the next three-way junction.

At a four-way junction with a map post, stay straight and hike along the creek. Bear left when the trail reconnects with Yellow Trail and follow this trail straight to the parking area to end your hike.

The Indian Seats viewpoint is one of the best views in metro Atlanta.

Sawnee Mountain Preserve

This 720-acre preserve is best known for a mountaintop viewpoint known to locals as Indian Seats. Sadly, most visitors only experience the Indian Seats Trail. The additional 6 miles of trails that loop around the 1,967-foot Sawnee Mountain are beautiful, challenging, and much less busy. Though the peak of Sawnee Mountain is privately owned, the rocky ridges, peaceful pond, and green forests will certainly entice you to continue your hike after visiting the iconic Indian Seats viewpoint.

HOW TO GET THERE

Driving Distance from Downtown Atlanta: 47 miles
Address: 4075 Spot Road, Cumming, GA 30040
Closest Highway: GA 400
City, County: Cumming, Forsyth
Parking: Large parking area near visitor center

HIKE DISTANCE

9-mile figure-8 loop (or 3.5-mile Indian Seats loop)

DIFFICULTY

Overall: Strenuous
Navigation: Maps at trailheads, diamond blazes; trails are wide and easy to follow
Terrain: Hard-packed dirt or gravel with lots of roots and rocks
Elevation Change: Several steep and extended ascents and descents

SAFETY

Usage ★★★★★
Visibility ★★★★★
Upkeep ★★★★★
Parking ★★★★★

HOURS

- March through October, 6:00 am to 9:30 pm; November through February, 6:00 am to 7:00 pm
- Visitor center

DOGS

Dogs not allowed

FACILITIES

- Toilets at each trailhead

- Visitor center, picnic tables, drinking fountains, information boards, outdoor classroom, playground

FEES & PERMITS None

LAND MANAGER Forsyth County Parks & Recreation

Landmarks

ABANDONED MINES

Twenty years before the California gold rush, gold was discovered in Dahlonega, Georgia, in 1828. Several gold mines were built on the sides of Sawnee Mountain, and you'll pass the barricaded entrances to two of them along this hike.

INDIAN SEATS

Though indigenous people likely used the ridge now known popularly as Indian Seats, this name was chosen by European colonizers. The depressions in the rock that look like seats were caused by hundreds of thousands of years of erosion.

POND

Because so much of this hike is along dry mountain ridges, this pond is a beautiful spot for humans and a great habitat for birds, frogs, and other wildlife.

Hike Route

Facing the visitor center entrance, start your hike on an asphalt trail to the right of the building, then turn right onto a dirt trail at three information boards. In 0.15 mile, reach an outdoor classroom, observation platform, and trail junction. Turn left on Indian Seats Trail, blazed with the letters IS and emergency responder codes on each diamond blaze.

Ascend on this steep trail, and do not use any side trails to avoid causing erosion damage to the mountain. In 0.8 mile, reach a junction with a bench and yellow post. Turn left and hike uphill. In 0.1 mile, pass an abandoned mine, then arrive at a junction with Yucca Trail. Go left to continue ascending toward Indian Seats.

In 0.6 mile, when you are almost at the peak, hike past an unofficial trail on the left to reach the official trail, marked with a yellow post. Turn left and hike the final few yards to the top of the mountain. Pass the seat-shaped divots in the rock that locals have

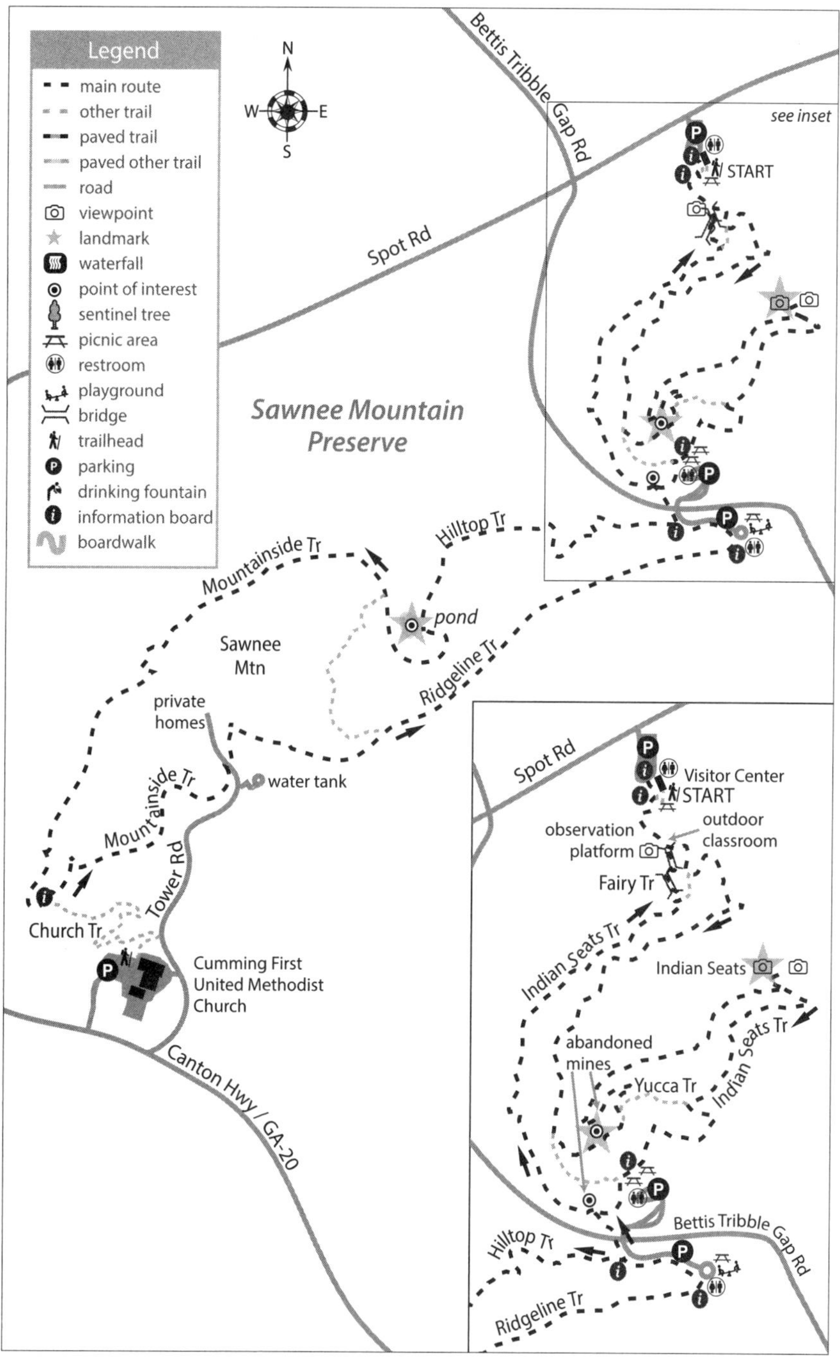
Legend
main route
other trail
paved trail
paved other trail
road
viewpoint
landmark
waterfall
point of interest
sentinel tree
picnic area
restroom
playground
bridge
trailhead
parking
drinking fountain
information board
boardwalk
N
W
E
S
Bettis Tribble Gap Rd
see inset
START
Spot Rd
Sawnee Mountain Preserve
Hilltop Tr
Mountainside Tr
pond
Sawnee Mtn
Ridgeline Tr
private homes
water tank
Mountainside Tr
Mountainside Tr
Tower Rd
Church Tr
Cumming First United Methodist Church
Canton Hwy / GA-20
Spot Rd
Visitor Center
START
observation platform
outdoor classroom
Fairy Tr
Indian Seats Tr
Indian Seats
abandoned mines
Yucca Tr
Indian Seats Tr
Bettis Tribble Gap Rd
Hilltop Tr
Ridgeline Tr

You'll pass two abandoned gold mines on your hike at Sawnee Mountain.

named Indian Seats and then arrive at a wooden observation deck with great views to the north.

Hike back downhill to the previous junction and turn left to descend the mountain. At a junction with Yucca Trail in 0.4 mile, turn left and continue hiking downhill for another 0.3 mile to reach a parking area with picnic pavilions, a restroom, and an information board. Stay straight, passing the information board on your left, then turn left at a yellow post to hike downhill, following an arrow for the visitor center. At a junction near an abandoned mine in 0.1 mile, take a hard left to hike downhill to Bettis Tribble Gap Road. (Stay straight here if you are ready to turn back to the visitor center.)

Carefully cross the road at the crosswalk, then walk the sidewalk to an information board that serves as a trailhead for Hilltop Trail. Turn right into the woods and hike 1.2 miles to reach a junction near the edge of a small pond. Turn left to continue on Hilltop Trail.

Hilltop Trail meets Mountainside Trail in 0.4 mile. Continue straight on Mountainside Trail and hike along the northwest side of Sawnee Mountain for 1.5 miles to reach a junction with Church Connector Trail and a map sign. Continue straight, and the trail ascends along the Sawnee Mountain ridge.

In 0.75 mile, as you near a road, you'll see a large water tank next to the road below you. Hike down the rock stairs and across the road, then continue another 0.5 mile to reach Ridgeline Trail. Go straight to hike Ridgeline Trail 1 mile to the parking lot along Bettis Tribble Gap Road. There are pavilions, a playground, an information board, and a restroom at the parking lot. Turn left and hike the sidewalk back to the road. Cross the road at the crosswalk and hike the short trail back to a junction with Indian Seats Trail near the abandoned mine. Turn left to return to the visitor center. In 0.8 mile, reach a junction with Fairy Trail on the left. For a whimsical end to your hike, turn left and hike downhill on this trail, which is lined with fairy houses built by children.

When Fairy Trail ends near the observation platform and outdoor classroom, continue straight for 0.15 mile to end your hike at the visitor center.

I-85 NORTH

Simpsonwood Park has over 8 miles of trails.

Simpsonwood Park

Whenever you visit Simpsonwood you'll pass joggers, hikers, bikers, and neighbors walking their dogs. This 300-acre-plus park along the Chattahoochee River was originally donated to the Methodist Church by Miss Ludie Simpson and is now owned by Gwinnett County, which is implementing a new master plan for the park that follows Miss Ludie's vision: "to keep the land so that all people [can] enjoy God's beautiful creation." After hiking at Simpsonwood, you'll likely agree that the trails do just that.

HOW TO GET THERE

Driving Distance from Downtown Atlanta: 25 miles

Address: 4511 Jones Bridge Circle NW, Peachtree Corners, GA 30092

Closest Interstate: I-85

City, County: Peachtree Corners, Gwinnett

Parking: Gravel parking along the paved park road near the park entrance and restrooms

HIKE DISTANCE

2.5-mile loop

DIFFICULTY

Overall: Moderate

Navigation: No blazes, maps, or other signage; mile marker posts left over from a previous era still exist but are no longer accurate

Terrain: Hard-packed dirt or gravel trails, which can be muddy or overgrown in places

Elevation Change: Rolling hills, but no major ascents or descents

SAFETY

Usage ★★★★☆

Visibility ★★★☆☆

Upkeep ★★★☆☆

Parking ★★★★☆

HOURS

Sunrise to sunset

DOGS

Leashed dogs allowed

FACILITIES	• Toilets near the trailhead • Picnic tables and benches
FEES & PERMITS	None
LAND MANAGER	Gwinnett County Parks & Recreation

Landmarks

HARDWOOD FOREST

How can you tell that this section of forest is particularly healthy? Look for large trees, minimal underbrush, and a diversity of species. Just among the trees, you'll find southern red oak, white oak, sweetgum, American beech, and tulip tree (commonly known as tulip poplar).

SENTINEL UMBRELLA MAGNOLIAS

One of Atlanta's deciduous magnolias, these two umbrella magnolias growing along the banks of the Chattahoochee are particularly large for their species. But it's not the trunk size you'll likely notice. These trees have giant leaves that can grow up to 2 feet long.

CHATTAHOOCHEE VIEWPOINT

There are fewer places than one might expect to view the most iconic river of the Atlanta metro area. Other than the Chattahoochee River National Recreation Area units, much of the land along the river is in private hands. We can be thankful that Gwinnett County has protected this large and beautiful stretch of river.

Hike Route

Though this route is only 2.25 miles, Simpsonwood Park contains over 8 miles of trails, which can make this loop confusing and complicated to follow. Refer to the map as you hike, and if you get turned around, hiking to the left will usually lead you back to the main park road.

Begin your hike across the road from the restrooms. Within 100 feet, the trail splits. Take the left fork and stay on the main trail. Over the next 0.3 mile, you'll encounter two junctions. Bear right at both. When you reach a green metal gate, turn right and hike downhill into a valley with a mature hardwood forest. Look for many large beech, oak, sweetgum, and tulip trees. Stay straight on this trail through the valley until you reach a wide access road.

The next portion of this hike allows you to walk along the banks of

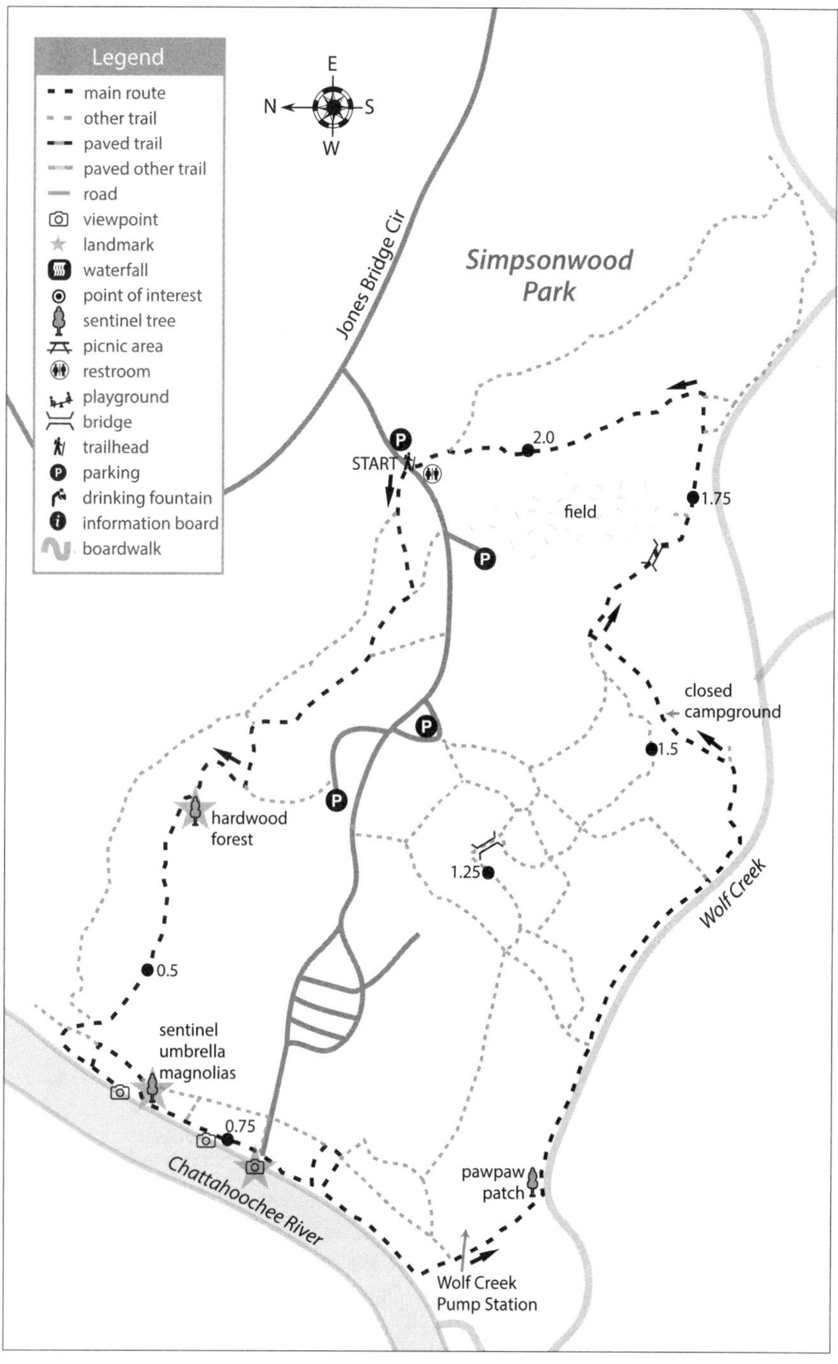
Legend
main route
other trail
paved trail
paved other trail
road
viewpoint
landmark
waterfall
point of interest
sentinel tree
picnic area
restroom
playground
bridge
trailhead
parking
drinking fountain
information board
boardwalk
E
N
S
W
Jones Bridge Cir
Simpsonwood Park
START
2.0
field
1.75
closed campground
1.5
hardwood forest
1.25
Wolf Creek
0.5
sentinel umbrella magnolias
0.75
Chattahoochee River
pawpaw patch
Wolf Creek Pump Station

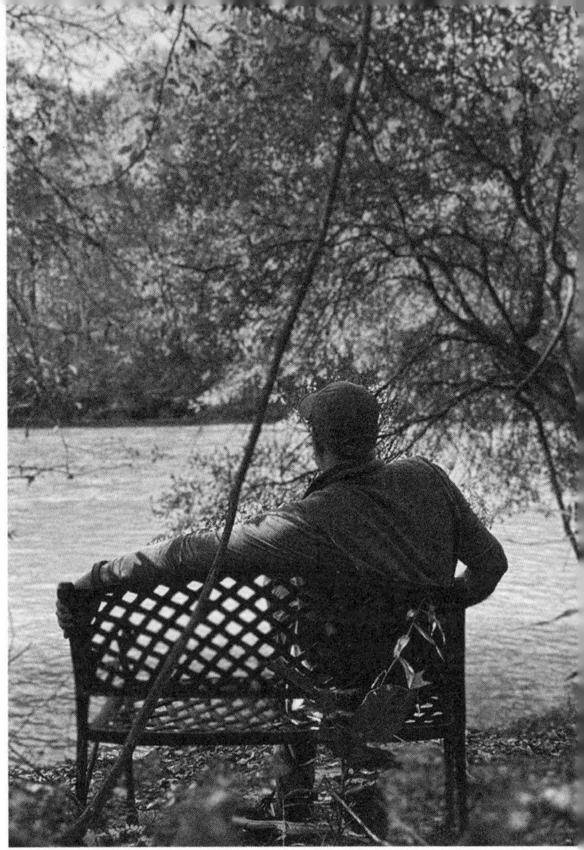

A long stretch of this trail is along the Chattahoochee River.

the Chattahoochee River in three sections, connected by this access road. Cross the access road and follow the single-track trail to the edge of the Chattahoochee River. Enjoy the view of the river until the trail ends, then turn around and retrace your steps to the access road, or take a trail that leads up over the rise to the access road. Either way, turn right on the access road and hike to the top of a rise, where you'll reach stairs leading downhill to the right.

Hike down the stairs and curve left. Once you are parallel to the river, look on your left for two sentinel umbrella magnolia trees with very large leaves. Then continue to parallel the river for 0.3 mile, passing several benches and viewpoints. Stay alongside the river past each side trail that leads back to the access road. Finally, the trail curves sharply left and emerges from the forest onto the access road again. Turn right and walk only 10 yards before turning right again onto a dirt trail that leads back to the river's edge. Enjoy this final 0.15-mile section of river views. The trail then curves left, away from the Chattahoochee and along the southern edge of the park. To your right is private property, and to the left is the Wolf Creek pump station.

In 0.1 mile, the trail begins paralleling Wolf Creek. If you are interested in native fruit trees, there is a sizable pawpaw patch here. Continue along Wolf Creek for 0.4 mile. When you start seeing houses, look for a single-track trail on the left. The wide path you are on leads into private property, so pay close attention for this turn.

Hike this trail uphill and through an area that used to be a campground, then bear right on the main trail. In 0.1 mile, cross a narrow wooden bridge, curve right, and then stay straight, past a trail that leads into a large grassy field on the left.

After passing an inaccurate 1.75-mile marker (you've hiked more than 2 miles already), the trail follows the crest of a small ridge. At the end of the ridge, turn left and hike 0.3 mile, past an inaccurate 2-mile marker, to reach a junction below the restrooms. Stay left and hike uphill to the restrooms and parking area, where you'll end your hike.

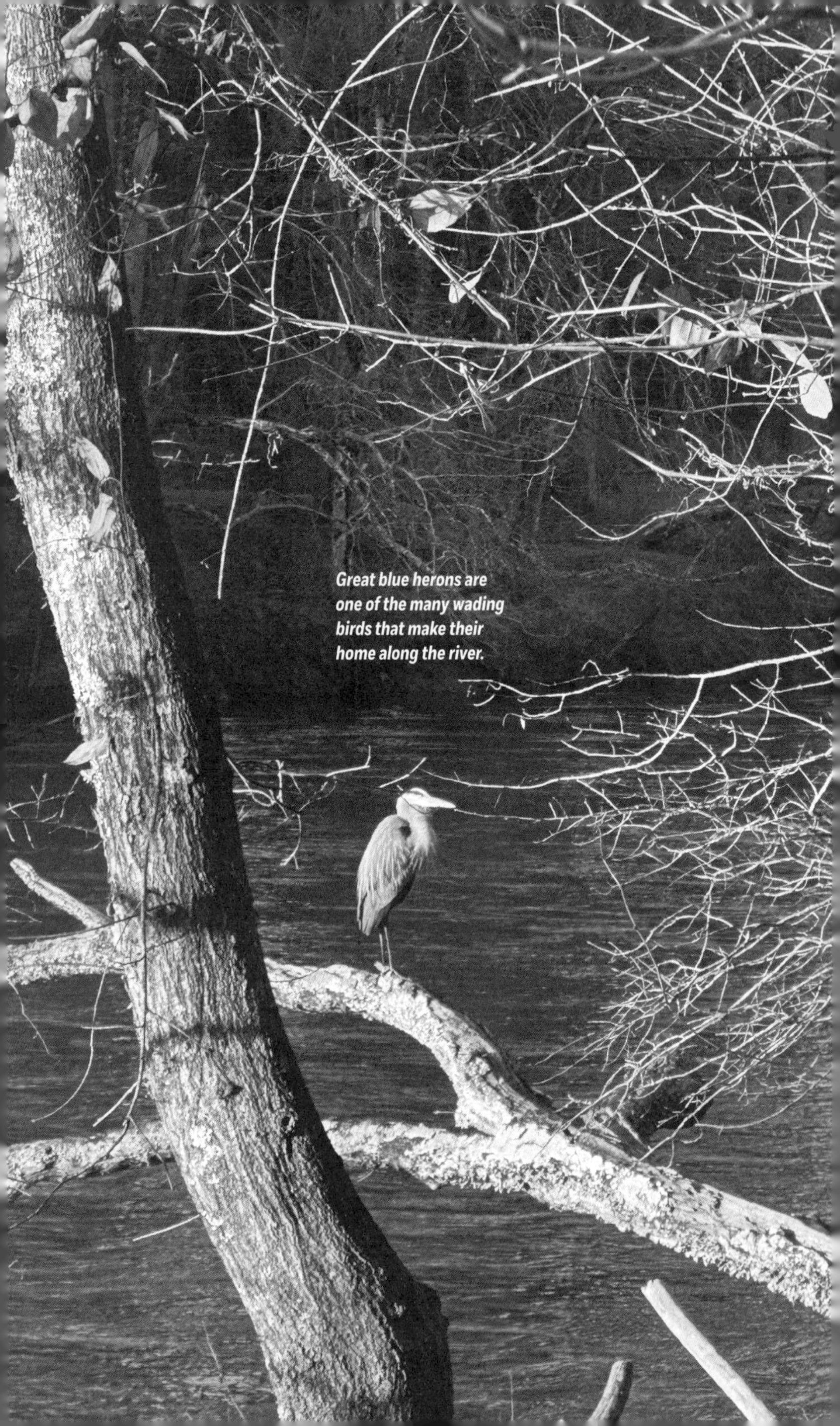

Great blue herons are one of the many wading birds that make their home along the river.

Jones Bridge

CHATTAHOOCHEE RIVER NATIONAL RECREATION AREA

This protected area of land in the midst of multi-million-dollar housing developments has many miles of hiking trails and a storied past; half of the original Jones Bridge was actually stolen in the 1940s. (The remainder was recently removed by the National Park Service.) And if you venture beyond the first mile of riverside trails you'll reach a remote area of interconnecting routes that wind over Piedmont ridges and through an old-growth oak forest along the river's edge.

HOW TO GET THERE	**Driving Distance from Downtown Atlanta:** 26 miles **Address:** Entrance near 8165 Barnwell Road, Johns Creek, GA 30022; parking at GPS 34.001200, -84.239661 **Closest Interstate:** I-85 **City, County:** Johns Creek, Fulton **Parking:** Gravel parking area at the end of a long access road
HIKE DISTANCE	5.25-mile lollipop loop
DIFFICULTY	**Overall:** Moderate **Navigation:** Map posts at most junctions **Terrain:** Hard-packed dirt trails with rocks and roots; some areas can be muddy after rain **Elevation Change:** Mostly flat with a few short but steep ascents and descents
SAFETY	**Usage** ★★★★☆ **Visibility** ★★★★☆ **Upkeep** ★★★★☆ **Parking** ★★★★☆
HOURS	Dawn to dusk
DOGS	Leashed dogs allowed
FACILITIES	• Toilets near parking and trailhead • Picnic tables, information boards

FEES & PERMITS	$5 daily fee—purchase at recreation.gov
LAND MANAGER	Chattahoochee River National Recreation Area—National Park Service

Landmarks

CHATTAHOOCHEE VIEWPOINT

Half a bridge used to be visible on this section of river. A rogue salvage company stole the other half in the 1940s. Finally, in 2018, the remaining span of the bridge collapsed and was removed by the National Park Service.

AMERICAN BEECH AND WHITE OAK

Beech trees have smooth gray bark, but white oaks have thick flaky bark. Both trees are over 10 feet in circumference and are a sign that this forest hasn't been disturbed in a long time. Can you find other large trees on this portion of the hike?

PRIVATE PONDS

Though the trails around these ponds are private, these bodies of water are beautiful and provide a great habitat for birds. Listen for the rattling call of belted kingfishers and the quacks of mallard ducks, and watch for the methodical movements of great blue herons.

Hike Route

Begin your hike at the second parking area. (The first parking area you pass is for boat trailers.) The trail begins at the back gate of the parking area (JB 5) and winds uphill on an old road. In 0.15 mile, the trail curves right and continues uphill to the crest of the ridge, then descends.

The trail exits the woods in a small clearing near the river. At the first map post (JB 1), bear left and rockhop across the creek, continuing through a picnic area to where the old Jones Bridge was located (now a defunct boat ramp) and then circling back in 0.1 mile to a footbridge in the clearing.

Continue straight across the bridge, then reach an observation deck on your left that provides great views of the Chattahoochee River. At junction JB 2, stay left on the trail along the river's edge.

In 0.2 mile, pass a side trail to the parking lot and continue straight, then cross another footbridge.

Cross another bridge in 0.3 mile. When you reach the boat trailer

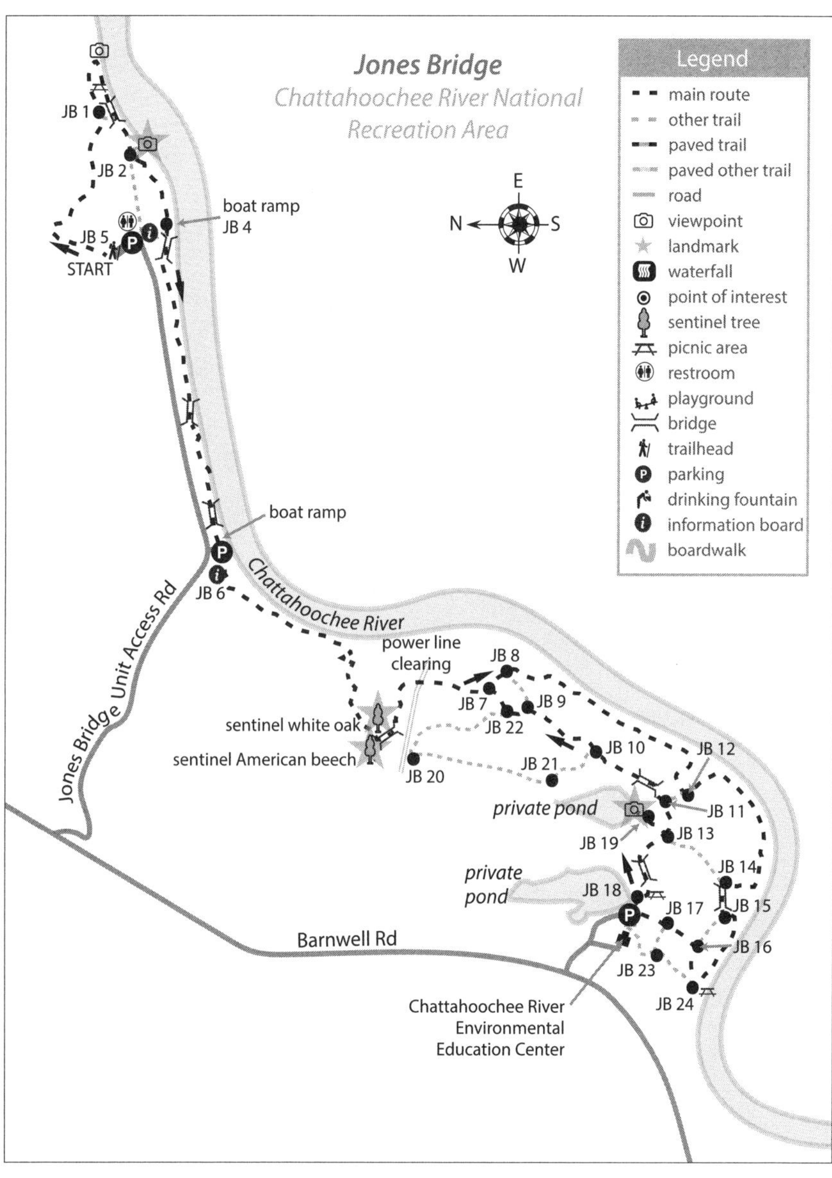
Jones Bridge
Chattahoochee River National Recreation Area
Legend
main route
other trail
paved trail
paved other trail
road
viewpoint
landmark
waterfall
point of interest
sentinel tree
picnic area
restroom
playground
bridge
trailhead
parking
drinking fountain
information board
boardwalk
E
N
S
W
JB 1
JB 2
boat ramp
JB 4
JB 5
START
boat ramp
JB 6
Chattahoochee River
Jones Bridge Unit Access Rd
power line clearing
JB 8
JB 7
JB 9
JB 22
sentinel white oak
sentinel American beech
JB 10
JB 12
JB 20
JB 21
private pond
JB 11
JB 19
JB 13
private pond
JB 14
JB 18
JB 17
JB 15
JB 16
Barnwell Rd
JB 23
JB 24
Chattahoochee River Environmental Education Center

Much of this hike is along the scenic banks of the Chattahoochee River.

parking lot, walk to the information board (JB 6) and cross a bridge to continue your hike.

Hike 0.3 mile, then curve right to climb steps and follow a switchback to the crest of the ridge. The trail immediately dips back down to a private gravel road. Cross this road and hike uphill for 0.1 mile before reaching a small footbridge between two large trees. From the bridge, an American beech stands 30 feet uphill, and a white oak is 100 feet downhill.

Take the left fork at the junction just beyond the bridge and hike 0.25 mile, passing under a power line, to reach junction JB 7. At this junction, go left and downhill, then turn left again at junction JB 8.

For the next 0.75 mile, the trail parallels the river through an area of many large old oak trees. Stay left at junction JB 12, left again at JB 14, and take another left at JB 15.

At junction JB 24 near a picnic table, turn right and follow the trail to a small clearing. As you enter the clearing, you will see the sign for JB 16 on your left, but it may be obscured by foliage. (There is a large interpretive sign at the far side of the clearing—if you reach it, you've gone too far.) Turn left at junction JB 16, go straight at junction JB 17, and cross a large clearing to reach an information board (JB 18) near the Chattahoochee River Environmental Education Center (CREEC). From here, you'll have views of a beautiful private pond. Turn around and hike back downhill and to the left through the clearing toward a cluster of picnic tables under an oak tree. At the tables, the trail curves left and into the forest. Hike to junction JB 13 and turn left to visit a viewpoint of another private pond. Then backtrack to JB 13 and turn left.

Stay straight at junction JB 11 and straight again at JB 10. At junction JB 9, turn left, then right at JB 22, then left at JB 7 to begin hiking back to the parking area. Pass under the power line again, cross the private gravel road, hike through the boat trailer parking lot, and then finally return to junction JB 4. Turn left to return to the parking lot and end your hike.

The trails of Medlock Bridge provide access to a tight curve of the Chattahoochee River.

Medlock Bridge

CHATTAHOOCHEE RIVER NATIONAL RECREATION AREA

Though not one of the most famous or popular units of the Chattahoochee River National Recreation Area, Medlock Bridge is still one of the most beautiful. Situated along the river at a spot where the channel makes a hairpin turn north, this area includes scenic views and peaceful forests. Many of the trails in this unit are along the water, and the other trails traverse an interesting rocky ridge in the park's interior.

HOW TO GET THERE

Driving Distance from Downtown Atlanta: 25 miles

Address: Entrance 0.3 mile north of the intersection of Medlock Bridge Road and Ridgegate Drive; GPS 33.995267, -84.204822

Closest Interstate: I-85

City, County: Peachtree Corners, Gwinnett

Parking: Paved parking area in the forest at the end of a 0.25-mile driveway

HIKE DISTANCE

1.75-mile lollipop loop

DIFFICULTY

Overall: Easy to moderate

Navigation: Map posts at most junctions

Terrain: Hard-packed dirt trails with rocks and roots

Elevation Change: Rolling hills, but no major ascents or descents

SAFETY

Usage ★★★☆☆

Visibility ★★★★☆

Upkeep ★★★★☆

Parking ★★★☆☆

HOURS

Dawn to dusk

DOGS

Leashed dogs allowed

FACILITIES

- No toilets
- Picnic tables, information kiosk

FEES & PERMITS $5 daily fee—purchase at recreation.gov

LAND MANAGER Chattahoochee River National Recreation Area—National Park Service

Landmarks

RIVER BEND VIEWPOINT

The Chattahoochee River, which generally flows southwest, takes a sharp curve at Medlock Bridge and flows northwest here. This viewpoint provides a great view of this bend in the river.

CHATTAHOOCHEE VIEWPOINT

From this vantage point on a small ridge about 30 feet above the water, you can take in a scenic view of Atlanta's most iconic river.

ROCK LEDGE

This rock ledge on top of the park's central ridge juts out over the ravine below. You can carefully step out onto the ledge for a heart-pounding woodland view.

Hike Route

Start your hike at the fee station and information boards on the north end of the parking area and walk toward the boat ramp and river to reach junction MB 1. Turn right and hike the dirt trail parallel to the river. You'll pass several unofficial trails on the left that lead down to the river's edge. Picnic tables are available on the right.

Continue straight at junction MB 2 and hike 0.2 mile to junction MB 4. Turn left here, then in 50 yards, a small unofficial trail on the left leads to a beautiful viewpoint of the bend in the river. Continue along the trail until you arrive at junction MB 5.

Bear left along the river, hike across a bridge, and climb the stairs to continue hiking on a small ridge above the Chattahoochee River. After another 0.1 mile, just before the trail curves right and descends, a short unofficial trail leads to another fantastic viewpoint above the river. When you reach the map post at MB 10, turn around and hike back the way you came, to junction MB 5.

This time, turn left and hike 0.1 mile to junction MB 6. Turn right here to hike the interior ridge of the park, which lessens obtrusive traffic noise and offers pleasant scenery. In just over 100 yards, crest the high point of the park and descend to junction MB 9. Go

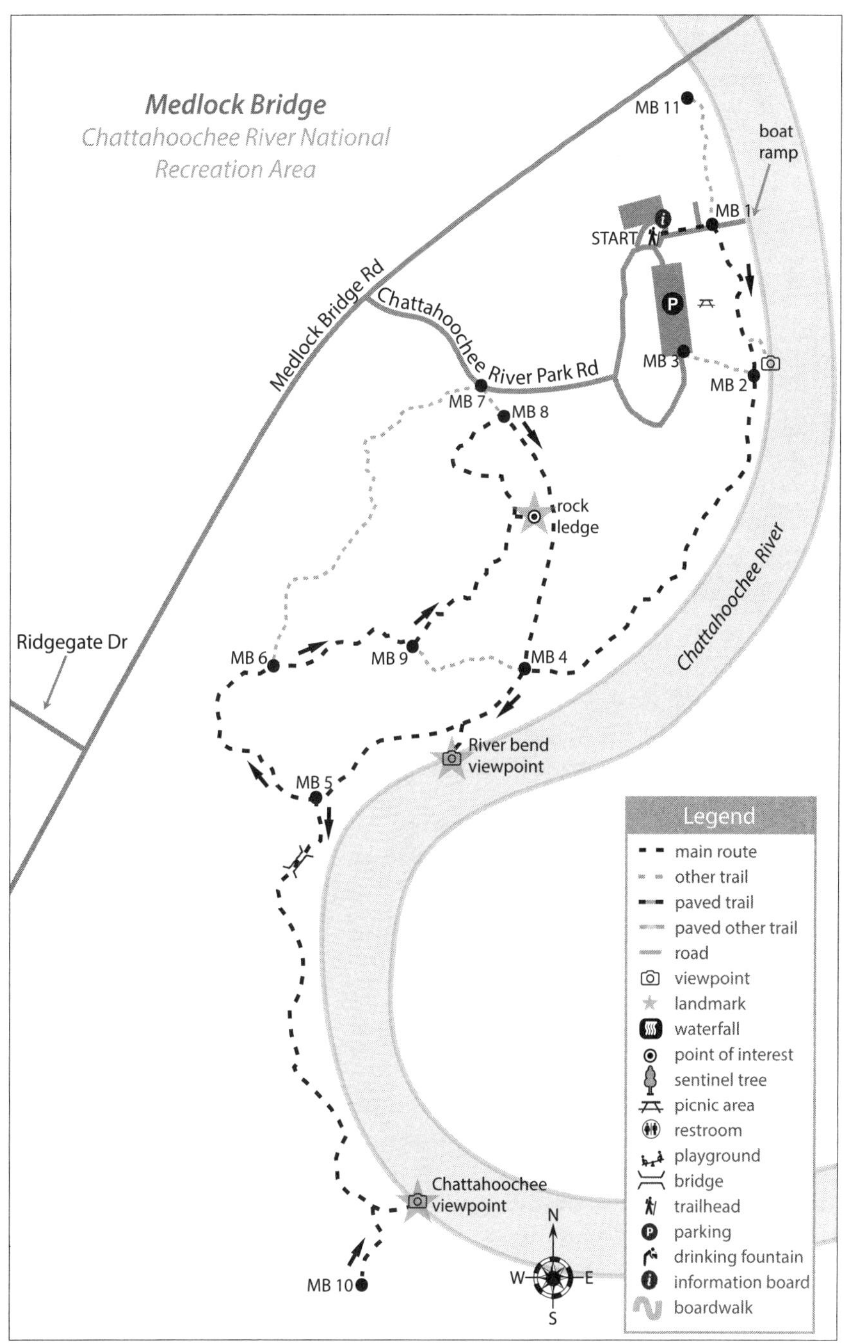
Medlock Bridge
Chattahoochee River National
Recreation Area
MB 11
boat
ramp
MB 1
START
Medlock Bridge Rd
Chattahoochee River Park Rd
MB 3
MB 2
MB 7
MB 8
rock
ledge
Chattahoochee River
Ridgegate Dr
MB 6
MB 9
MB 4
River bend
viewpoint
MB 5
Legend
main route
other trail
paved trail
paved other trail
road
viewpoint
landmark
waterfall
point of interest
sentinel tree
picnic area
restroom
playground
bridge
trailhead
parking
drinking fountain
information board
boardwalk
Chattahoochee
viewpoint
N
W
E
S
MB 10

The rock ledge on the park's central ridge has great forest views.

left and follow the trail along the edge of a steep ridge. In 0.1 mile, pass a rock ledge on the right that provides nice views of the land below.

Descend the steep ridge and arrive at junction MB 8. Turn right and hike 0.1 mile to junction MB 4. Look up to your right, and you can see the rock ledge you visited earlier. At junction MB 4, turn left and hike 0.3 mile back to the boat ramp, then left to end your hike at the information boards where you started.

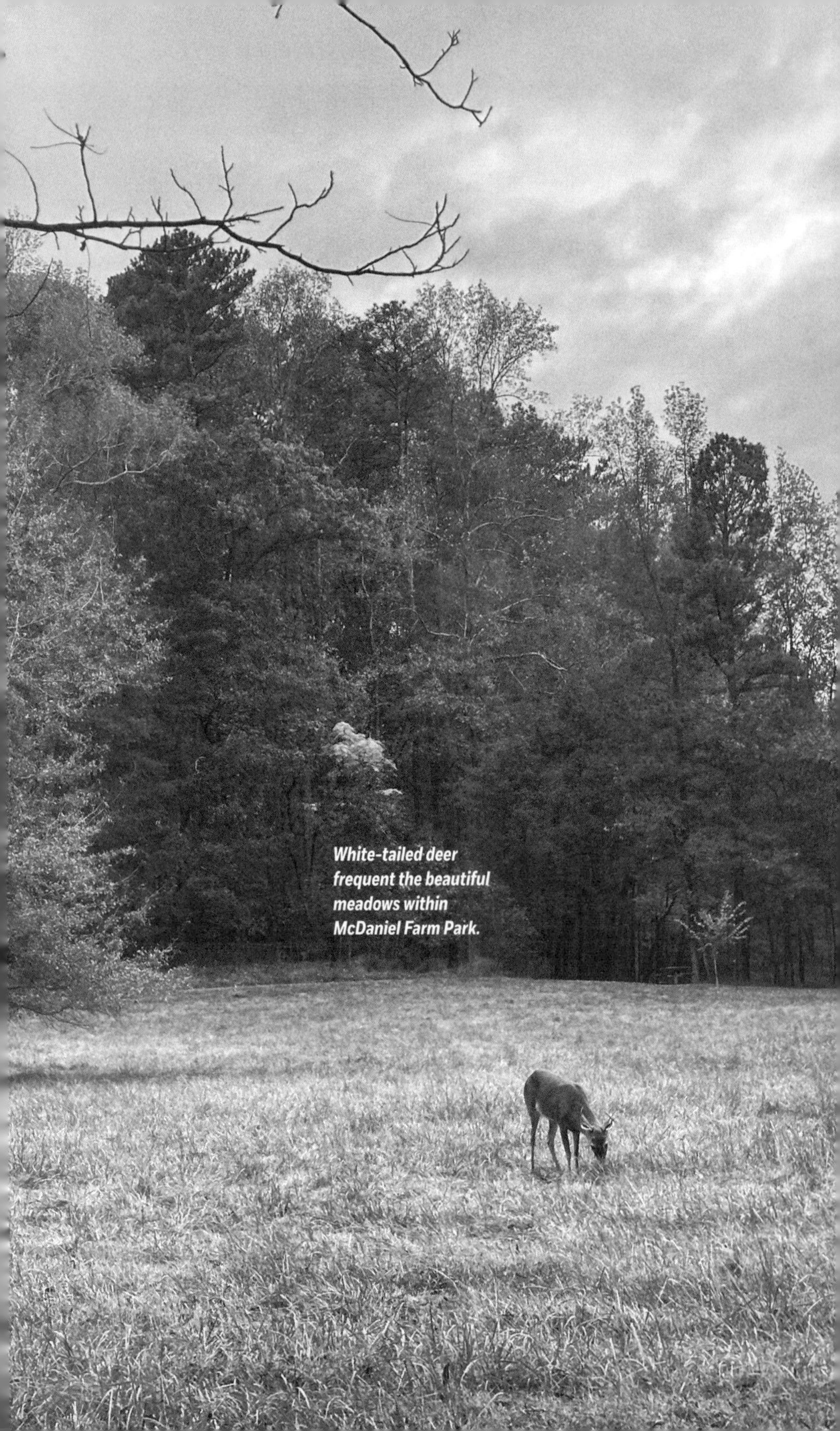

White-tailed deer frequent the beautiful meadows within McDaniel Farm Park.

McDaniel Farm Park

This 130-acre greenspace is a pleasant and unexpected surprise. Bordered by the sprawling Gwinnett Place Mall complex, the park is a quiet gem of woodland, babbling streams, and peaceful meadows. Once you're on the trails it's easy to forget the bustling development next door. The paved trails wind through fields and forests, along creeks, and through a restored farmstead area. This parcel of land was owned by the McDaniel family since 1859 and is now owned and preserved by Gwinnett County. This hiking route is friendly for chair users, bicyclists, and parents with strollers, but there are miles of dirt trails, too, if you want a more rugged adventure.

HOW TO GET THERE

Driving Distance from Downtown Atlanta: 25 miles
Address: 3251 McDaniel Road, Duluth, GA 30096
Closest Interstate: I-85
City, County: Duluth, Gwinnett
Public Transit: Ride Gwinnett 10A/10B bus + 0.5-mile walk
Parking: Paved parking area at the end of McDaniel Road

HIKE DISTANCE

2.3-mile figure-8 loop

DIFFICULTY

Overall: Easy to moderate
Navigation: Map posted at trailhead; trail markers at most junctions
Terrain: This route is all on paved multiuse trails, but there are many hard-packed dirt side trails
Elevation Change: Rolling hills with a few short but steep ascents and descents

SAFETY

Usage ★★★★★
Visibility ★★★★★
Upkeep ★★★★★
Parking ★★★★★

HOURS

- Trails open sunrise to sunset
- Heritage preservation farm open 10:00 am to 4:00 pm

DOGS

- Leashed dogs allowed

- Fenced off-leash dog park along this hike route at northeast corner of the park

FACILITIES	• Toilets at trailhead • Playground, picnic areas, swinging benches, water fountains, information kiosks, bicycle racks, historic farm and interpretive signage; shelters located at or adjacent to both parking areas
FEES & PERMITS	None
LAND MANAGER	Gwinnett County Parks & Recreation

Landmarks

SENTINEL SWEETGUM

Sweetgums are one of the tallest-growing tree species in the Atlanta metro area. Sweetgum can be identified by its star-shaped leaves and spiky round seed pods littering the ground. Find this double-trunked specimen on the right of the paved trail, just before a junction.

MEADOW

Because most Atlanta-area trails are forested, the large meadows at McDaniel Farm Park are a unique and beautiful feature that provide habitat and feeding areas for mammals, including white-tailed deer, and many species of birds.

HERITAGE PRESERVATION FARM

The McDaniel family's farm has been restored by Gwinnett County to demonstrate an example of farm life from the early 1900s. Visit the gardens, barn, farmhouse, and tenant house and read the interpretive signs along the way to learn more. This area of the park is open from 10:00 am to 4:00 pm daily.

Hike Route

McDaniel Farm Park has an extensive network of paved and dirt trails that allow more than 5 miles of hiking. This 2.3-mile route stays on the paved trails and is friendly for chair users, bicyclists, and parents with strollers. If you want a more rugged hike, use the map to explore the dirt trails.

Start your hike next to the information board to the left of the restrooms. Pass a barn on the right and boardwalk on the left that leads to a picnic pavilion. Continue straight on the paved path,

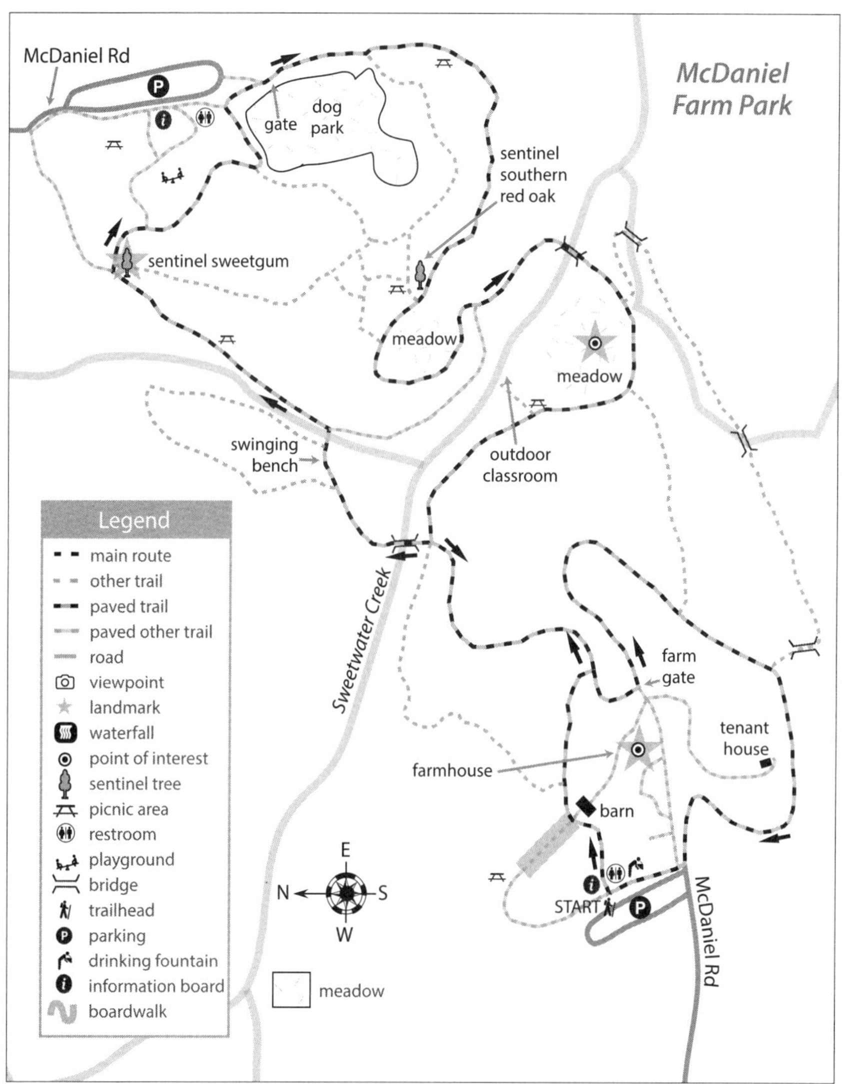
McDaniel Farm Park
McDaniel Rd
gate
dog
park
sentinel
southern
red oak
sentinel sweetgum
meadow
meadow
swinging
bench
outdoor
classroom
Sweetwater Creek
farm
gate
tenant
house
farmhouse
barn
START
McDaniel Rd
E
N
S
W
meadow
Legend
main route
other trail
paved trail
paved other trail
road
viewpoint
landmark
waterfall
point of interest
sentinel tree
picnic area
restroom
playground
bridge
trailhead
parking
drinking fountain
information board
boardwalk

This historic tenant farmhouse is in the middle of the suburbs.

passing a dirt trail on the left and skirting the edge of the farm. At a junction with another paved trail, turn left and hike downhill.

Reach a junction at the bottom of the hill in 0.15 mile. Stay straight on the paved trail and cross a bridge. Pass a dirt trail on the left in 0.1 mile, then pass a picnic table and swinging bench before reaching another paved junction. Turn left and pass another picnic table in 0.1 mile, then arrive at a junction near a large double-trunked sweetgum tree with two eastern red cedars at its base. Stay right on the paved trail.

Pass a paved trail on the left that leads to a playground, picnic pavilion, restrooms, and parking area. Stay on the main paved path for 0.2 mile, passing several more paved trails that lead left to the playground and picnic area and a dirt trail on the right that leads into the interior of the park. After passing the entrance to the dog park, pass another dirt trail on the right and hike the winding paved path through a mature forest to reach a meadow with a swinging bench and picnic table on the right. Near the bench, look for a southern red oak tree with outstretched branches that seem to defy gravity.

The paved trail curves left around the clearing and descends. At a junction in 0.1 mile, turn left, hike another 0.1 mile to cross a bridge over Sweetwater Creek, and enter a larger meadow. Keep your eye out for deer, which often graze in this meadow. As you circle the clearing, pass two dirt trails on your left that lead uphill to the farm. Stay on the paved path past a picnic area and outdoor classroom to reach a junction near another bridge over Sweetwater Creek.

Turn left and hike uphill on the paved trail. Continue straight at the junction near the top of the hill. The trail curves left along a fence covered with muscadine vines, then reaches the farm gate. If the gate is open (10:00 am to 4:00 pm daily), you should definitely explore the historic farm and read the interpretive signs about the McDaniel family. Then continue on the main paved trail.

Over the final 0.5 mile of the route, the trail winds around the perimeter of the farm past two dirt trails on the left that lead downhill to the large meadow. End your hike at the parking area and restrooms.

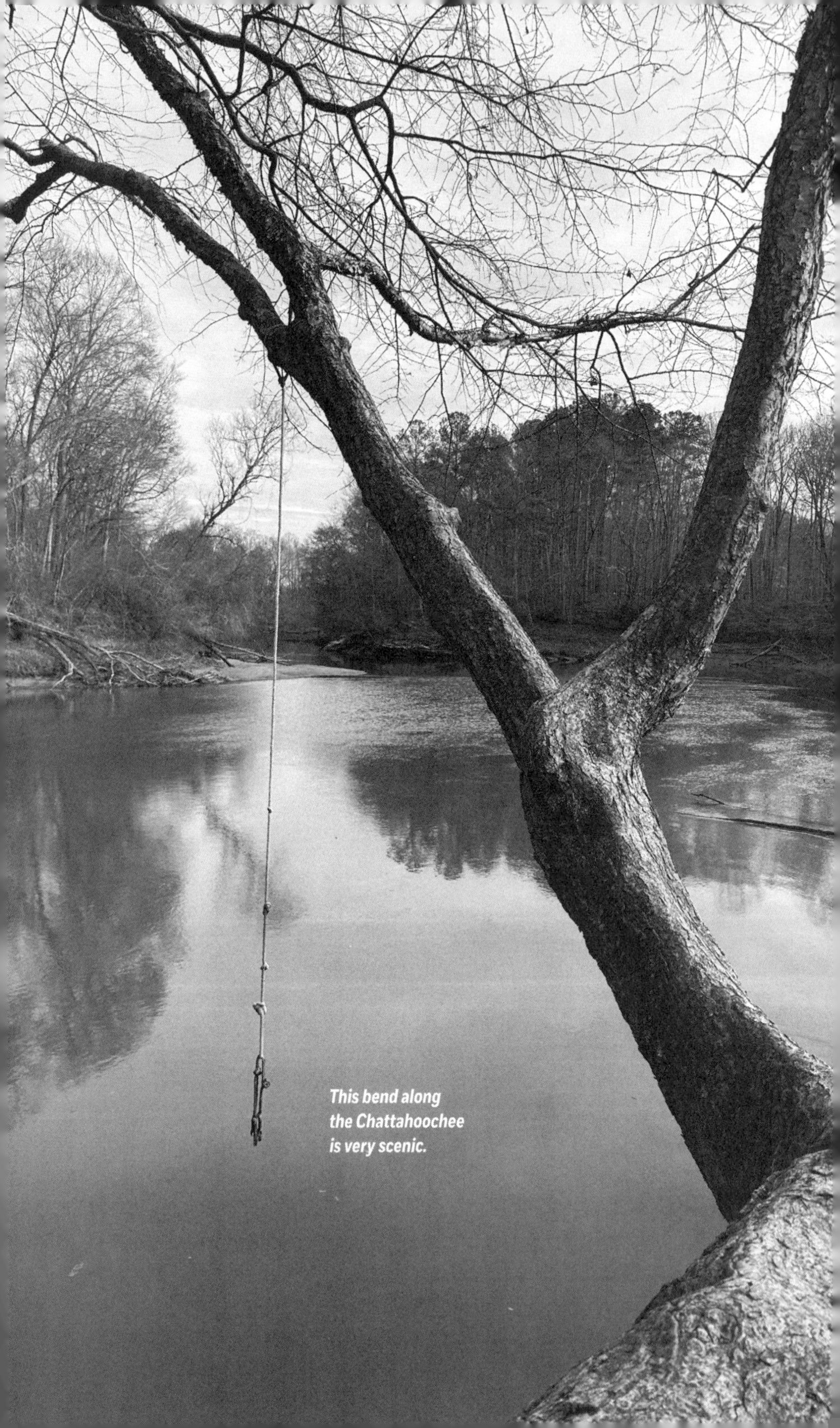

This bend along the Chattahoochee is very scenic.

Chattahoochee Pointe Park

This Forsyth County Park is a great entryway for new hikers wanting to experience the Chattahoochee River. The 3-mile crushed gravel loop trail will lead you through former farm fields and forest edges and along Dick Creek and the Chattahoochee River. Though you are never far away from the parking lot and adjacent subdivisions, you will enjoy this easy, fun, and scenic hike. There is something for everyone at Chattahoochee Pointe, whether you're a hiker, jogger, dog walker, birder, paddler, or disc golfer.

HOW TO GET THERE

Driving Distance from Downtown Atlanta: 35 miles

Address: 5790 Chattahoochee Pointe Drive, Suwanee, GA 30024

Closest Interstate: I-85

City, County: Near Suwanee, in Forsyth County

Parking: Multiple large gravel parking areas upon entering the park; park near restrooms for best access to the trail

HIKE DISTANCE

3.3-mile loop

DIFFICULTY

Overall: Easy

Navigation: Map at an information board near the parking area; kilometer markers along the trail; the trail is wide and easy to follow

Terrain: Wide crushed gravel paths with a section of boardwalk; two short hard-packed dirt side trails

Elevation Change: Minimal elevation change—very level

SAFETY

Usage ★★★★★

Visibility ★★★★★

Upkeep ★★★★★

Parking ★★★★★

HOURS

March through October, 6:00 am to 9:30 pm; November through February, 6:00 am to 7:00 pm

DOGS

Leashed dogs allowed

FACILITIES	• Toilets at far end of parking area • Playground, picnic areas, drinking fountain, information kiosk, disc golf course, boat ramp
FEES & PERMITS	None
LAND MANAGER	Forsyth County Parks & Recreation

Landmarks

SENTINEL WATER OAK

Water oaks are one of the most common oak species in the Atlanta area. Fast growing and tolerant of moist soil, these trees are commonly found on the edge of fields. This particular tree is hollow, craggy, and almost spooky looking.

CHATTAHOOCHEE BOAT RAMP & VIEWPOINT

This section of the Chattahoochee River is a 48-mile national water trail contained within the national recreation area and is 341 river miles from the Gulf of Mexico. This park offers one of the access points for paddling the water trail.

CHATTAHOOCHEE VIEWPOINT

Notice the difference in the color of the water at this section of river. At the boat ramp, the river cuts a deep channel, and the water is deep green. Here, the relatively more shallow water has a browner tint.

Hike Route

Start your hike near the restrooms. Cross the parking area and access the crushed gravel path through a gap in the split-rail fence, then turn right to begin your hike. In about 100 yards, the trail crosses the gravel drive and curves around the edge of a large field. In 0.3 mile, an old grass-and-dirt trail splits off to the left. Stay straight on the gravel path.

In 0.1 mile, pass through a line of trees that used to separate farm fields. On your right is a giant crooked water oak tree with a hollow trunk. Its shape is interesting and kind of spooky. Continue straight when the grassy side trail reconnects with the gravel path.

Over the next 0.25 mile, you'll pass a fenced utility area and a plaque that memorializes the Gilstrap farm, which was on this land from 1908 to 2015. Then reach a junction with a private trail that provides access to this park from the adjacent subdivision. Stay straight. The trail then curves left to parallel Dick Creek. You'll see

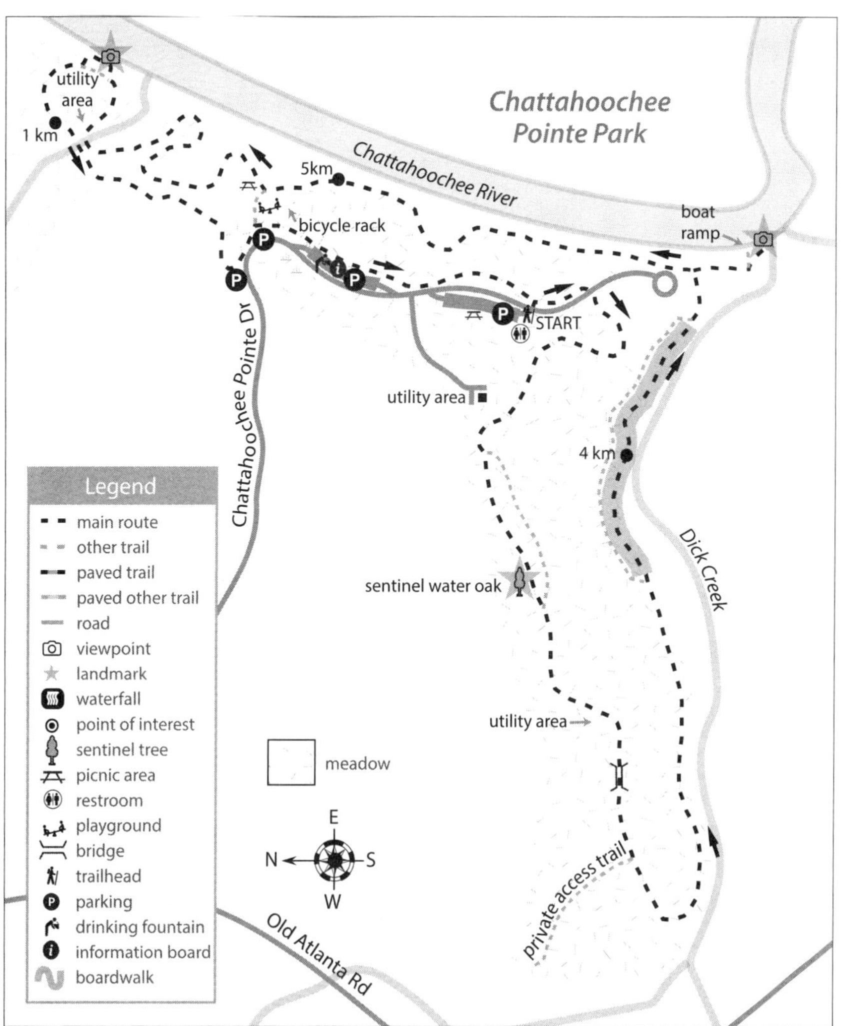

Chattahoochee
Pointe Park
Chattahoochee River
utility
area
1 km
5km
bicycle rack
boat
ramp
START
utility area
4 km
Chattahoochee Pointe Dr
sentinel water oak
Dick Creek
utility area
meadow
E
N
S
W
private access trail
Old Atlanta Rd
Legend
main route
other trail
paved trail
paved other trail
road
viewpoint
landmark
waterfall
point of interest
sentinel tree
picnic area
restroom
playground
bridge
trailhead
parking
drinking fountain
information board
boardwalk

An old and unusually shaped water oak grows on the edge of this trail.

several disc golf baskets and tees nearby. This is a good area to leave the trail and visit the banks of Dick Creek to your right.

In 0.3 mile, a raised wooden boardwalk branches off to the left of the trail. You can stay on the crushed gravel path or walk the boardwalk for the next 0.3 mile. When the boardwalk ends, hike another 100 yards to reach a junction with the boat ramp access road. Turn right and hike 100 yards to the boat ramp. Look to the right of the ramp for a small unofficial trail that leads to a great view of a bend in the Chattahoochee River. Footprints and rope swings indicate that locals play in the water here.

After enjoying the view, backtrack to the previous junction and turn right to continue on the crushed gravel trail. The trail parallels the banks of the Chattahoochee and offers sporadic views of the river. Pass a 5-kilometer marker in 0.4 mile, then stay on the gravel trail as disc golf paths cross the trail.

At a picnic pavilion near the playground, turn right. The trail continues to wind through fields and forest edges along the banks of the Chattahoochee. In the farthest field, after passing a fenced utility area, look for a bench and narrow single-track trail leading right to a viewpoint of the Chattahoochee River. Continue on the crushed gravel trail for 0.4 mile, passing a 1-kilometer marker, and then reach the playground again. Stay straight for 0.3 mile parallel to the parking area and then end your hike near the restrooms.

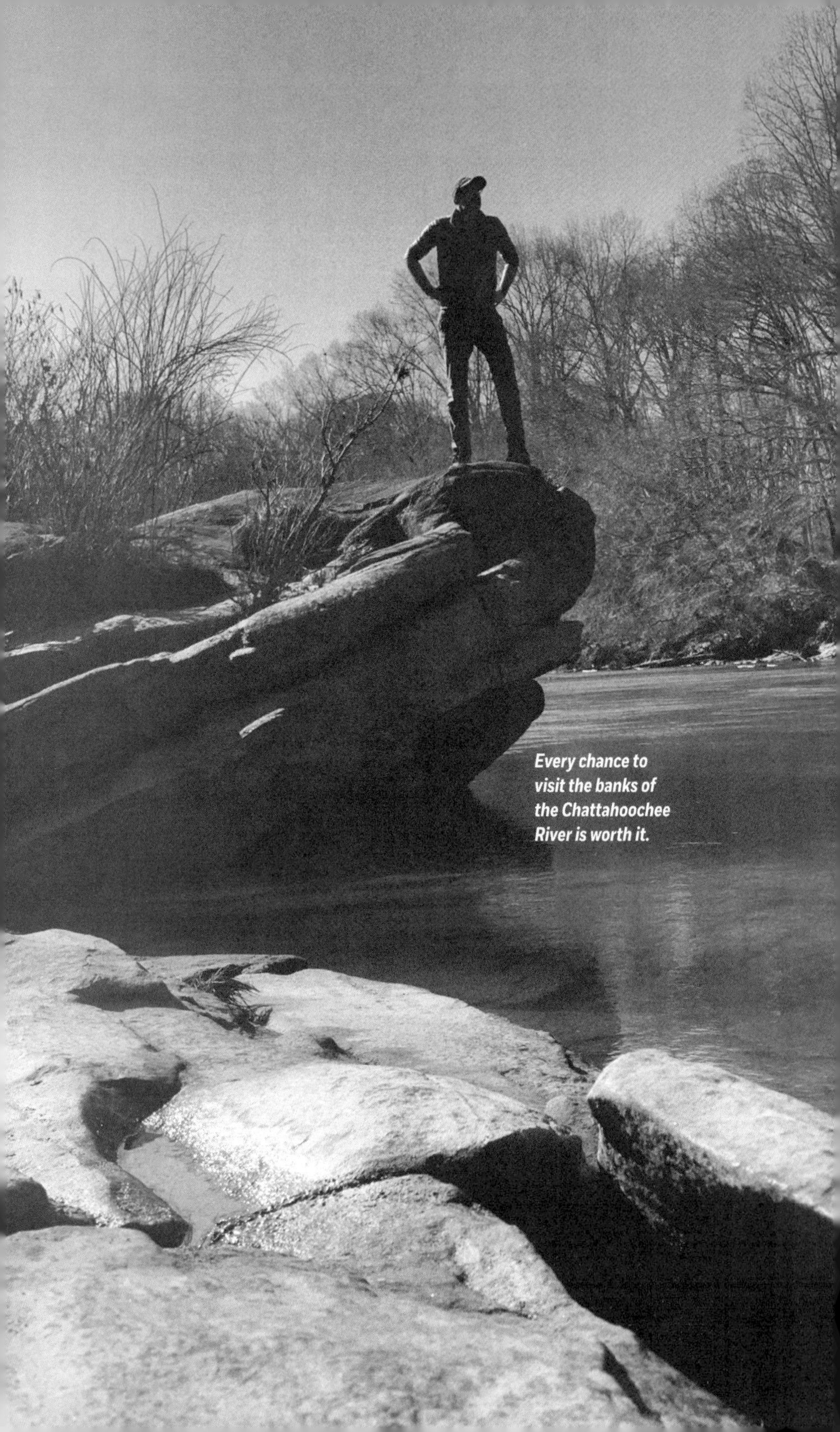

Every chance to visit the banks of the Chattahoochee River is worth it.

Settles Bridge Park

This hike spans two beautiful parks. The 2 miles of well-maintained trails within Settles Bridge Park connect with 2 additional miles of unofficial but well-traveled paths of the Settles Bridge Unit of the Chattahoochee River National Recreation Area. You can walk the paved multiuse path through the young forest, hike the crushed gravel trails over hills and through valleys in the county park, and explore the unofficial trails along the Chattahoochee River on national recreation area land. Best of all, this hike includes a visit to the oldest still-standing bridge across this section of the Chattahoochee.

HOW TO GET THERE

Driving Distance from Downtown Atlanta: 36 miles

Address: 380 Johnson Road, Suwanee, GA 30024

Closest Interstate: I-85

City, County: Suwanee, Gwinnett

Parking: Paved parking area near the skate park, playground, and trailhead

HIKE DISTANCE

4-mile loop

DIFFICULTY

Overall: Moderate

Navigation: Trail map at entrance and posted at many junctions within Settles Bridge Park; the national recreation area has no directional signage, and navigation is more complicated

Terrain: Hard-packed gravel and dirt trails with concrete options; at least one creek crossing on stones

Elevation Change: Rolling hills, but no major ascents or descents

SAFETY

Usage ★★★★☆

Visibility ★★★★☆

Upkeep ★★★★☆

Parking ★★★★★

HOURS

Sunrise to sunset

DOGS	Leashed dogs allowed; off-leash dog park in the center of Settles Bridge Park can be accessed by the paved multiuse trail
FACILITIES	• Toilets near parking lot • Skate park, basketball court, playgrounds, multiuse path, picnic pavilion, dog park
FEES & PERMITS	None
LAND MANAGER	Gwinnett County Parks & Recreation and Chattahoochee River National Recreation Area—National Park Service

Landmarks

CHURCH

Though this small, well-maintained church is on private property, the trail passes no more than 50 feet from its front doors. Because there is no sign or other information posted, the church is a fun mystery and opportunity for imagination while hiking.

ROCK OUTCROP

The U.S. Army Corps of Engineers manages the water flow in the Chattahoochee, so this rock outcrop in the river below the trail is accessible when the water is low, but it is almost completely submerged during high flow.

HISTORIC SETTLES BRIDGE

Fords and ferries were the only way to cross the Chattahoochee River until the late 1800s, when bridges started being built. Settles Bridge, built in 1880, is the oldest still-standing bridge in the national recreation area. The steel trusses are visible, but the wooden decking is no longer there.

Hike Route

Start your hike at the paved multiuse path trailhead near the park's entrance. Walk a few steps on the pavement but almost immediately turn right onto a crushed gravel path and hike downhill into the forest. In 0.25 mile, the trail splits and reconnects on a steep uphill. The left path is slightly easier to hike. Just after the trails reconnect, reach a junction and turn right.

In 0.1 mile, pass a small church on private property to the right, then arrive at a trail junction with a map and help locator sign. Turn left, hike 0.25 mile, then turn left at the next junction. The trail

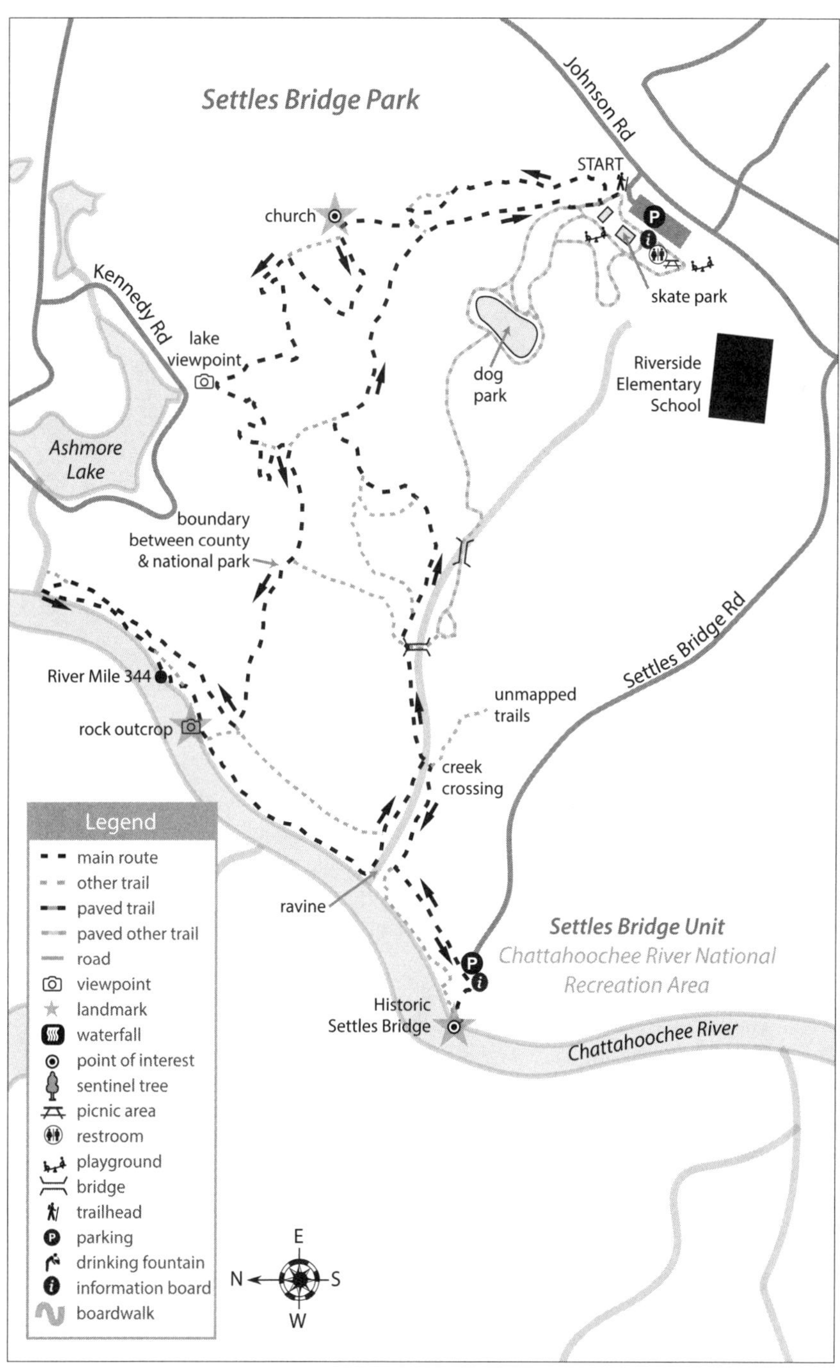
Settles Bridge Park
Johnson Rd
START
church
Kennedy Rd
lake viewpoint
skate park
dog park
Riverside Elementary School
Ashmore Lake
boundary between county & national park
Settles Bridge Rd
River Mile 344
rock outcrop
unmapped trails
creek crossing
ravine
Settles Bridge Unit
Chattahoochee River National Recreation Area
Historic Settles Bridge
Chattahoochee River
Legend
main route
other trail
paved trail
paved other trail
road
viewpoint
landmark
waterfall
point of interest
sentinel tree
picnic area
restroom
playground
bridge
trailhead
parking
drinking fountain
information board
boardwalk
E
N
S
W

The steel trusses of the historic Settles Bridge were originally built in 1880.

descends past a spot where you can see Ashmore Lake, then curves left and begins a steep ascent. Near the top of the hill, turn right at a bench, then right again to arrive at a junction marked with help locator 1144. Turn right here and hike 0.15 mile to reach a large sign marking the boundary between the county park and the national recreation area.

Pass the sign and turn left at a stone monument honoring trail supporters. This trail leads generally downhill for 0.2 mile to reach a sewer line clearing that parallels the Chattahoochee. Use this clearing as a trail—turn right and hike 0.3 mile until you get to a larger clearing near a creek. Turn left on a single-track trail to reach a trail right next to the riverbank, then hike downstream along the river.

There are many unofficial trails in this area, so generally stay on the path closest to the river. Pass mile marker 344 on the river (this is for boats), then a large rock outcrop in the river below you on the right. Continue to hike along the edge of the river for 0.25 mile to reach a creek ravine with steep banks. Do not attempt to cross here. Follow the trail as it curves left, away from the river. In 0.15 mile, there is an easy rock crossing to the right. Cross the creek and hike to the right along the opposite bank. Curve left into a wide pine-tree-lined path that leads you to the national recreation area parking area.

Hike the trail behind the information board to visit the historic Settles Bridge, then backtrack to the creek crossing. After crossing the water, turn right to hike 0.15 mile to a junction in the county park. This hike turns left, then immediately right to follow the main nature trail back to the park entrance. (If you turn right, you can walk the paved multiuse path back.)

Stay straight at each subsequent junction until you reach a T-junction with a wide gravel trail. Turn right and hike almost 0.5 mile before this trail joins the paved path. Continue straight on the pavement to return to the parking lot and end your hike.

This is where the Chattahoochee River emerges from Lake Lanier below Buford Dam.

Bowmans Island & Laurel Ridge Trail

CHATTAHOOCHEE RIVER NATIONAL RECREATION AREA

Whether you are looking for an afternoon hike or a full-day trek, these two trails provide an exceptional adventure along the banks of both Lake Lanier and the Chattahoochee River. Starting in the shadow of Buford Dam, the trails of Bowmans Island provide rolling hills and plenty of river views. Just across the river, the Laurel Ridge Trail follows the panoramic lakeshore and then delights you with a cascading waterfall to end the hike. Only have a few hours? This hike can easily be split in two.

HOW TO GET THERE

Driving Distance from Downtown Atlanta: 44 miles

Address: Parking on Lower Pool Road, Cumming, GA 30041; GPS 34.158222, -84.077667

Closest Interstate: I-85

City, County: Cumming, Forsyth

Parking: Gravel parking area near the U.S. Army Corps of Engineers boat ramp at the end of Lower Pool Road; alternative parking in a national recreation area gravel lot just off Lower Pool Road

HIKE DISTANCE

9.75-mile multiple figure-8 loops (5 miles on Bowmans Island trails, 4.75 miles on Laurel Ridge Trail)

DIFFICULTY

Overall: Strenuous

Navigation: In the national recreation area there are information boards at trailheads and maps posted at each trail junction; the Laurel Ridge Trail has some white blazes and some directional signage but is more difficult to navigate

Terrain: Hard-packed dirt and gravel trails with short sections on pavement; several sets of steep stairs

Elevation Change: Rolling hills and several short but steep ascents and descents

SAFETY

Usage ★★★★☆

Visibility ★★★★☆

Upkeep ★★★☆☆

Parking ★★★★☆

HOURS	Sunrise to sunset
DOGS	Leashed dogs allowed in national recreation area, but dogs are not allowed on Laurel Ridge Trail
FACILITIES	• Restrooms at trailhead and at several other places along Laurel Ridge Trail • Picnic areas, drinking fountains, and other park amenities along Laurel Ridge Trail
FEES & PERMITS	$8 daily fee—purchase at U.S. Army Corps of Engineers kiosk on Lower Pool Road or purchase Chattahoochee River National Recreation Area day pass on recreation .gov
LAND MANAGER	Chattahoochee River National Recreation Area—National Park Service and U.S. Army Corps of Engineers

Landmarks

BOWMANS ISLAND VIEWPOINT

Bowmans Island is one of the largest islands in the metro Atlanta section of the Chattahoochee. The island was used by European settlers to help them ford the river, and a fishing weir built by indigenous people has been identified at the upstream tip of the island. Today there is no access to the island.

LAKE LANIER VIEWPOINT

Lake Lanier is Atlanta's primary reservoir for drinking water and a destination for water recreation. From this peaceful spot, you can sit on a swinging bench and watch families play on a sandy beach, listen to the wind in the trees, or watch birds. The lake was created in the 1950s when the U.S. Army Corps of Engineers built the earthen Buford Dam.

ROCKY CREEK CASCADE

This small cascade is a lovely way to end a long day of hiking. Pause on the wooden bridge and watch the flow of the water across the rocks. Listen to the sounds that surround you, and smell the lush forest scents. It's no wonder humans are drawn to waterfalls, right?

Hike Route

This hike combines two trail systems to create a nearly 10-mile route. Hike the Bowmans Island trails and Laurel Ridge Trail together or separately, depending on your stamina and sense of adventure. This route starts at the U.S. Army Corps of Engineers parking area at the end of Lower Pool Road. Walk back along the road, past the restrooms, to reach the gravel national recreation area parking area. Cross the parking lot, pass an information board, then cross a bridge to reach trail junction BI 1, where the trail curves left.

At junction BI 2, make a sharp right and hike uphill through an area that can be very overgrown in the summer. (If it doesn't look inviting, consider continuing straight ahead from junction BI 2 to BI 3 and southward from there as described at the end of the next paragraph to bypass this upland route.) The overgrowth ends in about 50 feet, and the forest opens up as the trail continues ascending the ridge. In 0.25 mile, reach the high point of the ridge, where there is a viewpoint. Haw Creek is visible below in the winter but hidden when leaves are on the trees.

Continue hiking for 0.3 mile to reach junction BI 9. Take the left fork and hike to BI 7, where you'll go straight to reach BI 6. Go right at BI 6, then left at BI 5, and continue hiking downhill. Pass a beautiful double-trunked American beech tree on the right, then arrive at junction BI 4. Stay straight for 50 yards before you come to junction BI 3, where you'll turn right and cross the creek on rocks, then curve left toward the river.

Over the next mile, you'll hike close to the banks of the Chattahoochee River, crossing several bridges and opportunities to view the river and Bowmans Island to your left. When you get to a cinder-block utility building, continue straight and hike this wide gravel trail 0.1 mile farther to reach junction BI 20. Turn left on the single-track trail and hike 0.2 mile to junction BI 22. Turn left on the wide gravel trail. As the trail approaches a chain-link fence near the Buford National Fish Hatchery, turn right and hike uphill at junction BI 23. Then, at junction BI 24, turn right.

In 0.4 mile, reach junction BI 25 near private residences. Turn right before the information board and hike to junction BI 21. Turn left and hike the wide gravel path to junction BI 20. Continue straight, back along this trail you've already hiked, to cross the creek and arrive at junction BI 3. Go right and hike past junctions BI 2 and BI 1 to reach the national recreation area parking lot. Backtrack along Lower Pond Road to the U.S. Army Corps of Engineers parking lot where you started.

To continue your hike on Laurel Ridge Trail, cross the parking lot and walk a faint path through the grass between the picnic tables. When you reach a steel bridge spanning the channel at the base of

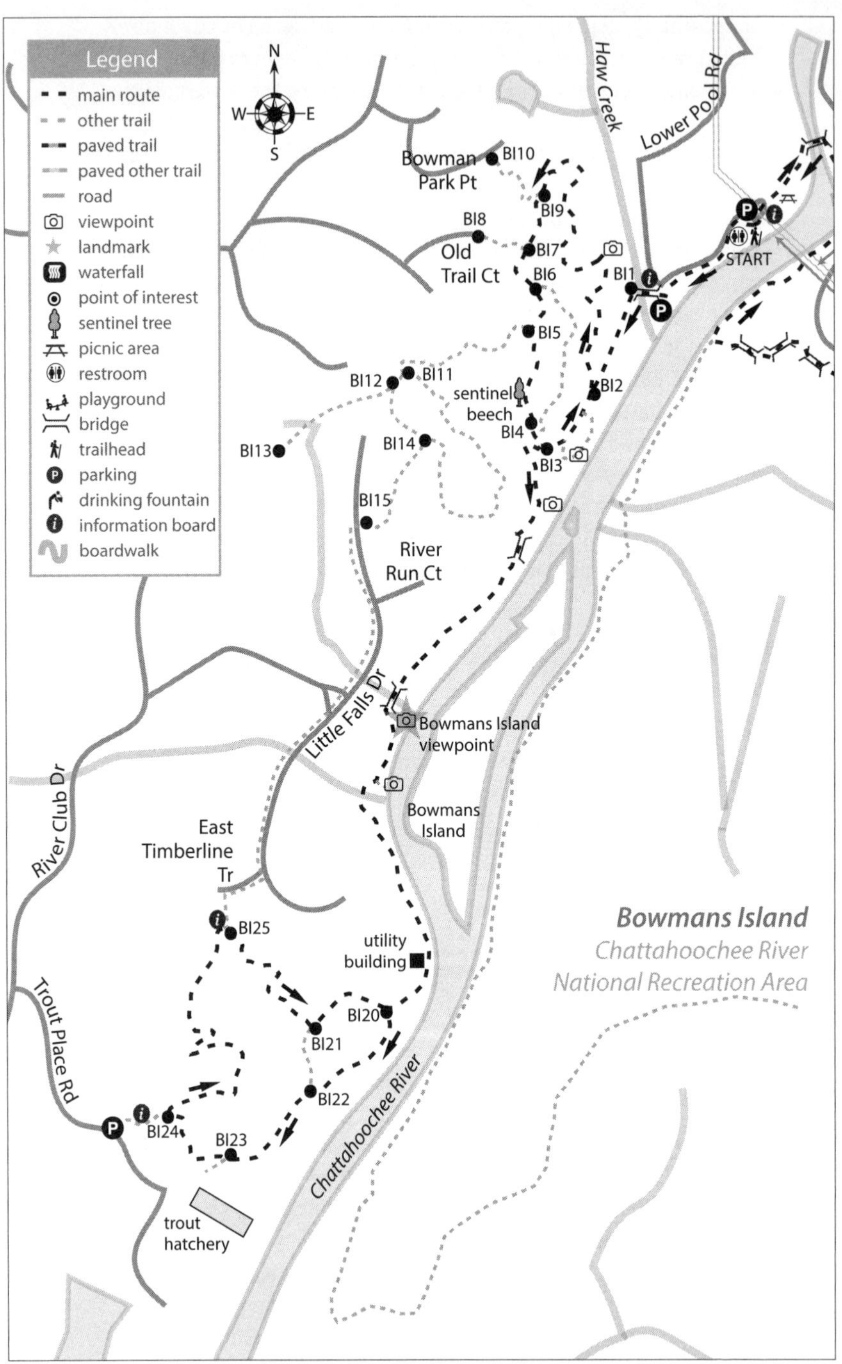
Legend
main route
other trail
paved trail
paved other trail
road
viewpoint
landmark
waterfall
point of interest
sentinel tree
picnic area
restroom
playground
bridge
trailhead
parking
drinking fountain
information board
boardwalk
N
W
E
S
Haw Creek
Lower Pool Rd
Bowman Park Pt
BI10
BI9
BI8
Old Trail Ct
BI7
BI6
BI1
START
BI5
BI12
BI11
sentinel beech
BI2
BI4
BI13
BI14
BI3
BI15
River Run Ct
Little Falls Dr
Bowmans Island viewpoint
River Club Dr
Bowmans Island
East Timberline Tr
BI25
utility building
Bowmans Island
Chattahoochee River National Recreation Area
Trout Place Rd
BI20
BI21
BI22
BI24
BI23
Chattahoochee River
trout hatchery

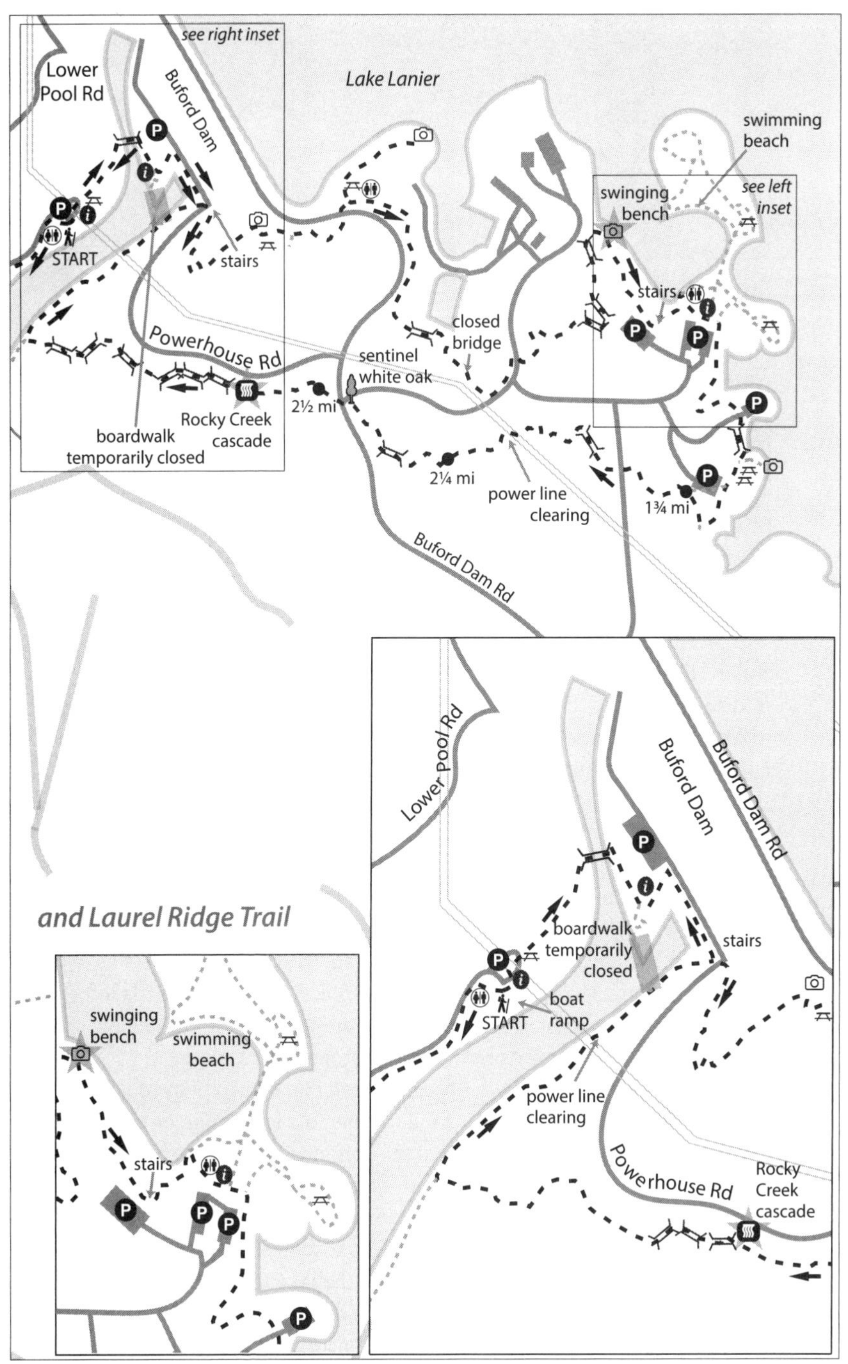

see right inset
Lower Pool Rd
Buford Dam
Lake Lanier
swimming beach
swinging bench
see left inset
START
stairs
stairs
closed bridge
Powerhouse Rd
sentinel white oak
2½ mi
Rocky Creek cascade
boardwalk temporarily closed
2¼ mi
power line clearing
1¾ mi
Buford Dam Rd
and Laurel Ridge Trail
swinging bench
swimming beach
stairs
Lower Pool Rd
Buford Dam
Buford Dam Rd
boardwalk temporarily closed
stairs
START
boat ramp
power line clearing
Powerhouse Rd
Rocky Creek cascade

Laurel Ridge Trail has many opportunities for beautiful views of Lake Lanier.

Buford Dam, cross the bridge and walk the paved ramp uphill to an information board. If the boardwalk below you is open, hike downhill and across the boardwalk, then turn left. If the boardwalk is closed, continue up the ramp and turn right on Powerhouse Road to bypass the closed trail.

When you reach steel stairs on the left of the road, hike uphill to begin Laurel Ridge Trail. After a short but steep climb, come to a bench where you can rest and soak in your first view of Lake Lanier. Continue uphill, then reach a junction with a stone wall below a picnic area. Turn left and hike to Buford Dam Road, where the trail crosses on a speed hump to reach another picnic area. A paved trail leads left to a fantastic viewpoint of the lake. Cross the driveway for the picnic area and reenter the woods between two stone pillars.

Keep an eye out for brown fiberglass trail markers to help you navigate through this area. In 0.4 mile, come to a footbridge on the left that was destroyed by a fallen tree. Continue straight to reach a road, then walk left along the edge of the road and through a vehicle gate. Turn right at a crosswalk and reenter the forest.

Cross several small bridges, then come to a lakeside viewpoint with a swinging bench where you can see the lake to the left and a sandy beach to the right. In 0.1 mile, you'll enter a developed recreation area where following this trail becomes more challenging.

Refer to the map as needed and look carefully for white blazes and trail directional signs.

Walk the sidewalk along the edge of a large parking lot, then head down a flight of stairs. When the trail reaches a paved sidewalk, turn right and walk toward another set of stairs leading to a restroom. Pass the restrooms and an information board and continue straight to a paved junction. Look to the right here and you'll see a white blaze on a tree near the lake on the right. This is Laurel Ridge Trail, so turn right here and hike 0.2 mile to another parking lot. Cross this lot, reenter the forest, then cross a bridge. Turn right and hike uphill past two large picnic pavilions to arrive at another large parking lot. A directional sign points diagonally across the parking lot, but if you continue straight on the obvious trail, you can hike through the woods around the parking lot instead of crossing the asphalt.

At the far side of the parking lot, Laurel Ridge Trail reenters the woods near a small sign that reads "1¾ mile." From here, trail navigation becomes easier. Cross a road in 0.15 mile, hike through a power line clearing, then reach Buford Dam Road, where there is a beautiful old white oak tree near the road. Carefully cross this busy road, pass a 2½ mile marker, and hike onward.

The next 0.5 mile of this trail is along Rocky Creek, which cascades down the ridge in a series of beautiful small waterfalls. Crisscross the creek on bridges and then reach a trail junction near the Chattahoochee River. Turn right and follow the bank of the river for 0.25 mile, when you'll reach a junction on the left with the boardwalk trail. If it is closed, hike 100 yards uphill to Powerhouse Road, turn left, and hike back the way you came, across the Chattahoochee River, then across the grassy field to return to the Lower Pool Road parking area and end your hike.

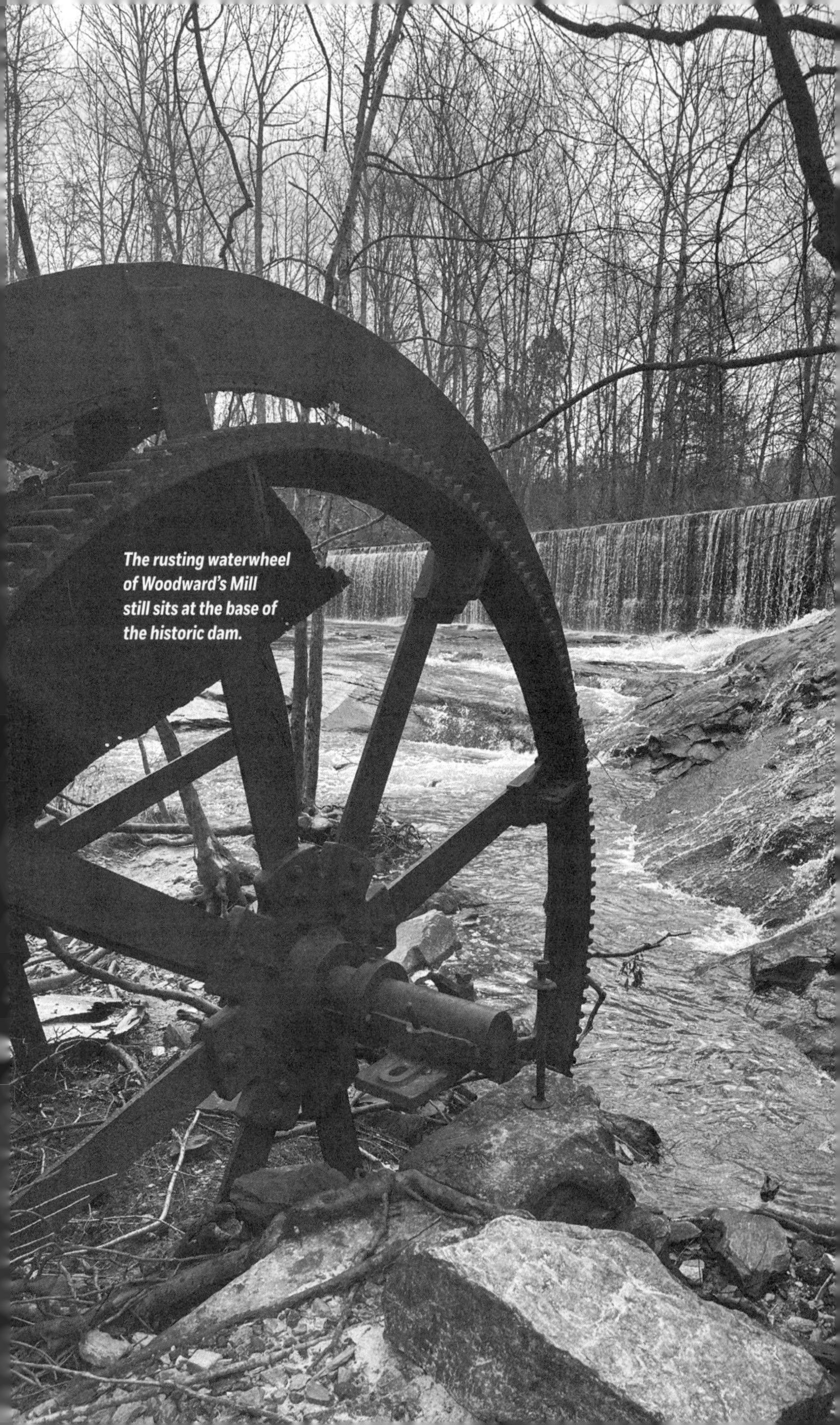

The rusting waterwheel of Woodward's Mill still sits at the base of the historic dam.

Gwinnett Environmental and Heritage Center & Ivy Creek Greenway

This trail system is a tribute to far-sighted urban master planning. Instead of building homes in the wedge of land between I-85 and I-985, Gwinnett County protected this beautiful Piedmont forest. Today, over 12 miles of trails connect the Gwinnett Environmental and Heritage Center, Mill Creek Nature Center, and Ivy Creek Greenway. You'll find amazing trees, a large waterfall, extensive wetlands, a 270-foot suspension bridge, and a historic mill dam. These trails are great for all ages and abilities, and you can design pretty much any adventure you want.

HOW TO GET THERE

Driving Distance from Downtown Atlanta: 36 miles

Address: 2020 Clean Water Drive, Buford, GA 30519

Closest Interstate: I-85

City, County: Buford, Gwinnett

Public Transit: Mill Creek Trailhead can be accessed via Ride Gwinnett bus 50

Parking: Large paved parking area at the Gwinnett Environmental and Heritage Center

HIKE DISTANCE

7.75-mile triple loop (shorter hike options available as well)

DIFFICULTY

Overall: Moderate

Navigation: Color-coded blazes and some trails and maps posted at many locations

Terrain: Dirt, gravel, paved, and boardwalk trails; some dirt trails can be muddy after rain

Elevation Change: Rolling hills with a few short but steep ascents and descents

SAFETY

Usage ★★★☆☆

Visibility ★★★★☆

Upkeep ★★★☆☆

Parking ★★★★★

HOURS

- Trails open daily, sunrise to sunset
- Center open Monday through Saturday, 9:00 am to 4:00 pm

DOGS	Leashed dogs allowed
FACILITIES	• Restrooms in the Heritage Center and along Ivy Creek Greenway • Museum, Treetop Quest, picnic pavilions, outdoor classrooms, observation platforms
FEES & PERMITS	None
LAND MANAGER	Gwinnett County Parks & Recreation and Mill Creek Nature Center

Landmarks

SENTINEL WHITE OAK

Over the years, at least three 19th-century homesites were present in this area of the park. Located on the aptly named Homesite Trail, this impressive white oak was likely a yard tree on one of the homesites. This tree is over 150 years old and more than 15 feet in circumference.

SUSPENSION BRIDGE

This 270-foot cable-stayed suspension bridge over Ivy Creek is impressive in and of itself, but it will also allow the county to eventually connect this trail to the greenspace and trail in George Pierce Park. Across the creek are giant domed water treatment facilities.

WOODWARD'S MILL DAM

This dam and rusting waterwheel are all that remain of William Ivory Woodward's mill, which operated here from the 1850s until the 1960s.

Hike Route

This hike combines three segments of trail that can be hiked together or separately: (1) the Gwinnett Environmental and Heritage Center (GEHC) trail system; (2) the Ivy Creek Greenway and Wildlife Observation Trail; and (3) the Ivy Creek Greenway to Mill Creek Nature Center. It is worth stepping inside the GEHC before or after your walk.

SEGMENT 1

Start your hike at the information board near the parking lot entrance, adjacent to Treetop Quest. Walk away from the information board and into the Treetop Quest area toward the picnic pavilion, then hike the purple-blazed Stream Ecology Trail to the right. Pass a junction with Dogwood Trail, cross a bridge, and then hike uphill. The trail descends the hill and up another before passing a picnic pavilion on the right and then a side trail to a council ring on the left. Stay on Stream Ecology Trail as it winds back through Treetop Quest to reach the information board where you started. Turn left and hike the paved connector trail 0.3 mile to Woodward Mill Road (a closed-access road). Turn left on the road and cross a water authority access road to reach the next segment of this hike.

SEGMENT 2

After crossing the access road and beginning the paved Ivy Creek Greenway, turn right onto Homesite Trail. Walk this dirt path a few hundred feet to a junction and turn left. Pass a huge white oak tree on the right, then a council ring, and continue straight to reach Ivy Creek Greenway again. Turn right and hike the paved path for 0.6 mile to reach an observation deck with views of Ivy Creek, a very impressive suspension bridge, and large water treatment facility domes on the hillside across the creek.

Cross the suspension bridge and curve left onto Wildlife Observation Trail when the pavement ends. Walk for 0.5 mile through a mature forest. Even though you can hear the interstate traffic, it's easy to be enamored by the beauty of this forest. At a junction, turn right to hike a 0.3-mile loop and then hike 0.5 mile back to the paved Ivy Creek Greenway. Follow the greenway back to a picnic pavilion near the Homesite Trail junction to reach the third segment of this hike.

SEGMENT 3

After passing the pavilion, turn right onto the long boardwalk bridge over Ivy Creek. The greenway passes through an apartment complex with picnic tables and a view of the Ivy Creek waterfall on the left. Continue for 0.4 mile on Ivy Creek Greenway under two road bridges to reach the Woodward's Mill Dam. The waterfall created by the dam is picturesque, and the rusted metal waterwheel is a unique artifact.

Beyond the dam, the trail crosses a bridge over the creek, then curves to the right and dips below Buford Drive. Hike another 0.2 mile before the pavement ends. Continue on the gravel greenway through an open chain-link gate and hike 0.4 mile to reach the trails of Mill Creek Nature Center. This series of narrow boardwalk trails through wetlands on either side of Ivy Creek is beautiful and is a fantastic spot for birding. Turn right and hike into the wetlands. Cross

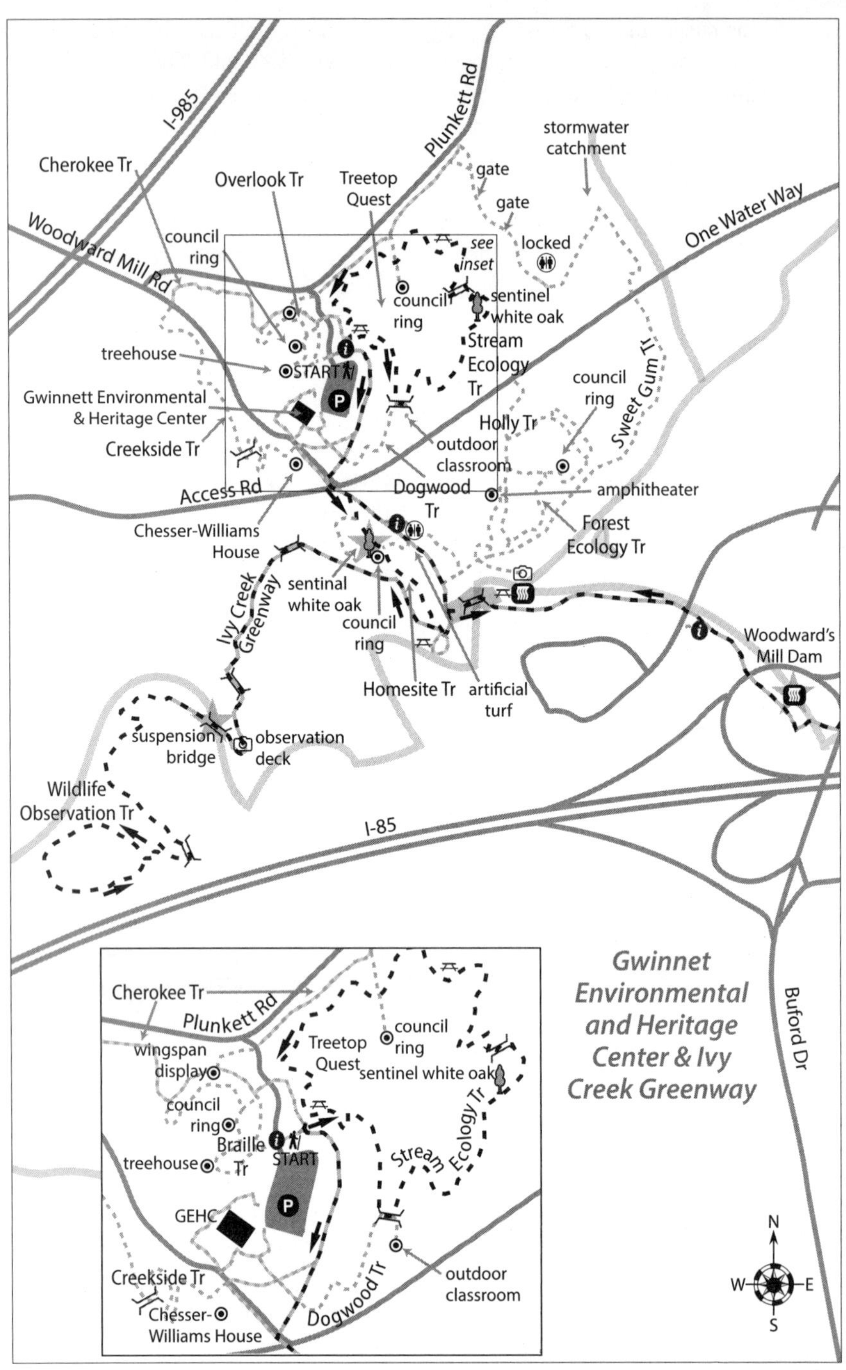
I-985
Plunkett Rd
stormwater catchment
Cherokee Tr
Overlook Tr
Treetop Quest
gate
gate
Woodward Mill Rd
council ring
see inset
locked
One Water Way
council ring
sentinel white oak
treehouse
START
Stream Ecology Tr
Sweet Gum Tr
council ring
Gwinnett Environmental & Heritage Center
Holly Tr
Creekside Tr
outdoor classroom
Access Rd
Dogwood Tr
amphitheater
Chesser-Williams House
Forest Ecology Tr
Ivy Creek Greenway
sentinal white oak
council ring
Woodward's Mill Dam
Homesite Tr
artificial turf
suspension bridge
observation deck
Wildlife Observation Tr
I-85
Cherokee Tr
Plunkett Rd
wingspan display
Treetop Quest
council ring
sentinel white oak
council ring
Braille Tr
START
treehouse
Stream Ecology Tr
GEHC
Creekside Tr
Dogwood Tr
outdoor classroom
Chesser-Williams House
Gwinnet Environmental and Heritage Center & Ivy Creek Greenway
Buford Dr
N
W
E
S

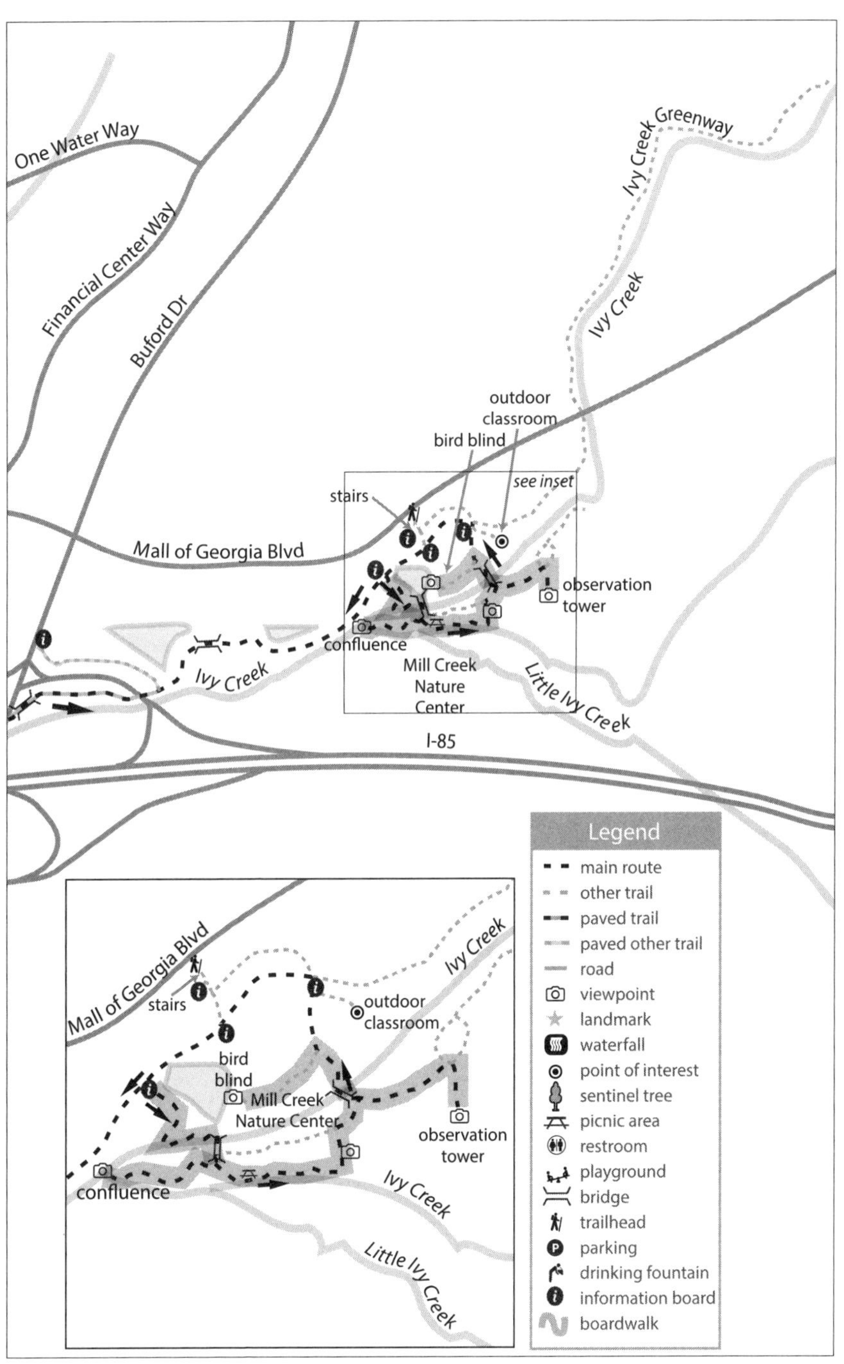
One Water Way
Financial Center Way
Buford Dr
Ivy Creek Greenway
Ivy Creek
outdoor classroom
bird blind
see inset
stairs
Mall of Georgia Blvd
observation tower
confluence
Ivy Creek
Mill Creek Nature Center
Little Ivy Creek
I-85
Legend
main route
other trail
paved trail
paved other trail
road
viewpoint
landmark
waterfall
point of interest
sentinel tree
picnic area
restroom
playground
bridge
trailhead
parking
drinking fountain
information board
boardwalk
Mall of Georgia Blvd
stairs
Ivy Creek
outdoor classroom
bird blind
Mill Creek Nature Center
observation tower
confluence
Ivy Creek
Little Ivy Creek

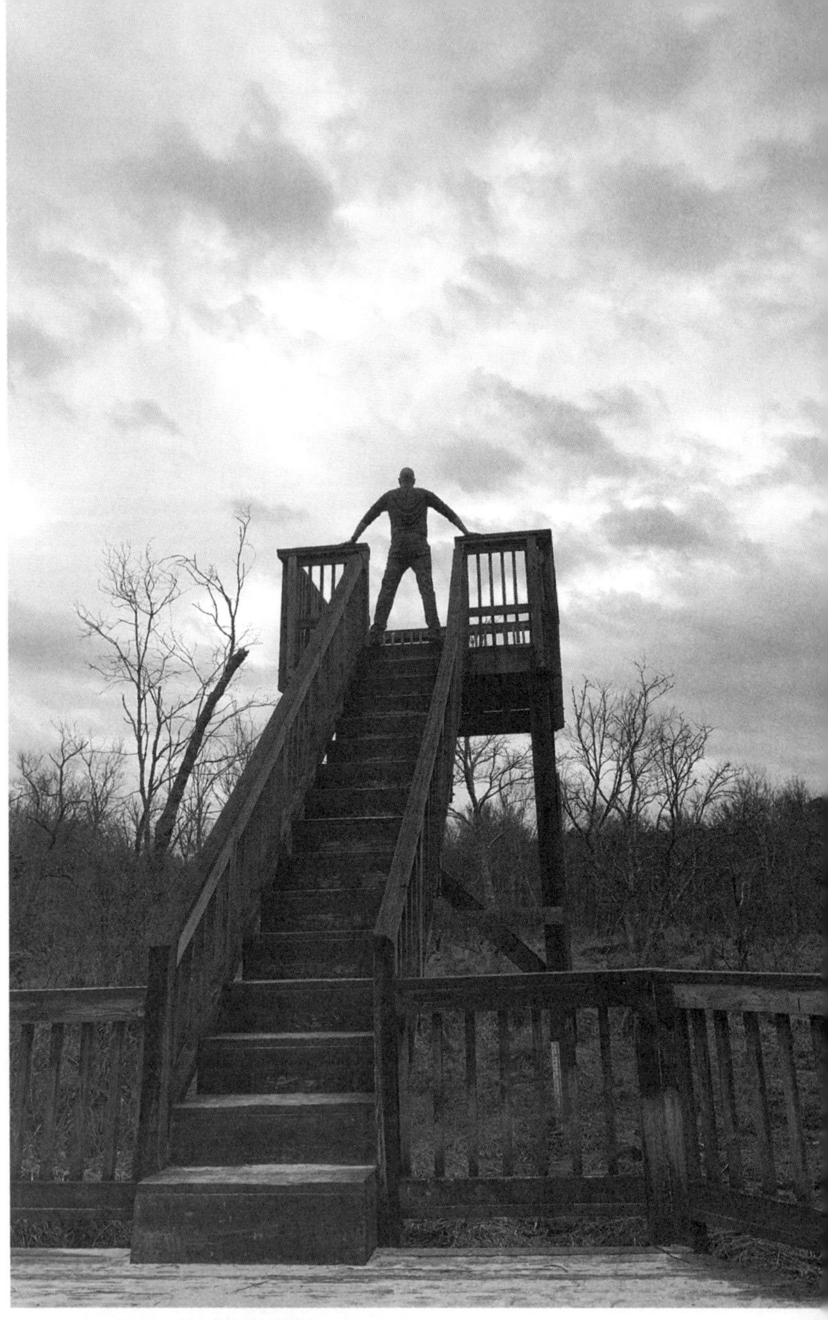

A two-story observation tower provides great views of the Mill Creek Nature Center wetlands.

a large bridge over Ivy Creek, then take a right on a trail that leads to an observation deck at the confluence of Ivy Creek and Little Ivy Creek.

Turn back and go right at the junction to follow the banks of Little Ivy Creek. Just before reaching another large bridge over Ivy Creek, turn right, then right again to visit a two-story observation tower.

Backtrack to the bridge and cross to continue straight back to Ivy Creek Greenway. Turn left and hike the greenway 1 mile back to the boardwalk bridge over Ivy Creek near the apartment complex and waterfall. After crossing the bridge, turn right on the paved path. It's 0.3 mile, past a restroom, across the access road, then right on the first paved path to return to the GEHC parking lot, where you'll end your hike.

Look for a picturesque waterfall along the Ravine Loop Trail.

Little Mulberry Park

There is so much great hiking at Little Mulberry Park that you'll have to visit multiple times to experience it all. This route leads you past many of the park's highlights along paved and dirt trails. You'll walk through peaceful forests and picturesque meadows, around a quiet pond and along bubbling brooks, past historic stone structures, and past a waterfall. And if that's not enough, next time, you can explore hilltop meadows, a second waterfall, wetlands, forests, and a trail that circles Miller Lake. If it wasn't on your radar before, Little Mulberry Park will soon become a family favorite for outdoor activities.

HOW TO GET THERE

Driving Distance from Downtown Atlanta: 41 miles
Address: 3855 Fence Road NE, Dacula, GA 30019
Closest Interstate: I-85
City, County: Dacula, Gwinnett
Parking: Paved parking area

HIKE DISTANCE

6-mile figure-8 loop

DIFFICULTY

Overall: Moderate to strenuous
Navigation: Trail map posted at trailhead and on information boards throughout the park; wayfinding signs at many trail junctions
Terrain: Wide asphalt multiuse trails, narrow paved trails, and hard-packed dirt trails with roots and rocks
Elevation Change: Rolling hills with many extended ascents and descents

SAFETY

Usage ★★★★★
Visibility ★★★★★
Upkeep ★★★★★
Parking ★★★★★

HOURS

Sunrise to sunset

DOGS

Leashed dogs allowed

FACILITIES

- Restrooms near trailhead

- Picnic pavilions, drinking fountain, interpretive signs

FEES & PERMITS None

LAND MANAGER Gwinnett County Parks & Recreation

Landmarks

RAVINE WATERFALL VIEWPOINT

Although its water only falls 8 to 10 feet vertically, after a rain this waterfall forms a much longer cascade and is a wonderful sight in this deep forest. After gazing at its falling waters, close your eyes and listen to the sounds of the forest, creek, and waterfall below you.

HISTORIC STONE STRUCTURES

Look for neatly stacked stone structures and rock piles to the side of the trail. No human artifacts or remains have been found nearby, but park officials are confident that these structures were built by indigenous people. For what purpose, no one knows.

MILLER LAKE VALLEY VIEWPOINT

Even though this hike route doesn't lead you past Miller Lake, when the trees are bare of leaves in winter and spring, you might get a glimpse of the lake below you. Stand on the boulder here, and you'll feel like the king or queen of the mountain.

Hike Route

Start your hike at the paved trailhead opposite the Fence Road parking lot entrance. Turn left at a junction with an information board, pavilion, and restrooms, then turn right on West Meadow Trail. Hike to a four-way junction near a picnic pavilion, where you'll turn left (toward the pavilion) and hike uphill on the paved trail, which circles a grassy hill. In 0.4 mile, pass an information board and junction with Beech Tree Trail. Continue straight another 0.1 mile to the junction with Ravine Loop Trail.

Turn right to begin Ravine Loop, which after a short period of gravel surface becomes a sidewalk-width concrete path. In 0.2 mile, pass a large white oak tree on the left with an interpretive sign, then come to a trail junction. Bear right and hike to a junction with two side trails on the left that lead to observation platforms over the ravine. The first platform provides views of a gorgeous waterfall. The other viewpoint offers sweeping views of a beech, oak, and hickory valley. After enjoying the views, continue on Ravine Loop Trail to a

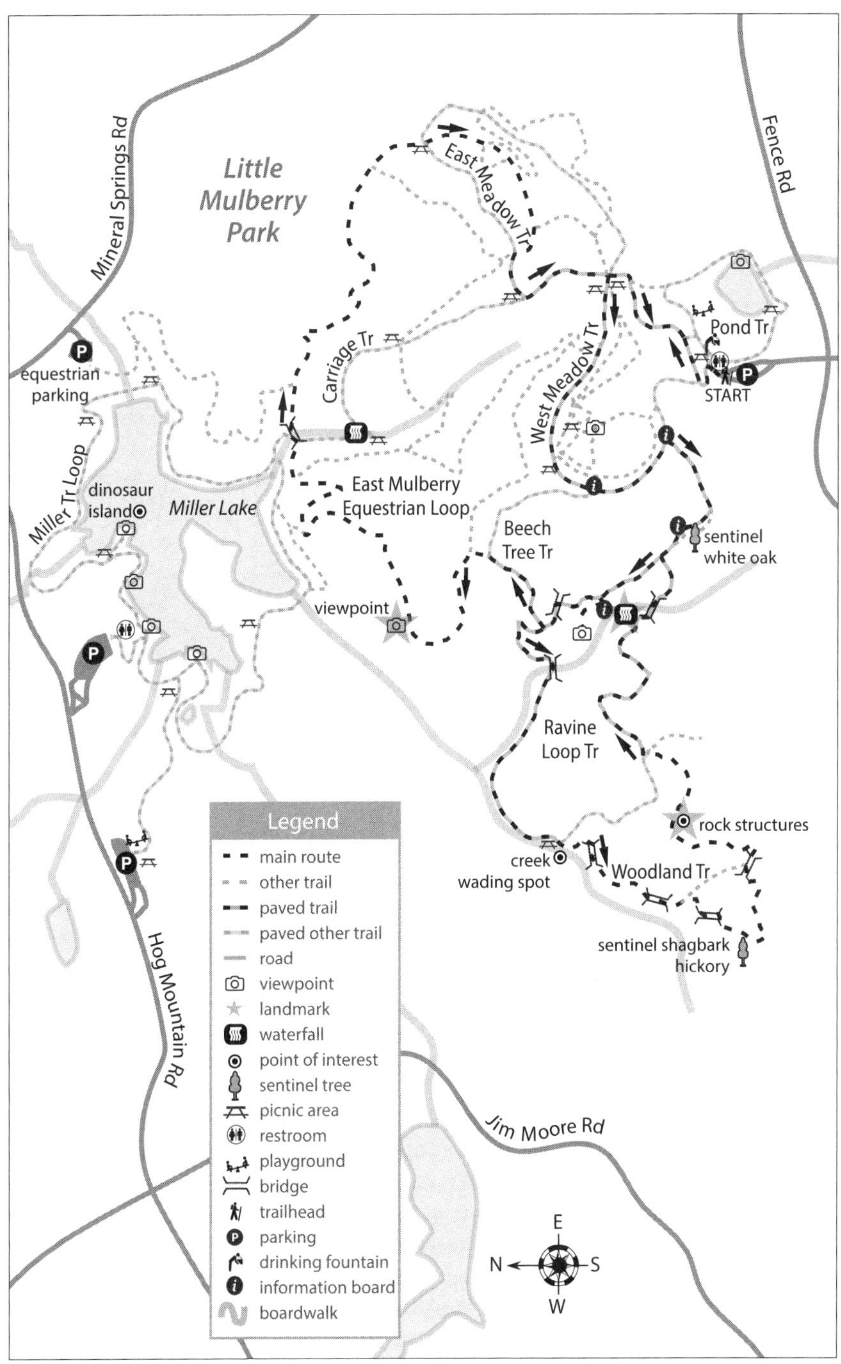

Little Mulberry Park
Mineral Springs Rd
Fence Rd
East Meadow Tr
Carriage Tr
West Meadow Tr
Pond Tr
START
equestrian parking
Miller Tr Loop
dinosaur island
Miller Lake
East Mulberry Equestrian Loop
Beech Tree Tr
sentinel white oak
viewpoint
Ravine Loop Tr
rock structures
creek wading spot
Woodland Tr
sentinel shagbark hickory
Hog Mountain Rd
Jim Moore Rd
Legend
main route
other trail
paved trail
paved other trail
road
viewpoint
landmark
waterfall
point of interest
sentinel tree
picnic area
restroom
playground
bridge
trailhead
parking
drinking fountain
information board
boardwalk
E
N
S
W

The forests of Little Mulberry Park are a beauty to behold.

junction with Beech Tree Trail, when you'll bear left and hike the very steep paved trail downhill.

After hiking 0.5 mile, reach a junction with Woodland Trail at an interpretive sign. Stay straight and hike the dirt trail through the peaceful forest for 0.3 mile to a signed trail junction. Bear right and continue uphill on Woodland Trail for 0.3 mile. Keep an eye out for unique shagbark hickory trees in the forest to your right. Cross a bridge just before reaching the next junction and turn right to continue hiking Woodland Trail. This trail passes several unusual rock structures that were likely built by indigenous people.

The next junction is with the paved Ravine Loop Trail. A smaller paved trail leads hard right into a subdivision. If you want to learn more about the rock structures, a quick detour to the left leads 0.1 mile to an interpretive sign and even taller rock structures. This route bears softly right at this junction and continues 0.5 mile to the next Ravine Loop Trail junction. Turn left and hike past the ravine viewpoints again to reach the Beech Tree Trail junction. This time, turn right and hike almost 0.2 mile to reach an unmarked dirt trail on the left just past a rock pile. Turn left and hike this trail through a narrow gap in a fence to reach East Mulberry Equestrian Loop. Turn left and hike 0.25 mile to a bench and boulder that provide a nice viewpoint of the Miller Lake valley.

Stay on East Mulberry Equestrian Loop for 0.6 mile until it intersects with the paved Carriage Trail. At the pavement, look for a bridge on your left. Hike left on the pavement, cross the bridge, then turn right on the dirt East Mulberry Equestrian Loop. Stay straight on this trail as it makes a long, slow ascent up the ridge. In 0.6 mile, you'll emerge into a meadow and then meet the paved East Meadow Trail near a picnic table. Cross the paved trail to stay on East Mulberry Equestrian Loop, which leads you through the grassy meadow on top of the ridge. Smaller cross-country trails branch off on the right and left. Stay straight on the widest path until you reach the paved East Meadow Trail again. Turn left on the pavement and hike 0.1 mile to a junction with Carriage Trail. Turn left and hike 0.2 mile to a four-way junction. Stay straight to hike West Meadow Trail back to the picnic pavilion and restrooms, where you'll end your hike.

BONUS HIKES

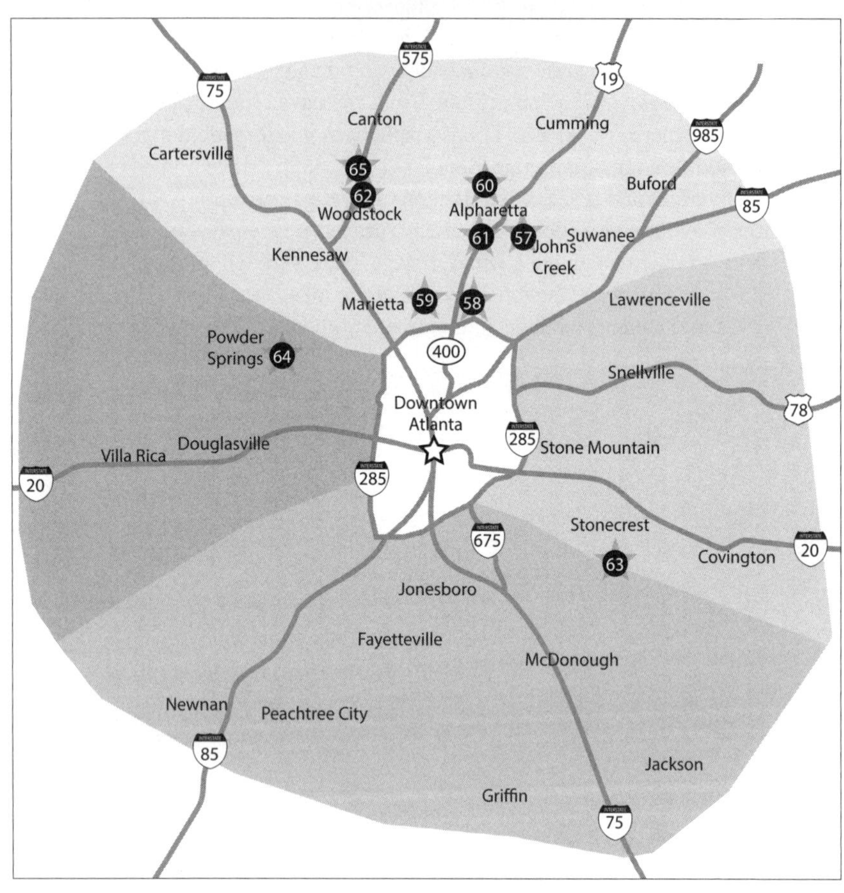

57 Autrey Mill Nature Preserve and Heritage Center

58 Dunwoody Nature Center

59 Lost Corner Preserve

60 Providence Park

61 Big Creek Greenway

62 Noonday Creek Trail

63 Rockdale River Trail

64 Wildhorse Trail

65 Olde Rope Mill Park

SHORT BUT SWEET HIKES

Autrey Mill Nature Preserve and Heritage Center

Besides providing a perfect spot to picnic along a bubbling brook, this nature preserve is a wonderful place to learn—and to hike. Its network of interconnecting trails has wildlife viewing stations and informative signs about trees, birds, history, and wildflowers. The forest is peaceful, and the trails are well marked and maintained, so you can enjoy your hike without worrying about getting lost. Back at the nature center, visitors can learn about Georgia history and see reptiles and amphibians in a special exhibit.

HOW TO GET THERE	**Driving Distance from Downtown Atlanta:** 28 miles **Address:** 9770 Autrey Mill Road, Johns Creek, GA 30022 **Closest Interstate:** I-85 **City, County:** Johns Creek, Fulton **Parking:** Gravel parking area near the visitor center
MILES OF TRAIL	2 miles
DIFFICULTY	Easy
POPULARITY	★★★★☆
HOURS	• Trails open daily, 8:00 am to 9:00 pm • Visitor center and farm museum open Tuesday through Saturday, 10:00 am to 4:00 pm, and Sunday, 12:00 pm to 4:00 pm
DOGS	Leashed dogs allowed
FACILITIES	• Restrooms near parking area • Picnic tables and pavilion, many outdoor classrooms, gardens, historic houses, visitor center
FEES & PERMITS	None
LAND MANAGER	Johns Creek Parks & Recreation in partnership with Autrey Mill Nature Preserve Association

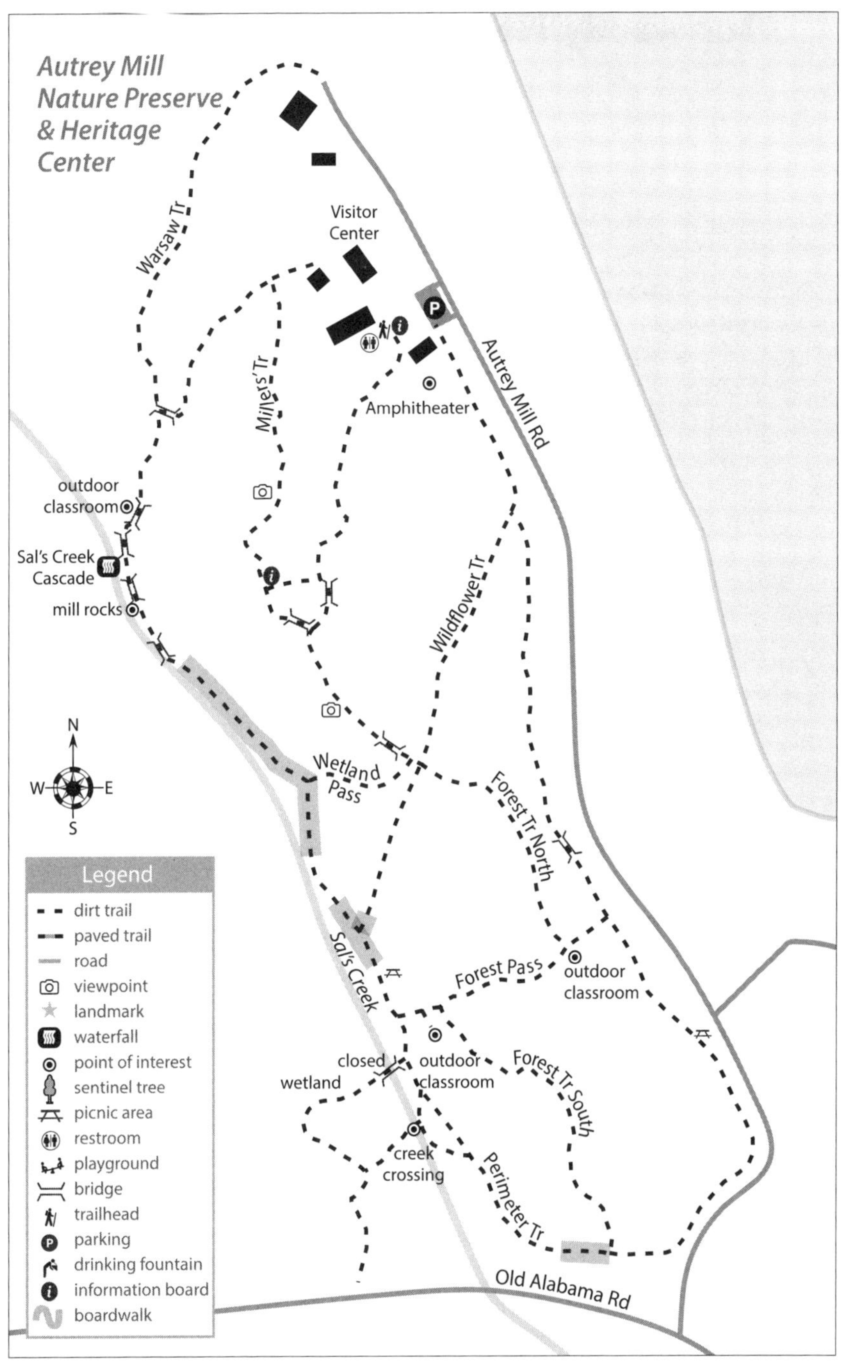
Autrey Mill Nature Preserve & Heritage Center
Warsaw Tr
Visitor Center
Miller's Tr
Amphitheater
Autrey Mill Rd
outdoor classroom
Sal's Creek Cascade
mill rocks
Wildflower Tr
Wetland Pass
Forest Tr North
N
W
E
S
Legend
dirt trail
paved trail
road
viewpoint
landmark
waterfall
point of interest
sentinel tree
picnic area
restroom
playground
bridge
trailhead
parking
drinking fountain
information board
boardwalk
Sal's Creek
Forest Pass
outdoor classroom
closed
wetland
outdoor classroom
Forest Tr South
creek crossing
Perimeter Tr
Old Alabama Rd

Dunwoody Nature Center

You might have attended camp here or visited it on a school field trip, but surprisingly few people know the trails at the Dunwoody Nature Center. It's worth a visit! Besides the sheer joy of spending time in the woods, hiking here is fun because trees are labeled with plaques. You'll pass families walking with young children, and there is plenty of information available if you'd like to learn more about forest and stream ecology.

HOW TO GET THERE	**Driving Distance from Downtown Atlanta:** 20 miles **Address:** 5343 Roberts Drive, Dunwoody, GA 30338 **Closest Interstate:** GA 400 **City, County:** Dunwoody, DeKalb **Parking:** Paved parking lot near the nature center building
MILES OF TRAIL	1.5 miles
DIFFICULTY	Easy
POPULARITY	★★★★★
HOURS	Dawn to dusk; office open Monday through Friday, 9:00 am to 5:00 pm
DOGS	Leashed dogs allowed
FACILITIES	• Toilets available in nature center during office hours • Picnic tables, outdoor classrooms, playground, hammocks
FEES & PERMITS	None
LAND MANAGER	Dunwoody Nature Center and City of Dunwoody Parks & Recreation

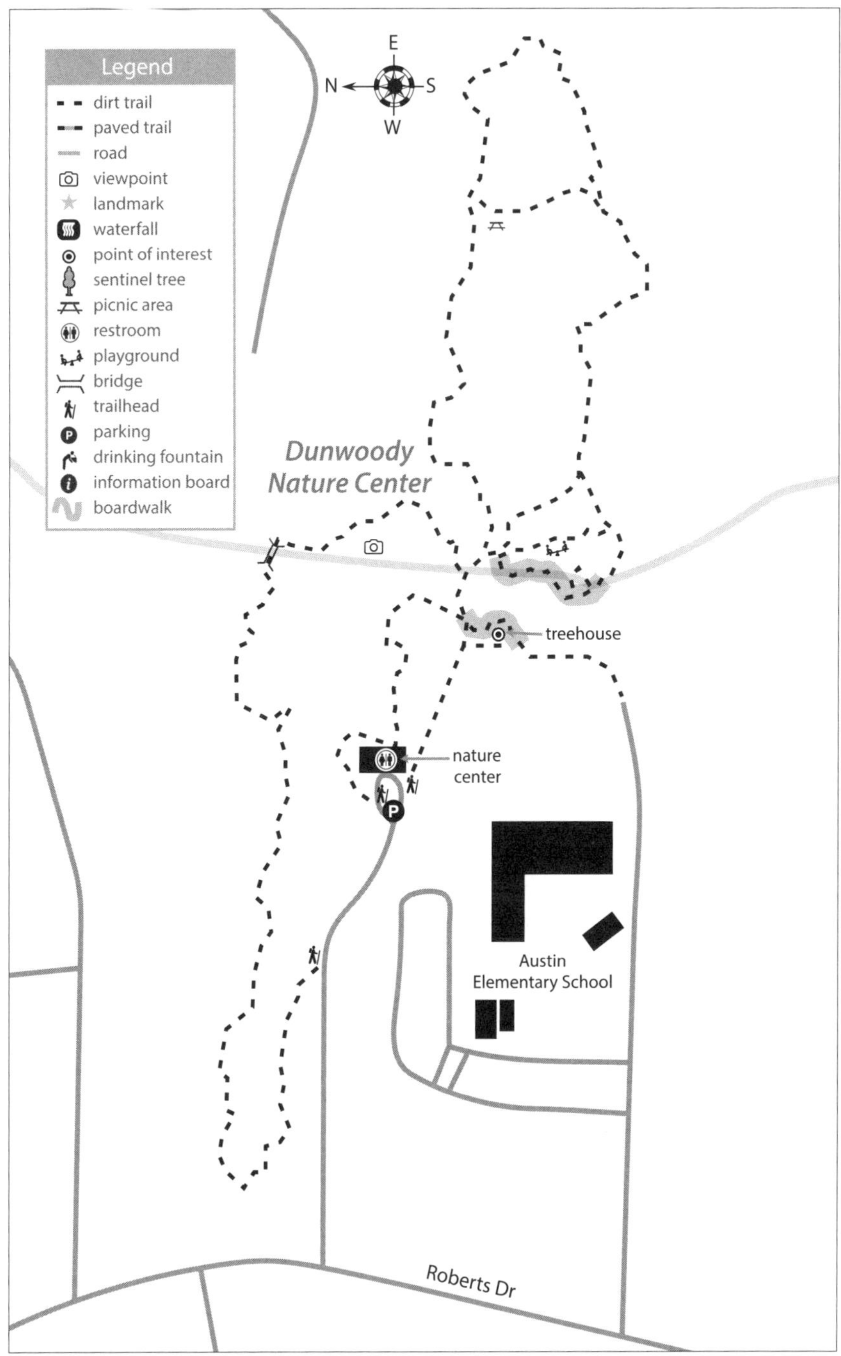
Legend
dirt trail
paved trail
road
viewpoint
landmark
waterfall
point of interest
sentinel tree
picnic area
restroom
playground
bridge
trailhead
parking
drinking fountain
information board
boardwalk
E
N
S
W
Dunwoody Nature Center
treehouse
nature center
Austin Elementary School
Roberts Dr

Lost Corner Preserve

What Lost Corner Preserve lacks in trail mileage, it more than makes up for in character. The previous landowner, Peggy Miles, deeded her property to the Trust for Public Land and City of Sandy Springs in the early 2000s to create this 24-acre nature preserve. This unassuming park is a well-preserved old-growth forest with many massive trees. And as you explore you'll find clues about the land's history from a 170-year-old spring house to the 1920s-era cottage at the preserve entrance. Enjoy a scenic hike, then stick around for one of the many educational programs offered in the apiary and community garden and on the trails.

HOW TO GET THERE

Driving Distance from Downtown Atlanta: 19 miles
Address: 7300 Brandon Mill Road NW, Sandy Springs, GA 30328
Closest Highway: GA 400
City, County: Sandy Springs, Fulton
Parking: Paved parking area

MILES OF TRAIL 1 mile

DIFFICULTY Easy

POPULARITY ★★★★☆

HOURS 8:00 am to dusk

DOGS Leashed dogs allowed

FACILITIES

- Toilets available at cottage
- Pavilion, community garden, benches

FEES & PERMITS None

LAND MANAGER Sandy Springs Parks & Recreation in partnership with Friends of Lost Corner

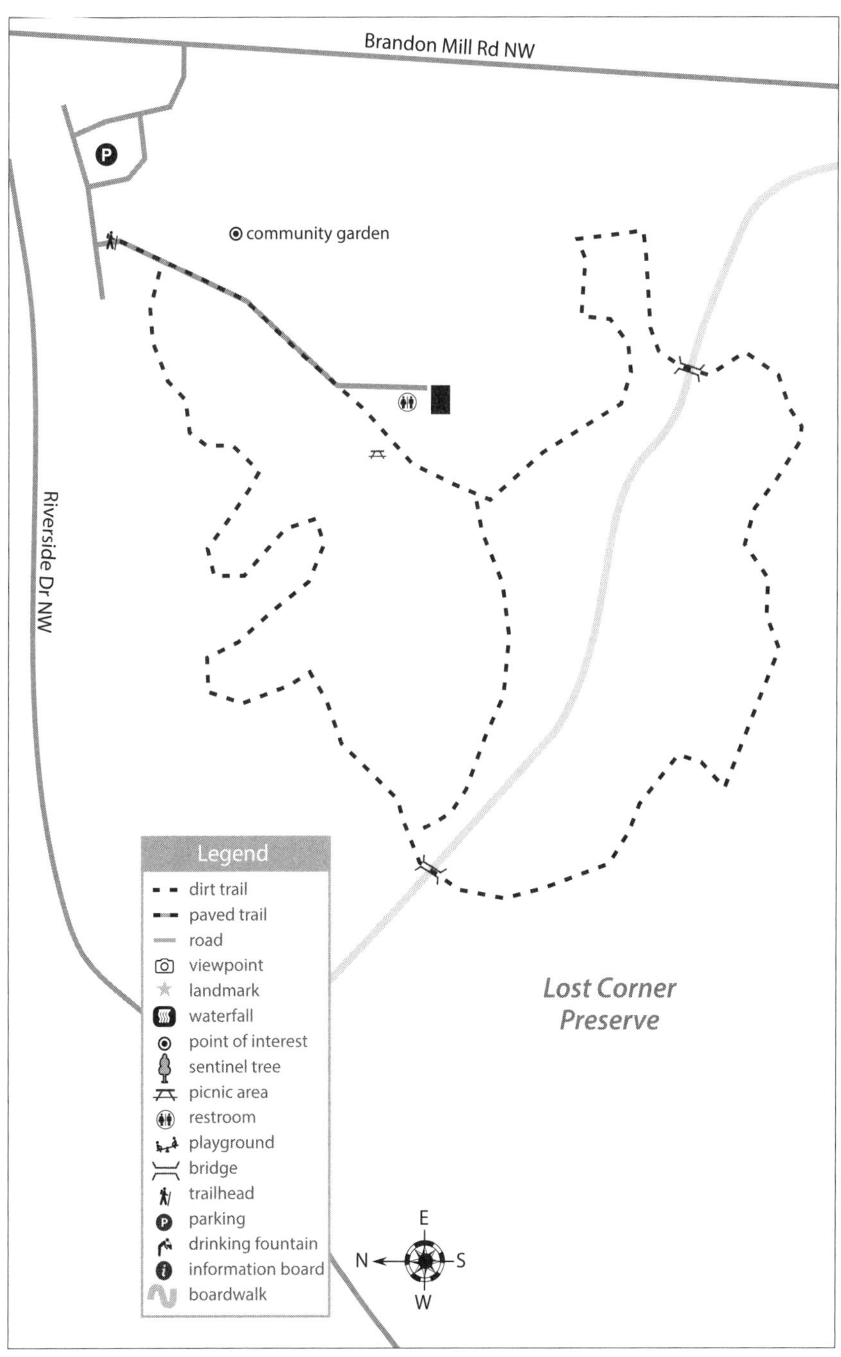
Brandon Mill Rd NW
community garden
Riverside Dr NW
Legend
dirt trail
paved trail
road
viewpoint
landmark
waterfall
point of interest
sentinel tree
picnic area
restroom
playground
bridge
trailhead
parking
drinking fountain
information board
boardwalk
E
N
S
W
Lost Corner Preserve

Providence Park

Providence Park is a 42-acre greenspace tucked into a residential neighborhood in Milton, Georgia. The trails wind through forests and by a lake with a fishing pier, including a paved route to the lake that is ADA accessible. The interpretive signs along the trails add to the fun and provide an easy way to learn about the native plants and animals in a Piedmont forest.

HOW TO GET THERE	**Driving Distance from Downtown Atlanta:** 30 miles **Address:** 13440 Providence Park Drive, Milton, GA 30009 **Closest Highway:** GA 400 **City, County:** Milton, Fulton **Parking:** Large paved parking area
MILES OF TRAIL	2 miles
DIFFICULTY	Easy
POPULARITY	★★★★☆
HOURS	Dawn to dusk
DOGS	Leashed dogs allowed
FACILITIES	• Toilets at parking lot • Water fountain, picnic areas, dog waste station
FEES & PERMITS	None
LAND MANAGER	Milton Parks & Recreation

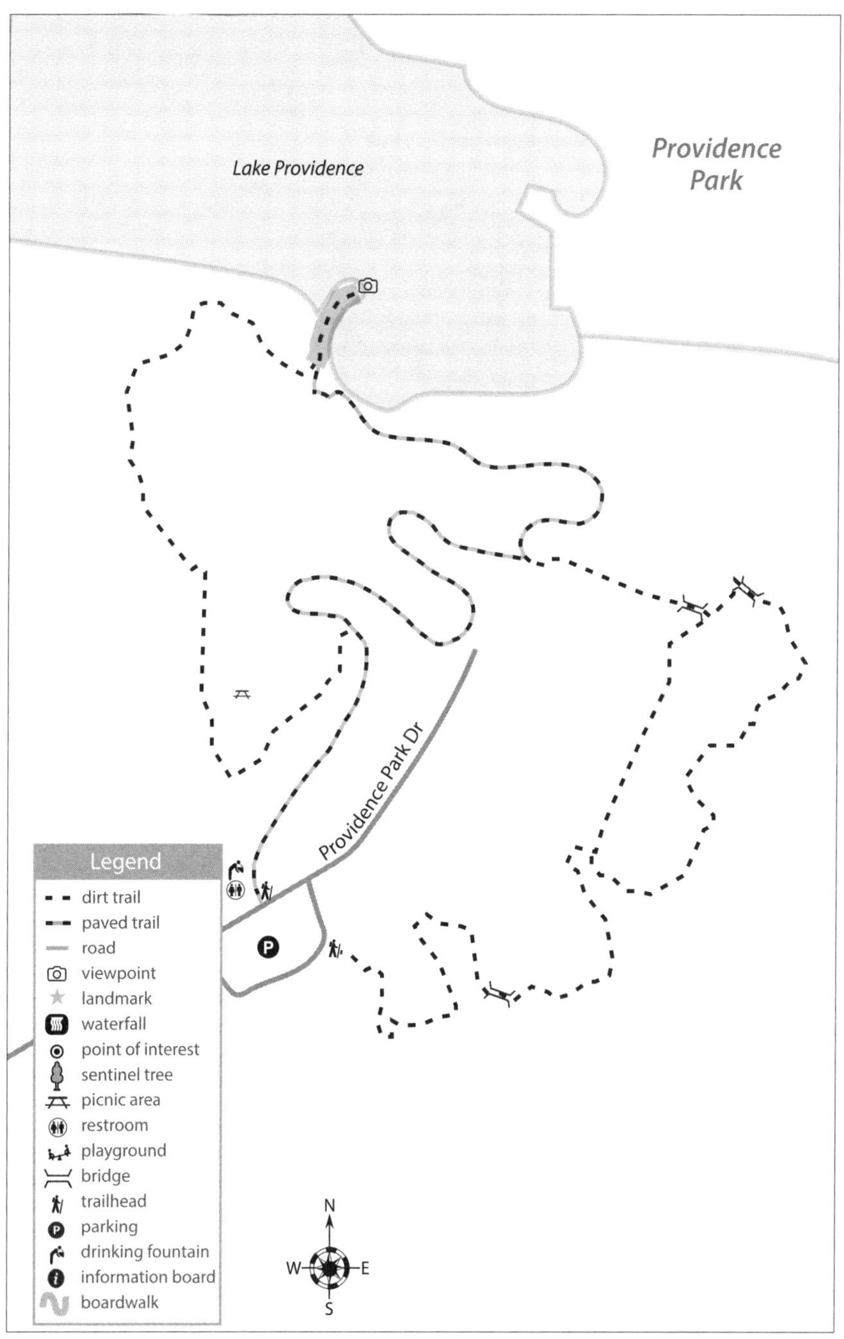
Providence Park
Lake Providence
Providence Park Dr
Legend
dirt trail
paved trail
road
viewpoint
landmark
waterfall
point of interest
sentinel tree
picnic area
restroom
playground
bridge
trailhead
parking
drinking fountain
information board
boardwalk
N
W
E
S

OTHER SHORT TRAILS TO EXPLORE

Southside

Hutcheson Ferry Park
Indian Springs State Park
Serenbe Trails

Eastside

Alcovy Conservation Center
Charlie Elliot Wildlife Center
Graves Park
Hard Labor Creek State Park
Muscogee Trail–Stone Mountain Park
Tucker Nature Preserve

Westside

Blue Trail–Sweetwater Creek State Park
Boat Rock Preserve

Northside

Abbotts Bridge–CRNRA
Allatoona Pass Battlefield
Caney Creek Preserve
Cooper's Furnace Day Use Area
Garrard Landing Park
Leone Hall Price Park
Morgan Falls Park
Shakerag Park
Webb Bridge Park
W.P. Jones Memorial Park

PAVED MULTIUSE TRAILS

Big Creek Greenway

The Big Creek Greenway spans two counties over nearly 15 miles of paved multiuse trails with future plans to connect the north and south sections of trails. The wide paved trail and minimal elevation gain make this a great hike (or bike) for families and hikers of all levels. The trail runs through several areas of wetland and along Big Creek. You can reach the trail from multiple neighborhood access points, and you're never too far from shopping areas and restaurants. This is a true urban hike.

HOW TO GET THERE	**Driving Distance from Downtown Atlanta:** 24 miles **Address:** Greenway access to the left of 6800 North Point Parkway, Alpharetta, GA 30022 **Closest Highway:** GA 400 **City, County:** Alpharetta, Fulton and Forsyth Counties **Parking:** Large paved and gravel parking areas
MILES OF TRAIL	15 miles
DIFFICULTY	Easy to moderate
POPULARITY	★★★★★
HOURS	Dawn to dusk
DOGS	Leashed dogs allowed
FACILITIES	• Toilets at many trailhead parking areas • Water fountain, picnic area, bike repair station
FEES & PERMITS	None
LAND MANAGER	Alpharetta Recreation, Parks & Culture and Forsyth County Parks & Recreation

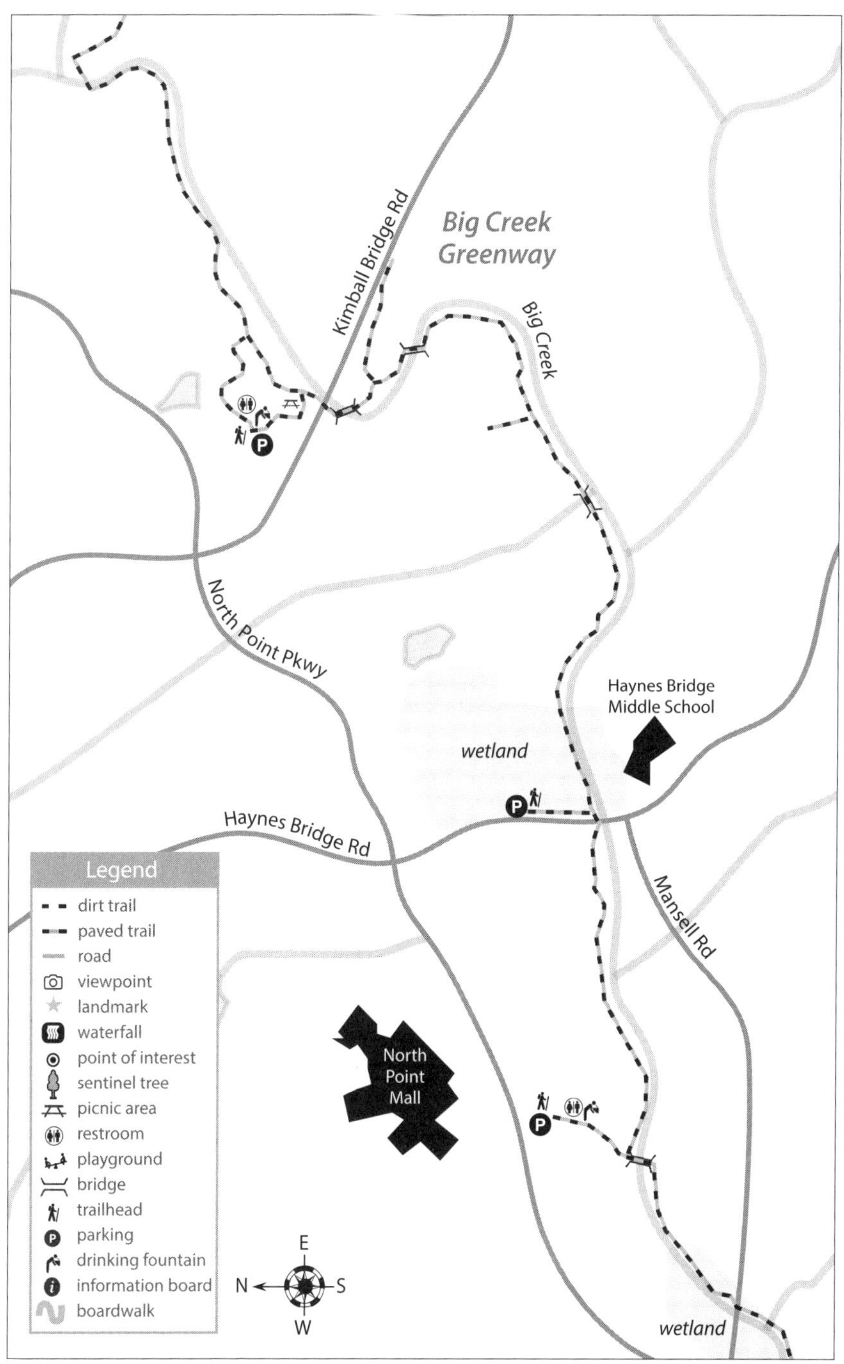
Big Creek Greenway
Kimball Bridge Rd
Big Creek
North Point Pkwy
Haynes Bridge Middle School
wetland
Haynes Bridge Rd
Mansell Rd
North Point Mall
wetland
Legend
dirt trail
paved trail
road
viewpoint
landmark
waterfall
point of interest
sentinel tree
picnic area
restroom
playground
bridge
trailhead
parking
drinking fountain
information board
boardwalk
E
N
S
W

Nooday Creek Trail

If you're interested in an urban hike through a suburban town center, this paved multiuse trail is perfect. Woodstock, Georgia's historic downtown is now a thriving commercial district with galleries, restaurants, and breweries. The Noonday Creek Trail starts one short block from Main Street, winds through neighborhoods, and then leads you to peaceful pockets of nature tucked into this bustling suburb. Visit a beaver wetland, the dog-themed Woofstock Park, and a small gorge along Noonday Creek.

HOW TO GET THERE	**Driving Distance from Downtown Atlanta:** 31 miles **Address:** 111 Elm Street, Woodstock, GA 30188 **Closest Interstate:** I-575 **City, County:** Woodstock, Cherokee **Parking:** Street parking on Market Street or a public lot at Market and Elm Streets
MILES OF TRAIL	2.75 miles
DIFFICULTY	Easy
POPULARITY	★★★★★
HOURS	Dawn to dusk
DOGS	• Leashed dogs allowed • Large off-leash dog park at Woofstock Park
FACILITIES	• Toilets near Market Street trailhead and at Woofstock Park • Playground, picnic tables, public art, dog park
FEES & PERMITS	None
LAND MANAGER	City of Woodstock Parks & Recreation

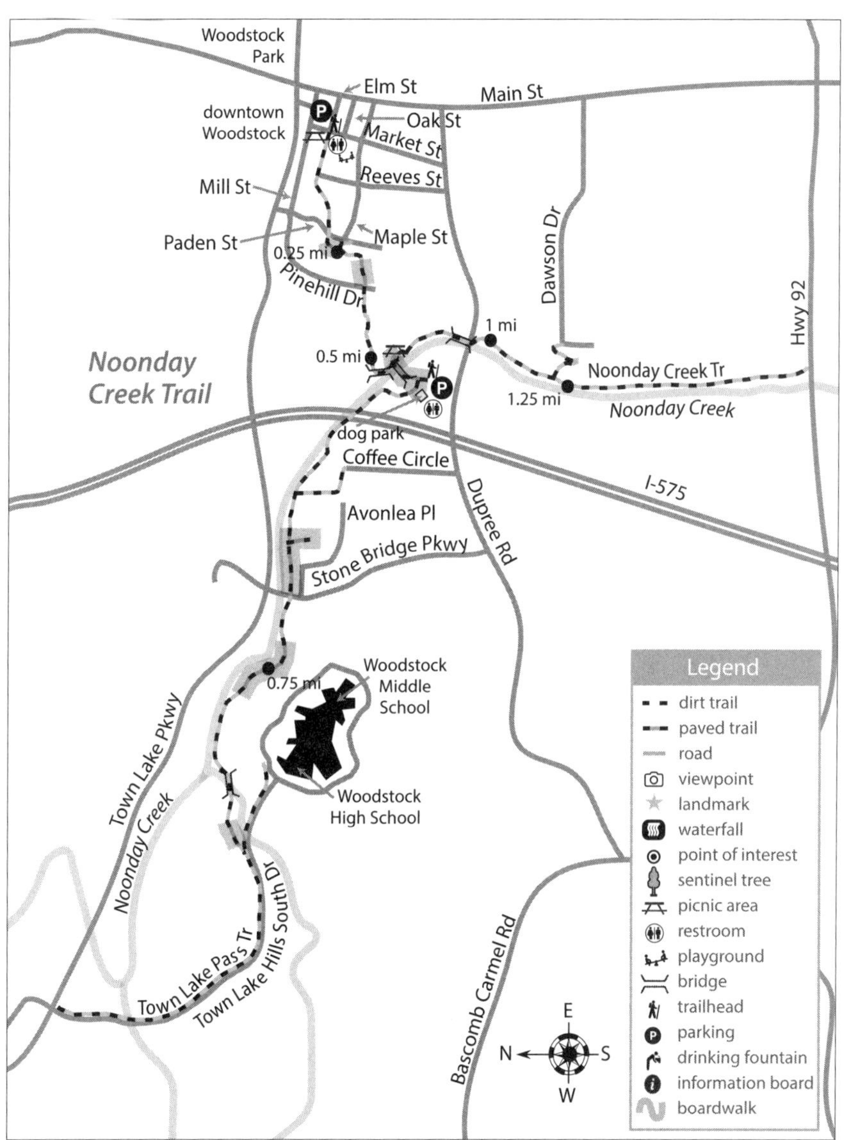
Woodstock
Park
Elm St
Main St
downtown
Woodstock
Oak St
Market St
Reeves St
Mill St
Paden St
Maple St
0.25 mi
Pinehill Dr
Dawson Dr
Hwy 92
1 mi
Noonday
Creek Trail
0.5 mi
Noonday Creek Tr
1.25 mi
Noonday Creek
dog park
Coffee Circle
I-575
Dupree Rd
Avonlea Pl
Stone Bridge Pkwy
Woodstock
Middle
School
0.75 mi
Woodstock
High School
Town Lake Pkwy
Noonday Creek
Town Lake Hills South Dr
Town Lake Pass Tr
Bascomb Carmel Rd
E
N
S
W
Legend
dirt trail
paved trail
road
viewpoint
landmark
waterfall
point of interest
sentinel tree
picnic area
restroom
playground
bridge
trailhead
parking
drinking fountain
information board
boardwalk

Rockdale River Trail

The Rockdale River Trail is a paved multiuse path that runs through south Rockdale County from the Monastery of the Holy Spirit to Panola Mountain State Park, with several trailheads in between. The trail can be entered at any trailhead along the trail, but we recommend starting at the monastery, whose grounds and gift shop are open to the public. This allows you to enjoy the less trafficked section of trail as it winds through forests, past meadows, and crosses the South River.

HOW TO GET THERE
Driving Distance from Downtown Atlanta: 30 miles
Address: 2625 Highway 212 SW, Conyers, GA 30094
Closest Interstate: I-20
City, County: Conyers, Rockdale
Parking: Small gravel parking lot

MILES OF TRAIL 18 miles

DIFFICULTY Easy to strenuous, depending on mileage

POPULARITY ★★★★☆

HOURS Dawn to dusk

DOGS Leashed dogs allowed

FACILITIES
- Toilets at Lorraine Park Trailhead and in monastery gift shop
- Café in monastery (hours posted online), playground, water fountain, picnic area at Lorraine Park

FEES & PERMITS None

LAND MANAGER Rockdale County Parks & Recreation in partnership with Arabia Mountain National Heritage Area

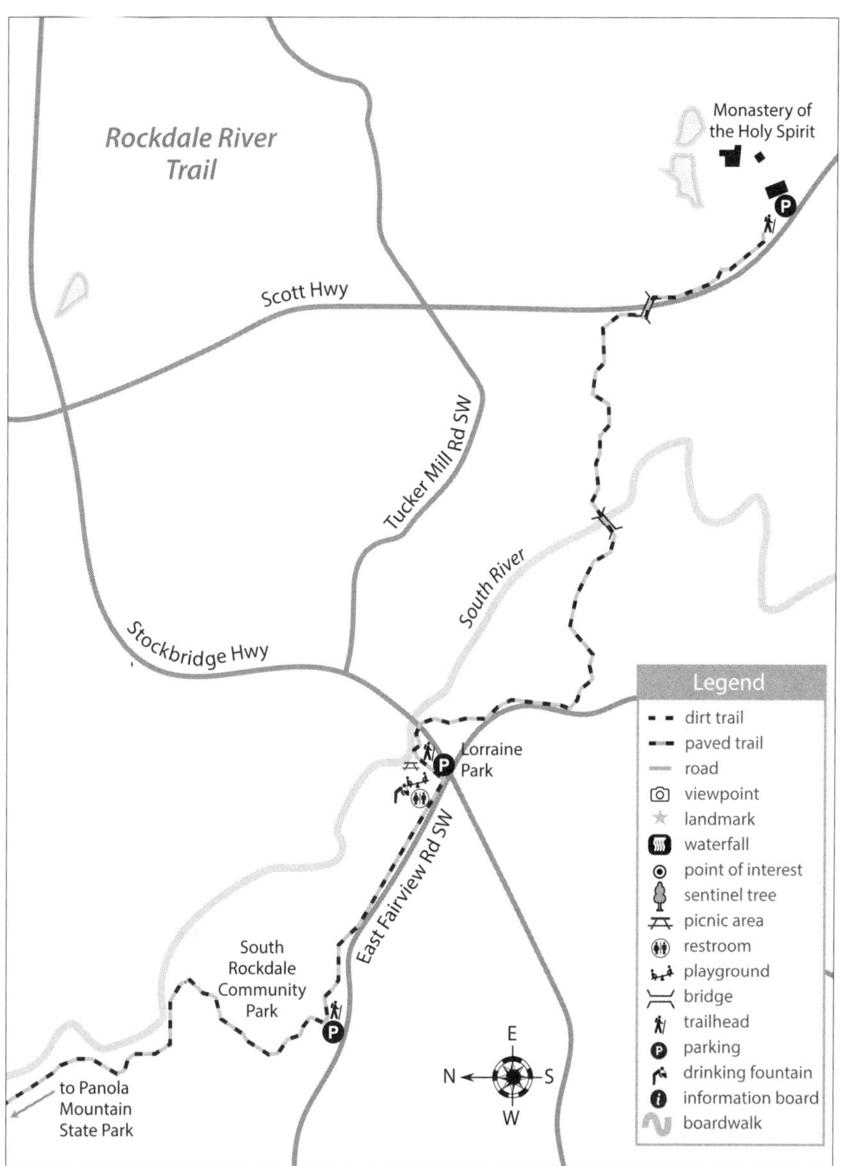
Rockdale River Trail
Monastery of the Holy Spirit
Scott Hwy
Tucker Mill Rd SW
South River
Stockbridge Hwy
Lorraine Park
East Fairview Rd SW
South Rockdale Community Park
to Panola Mountain State Park
E
N
S
W
Legend
dirt trail
paved trail
road
viewpoint
landmark
waterfall
point of interest
sentinel tree
picnic area
restroom
playground
bridge
trailhead
parking
drinking fountain
information board
boardwalk

Wildhorse Trail

Wildhorse Trail is a wide multiuse trail in Powder Springs that connects Wild Horse Creek Park to the Silver Comet Trail and is a popular route for bikers, walkers, and runners. The trail's proximity to residential areas makes it an accessible hike for neighbors. Visitors from across the metro area will appreciate this trail's urban art and forested creekside scenery.

HOW TO GET THERE

Driving Distance from Downtown Atlanta: 23 miles

Address: Closest address is 3820 Macedonia Road, Powder Springs, GA 30127; parking at GPS 33.876152, -84.662383

Closest Interstate: I-20

City, County: Powder Springs, Cobb

Parking: Large paved parking lot

MILES OF TRAIL 1.7 miles

DIFFICULTY Easy

POPULARITY ★★★☆☆

HOURS Dawn to dusk

DOGS Leashed dogs allowed

FACILITIES

- Toilets at concession building
- Benches, sports fields, water fountain

FEES & PERMITS None

LAND MANAGER Powder Springs Parks & Recreation

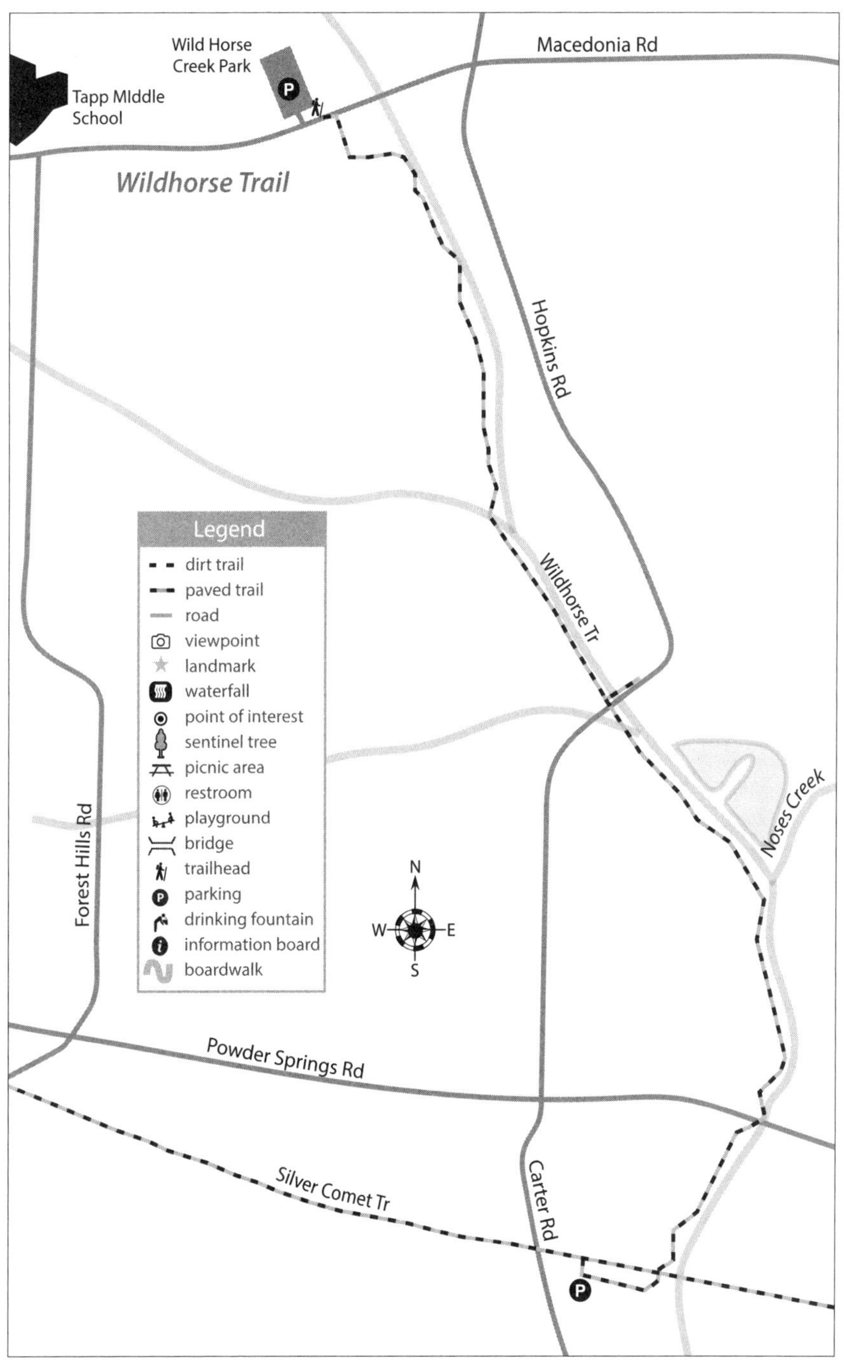

Wild Horse
Creek Park
Macedonia Rd
Tapp MIddle
School
Wildhorse Trail
Hopkins Rd
Legend
dirt trail
paved trail
road
viewpoint
landmark
waterfall
point of interest
sentinel tree
picnic area
restroom
playground
bridge
trailhead
parking
drinking fountain
information board
boardwalk
Wildhorse Tr
Noses Creek
Forest Hills Rd
N
W
E
S
Powder Springs Rd
Silver Comet Tr
Carter Rd

OTHER PAVED TRAILS TO EXPLORE

Southside

Clayton County International Park
Newnan LINC

Eastside

Covington Cricket Frog Trail
Olde Town Conyers Trail
Wilkins Greenway

Westside

Carrollton Greenbelt
Silver Comet Trail

Northside

Camp Creek Greenway Trail
Pinckneyville Park
Rogers Bridge & Cauley Creek Parks
Roswell Riverwalk
Suwanee Creek Greenway at George Pierce Park
Swift Cantrell Park

TRAILS SHARED WITH MOUNTAIN BIKES

Olde Rope Mill Park

This park is well known to mountain bikers and to locals in Cherokee County, but it should be known to all Atlantans. This extensive park is named for a cotton mill that spun fibers into rope on this site until 1950. The ruins along the Little River are still visible, and this park has an extensive trail system for both hikers and bikers. There is even a kayak launch if you want to paddle the Little River into Lake Allatoona. Because these trails share use with mountain bikers, pay special attention when hiking at Olde Rope Mill Park.

HOW TO GET THERE	**Driving Distance from Downtown Atlanta:** 32 miles **Address:** 690 Olde Rope Mill Park Road, Woodstock, GA 30188 **Closest Interstate:** I-575 **City, County:** Woodstock, Cherokee **Parking:** Paved parking area near the trailhead and a large overflow lot up the hill if the lower lot is full
MILES OF TRAIL	17 miles
DIFFICULTY	Easy to strenuous, depending on route
POPULARITY	★★★★★
HOURS	• 7:00 am to 11:00 pm • Explorer, Avalanche, Moore's Pass, Turbine, Raceway, and Powerhouse Trails are closed to bikes and foot traffic when rainy or muddy; visit sorbawoodstock.org for up-to-date trail status
DOGS	Leashed dogs allowed
FACILITIES	• Restrooms • Picnic tables, water fountain, information board, mountain bike trails
FEES & PERMITS	None
LAND MANAGER	City of Woodstock Parks & Recreation in partnership with SORBA Woodstock

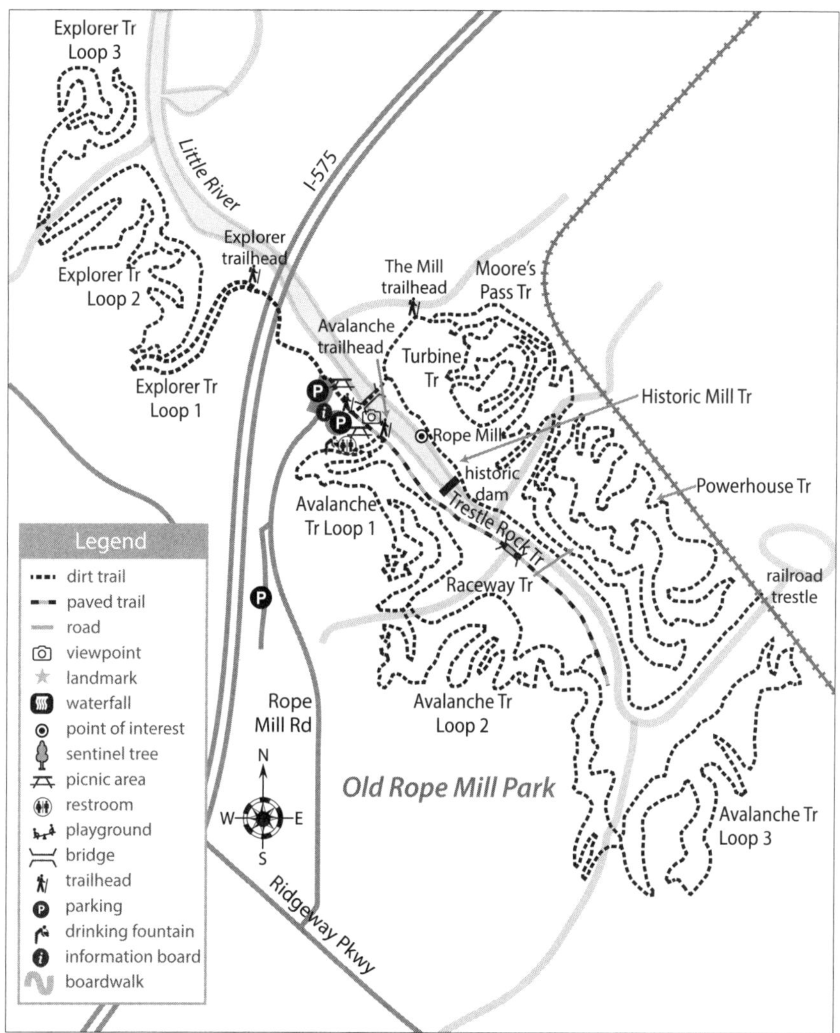
Explorer Tr Loop 3
Little River
I-575
Explorer trailhead
Explorer Tr Loop 2
Explorer Tr Loop 1
The Mill trailhead
Moore's Pass Tr
Avalanche trailhead
Turbine Tr
Historic Mill Tr
Rope Mill
historic dam
Powerhouse Tr
Avalanche Tr Loop 1
Trestle Rock Tr
Raceway Tr
railroad trestle
Legend
dirt trail
paved trail
road
viewpoint
landmark
waterfall
point of interest
sentinel tree
picnic area
restroom
playground
bridge
trailhead
parking
drinking fountain
information board
boardwalk
Rope Mill Rd
Avalanche Tr Loop 2
N
W
E
S
Old Rope Mill Park
Avalanche Tr Loop 3
Ridgeway Pkwy

OTHER SHARED TRAILS TO EXPLORE

Southside

Brown's Mill Battlefield
Moore's Bridge Park

Eastside

Harbins Park
South Rockdale Park
Fort Yargo State Park

Westside

Aerotropolis Nature Park
Campbellton Creek Nature Park

Northside

A.L. Burruss Nature Park
Allatoona Creek Park
Blankets Creek Park
Mount Tabor Park

ABOUT THE AUTHORS

Jonah McDonald

Jonah McDonald arrived in Atlanta on foot over two decades ago. After completing his 2,172-mile southbound thru-hike on the Appalachian Trail, he put down roots in Atlanta. Today, he serves as the DeKalb County park naturalist at Mason Mill Park. He published the first edition of *Hiking Atlanta's Hidden Forests: Intown and Out* in 2014. His second book, published in 2020, is titled *Secret Atlanta: A Guide to the Weird, Wonderful, and Obscure*.

Jonah is also a storyteller, television host, and tour guide. He loves exploring his city via bicycle or canoe or on foot and believes that there is a new story to learn and tell around every bend. When he's not already on an adventure, Jonah loves finding a new one. Connect with him at jonahmcdonald.com.

Zana Pouncey

Zana Pouncey is a native southerner and has lived in Atlanta for over 10 years. She loves city life with all her heart but is a passionate environmentalist at her core. Connecting people to nature is her calling. After graduating from Emory University with a degree in environmental science, Zana spent several years working in environmental advocacy and education for nonprofit organizations, including Trees Atlanta, Zoo Atlanta, and the Atlanta Botanical Garden. She has been awarded a Grosvenor Teacher Fellowship by the National Geographic Society, is on the board of the Atlanta Green Theater Alliance, has presented at environmental conferences and teacher workshops, and has written for the *National Geographic* Education Blog.

Zana finds enjoyment in most outdoor activities and is partial to riding bikes and kayaking with her husband, Matthew, as well as jogging, yoga, bird-watching from her porch, and gardening. She looks forward to the day her nieces and nephew are old enough to join her on hikes. Zana recently became a certified sound healing practitioner and aspires to become a certified herbalist.

Together, Jonah and Zana are also the authors of *Hiking Intown Atlanta's Hidden Forests: Inside and On the Perimeter*.